Janusz Zurakowski
Legend in the Skies

Janusz Zurakowski
Legend in the Skies

Bill Zuk with Janusz Zurakowski

Crécy Publishing Limited

Janusz Zurakowski
Legend in the Skies

First Canadian edition published 2004 by
Vanwell Publishing Limited, Ontario Canada
First English edition published 2007 by Crécy Publishing Ltd
Copyright © Bill Zuk 2004

A CIP record for this book is available from the British Library

ISBN 9 780859 791137

Cover photographs courtesy of Avro Aircraft Ltd, Geoff Worrall and
Janusz Zurakowski

Printed in the UK by Biddles

Crécy Publishing Limited
1a Ringway Trading Estate, Shadowmoss Road, Manchester M22 5LH
www.crecy.co.uk

To Dianne, the love of my life who has sustained me all these years.

CONTENTS

Foreword

In this book Bill Zuk has produced an in-depth and fascinating look into the life of a most remarkable man, Janusz Zurakowski – 'Zura' or 'Jan' to most who know him. Unlike the stereotype of a Second World War fighter pilot, Jan is a quiet-spoken and self-effacing man with all the grace and charm of his Polish ancestry. He also has a quick and sometimes 'wicked' sense of humour and is able to put in their places those who might not always agree with him, particularly in aviation matters.

Much has been written about him in books, magazines and newspaper articles and part of his life story has been included in a recent TV series, but this book is the definitive story on the life and times of Janusz Zurakowski. The author takes us through Jan's colourful and eventful life with care and attention to detail, some of which was no doubt provided by the great man himself.

In addition to being a superb test pilot – arguably the best aerobatic pilot in the world – Jan also took an engineering approach to flying and 'coaxed' an aircraft to the limit of its performance, often taking his 'mount' beyond the accepted limits – sometimes to the apprehension of the designers. They did not necessarily like to have their aircraft 'broken' by manoeuvres outside of the specified flight envelope for which it was designed. Jan's philosophy was based on his feeling that a service pilot may find himself in trouble if he inadvertently took the aircraft outside of its specified performance and Jan was anxious to examine the procedures for safe recovery. I personally believed that within reasonable limits, Jan's stance was correct. His wide knowledge of the engineering side of flight testing also enabled him to suggest corrections and follow-through procedures, particularly with respect to crew safety.

I was privileged to be associated with Jan during his career with Avro Canada, but lost touch with him after the cancellation of the Arrow programme in 1959, when Jan retired from flight testing and he and his family went to share the Madawaska Valley with their Polish compatriots. However, since my return to Canada in 1980, we have renewed our friendship and I have been intrigued by – and sometimes briefly involved in – recent products of his active mind: for example, his desire to design a sailing vessel that would capture the world's speed record for wind-driven water craft.

Like Peter Cope, another excellent Avro Canada test pilot, I am impressed by the depth of research that Bill Zuk has put into this book, particularly on Jan's early life, much of which I was not aware of. Bill has brought out the character of Jan and his supportive family in this book and provided an insight into the life and times of one of the world's most famous test pilots, and a very fine gentleman. A great read.

James C Floyd
Former Vice-President, Engineering (Avro Aircraft Limited)

I was associated with Jan Zurakowski from 1944 to 1960 and shared office space with him for some eight years in Canada. I would like to compliment Bill Zuk on this excellent biography of Jan. The research in this book has brought out many aspects of Jan's life that have not been covered in earlier accounts.

Jan is a great guy. You could not meet a more modest man. He does not like publicity and is always reluctant to talk about any of his personal accomplishments, both pre-war and post-war.

I have always maintained (and still do) that Jan was one of the world's greatest test pilots. He was a brilliant flyer with a very keen analytical sense for problem-solving, and he was also the best aerobatic pilot with high performance military aircraft that I have ever seen. I learned a great deal from Jan from the flying point of view and I feel honoured to consider him a personal friend.

Peter R Cope
Former Test Pilot of the CF-100 and CF-105 (Avro Aircraft Limited)

Preface

For most of my lifetime, the saga of the Avro Arrow and its pilot, Janusz Zurakowski, had resonated strongly with me. As an impressionable youth, I had followed Zurakowski's extraordinary feats, and when the fabled interceptor was cancelled, shock, bewilderment and remorse flooded over me, like many other Canadians. In the years to come, a stream of newspaper and magazine articles, books, documentary films and even a stage play kept the story alive. As my interest in the lore of the Avro Arrow grew, two fortuitous events brought the story to Winnipeg, my home town.

In 1996, the Western Canada Aviation Museum (WCAM) was chosen as a primary location for filming a television mini-series based on the Avro Arrow. The museum had been selected for its eerie resemblance to the old Avro Aircraft plant in Toronto. While writing a series of articles on the production for the museum, I was able to closely observe the filming. A particular scene that captivated me was the depiction of the first flight of the Avro Arrow. Actor Lubimar Mykitiuk, the stand-in for Zurakowski, appeared beside a full-scale prop of the Arrow to re-enact the maiden flight. Taxiing solemnly into place, the movie Arrow braked and the scene unfolded with a rousing reception of the triumphant test pilot by employees and press. When the film wrapped up later that summer, this scene remained as one of the most memorable aspects of the production. One of several articles I subsequently wrote was about Janusz Zurakowski, but I had never submitted it for publication.

Shortly after the mini-series aired, on 30 May 1997 the Western Canada Aviation Museum honoured Janusz Zurakowski as a 'Pioneer of Canadian Aviation'. Travelling with his son Mark from their home in Barry's Bay, Ontario, Zurakowski appeared at the award ceremony in Winnipeg. Although in his eighties, apart from a hearing loss he seemed remarkably fit for his age. Along with many admirers in the audience, I was enthralled by the account of Zurakowski's career as presented by the master of ceremonies, Mike McCourt. He said, in part, 'After all these years, with the Arrow simply a memory of what might have been, Zurakowski's extraordinary personal record of achievement in Canadian military aviation remains intact and undiminished. Indeed, he is an enduring symbol of the fearless determination and limitless ability which characterises all great men and that is why the Western Canada Aviation Museum has named Jan Zurakowski a Pioneer of Canadian Aviation.'

To the ringing of applause, Janusz Zurakowski made a brief address and later graciously signed autographs on programmes, photographs and memorabilia that members of the audience had brought. When my turn to meet Zurakowski came, I explained my interest in his exploits and expressed my hope that someone would write the story of his life and his role in aviation. I mentioned that I had already begun writing an article. He politely accepted my business card and signed his name on a photograph of himself and the Avro Arrow. My wife recorded our meeting on film and I moved aside to let the next person meet 'The Great Zura', as he had once been known.

The moment had been fleeting but had been more meaningful than I had expected. Three weeks later, a thick package labelled 'From the desk of Janusz Zurakowski' arrived at our home. As I slowly opened the package and examined its contents, I realised that the items were part of his personal files and scrapbook clippings. After reading and rereading the documents, I realised that the material represented a beginning to an incredible story. Although another book about Avro Canada occupied my writing for a period of time, the impetus to write the story of Janusz Zurakowski never left me.

Over the next three years, I travelled across Canada to gather information from archives and museums and conduct a series of interviews with the principals involved in a once-great aviation dream, and the man whose name was forever linked to it. Gradually, I realised that the focus of my work had shifted from recounting a legend to a personal account of a remarkable individual and the times in which he lived. During my research, I collaborated closely with Janusz Zurakowski and his wife, Anna Zurakowska. They generously shared their memories and gave me the unique opportunity to examine their photographs and personal records. With their kind assistance, numerous other contacts were made and 'doors were opened' across Canada, the United States, the United Kingdom and Poland. Direct quotations in the text following are linked to correspondence and interviews conducted with Janusz and Anna.

Acknowledgements

In undertaking this account of Janusz Zurakowski's life and times, there have been many individuals and organisations that offered assistance, encouragement and advice. Other authors and historians who have trod this path previously were invaluable colleagues. The list is made up of: Pierre Berton, Michael Bliss, Clinton Bomphray (playwright of *The Legend of the Avro Arrow*), Robert Bracken, Margaret Brodniewicz-Stawicki, June Callwood, Palmiro Campagna, Joan Dixon, James Dow, Christopher Gainor, Jack Granatstein, Russell Isinger, Marek Kusiba, Keith Ross Leckie, Julius Lukasiewicz, John Melady, Larry Milberry, Desmond P Morton, Murray Peden, Sean Rossiter, Greig Stewart, and Randall Whitcomb.

Interviewing people who were part of the Zurakowski story led me to a fascinating group from around the world. The list comprises those who flew with Zura as well as other friends: Bill Bialkowski, Robert D Cockfield, J R 'Roy' Combley, Mike Cooper-Slipper, Peter Cope, Neville Duke, Wilf Farrance, James C Floyd, Stan Haswell, Reg Kersey, Fred C Matthews, Vern Morse, Ron Page, John F Painter, Mario Pesando, Mark Robbins, Don Rogers, Lorne Ursel, Bill Waterton, Murray Willer, Lou Wise, Jack Woodman, Derek Woolley, Geoff Worrall and Elwy Yost.

Some individuals should be noted as 'keepers of the flame' who have ensured that the legacy of the Avro Arrow will continue. These include Jason Eldridge, Doug and Donette Hyslip, David Mackechnie, Kyle Schmidt, Claude Sherwood, Les Wilkinson, Brian Willer, and Peter Zuuring.

During the process of collecting data, several organisations were willing to share their resources, chief among them being the Western Canada Aviation Museum with its extensive library. Others included the Canada Aviation Museum, Canadian Warplane Heritage Museum and the Toronto Aerospace Museum. I would also like to acknowledge Jarek Gwardys, Jerzy Topor-Jasinski and Teresa Jasiewicz for their assistance in translating many Polish documents.

Finally, this story could not have been told without the participation of the extraordinary Zurakowski family. While each member contributed in some way, Anna and Janusz provided sage, kindly and knowledgeable analysis. I am forever indebted to them for their friendship and counsel.

Chapter One

First Flight

For many Canadians the epic of the Avro Arrow actually began on 25 March 1958. At the Avro Aircraft Limited plant in Malton, Ontario, a small Toronto suburb, a flurry of activity had already taken place early that cloudy Tuesday morning. For nearly six months the aircraft manufacturer had been readying the first production Avro Arrow Mk 1, S/N 25201, carrying the markings 'RL-201', for its maiden flight.

(L-R) Test pilots Peter Cope, Don Rogers and Janusz Zurakowski plan the first flight of the Avro Arrow. *(Western Canada Aviation Museum archives)*

At the company control tower, an anxious group of Avro workers and a small number of press and visitors were on hand. Foremost amongst this group was Air Marshal (Ret) W A Curtis, a member of the Board of Directors of A V Roe Canada Limited and the Vice-Chairman of the parent company, Hawker Siddeley Canada. Eight years earlier, in the capacity of Chief of Air Staff, Curtis had watched a similar scene at the Avro plant when the Avro CF-100 had made its first flight. The CF-100 had ended up as a successful aircraft programme, becoming the backbone of Canada's air defence. The Arrow, however, would be an incredible leap forward in aeronautical technology and performance. Janusz Zurakowski described it in these terms: 'It was expected to reach Mach 2 (twice the speed of sound): more than twice the performance of the CF-100 at MN [Mach Number] .85.' A lot of hopes and dreams were carried on the wings of the new fighter.

The normal clatter of typewriters, rivet guns and stamping machines seemed subdued that day as many employees were anticipating that this would be 'the day'. Kay Shaw, one of the engineers at Avro, recalled: 'The rumour went around that the Arrow was going to fly. The roof of one of the low buildings was a good vantage point and it was soon crowded with personnel.'[1] Word had spread that Victor John 'Shorty' Hatton, the company's Chief Experimental and Test Flight Inspector, had checked and cleared RL-201, with the Royal Canadian Air Force (RCAF) Inspector countersigning the all-important 'Cleared for Flight' document. Shortly after, management announced over the loudspeakers that 'non-essential' employees could leave their workplaces to see the test flight. Up to ten thousand employees from the sprawling complex of Avro Aircraft and the nearby Avro Orenda Engines plant rushed outside to witness a momentous event – the first flight of their beloved Arrow.

Some workers had already positioned themselves down the grassy verge of the longest runway at Malton Airport. The best locations were taken up early, but from the end of the runway one of the optimal viewing areas was actually a parking lot at the end of the service road that provided access to the south hangars' side. Only the last three-quarters of the recently extended runway was visible because a slight rise to the north of the runway blocked the view of the first section. However, if viewers were to focus at that point, they would be able to see the magnificent delta-winged 'bird' take-off in a spectacular leap into the air.

Most Avro workers waited patiently in the airport area but a few 'Avroites', as they had been called, had some special tasks to perform to record the flight. The Avro Photographic Department, directed by

---

[1] E K Shaw, *There Never Was an Arrow* (Brampton, Ontario: Steel Rail, 1981), 57.

Lou Wise, readied fourteen camera stations on the ground. These included both normal and high-speed still and 16mm motion picture cameras. Hugh Mackechnie, the company photographer usually responsible for aerial work, secured two movie and two still cameras on the Avro CF-100 Mk 5 chase plane (S/N 18513). Mackechnie's job would be to record the flight in black and white stills and in colour slides, using modified Speed Graphic cameras, as well as on 16mm movie film. The CF-100 chase plane was to be flown by Wladyslaw Jan 'Spud' Potocki, Avro company test pilot. Potocki put on his trademark leather flying helmet that had served him well in his war years as a Polish fighter pilot in the Royal Air Force (RAF).

The other chase plane was a Canadair Sabre Mk 6 (S/N 23744) piloted by RCAF Flight Lieutenant Jack Woodman, Central Experimental and Proving Establishment Chief Test Pilot. He was assigned to the Avro Arrow programme, serving as the RCAF acceptance pilot. Woodman wore a special helmet, with a 16mm gunsight aiming point (GSAP) movie camera strapped to the top. The day before, he had had a harrowing escape, crash landing a CF-100 at Malton in a shower of sparks and flames. Potocki, accompanying him in a chase plane on his test flight, had spotted fluid pouring from the stricken aircraft, the result of a massive hydraulic failure. Woodman calmly 'pancaked' the CF-100 in and brushed off the incident as just a part of the business of test flying. The next morning Woodman was ready to go again, especially for the first flight of the Arrow.

Members of the Flight Test Section were involved in a myriad of details prior to the maiden flight. The flight test engineering team worked closely with the telemetring labs, since the first flight would involve recording the flight data with instrumentation packed into the weapons bay. Every function of the aircraft in flight would be monitored and transmitted to a telemetry trailer.

When the flight test crew was given authorisation to tow the first Arrow out of the hangar, anxious faces in the machine shop and assembly areas watched its slow passage. At the engine run-up shed, engines were started and primary systems were checked. The ground crew, consisting of seasoned hands Arnold Banks, Art Cowper, Bill Forrester, Jack Gary, Bob Levitt, John Salmon, Bill Seggie, Doc Staly and Johnnie Straboe, completed the last checks of the aircraft. They had been at work on the aircraft since six o'clock that morning. With satisfactory completion of the preliminary tests, the flight test crew pronounced that all was ready for flight.

At a distance, most observers could make out the slight figure of a test pilot approaching the Arrow. He slowly made his way around the rescue vehicles and fire trucks parked next to the gleaming white, delta-shaped aircraft. As he walked around the perimeter of the aircraft, a 'walk-around' ground check of controls and undercarriage was completed. Conferring briefly with the flight crew and the engineering staff, he smiled and joked with them. Then slowly the figure climbed the tall boarding ladder hooked onto the side of the aircraft. When the pilot finished his climb up the steep ladder, he stepped over to the cockpit and dropped into the opening left by the split clamshell door canopies. Line Chief Ray Hopper helped adjust his belts and gave him a reassuring pat on the back as he left him.

Then he was alone. Avro Aircraft Limited's Chief Development Test Pilot assigned to the Avro Arrow was Jan Zurakowski, known simply as 'Zura' by many (his Christian or given name was 'Janusz', but few outside of family and close friends used that name). Zurakowski had been preparing for this day for more than a year. It was his tenacity and indomitable spirit that had kept the flight test programme on schedule even after the engineers in the Arrow Project Office under Fred Mitchell had wanted to postpone flight testing. The Arrow simulator, hooked up to an IBM 704 digital computer, had shown that the aircraft would be unflyable. After only seconds, Potocki and Zura had 'crashed' in the simulator runs. An expert from the United States wasn't sure why the pilots were doing so badly. Simulator supervisor Stan Kwiatkowski and members of his staff had doubted the accuracy of the tests. Zurakowski flatly rejected them.

After conferring with Jim Floyd, Vice-President of Engineering, Zurakowski said that things would straighten themselves out; he had flown so-called unstable aircraft earlier in England and survived. The Arrow simulator programme was shelved for the time being and the test pilots went back to what they knew best – flying aircraft.

On 4 December 1957, RL-201 had commenced ground-running tests with the interim twin Pratt and Whitney J75 P3 engines installed. Taxi tests were begun on Christmas Eve 1957, and over the next few months low-speed trials had taken the first aircraft up to 100 knots, still well below take-off speeds. The initial taxi runs had proved that the aircraft was stable in its runs and the engines performed satisfactorily. The only problems came in the operation of the drag chute, which had released properly only twice in five tests after its deployment, and a series of tyre explosions. Due to the Arrow's all-up weight and relatively high touchdown speed, a drag chute was required to shorten its landing rollout, thus providing a safety factor in landing. The taxi tests had resulted in a modified drag-chute release mechanism and an adjustment of the length of the chute lines. Other than minor adjustments to brakes, flight control systems and engine flow control units, everything was proceeding normally.

Earlier that day Zurakowski had gone about his morning routines, with his wife and his family kept unaware that the first flight might be imminent. However, when he kissed her goodbye, his wife Anna (Hanka) seemed to sense that something was different. She later reported, 'I really did not know it would be for sure today. He never tells me the real day.'[2] She would not go to the plant; instead she busied herself at home with sending off the two young Zurakowski boys, nine-year-old George and six-year-old Mark, to St Vincent de Paul School in Toronto. She didn't tell the boys what she had guessed, not wishing to worry them. Anna returned to her household chores and occupied herself with ironing, keeping her thoughts in check.

Her husband now had his mind on his job. In his customary calm and methodical fashion Zurakowski completed his cockpit check. One week before, a similar procedure had uncovered a hydraulic leak that had resulted in the flight being 'scrubbed'. He scanned the instruments; everything looked right. After eighteen months of preparation, Avro Arrow RL-201 was ready for its maiden flight, the beginning of Phase 1 of the flight test programme, involving the contractor's test and development flying.

Two Avro Aircraft fire trucks rolled away and took up their stations at a midway point just off Runway 32. It was 9.30am. Right on schedule, Zurakowski signalled the Malton control tower that he was taxiing. In the Avro control tower, Don Rogers, Chief of Flight Operations, joined Fred Lake, the company's radio operator, to maintain a radio link for the flight, thereby 'monitoring the progress of this very critical first flight'.[3] As Zura scanned the sky in front of him, it looked good: hazy, but sunshine was poking through the high cloud cover. The radio crackled with the message, 'Number 201, you are cleared for Runway 32. Winds are north-east, 10 to 20 knots.'

---

[2] Helen Allen, 'Jan's Wife had Pressing Job, Too', *Toronto Telegram*, 25 March 1958.
[3] Don Rogers, conversation with the author, 2001.

In company with an Avro fire truck, the sleek, delta-winged aircraft rolled to the end of Runway 32, the longest runway at Malton. No special arrangements had been made for the Arrow's flight. It would merely enter the normal air traffic operating that day at Malton Airport, which was shared by Avro Aircraft's facilities.

Huddled on the ground by the company's control tower was a group of the flight test engineers. One of them, Derek Woolley, tried to crack a joke, but no one seemed to be listening. At that point, someone from the Employee Services Department joined the group and blew into his hands to take away the chill. Woolley recognised him as Elwy Yost. Not far from them was a smaller group that was equally sombre. All of the Avro executive officers were there, sweating out the next few moments: A V Roe Canada's President, Crawford Gordon Jr; and from the Avro Aircraft Division, John L Plant, President and General Manager; Fred T Smye, Executive Vice-President; and James C Floyd, Vice-President and Director of Engineering, the Chief Designer responsible for the Avro Arrow.

The two chase planes roared off the runway, then the crowd shifted nervously as they watched the Arrow at the end of Runway 32.

While the chase planes circled overhead, at the end of the runway Zurakowski wound up the powerful J75 engines. Although afterburning could have been used, the first flight did not require the additional engine power. William T 'Bill' Gunston, Technical Editor of the prestigious British magazine *Flight* stationed at the parking lot near the service road, described the take-off: 'The crescendo of engines signalled the start of the take-off run. Simultaneously, the two chase planes straightened out, taking up courses low on either side of the runway, the CF-100 to the Arrow's right, the Sabre to the left, the signal that the Arrow was beginning its take-off roll.'[4] At 9.51am the brakes were released and the white interceptor streaked down the concrete runway. In a car parked near the edge of the runway, John Painter, a member of Avro's service department, recalled: 'The big white delta thundered past me down the runway...'[5]

Gunston's first view of the Arrow was dramatic. He reported, 'Suddenly, the Arrow burst into view behind the view-obstructing rise in the ground. It was rolling along at a steep angle of attack,

[4] 'He did it', *Aircraft*, April 1958.
[5] John F Painter, 'Zura: Turning Cartwheels in the Sky', *Aeroplane Monthly*, Pt 3 (March 2002), 66.

nose wheel already high off the runway. Then it simply flew off in one clean motion that was at once smoothly continuous, yet positive.'[6] Reaching 120 knots, Zurakowski had raised the nose wheel and, at 170 knots, smoothly lifted off, less than half of the way down the lengthened 11,050-foot runway.

Momentarily the giant delta flew just above and parallel to the runway before beginning a climb to altitude. The Malton tower laconically intoned: 'Avro 201 off at 9.51 and cleared to company tower.' Zurakowski pointed the Arrow skyward on a northerly course at an initial rate of climb of 3,000fpm, cautiously testing the plane at 200 knots. Approaching from above and behind were Woodman, who took station on the left, and Potocki, sliding into position on the right, checking the Arrow. Raymond Boone, who worked in Procurement, vividly recalled that 'The staff were all invited to go outside to watch, and as I looked around my immediate area, I could see grown men and women wiping away the tears. Over the years these dedicated men and women gave blood, sweat and tears as their contribution to that day. And now, it really happened: our beloved bird was in the air.'[7]

Climbing steeply to 5,000 feet with the undercarriage still extended, Zura maintained 200 knots as the chase planes bobbed close by. With most of the Arrow's first flight scheduled to be in low speed and landing configuration, the chase aircraft had flaps down to keep position. In the control tower, Zurakowski's emotionless voice started to come through with vital information. When he retracted the landing gear, suddenly the nose gear uplock's warning light blinked red in the cockpit.

Zurakowski asked Potocki for a positive visual confirmation of the nose wheel's retraction. In the CF-100 chase plane Potocki moved in closer for a look. He reported that the gear had retracted and the nose wheel gear door had closed properly. Woodman confirmed the check. Zura gave a crisp 'Thank you' before moving on to the other basic manoeuvres of a first test flight. After a while, he reported formally, 'The controls are behaving quite nicely. I can see no oscillatory motions of any description.'[8]

---

[6] 'He did it'.
[7] Raymond Boone, conversation with the author, 2001.
[8] *There Never Was an Arrow*, produced by George Robertson, 44 min, CBC Film Production, 1980.

The Avro Arrow over the Avro factory during the first flight.
(Toronto Aerospace Museum)

The speed was then boosted to 250 knots, and the Arrow moved
up to 11,000 feet altitude.

The first flight had been denoted as a familiarisation flight. Each
new experimental aircraft went through a similar process. No two
types of aircraft have the same 'feel', and flying characteristics have
to be established before testing can continue. A routine of gentle
manoeuvres tested the responsiveness of the controls and the flight
characteristics of the plane. Zura went through his list of checks: air
brakes, automatic flight control in normal and emergency modes,
low-speed handling, undercarriage operation. All seemed normal.
The interim J75 engines were also tested. Zura reported, 'The
engines are behaving quite nicely. They are occasionally giving me a
bit of a black puff of smoke coming out in the mirror but otherwise,
I can see there is no problem.'[9]

[9] *Arrow: From Dream to Destruction*, ed Jim Lloyd, A-V Studio, Video
Production, 1992.

'Wind tunnels, test rigs, electronic simulators and engineering opinion, notwithstanding, once a new type of airplane is in the air for the first time, the flight becomes a voyage of discovery for the test pilot. There is no room in the cockpit for inexperience or brashness. With an untried and unproven airplane, familiarisation flights demand a master's touch.'[10] Zurakowski was such a master.

Signals from the heavily instrumented aircraft were sent to a telemetry van where Ray Gibson, John Lockyer, Al Maddock and Bill Moore from the Flight Test Instrument Section manned complex electronic equipment. A nearly instantaneous analysis of the aircraft's flight was being recorded. The data would later be matched to the pilot's reports and the chase planes' photographs and films. More importantly, the telemetry system monitored a vast number of the flight's parameters and could instantly relay to the pilot a warning of any potential problems.

With the initial flight programme completed, Zurakowski turned back towards Malton. Marina Edgar, who worked at Orenda Engines, saw the Arrow overhead 'with the chase planes close by, and all of us were outside squinting up into the sunlight and cheering like mad. It was an exciting day.'[11] After making several passes over the factory, Zurakowski lined the aircraft up for landing. Still concerned with shepherding the first Arrow home, Zura flared into a final approach with his air brakes extended at a slightly 'hot' 180 knots – a necessary precaution. Potocki exclaimed excitedly on the intercom, 'Wonderful, Jan!'[12] The Arrow touched down 'on the button' at 160 knots, streaming the brilliantly coloured red and white drag chute. RCAF Group Captain Reg Lane, who was attached to the Arrow programme, remarked, 'It was absolutely magnificent.'[13] Zurakowski brought the streaking aircraft to a halt well before the end of the runway, ending a mainly routine, thirty-five-minute first flight.

The two chase planes made a low pass in front of the Malton passenger terminal building, with Woodman executing an exuberant victory roll in the Sabre before joining Potocki. As the Arrow rolled to the end of the runway, the immense crowd of supporters let out a

[10] Jim McLean, 'Each Move Experimental on Arrow's First Flight', *Avro Newsmagazine*, 4, 4 (2 April 1958), 10.
[11] Marina Edgar, conversation with the author, 2001.
[12] *Arrow: From Dream to Destruction.*
[13] *There Never Was an Arrow.*

collective sigh and cheered. Don Rogers took off his headset and realised, 'My knees were shaking a little bit ... it was such an important occasion.'[14] When the plane came to a stop at the run-up area of the Avro plant, Zura shut down the engines and opened the canopy. Standing up in the seat, he grinned and waved triumphantly to the group of Avro employees who were descending on the Arrow. Beginning his climb down the boarding ladder, Zurakowski was mobbed by Avro workers. Hands clutched at him as he was lifted high on the shoulders of Derek Woolley, Peter Martin and the other flight test engineers. Richard R Carley, one of the engineers assigned to the simulator programme, anxiously asked him how it flew. Zurakowski thought for a second and said, 'It's a lot easier flying the airplane than it was a simulator.'[15]

The Toronto Telegram reported that the scene was a 'football hero's ovation from overjoyed Avro Aircraft workers.'[16] In the *Toronto Daily Star* was a more portentous description of their emotions: 'The first flight was the climax of four years of research and building. On it was pinned the hopes of more than 600 separate companies who had built parts for this machine.'[17]

The first flight debriefing was a short affair. Zura made his typical, brief but accurate report on the flight: 'The first flight of the Arrow was very simple: check the control response, engines, undercarriage and air brakes, handling in speed up to 400 knots, and low speed in a landing configuration.'[18] With virtually nothing to report on in terms of problems, Zura was whisked by Arthur H Stewart, the Public Relations Manager, into a press conference. Media from the Toronto and Hamilton areas were filing local, national and international stories featuring Zurakowski and the Avro Arrow. In the Avro head office Zurakowski and Potocki were joined by a jubilant group of Avro executives who included Plant, Floyd and Duke Riggs, Vice-President of Manufacturing.

---

[14] *Straight Arrow: the Janusz Zurakowski Story*, directed by George and Anna Prodanou, White Pine Pictures, Toronto, 1998.

[15] Chris Gainor, *Arrows to the Moon: Avro's Engineers and the Space Race* (Burlington, Ontario: Apogee Books), 29.

[16] 'He did it'.

[17] Ibid.

[18] Jan Zurakowski, 'Flying the Arrow', 35th Anniversary Celebration of the Roll-Out of the 'Avro Arrow' CF-105, souvenir booklet, 1992.

After being pressed later for a statement, Zurakowski offered: 'There certainly was more excitement for the several thousand Avro employees watching my first flight than for myself seated in the cockpit trying to remember hundreds of dos and don'ts. The unpleasant part of my first flight was my feeling of responsibility, combined with the realisation that the success of this aircraft depended on thousands of components, especially electronic and hydraulic, with only a small percentage under my direct control. But total responsibility for the flight was mine.'[19] Plant laughed and said, 'Zurakowski must have been the only one who wasn't nervous.'[20]

Janusz Zurakowski being carried on the shoulders of Avro employees after the first flight. *(DND)*

Within two hours of the Arrow's first flight, more than half a million readers and listeners in the Toronto area were following the events of the day in newspapers and on the radio, and by evening more than a million Canadian viewers had seen the story on CBC Television. An Avro media campaign that had been blanketing media outlets worldwide ensured that the story was also picked up by Associated Press, United Press and the International News

[19] Ibid.
[20] 'Arrow', *Toronto Daily Star*, 25 March 1958.

Service across the United States, and by Canadian Press throughout Europe and Asia. Invitations to James S Butz from the prestigious trade magazine *Aviation Week* and to Bill Gunston, renowned British aviation author and frequent contributor to *Flight* magazine, led to a number of feature newspaper and magazine articles that appeared in both the United States and the United Kingdom.

In the United States, an estimated audience of ten million or more watched the Arrow's maiden flight on the *Today* show hosted by Dave Garroway. In an era when families were buying television sets for the very first time, the *Today* show on NBC emerged as the first news-entertainment programme, and forever changed the way that people both make and watch television. Earlier in the fall of 1957, Garroway had completed a live broadcast from Toronto that had included a story about Avro Aircraft. He had commented that 'behind these doors [Avro] is developing a tremendous achievement in world aviation; but it is top secret.'[21] On Wednesday 26 March 1958, Garroway's morning audience was told, 'And now the doors have opened and this is what happened...'[22] With that comment, the screen changed to reveal the Arrow lifting off gracefully from the runway.

The flight had been nearly flawless. Zurakowski remembered: 'I had a lot to keep me busy, with a multitude of switches and indicators in front of me. I liked the layout of the cockpit; things were easy to see and reach.'[23] Jim Floyd recalled, 'We were concerned, but not apprehensive; we had confidence in our airplane.'[24] When interviewed after the flight, Potocki, Zura's friend and 'second', made the taciturn reply of the test pilot: 'The plan for the test flight went exactly on schedule.'[25] In response to questions about the flight characteristics of the Arrow, the soft-spoken Zurakowski remembers saying simply, 'It handled very nicely.'[26]

The flight problems or 'snags' Zura reported were 'minor: buffeting when the landing gears opened in flight, no 'up and

---

[21] Jim McLean, 'Each Move Experimental'.

[22] Ibid.

[23] John Thompson, 'Captains of the Clouds: Remembering that day 40 years ago when the Arrow first took flight', *Toronto Sun*, 21 March 1998.

[24] Ibid.

[25] Jim McLean, 'Each Move Experimental', 11.

[26] Jan Zurakowski, 'Flying the Arrow'.

locked' display of the landing gear and failure of the air conditioner's temperature control.'[27] Floyd was incredulous at the smooth first flight. 'I remember the test of a new plane in England when the snag sheet was 13 pages long. The Arrow's took only one page, including Zura's request for a clock in the cockpit. We kidded him that he wanted it so he'd know when it was time to head back for lunch.'[28] Engineering staff later framed the first flight snag sheet and hung it proudly in the flight test office. (Today, the framed snag sheet resides in Floyd's home office.)

Avro company executives warily began to describe the Arrow as 'a world-beater'.

The first flight was chronicled in a unique 16mm promotional film, *Supersonic Sentinel*, put out by A V Roe Canada's photographic department as an initiative supported and funded by the Engineering Division (under Ron Adey as the Chief Administrative Engineer). Lou Wise had asked Floyd for permission to make a series of films. 'I told him it would be useful to film all activity related to the project so that periodically we could edit a progress report film to go along with engineering documents that had to be submitted to RCAF and DND [Department of National Defence] from time to time... He agreed with the idea, and that was the start of a series of several films over a period of years.'[29]

The film sequence of the first flight which dominated the 23-minute production was made up of raw footage shot that day by Mackechnie and Woodman as well as film shot from the ground by a number of Lou Wise's crew members. Although the primary purpose for the aerial photography was 'engineering coverage', another reason for the filming was publicity. At a meeting with Zurakowski, Potocki and Woodman, the photographic department directed that at least five minutes of the maiden flight was to be devoted to aerial cinematography and still shots from the chase planes for publicity use. The *Supersonic Sentinel* film was completed with footage of test flights by the RL-202 and the RL-203, the second and third Arrows. Wise served as producer, director and narrator of the project, albeit uncredited. The public relations department released the film in

---

[27] James Dow, *The Arrow* (Toronto: James Lorrimer and Co, 1979), 115.

[28] John Thompson, 'Captains of the Clouds'.

[29] Lou Wise, conversation with the author, 2001.

August 1958 as part of a massive advertising and marketing campaign that accompanied the Avro Arrow during its short life.

Along with all of the company's records that were later destroyed, *Supersonic Sentinel* disappeared from the public eye for decades. It was rumoured that an original print had escaped destruction, and years later, in 1996, the film once again became part of the Avro Arrow saga. If you listen carefully to the voice narrating the CBC *Arrow* production, you will hear Lou Wise again telling the story of a dream that once was.

A tribute from the man on the ground to the man in the air

Years later, on 26 June 1990, at a special night for Janusz Zurakowski, the Madawaska Valley Lions Club sponsored a Testimonial Dinner. In an eloquent address, Jim Floyd remembered the occasion of the Arrow's maiden flight:

> The date is March 25, 1958. The Man on the Ground is feeling lonely today as a man, in whose trust and skills he must place his reputation and future, climbs into the tiny cockpit of the white monster with wings, ready to take it from Mother Earth into the blue skies for the first time.
>
> As the bird goes up and away, the Man in the Air is also feeling the unique sense of loneliness that comes with the knowledge that he is now in sole charge of this incredibly complex piece of flying machinery and that his skills and courage in taking it through the vital first-flight performance checks could be a major factor in the future of the project. Yet much of the decision making was outside of his control and he had to trust that the Man on the Ground had made all the right decisions to ensure that he had a safe aircraft that would meet the stringent performance specifications.
>
> As he takes the bird through the paces, the loneliness of the Man in the Air gradually relaxes, since he is giving his undivided attention to the flying of the aircraft and is in constant communication with the chase planes beside him and the technicians on the ground.
>
> But the Man on the Ground is still feeling lonely, even though surrounded by colleagues who were involved in the design and build of this state-of-the-art airplane. He is thinking of the thirty-eight thousand

parts that are going to have to work perfectly to prove the aircraft and keep his friend safe on this important flight, thinking of the thousand and one problems encountered in the five years of designing and building this megabuck project, and the hopes that go with its success. He is also aware that, in spite of the fact that the creation of this edge-of-technology airplane was the work of an incredibly talented team, the final responsibility rests squarely on his shoulders and if anything should go wrong on this or any future flight, the buck would come to rest at his feet.

There is an unspoken bond between this Man on the Ground and the Man in the Air, since theirs is the kind of loneliness only understood by those who have faced almost unbearable responsibility alone – and yet together.

Tonight on this special occasion, the Man on the Ground salutes the Man in the Air and joins all attendees in offering Jan Zurakowski the affection and respect he so rightfully deserves.

(The Man on the Ground: Jim Floyd, Former VP Engineering, Avro)[30]

---

[30] James C Floyd, conversation with the author, 2001.

Chapter Two

Forged in Fire

Janusz Zurakowski's story began on 12 September 1914 when he was born to Polish parents in Ryzawka, in the most eastern part of the Russian territories previously belonging to Poland. Today his birthplace is part of Ukraine. The patriarch of the family was his grandfather, Edmund Zurakowski, one of the landed gentry. The family bore the 'Sas' coat of arms, dating back to the 1600s. The coat of arms features two golden arrows, one piercing the plumage of the crown as if symbolising war and the other rampant on a blue shield bearing two golden stars and a half moon. The arrows are perhaps a prophetic sign of Janusz Zurakowski's life to come.

Poland in the 1900s

Janusz had kept extensive diaries, and much of his family's story comes from these memoirs. For many generations, the Zurakowskis had been a well-known family in the community. Their land holdings comprised the beautiful country estate, Zytniki (not far from Human). The family were renowned for their quick tempers as well as large numbers of children. The locals had a clever saying that 'behind every bush there is a Zuraczek'. Over time the family grew but became poorer, such that when a marriage was arranged for Maria Juriewicz and Edmund Zurakowski, the bride's father, Teofil Juriewicz, worried that his daughter might have made a poor choice.

The Zytniki estate was the dowry, and although the fortunes of the newlyweds were assured, the prospects for their family were not promising. Edmund realised that the old family estate was not sufficient to provide a secure living for his five sons and three daughters, and he strived to find them a new future. Education for his sons was a priority. One of the sons, Adam Victor, the second-last child born, was to become a doctor.

Adam Zurakowski was born and spent his childhood in Zytniki and later was educated in Human. In 1911 he obtained his degree in medicine at Kiev University. It was in Kiev that Adam was to meet his future wife. Janusz's mother, Maria Antonina Szawlowska, was the eldest daughter in a family with five children living in a small town, Hajsyn. As a child she loved music and her family ensured that she studied music at the Kiev Conservatory. She was fifteen years old when she met Adam Zurakowski. One of Janusz's earliest family stories involves the first encounter of his mother and father. 'They lived with the same family who ran a students' lodging house. The family was always joking that my mother purposefully crushed her finger in the door to ask for help from her neighbour, a handsome medical student. After this meeting, the two young people fell in love.' They wed in Kuny, close to Hajsyn, in 1910. Adam was still to complete his studies at the university, then the two young people set out to begin their life together in a new community.

Ryzawka was the site of a large sugar refinery, which hired Adam Zurakowski as a doctor. Young Maria became a homemaker and shortly afterward a mother, when their first child was born. Bronislaw and Justyna were the first two offspring before the birth of Janusz, who was followed by Jadwiga and Kazimiera. Janusz's memories of the family home were documented much later with the comments: 'My recollections from the time when we lived in Ryzawka are hazy. I know that we often visited Zytniki, where my father's family stayed till the revolution. Somehow I don't remember the house except for the vast fields and the orchards of sour cherries. The cherries were gathered into big baskets and poured right into the wagons that moved slowly along the lines of trees. I do remember the same wagons full of ripe watermelons.' Just before 1914 a mortgage of eight thousand roubles in gold, with a duration of forty years, was issued against the estate. As the world entered the First World War, the family's fortunes looked favourable.

Being a Pole in that period was a measure of culture, beliefs and language but not of a homeland. In the 1600s the Polish Commonwealth had been the largest European state, but then came a time of struggles and misfortunes under a succession of rulers. By the end of the eighteenth century Russia, Prussia and Austria had succeeded in partitioning the territory and Poland had ceased to exist as an independent state. The long period of Poland's partition by the Three Powers failed to destroy the Polish longing for a linguistic and spiritual identity. Although successive bloody uprisings (1830-1831 and 1863) were viciously suppressed and thousands of Poles were forced to flee to the West, 'attempts to repress the national culture were not very successful. The various methods used during the partitions to change the character of the society tended instead to fuel the national spirit – those were the years when the best Polish literature was created, partly in the occupied country, partly abroad especially in France, where the Polish emigration was very strong.'

The tumultuous First World War years shortly after Janusz's birth were a distressing time as the area in which the Zurakowski family lived was drawn into war. He remembered: 'It was wartime but I was too small to understand the meaning of it. However, I know from my family's recollections that everybody was waiting for news from the fronts.' Although Janusz's father was a medical doctor and, therefore, of the gentry, or at least the intelligentsia, there would be no guarantees that the family would be spared the hardships and deprivation that befell their region. Many of the Polish peasants and middle class of the time had fallen on hard times, as crops had failed and the younger generations had been drafted into military service. Three different armies, Austrian-Hungarian, German and Russian, conscripted Polish youth. Often these young men would be facing each other across the battlefront. Their small community was put in peril as the shifting fortunes of conflict eventually led to much of the populace fleeing to the West. The fervent dreams of a new Poland had not been extinguished; rather, it was a momentous opportunity for it to arise again as a nation from the pyres of war.

A new Poland arises

With the leadership of General Józef Pilsudski, who had formed the Polish Legions under Austrian sponsorship, Polish claims to national emancipation were raised. In 1918, when at Brest Litovsk the Central Powers (Germany, Austria-Hungary, Bulgaria and Turkey) signed a peace treaty with Russia, which was detrimental to a new Poland, the Polish Legions rebelled, led by General Józef Haller. They marched into Ukraine to join other Polish forces fighting against the Germans. Haller's forces eventually were surrounded and defeated. This act of courage and sacrifice may have moved the victorious Allied Powers (Great Britain, France, Italy and the United States) to recognise the national goals of the Poles. In US President Woodrow Wilson's Fourteen Points (1918), which subsequently formed the basis of the Peace Treaty of Versailles at the end of hostilities, Wilson acknowledged the right to an independent Poland that would 'include territories indisputably Polish, with free and secure access to the sea'.

On 11 November 1918, Józef Pilsudski proclaimed Polish independence and became Head of State and Commander-in-Chief, with Ignacy Jan Paderewski as Prime Minister. An uprising liberated

Poznan and, shortly afterwards, Pomerania, which gave access to the Baltic Sea. In the chaos that followed the Russian Revolution and the collapse of the Central Powers, new states arose, the Soviet Union, Lithuania, Czechoslovakia and the Ukrainian Republic. All these states laid claims to territory occupied by Poles.

Even for a young child, Janusz's memories of this period are vibrant. The following comments come from his memoirs (translated by his wife, Anna): 'I don't remember when the revolution reached us. The Bolsheviks left my father in peace as a factory doctor, but my family remembered that they had sought the director of the factory, Grzybowski, and that my father had risked his life giving him shelter in our house.

'My own first recollection from this time is not at all dramatic. A big Bolshevik vehicle stopped in the middle of the factory yard. I stayed close to it and observed in fascination. I was especially excited by the puffs of black smoke coming from the back of this strange monster. This was the first car that I had seen in my life and my first encounter with a motor vehicle.

'With the revolution came disaster and fear into the lives of the estate owners across the country. Their houses and mansions were set on fire, and very often this was the end of their life. They were often murdered by the wild crowds. However, a large number of Polish owners were able to escape to the large cities, especially Kiev.'

A race for freedom

Anna described the times: 'In 1918, when independent Poland was declared, the Bolsheviks opened the frontier for a short time and Poles could then leave Ukraine. Not too many people decided to do so. They still had some hope that the revolution would end and that they would be able to go back to their homes. Very soon the frontier was closed again, but in 1919 the Bolsheviks agreed to release several rail transports of cargo and people to Poland. The conditions in those transports were deplorable. The perilous journey took weeks. The Bolsheviks purposefully left the cars on side tracks for gangs of hoodlums to rob the people of all their possessions. Sometimes they even took the clothes from the people's backs. We had relatives who came to Poland with their clothes stitched from old sacks.'

For the Zurakowski family an imminent move would soon change their lives. 'In the meantime my family was still staying in Ryzawka. It seemed that the fate of this part of Ukraine was yet undecided. There was news that General Pilsudski had an understanding with Ataman Petlura to create a free Ukraine.'

The Poles had liberated Wilno from the Lithuanians in 1919, reoccupied the area around Cieszyn (which had been invaded by the Czechs) and annexed the Western Ukraine, when the Ukrainian Republic, which had been supported by Poland, collapsed under attack from Soviet forces. At the beginning of 1920 the Polish Army started an offensive to the east. Zurakowski's memoirs note: 'When in May 1920, this army reached Kiev, our people were full of hope. Unfortunately, this army never reached us! And later worse news came.' The Red Army, having crushed all counter-revolutionary forces inside Russia, now turned its attention to Poland. The Polish offensive was crushed, the Bolsheviks pushed to the west and reached the heart of Poland, approaching Warsaw.

By August 1920 the Russian forces were at the gates of Warsaw. Their bloody advance through Poland had been accompanied by savage atrocities. Lenin even deliberated over greater retribution. In a note to Comrade Skylansky (Efraim Markovich), Chairman of the Fifth Army in Dvinsk, he wrote, 'We shall move forward 10-20 versts [0.7 miles] and hang the Kulaks [wealthy landowners], priests and landowners. Bounty: 100,000 roubles for each man hanged.'[1] With the very survival of Poland at stake, on 15 August the Battle of Warsaw became 'the Miracle on the Vistula': the Polish Army routed the Red Army and saved an impotent and weakened Europe from Soviet conquest.

Janusz remembered, 'Everybody in our family was feeling relief when the Polish Army was able to push the Red Army back and out of Poland. Only after the Peace Treaty of Riga in 1921, when the Polish eastern frontiers were settled, did my parents decide to escape to Poland.'

From a passage in Janusz's memoirs comes this account: 'Very quietly, our parents started preparations for departure, although we children knew nothing about it. I remember only that they prepared for us small camisoles with some money sewed inside. And one day, disguised in country clothes, we mounted a large wagon drawn by a

---

[1] Martin McCauley, *The Russian Revolution and the Soviet State 1917-1921 Documents* (New York: Barnes & Noble Books, 1975), 165.

pair of strong horses and we started our journey to the west. On the wagon were eight people including five children, because during the war our two little sisters, Jadwiga and Kazimiera, were born, and our young cousin Jozia travelled with us.

The Zurakowski family in 1921 on the wagon that bore them to freedom with Janusz in the centre. *(Zurakowski collection)*

'Very often we were travelling during the night, when the children slept. We were saying that we were going to visit our relatives in the next village. In this way, slowly we were moving ahead, and the names of villages were changing all the time. This journey lasted three weeks and we covered six hundred kilometres. I can imagine now how difficult and nerve-racking a time this was for my parents!

'Close to the Polish border, my father found a guide. This was a new frontier and the people from both sides could visit without much trouble. We crossed the border with our wagon during the night or rather early morning before the sunrise.

'We were travelling in complete silence and the wagon was shaking terribly on the rough trail. After some time the guide left us, saying that we were already on Polish soil. Somehow my father did not believe him, and when we heard hoof beats behind us, we started to go ahead very quickly. Even today I remember this frantic drive! The wagon was jumping so badly that we thought that it would go to pieces in the next moment. But escaping the cavalry was impossible. The horsemen caught up with us, and then we saw that it was the Polish cavalry (*ulani*). We were in Poland!'

In Rowne, a small community along the way, Janusz's father sold the horses, and the family then travelled to Warsaw by train, staying there with the Grzybowski family (the same Grzybowski whom they had saved during the revolution). Soon after, Adam Zurakowski obtained the post of District Doctor in Garwolin, a small town located between Warsaw and Lublin.

An uneasy peace

The armistice between Poland and the Soviet Union that had been signed at Riga was followed in March 1921 by a peace treaty that determined and secured Poland's eastern frontiers. On 17 March 1921 a modern, democratic constitution was voted in for Poland. The task that lay ahead would be difficult. The new nation was still in turmoil, with the land in economic ruin, a chaotic political situation and, after a hundred and twenty years of foreign rule, no tradition of civil service. Only the army and the Church acted as stabilising forces.

It was shortly after the conflict between Poland and the Soviet Union was resolved that the Zurakowski family settled in the town of Garwolin. There, Janusz's youngest brother, Adam, was born and Janusz began his school years. His father and mother had high hopes for their children in the reborn Polish state.

Young Janusz had a vivid memory of his first sight of an aircraft over Garwolin. As the seven-year-old trudged home from school one day, a white airplane gracefully traced its way above the startled and amazed youngster. Janusz ran breathlessly after the humming 'white bird' until it was out of sight. He never forgot that first glimpse of a flying machine.

In 1927 the Zurakowski family moved again, to a permanent home in the city of Lublin, 110 miles south of Warsaw, where Adam Zurakowski was now a district medical inspector. Janusz and Anna Alina Danielski (his future wife) came to know each other in Lublin because their fathers worked together as doctors. In Lublin, Janusz attended the Stanislaw Staszic High School but did not take a great interest in his studies. He loved skating, skiing and swimming, but he commented later, 'I didn't show too much enthusiasm for learning; I would rather follow in the footsteps of my brother'[2] who had developed a love of flying. Like many young people of the time, their imaginations were inspired by the aerial feats that were taking place in Poland and Europe.

In the 1920s the support of Polish government agencies had resulted in the establishment of an aviation industry producing 'home' designs for both civil and military aviation demands. 'Polish designers soon gained a worldwide reputation for ingenious approaches to various problems.'[3] Civil aviation in Poland developed along the lines of other European nations. Recreational flying in both glider and powered aircraft was undertaken at civilian airfields, which also provided training facilities. Indigenous aircraft – such as the RWD-4 touring airplane and, a development of this design, the RWD-5 – played an important role in this period. Polskie Linie Lotnicze (LOT), the state airline established at Strachowice Airfield in 1928, began to provide a national and international service.

The Polish military aircraft industry produced a number of unique bomber and fighter aircraft in the 1930s for both domestic and foreign orders. Panstowe Zaklady Lotnicze (PZL), or the state aircraft factory known as Polish National Aviation Establishments, was established in 1927 to undertake design and production of indigenous aircraft. Designer Zygmunt Pulawski developed a series of revolutionary fighters (P1 to P 24) with a characteristic high-mounted gull wing known as the 'Pulawski wing'. The wing was mated to a simple but robust metal fuselage that had a fixed scissors undercarriage and a tightly cowled Jupiter or Mercury radial engine. Extensive testing and refinement led to the P7a, which entered production in 1931 with an order for 150 aircraft. In September 1939, 205 of the more advanced P11a and P11c variants were the principal Polish fighters opposing the Luftwaffe. After Pulawski was killed in a crash in 1931, the development of the fighter series was undertaken by Wsiewolod Jakimiuk. An export version, the P24, with slightly increased performance, went into service in Bulgaria, Greece, Romania and Turkey in the years before conflict engulfed Europe. The PZL-23 'Karas' bomber and reconnaissance aircraft and the PZL-37 'Los'

[2] Marek Kusiba, 'ZURA' Opisanie Janusza Zurakowskiego, October 2001.
[3] Jerzy B Cynk, 'Pictorial Museum of Polish Aviation', *Air Progress* (May 1959), 63.

medium bomber (one of the most modern types in Europe in the inter-war years) were also produced by the company. Other Polish manufacturers produced training and light aircraft used by the military.

During this exciting period in aviation history, Janusz's brother Bronislaw, who was three years his senior, was an aviation enthusiast who studied aeronautics at Warsaw Polytechnic. Janusz emulated his brother's interest in flying and began to build flying models at an early age. Both he and Bronislaw were members of a school model club where larger and more elaborate models were constructed. This hobby became Janusz's preoccupation, and he excelled at the construction of intricate balsa and cloth models. His memories of that period reveal that there were numerous model plane competitions between schools and at regional and national levels. In 1929, when Janusz was fifteen years old, he won first prize in a national competition for flying models. His award included a flight in a small single-engine Lublin LKL-5 trainer at the Lublin Flying Club, piloted by a First World War veteran, Sergeant Zuromski. His account of the flight came later in 1959 when he wrote: 'I remember what was surprising to me as we got up – that everything on the ground seemed to move very slowly. We were up twenty minutes. Coming down everything moved faster... I knew two things: that I had to finish school and that then I would fly!'[4] This brief first flight was the beginning of Janusz's lifelong passion for flying.

One obstacle had to be overcome, however. Janusz intimated that 'the idea of becoming a pilot met strong opposition from my father, who made sure that his doctor friends at the Aviation Medical Examination Centre in Warsaw refused my application. I allegedly suffered from tuberculosis in the collarbone.' Although upset over his treatment, Janusz persevered and in 1932, as a youth in high school, he gained flying skills at the controls of gliders. He signed on for a gliding course at the Gliding School in Polichno-Pinczow, instructed by Tadeusz Ciastula, attaining a Category A and B there. During his next holidays, after his matriculation exams, at another gliding club camp he attained his Category C, which called for greater proficiency and the ability to climb above the launch point.

[4] Janusz Zurakowski, quoted in Phyllis Griffith's 'In the Life of Zura', *The Toronto Telegram*, 4 May 1959.

His first piloting experiences were memorable. 'Flying in the right kind of weather over a beautiful countryside is wonderful. Seeing the sunset above the clouds is not to be forgotten, and flying is relaxing. It takes the tension out of me.'[5] 'The best flying really, which I remember, was flying gliders, sailplanes.'[6] The operation of the single-place glider involved a team of helpers stationed near the ramp at the apex of a hill. 'One started, without using a tow plane or take-off winch, just with the help of two rubber lines and six people, who on order pulled and ran downhill, stretching the lines, the tail of the glider being secured by a quick-release peg. On the pilot's command, 'Release,' the tail was released, and the glider shot in the air like from a catapult. The pilot started flying figure-eights trying to catch either up-draughts or thermals. Considering the low height of the launching field, that was quite an achievement.'[7]

By 1934 Janusz had completed his matriculation at Lublin. While his sisters intended to study in Warsaw, he now dreamed of becoming a pilot, although his father maintained a wish for his son to continue his studies in preparation for some other career. Janusz had determined that there was another way to achieve his goal. He volunteered to join the Army. 'As a graduate, I had a choice of service. Of course, I chose the Aviation Reserve Cadet Officers' School at Deblin and, as a twenty-year-old candidate, I joined the Polish Air Force.' That year he enrolled in Deblin as one of only forty successful applicants out of two thousand prospects. At that time, the fledgling air arm was part of the army, which had a long and proud history, and from 1935 to 1937 much of Zurakowski's studies prepared him for a military career.

Initially only graduates from the Aviation Reserve Cadet Officers' School were accepted for pilot training at Deblin, but from 1935 to 1937 this prerequisite was removed. However, new candidates had to complete a pilot course at an aeroclub, and the Reserve Pilots' School's training period was extended to three years. From 1936 training of pilots became the primary activity of the school.

General military training was introduced as the principal subject

[5] Kusiba, 'ZURA'.
[6] Peter Hum, 'The Man Who Flew the Arrow', *The Ottawa Citizen*, 9 January 1997.
[7] Kusiba, 'ZURA'.

in the first year. In the second and third years, mainly specialist-aviation training was provided for different groups of cadet pilots and observers. The pilot training course consisted of 2,200 hours of theoretical training in seven subjects as well as flying. Practical instruction, which made up forty per cent of the course, was conducted in French and Polish training planes. Zurakowski successfully soloed in May 1935 in a high-wing RWD8 monoplane. After completing his flight-training course under the able tutelage of Stefan Witozenc, he was promoted to the rank of Sub-Lieutenant. Like other cadets, Zurakowski's training at Deblin led to eventual transition to the Polish Air Force as a combat flier.

The Polish Air Force

During the First World War, numerous Poles had been drafted into the air arms of the three occupying powers (Russia, Austria and Germany), and Polish flying elements had been set up in these countries as well as in France. On 19 August 1917 a Polish aviation unit was incorporated into the Polish Army Corps, which was formed with the agreement of the Tsarist government. After the Russian revolution, this unit was dissolved.

Another aviation section was formed in October 1918 in territory held by White Russian forces and, making its way to Poland, seized a number of air bases from the retreating Austrian and German armies and began assembling a single coordinated air arm. In the meantime, after having completed training in France in the summer of 1918, a group of Polish aviators flying French-supplied aircraft arrived in Poland in June 1919. On 29 September 1919 the Polish Air Force (PAF), Polskie Powietrzne Sily Zbrojne, was officially established from the disparate units. It subsequently played a vital role in stalling the Soviet offensive of August 1920. In the peace that followed, the PAF was completely reorganised and expanded. In the inter-war period, when many of the European powers still relied on outmoded biplanes, the Polish Air Force was the first to use all-metal-construction monoplane fighters. In 1938 the PAF became independent of the army but remained a defensive force principally dedicated to army support.

Operational flying

Upon completion of his course in 1937, and graduating fifth in his class, Sub-Lieutenant Zurakowski was posted to Lwow (now Lvov

in Ukraine). Polish air bases were mainly concentrated in large
population centres and industrial areas, but a smaller network of
subsidiary fields and emergency bases was being developed at this
time. Zurakowski was attached to 161 Fighter Squadron of the Sixth
Air Regiment, Army Lodz, flying the PZL P11c fighter. For him,
flying a fighter was the epitome of the elite pilot, although
Zurakowski relates, 'Lots of people will probably dispute that ... but
when I was asked what I wanted to fly, I asked for fighters. I
remember that some of my friends tried to talk me out of it, though,
because they thought the day of the fighter was over.'[8]

Janusz Zurakowski serving in
the Polish Air Force, 1937.
(Zurakowki collection)

PZL P-11C, the frontline fighter in Poland in
1939. *(model by Tomasz Gronczewski)*

The squadron that Sub-Lieutenant Zurakowski joined was a
frontline unit involved in patrol duties on Poland's borders. In 1938
his squadron went on war alert as Germany pressured England and
France to abandon their commitments to Czechoslovakia. The
Soviets had reacted by clearing land and building fortifications at the
frontier area next to Czech territory. Polish military planners foresaw
either a redeployment of Soviet forces into the lands annexed by
Germany or, at the least, overflights of Polish territory by the
Soviets, to create a presence in the region. The 161 Squadron was
the closest unit to the Soviet border, and orders were drawn up to

[8] John Melady, *Pilots: Canadian Stories from the Cockpit from First Flights
to the Jet Age* (Toronto: McClelland and Stewart Inc, 1989), 98.

send the fighters north to Stanislawow to patrol the frontier. The PZL P11c was only able to maintain a patrol duration of forty-five to sixty minutes, which placed a severe limitation on its effectiveness at the border regions.

As one of the pilots charged with the defence of the sector, Zurakowski began to devise a solution to his fighter's lack of range. With a natural inclination to mechanics and 'tinkering', he began to develop new procedures to extend the 'on-station time' of the P11c. Using only a stopwatch and the fuel gauge for instrumentation, he experimented with different mixtures, settings and speeds until, as he recalled, 'I could patrol two hours and still meet the operating requirements of having a third of the fuel remaining in my tanks. At lower speed and richer mixture settings, I found I could extend my fuel range appreciably... After no enemy activity was evident and our squadron was ordered to report to Lvov, I asked the CO, 'May I check my actual range?' I flew to Warsaw, Krakow and Lvov on my flight back. In the end, I had made a five-and-a-half-hour flight with still a third of the fuel left.'

This first foray into experimental flying had only whetted his appetite for more. Zurakowski began to explore the capabilities of the P11c fighter, which many pilots had dubbed the 'bee' for its agility. His reasoning was, 'I was simply interested in the equipment we had and what it could do.' Despite the P11c's age and lack of speed, Janusz loved its responsiveness and manoeuvrability. It was still a potent fighter and the pilots in the squadron felt that the Soviet I-16s they would have faced would have been at a real disadvantage. A prominent German aerodynamicist and designer, C Weisselberger, had described what was called 'ground effect', the characteristic improvement in lift and reduction in drag as the aircraft is flying in close proximity to the ground. To check this phenomenon in practice, on the return flights from patrols at the Soviet frontier Zurakowski experimented with ground effect. 'Over the flat fields, I set the engine power at slow descend and trimmed the aircraft 'hands off'. When the aircraft reached a height less than ten feet above the ground, it stopped descending and even accelerated slightly.' These experimental test flights would be a precursor to Zurakowski's later career as a test pilot.

A gliding misadventure

Zurakowski loved the sheer exhilaration of flying and spent his holiday leave soaring in gliders at the Pinczow gliding field. 'There he carried out a fifteen-hour flight in a Komar [Mosquito] glider, which was extraordinary, considering the crude construction of gliders and primitive conditions of flying at the time.'[9]

In July 1938 Zurakowski went to the famous Gliding Academy in Bezmiechowa near the Carpathian Mountains. Earlier, in May of that year, the school had received worldwide acclaim when one of its young pilots, Tadeusz Gora, had set an international record. After starting from Bezmiechowa, Gora had reached the city of Wilno, his family home, establishing a new Polish record for the longest goal flying flight (578km). He became the first recipient of the Lilienthal Medal, the world's highest aviation award, established by the FAI in 1938. A year earlier, Wanda Molibowska had flown above Bezmiechowa for over a day (exactly 24 hours and 14 minutes), a record that wasn't surpassed for two decades.

Zurakowski was determined to leave his mark on Bezmiechowa, which almost led to tragedy. The school's gliders were constantly in use, so Zurakowski arranged to take a Delphin high-performance glider out at night when he had a better chance of having it for a long period of time. The dangers of a night launch were apparent, but with the proper use of the variometer, a climb indicator mounted in the glider, Zurakowski judged that he could manage the flight safely. He remembered recently that on the night he chose for his flight, 'It was pitch black and I could not see the top of the hills that I knew were just below.' Soon after the take-off, Zurakowski sensed that the wind had shifted and taken him over the hilltop. At the last moment he glimpsed the dim outline of the horizon and the hill in front of him. Banking the Delphin steeply, his wing tip caught the top branches of a fir tree on the slopes of Slone and he crashed heavily. 'The young pilot cracked his head and didn't remember how he managed to crawl back to the Academy buildings as he lost his memory for a couple of days.'[10]

After his head wound healed and as he slowly regained his memory, Zurakowski was released from the hospital in Przemysl to return to operational flying. He reported to his squadron and flew operationally throughout January and February 1939, but an X-ray

[9] Kusiba, 'ZURA'.
[10] Ibid.

taken earlier at the Warsaw Central Medical Aviation Institute resulted in his grounding. The X-ray revealed a crack at the back of his head and caused the military doctors to send him to Krynica in the mountains for recuperation. The diagnosis of the head injury by two different doctors varied greatly: one recommended rest while the other insisted that Zurakowski should undertake more exercise.

During his enforced 'holiday', Zurakowski passed his time in Lublin with his family and Anna Danielski. The two young people spent some time together and made arrangements to keep in touch, but for the present Zurakowski had to report back to his squadron. Despite his crash, gliders remained his first love in the air. Recalling them later, he remembered that he had begun his first aerobatics in gliders.

In early 1939 came news that Poland would field a team for a gliding competition at the 1940 Olympic Games to be held in Rome. Zurakowski was selected to be one of two military pilots that, along with two civilian flyers, would make up the Polish team. As war neared in the late summer of 1939, the plans for the Polish Olympic gliding team were suddenly dropped.

Anna Danielska and Janusz Zurakowski in 1939. *(Zurakowski collection)*

After his return to the squadron, Zurakowski learned that his skills in the P11c single-seater fighter had led his flight commander to identify him as a possible instructor. Orders for Zurakowski to return to the Central Flying School in Deblin as an instructor came in the spring of 1939. He bitterly complained to his commanding officer about the transfer. 'I asked him, 'Why would you lose a fully qualified fighter pilot at this time?' He stared at me and then pointed his finger at me, exclaiming, 'I had no choice. They asked for you.'' It would soon be evident why Zurakowski had been chosen.

Flight Instructor

In March 1939, Zurakowski became an instructor at the Air Training Centre in Deblin, known as the 'Eaglets School'. He was assigned to the Special Fighter Training unit in the Advanced Flying School at Grudziadz-Ulez near Deblin, joining four other experienced instructors. Until 1939 the Air Training Centre provided all the primary school and training centres for the air force. Due to the demands for modernisation of equipment and increased pilot recruiting, the Polish Air Force embarked on a more strenuous training programme utilising its most talented and able pilots in instructional units.

At Grudziadz-Ulez, teamed with his former instructor and friend, First Lieutenant Witozenc, Zurakowski flew the older PZL P7 as an advanced trainer for pilots who would transition to the operational PZL P11a and P11c fighters in squadron service. As his last summer of peace faded into the autumn of 1939, Zurakowski continued as an instructor. 'The number of students who were trained during those frantic last months of spring and summer increased. During that period the Deblin school was turning out combat pilots at a rate three times higher than previously.' In the desperate last months from March to September 1939 the school trained many of the pilots who would fight in France and England. Zurakowski realised that his job had now become vital to the defence of the nation.

During the period leading up to the outbreak of the Second World War, Polish pilots were possibly the best-trained in the world. Due to the relatively small size of the pre-war Polish Air Force (for a country comparable in population to France), only a select few of the many candidates made it through training to the combat units. From 1927 to September 1939 the Eaglets School produced thirteen commissions or graduating classes. Its 973 graduates included 707 air observers and 266 pilots.

The careers of such famous wartime Polish pilots as Lt-Col Jerzy Bajan, Lt-Col Witold Urbanowicz, Captain Stanislaw Skalski and Lt-Col Tadeusz Wicherkiewicz were intertwined with the school. During the Second World War, the school's graduates fought over Europe, Africa and Asia. Their heroism and sacrifice can be confirmed by the fact that only twenty of the one hundred and twenty airmen who graduated in 1939 survived the war. The operation of the school ended with the Nazi occupation of Poland, but was resumed during the Second World War, initially in Zamosc and, from the beginning of 1945, again in Deblin.

The training programme at the Aviation Cadets School in Deblin and the Advanced Flying School in Grudziadz-Ulez was very demanding with regard to flying and shooting skills. 'In practical training, a general rule held that only one instructor trained a cadet, which ensured continuous didactic, educational influence. This was the method of the so-called individualisation of training which took into consideration the personalities of particular cadets. A course in higher pilotage included aerobatics flights (first on a dual-control machine and then on a fighter plane), air shooting, night flights and flights without seeing the ground.'[11]

Until the outbreak of the war Eaglets School was one of the largest and best-organised aviation schools in Europe. Constant competition among the pilots pushed each candidate to do their best. One exercise, as recollected by Flight Lieutenant Stanislaw Bochniak, involved a small, coloured parachute being thrown out of the cockpit in flight. The trainee, always keeping the parachute in sight, had to climb 300 to 400 metres (1,000 feet) above it, stall into a spin and recover at just the right moment to fire exactly one shot with his gun camera. In most cases, not only did they not lose sight of the parachute, but they 'scored' on the shot!

The training of combat pilots in Poland was entrusted to the best of the pilots, the instructors, one of whom was Zurakowski. It was no coincidence that, when war broke out, the training units and their instructors were among the first into battle.

Poland on the precipice

Poland in the 1930s had been developing economic strength and building the framework of a modern industrial state. The infrastructure of roads, railways and airports was gradually being created, and although large numbers of the population were found in farming districts, and small towns still engaged in an agrarian life-style, small factories had blossomed. The very survival of the new nation of Poland would soon be put to the test.

Ringed by two great powers, Germany and the Soviet Union, the Polish government was acutely concerned with Europe's rapidly deteriorating political scene. At first, Pilsudski, then, after his death

---

[11] Jarek Gwardys, conversation with the author, 2001.

in 1935, a succession of Polish leaders, began to look for friends. France had always been a natural ally because of its historic ties to Poland. The Treaty of Locarno in 1925 and the Franco-Polish Alliance of 1926 provided for assistance to either nation in time of war. In an effort to diffuse the threat to its borders from the east, Poland made an alliance with its traditional enemy, Russia, signing a non-aggression agreement with the Soviet Union in 1931. England and France began to look to their own defences. On 22 February 1939, the British government authorised the creation of a British Expeditionary Force (BEF), which would be sent to France in the event of war. Poland firmed up its alliance with France by entering into a military convention on 19 May 1939. By this time ominous forces were gathering on Poland's borders.

Chapter Three

The World at War

The crisis leading up to the Second World War was dominated by a new series of German territorial demands regarding the Polish 'free' city of Gdansk, or Danzig as it was known by its German name, which Führer Adolf Hitler was eager to have returned to Germany. Poland also represented the 'Lebensraum' (living space) of the old German dream of expansion to the east. With the outbreak of war between Germany and Poland imminent, the German government manoeuvred to remove a threat on its borders and further isolate Poland. Unexpectedly the German and Soviet governments signed a ten-year non-aggression pact, the Ribbentrop-Molotov Agreement, in Moscow on 23 August 1939. Unknown to the world, a secret pact in the agreement had provided for the partition of Poland by Adolf Hitler and Josef Stalin.

Using the pretence of border provocations, German forces gathered at the Polish borders. The last days of summer became increasingly grim as staged incidents and alleged Polish 'atrocities' fuelled the call to arms in Germany. Many Poles could not, or would not, face the true implications of the constant warmongering. A young teen's account of the time indicated: 'It is difficult to recapture the atmosphere of those days and what governed my own thoughts that summer. There was obviously a threat of war. But this threat had been just as realistic the year before and then passed on by... We reasoned that the Führer must know, as we all did, that the Poles would fight rather than surrender Danzig. He might be infuriated by Warsaw's rejection of his modest demand; he might rant and rave, but surely he would not succeed in his blackmail.'[1] At the eleventh hour, on 25 August, Poland negotiated a guarantee of military assistance from Great Britain in the event of a German attack, but this arrangement 'scarcely caused a ripple in the tide of war now descending on Poland'.

Without a formal declaration of hostilities, on 1 September 1939, Germany invaded Poland. In Operation Weiss, German troops

[1] Adam Ulam, *Understanding the Cold War: A Historian's Personal Reflections* (Charlottesville, Virginia: Leopolis, 2000), 21.

attacked Poland on three fronts, East Prussia in the north, Germany in the west and Slovakia in the south. As German armoured columns drove deep into Poland, the German Luftwaffe (Air Force) established control of the air.

The Polish campaign

The Polish defenders faced impossible odds. The strength of the German forces amassed against Poland numbered about 1,850,000 soldiers, with 10,000 guns and mortars and 3,200 tanks and more than 2,000 Luftwaffe aircraft (approximately two-thirds of the total Luftwaffe force). Against the Nazi armada stood only approximately 800,000 soldiers, 180 operational tanks and 420 aircraft with scarcely 140 combat-ready fighter planes available, not including those of Zurakowski's outdated flying school trainers.

Poland on the eve of war, 1939. *(Polish Genealogical Society of America, 2003)*

Poland mobilised thirty-eight infantry divisions, three mountain brigades, two motorised armoured brigades, eleven cavalry brigades, and other specialised formations of artillery and engineers. Zurakowski described the belief commonly held in the military, 'that mobilisation efforts had been stalled when France and England demanded that Poland make no provocative actions against Germany.' Possibly only half of the brigades were at full strength, with reserves just being introduced as hostilities began. Other efforts were more successful. The Polish Navy had deployed a number of its ships to Britain in the build-up to war, and the Polish Air Force had dispersed many of its combat aircraft to thirty-eight emergency fields. Despite preliminary photo-reconnaissance missions carried out by the Luftwaffe in August 1939, at least four of the new bases had not been discovered. The reconnaissance flights had taken place unopposed, as the PZL fighters were not able to intercept the high-flying Dornier Do 17 aircraft. This clear show of force by the Germans was a portent of things to come.

The Luftwaffe aerial attack on the first day was delayed by a thick ground mist, but by mid-morning Junkers Ju 87 Stuka dive-bombers were in the air, bombing Poland's airfields and bases. The Luftwaffe's first airfield strikes destroyed a number of utility, training and civil aircraft, but were largely ineffective in their first objective of destroying the Polish Air Force because fighters and bombers had already been dispersed to camouflaged and concealed emergency airstrips. However, the secondary damage caused to the airfield infrastructures affected the vital fuel supplies and the repair and maintenance facilities needed to sustain a long campaign. The Luftwaffe had actually dealt a devastating blow to the Polish defenders, and within a week further German air attacks on railways and roads crippled the lines of communication.

First blood in the aerial conflict was drawn that morning at the Balice satellite airfield near Cracow when three PZL P11c fighters from the 121 Eskadra (Squadron) were caught on take-off. Although the lead P11c was shot down, Sub-Lieutenant Wladyslaw Gnys was able to damage one of the Stuka attackers. Gnys climbed above the airfield to encounter two Dornier Do 17 bombers returning from a raid on Cracow. He scored several hits on each of them before losing contact. The two German bombers collided after his attack and fell to the ground near the village of Zurada. His victories were the first over the Luftwaffe in the Second World War.

That day also marked a new milestone in military conflict as German panzer (armoured and mechanised) divisions advanced swiftly upon the Polish armies in what was soon to be called the 'blitzkrieg' strategy. In some ways, Poland began to resemble a proving ground for the combined land-air attack that had been practised previously in non-operational war games and manoeuvres. Later campaigns in the Low Countries and France that utilised the blitzkrieg attack duplicated strategies tried out first in Poland. German General Heinz Guderian, a proponent of massed armour attacks and the author of the groundbreaking *Actung Panzer*, commanded XIX Panzer Corps in the Polish attack and pushed forward the rapid armour advances.

Over the outskirts of Warsaw all fifty-two P11c aircraft of the Pursuit Brigade, aided by an early detection of an attack, intercepted a large formation of Heinkel He 111 bombers from KG27, escorted by Messerschmitt Bf 110s of I/LG1. 'As a result of a well-executed attack, six He 111s were shot down at the expense of one P11c, which crashed during a forced landing. What was supposed to be *Der Spaziergang über Warshau* – a stroll over Warsaw – turned into a bitter escape for the Luftwaffe bomber crews. During the fighting, Sub-Lieutenant Borowski of 113 Eskadra shot down a stray Messerschmitt Bf 109, which became the first aircraft of that type to be destroyed in the Second World War.

'Heavy fighting over Warsaw resumed in the afternoon when a second large German raid, escorted by both Bf 110 and Bf 109 fighters, was intercepted by the Pursuit Brigade. This time the escorts were able to engage Polish fighters before they reached the bombers, and soon the first German bombs fell on Warsaw. Before they were even able to enter the fight, four P7s of 123 Eskadra were shot down in a surprise attack by Bf 110s of I/LG1. Captain Olszewski, the C/O [Commanding Officer], was killed and the other three pilots bailed out, two of them shot at and heavily wounded by the Germans after opening their parachutes. These were the first victories for German fighter pilots in the Second World War. The fighting was fierce, and the Germans lost two Bf 109s, one of them shot down by Lt-Col Leopold Pamula, deputy C/O of the Brigade, who himself had to bail out soon afterwards. Polish losses additionally amounted to three P11s.'[2]

The German advances on the ground were sustained by close tactical support from the Luftwaffe. In a nearly textbook exercise, the fast-moving units of the Luftwaffe occupied available airstrips and flew from improvised runways to maintain a high rate of three to four sorties per day. The battlefront air commands were also able to rapidly react to new targets assigned by the army. Moreover, the technical and numerical superiority of the Luftwaffe and the German ground forces soon wore down the Polish resistance.

First combat

Zurakowski's training aircraft, along with other PZL P7s in Deblin and one P24 that was a prototype aircraft being evaluated at the training facility, were formed into a improvised combat unit. The newly formed 'Deblin Fighter Group', made up of instructors and approximately fifty

---

[2] Robert Postowicz, 'Polish Aviation History Page' [online], cited on 16 September 2001. <http://www.s-studio.net/polivhist/>.

cadets led by Sub-Lieutenant Witold Urbanowicz, was charged with the defence of the area. The mechanics readied three P7 trainers that had been used for air gunnery practice, to be flown at short notice. The two Vickers machine guns on each aircraft were elderly relics, of First World War ancestry, but that was all they had. The old guns would have to do, but more importantly the old ammunition supplied by the Polish Army was problematic. Constant difficulties with misspent shells and jammed rounds had plagued air gunnery training.

On 2 September Zurakowski would be in one of the 'ready-flight' P7s when a flight of seven Dornier Do 17Z bombers attacked Deblin. That morning at the base, the first indication that attackers were near was an explosion in one of the hangars. He vividly recalled, 'A bomb exploded and one aircraft jumped into the air.' Like most air force facilities, Deblin had a rudimentary chain of ground observer posts that provided early warning, but the effectiveness of this warning system was questionable. The bombers were already overhead and had released their bombs by the time Zurakowski took off in one of the trainers. He quickly established that the Dorniers were in a turning circle and were probably coming in for another bombing run on Deblin.

Zurakowski was able to climb his old fighter to 6,000 feet, a height above the bomber flight. When the bombers spotted him, they began defensive fire. His later report indicated, 'I was surprised that the bombers were firing, as they were out of range.' He could make out the distinctive outline of the pencil-thin Dornier Do 17Z bombers with their tails still bearing the Condor Legion white circles and black crosses that identified their service in the Spanish conflict. Selecting a target, the closest Dornier below him, he threw his P7 into a dive, approaching the bomber head-on, and opened fire.

As his bullets slammed into the bomber, the two Vickers machine guns jammed. With acrid smoke from the guns filling the cockpit, Zurakowski frantically began to recharge the guns to reload the old belt-fed ammunition. With both hands full, he tried to clear the breech-blocks of the guns and still control the aircraft. 'The breech-blocks of the P7's machine guns came back into the cockpit, on either side of the pilot. Stoppages, which were frequent, had to be cleared by hand while the aircraft was controlled as best as possible.'[3]

---

[3] John F Painter, 'Zura: Turning Cartwheels in the Sky', *Aeroplane Monthly*, Pt 2 (February 2002), 27.

The fighter began to porpoise up and down, inadvertently offering the bomber gunners a difficult target. Zurakowski noted, 'The enemy was probably confused by my actions.' With his aircraft in a vulnerable position and receiving return fire from a gunner on the Do 17, he watched helplessly as the formation of twin-engined bombers pulled away. The Do 17 bombers were faster and were playing 'cat-and-mouse' with Zurakowski, slowing so that the gunners could take a shot at the attacking Polish fighter. He now realised that his outdated fighter could not keep up with the enemy bombers in level flight.

As the Dorniers withdrew into the distance, Zurakowski's hopes were raised slightly: one of the aircraft was trailing white smoke and losing altitude as it entered a cloud. At first he wasn't sure what the white wisps meant, but later realised that the bomber had been leaking fuel from a damaged fuel tank. He thought, 'If only I could close in again,' but the bombers had now retreated. During the fight his aircraft had taken a number of hits. After landing at Deblin, Zurakowski saw that bullet holes in the wings had pierced the metal skins but had not caused serious damage.

His first combat had ended without a clear-cut victory and showed that the Polish fighters would be no match for their German opponents. Yet, once the rugged and manoeuvrable PZL fighters were among the best in the world. Although Polish fighter pilots fought valiantly against overwhelming numerical and technically superior odds, the obsolete PZL fighter aircraft were eventually forced to retreat.

With complete air superiority based on the Messerschmitt Bf 109 and, to a lesser extent, the Bf 110 fighters, medium bombers such as the Heinkel He 111, Junkers Ju 88 and Dornier Do 17 were able to fly missions in close formation, delivering their bombs with impunity. The Luftwaffe's most effective aerial weapons were the dive-bombers – the small numbers of the Henschel Hs 123 biplanes and the more modern Junkers JU-87 Stuka dive-bombers – which ranged at will. As retreating Polish troops ran into a terrified populace jamming the roads, Stukas exacted a terrifying toll both in destruction and sheer terror. The Ju 87 crews had utilised the frightening screams of sirens fitted to the wheel covers and of whistles mounted on the fins of the bombs to create panic below. Polish General Wladyslaw Anders described the scene as a 'sky [filled] with a menacing drone ... squadron after squadron of German planes like flocks of cranes swooping south in the direction of Warsaw.'[4]

From the new satellite airfields where they had hidden, the Polish aerial gladiators rose up to meet the Luftwaffe hordes. The smaller units either flew sweeps or small, detached formations of fighters from improvised airfields with the task of intercepting sighted German aircraft. The latter tactic, called an 'ambush', was soon abandoned, as the PZL fighters could not catch the German bombers once they were overhead. Coordination of flights was hampered by a lack of radio contact; once the pilots were in the air they used hand signals to direct an attack, and only the squadron commanders had radio contact with the home base. Not only were the Polish air defenders crippled by the lack of modern equipment, but their role had been strictly confined to that of tactical support for the army. Headquarters' directives to avoid aggressive acts against Germany hampered the air force's response. An order issued by the General Inspector of all Polish Forces even prohibited the PAF from bombing German territory. Polish headquarters had believed that a holding action would buy time for their allies to provide assistance.

On 3 September Britain and France demanded that Germany withdraw its troops. British Prime Minister Neville Chamberlain and French Premier Edouard Daladier promised aid to Poland. Adolf Hitler, in return for a withdrawal of German forces, demanded the return of Danzig to Germany and a strip of territory linking East Prussia with the rest of Germany. Poland refused to give in to these demands. When Germany refused the Allied demand to withdraw, Great Britain and France officially declared war on Germany.

Although Britain and France were now at war with Germany, they were unable to intervene effectively on Poland's behalf. On 8 September nine French divisions made a feint into Saarland, advancing beyond the Maginot Line, but immediately retreated without contact with the German defenders of the area. A half-hearted attack by French bombers was easily brushed aside by the Luftwaffe. The newly formed British Expeditionary Force (BEF) of army and air force units had not even embarked by the middle of September.

Poland was alone.

Shortly after the initial air attacks, the Luftwaffe changed its tactics. 'Taking advantage of the superior characteristics of its aircraft (German twin-engined bombers were faster than Polish

---

[4] Robert Wernick, ed, *Blitzkrieg* (New York: Time-Life Books, 1976), 20.

fighters), it used small groups of bomber aircraft approaching the target from several directions at different altitudes, while Bf 109s and Bf 110s flew sweeps in the area. These tactics proved quite successful.'[5] Attrition was also taking effect in the Polish fighter force. The PZL fighters that flew from improvised and satellite fields could not be serviced properly and malfunctions grounded many defenders. One problem was a frightening tendency for the synchronisation device to fail, causing pilots to shoot off their own propellers in mid-air. With the few resources on hand, ground crews continued to patch up the fighters and get them back into the fight.

'Despite its valiant efforts, the Fighter Brigade was unable to prevent German bombs from falling on Warsaw. Its pilots managed to shoot down 47 German planes from September 1 to 6, but combat attrition was very high, and on September 7 the remnants of the Brigade were moved to the Lublin area, leaving the capital virtually defenceless against heavy Luftwaffe raids (Warsaw was never captured by the Germans – it was to be bombed into submission during 20 days of successful defence against German assault).'[6]

Marshal Edward Smigly-Rydz, the Polish Commander-in-Chief, had a defence plan based on a thinly defended line known as the Polish Corridor – the flat stretch of land between the two parts of Germany. The plan relied on the rapid establishment of a stronger force of reserves along the more easily defended high ground around the Vistula and San Rivers. By the third day of battle, the German attack had severed the Polish Corridor. The two German armies of the north subsequently joined in a pincer attack that encircled the Polish Poznan army defenders caught in the middle. The trapped Poles fought back desperately but were overwhelmed by the swiftly advancing German units. When the defenders were isolated into smaller pockets and the reserves were unable to organise coordinated counter-attacks, the German forces concentrated their attack on the main Polish forces around Warsaw, the only strong point left by mid-September.

In Warsaw the trapped 1.3 million civilians and soldiers had refused to surrender their capital. The savage German reaction to this defiance was to systematically destroy Europe's 'City of Lights'. Saturation bombing by artillery and bombers began to

---

[5] Postowicz, 'Polish Aviation History Page'.
[6] Ibid.

pound the city into rubble, causing an estimated 40,000 dead and injured. The city, swollen by numerous refugees, with food and water for the defenders having run out, and facing famine and disease, only capitulated after the military garrison realised that the continued siege would mean death for all of Warsaw's inhabitants. If modern warfare had ever been considered chivalrous or honourable, the brutal conduct of the invading armies and air force was soon to put those arcane notions to rest. Polish pilots had first attempted to assist downed Luftwaffe crews, only to find that their own brethren had been machine-gunned when they took to parachutes. With the slaughter of military personnel and civilians evident all around them, an all-consuming hatred of the Germans took over.

At Deblin, the morale of the flyers was low as aircraft were in short supply. The supply of ammunition and fuel, which was controlled by the army, had also been interrupted and delayed, thereby hampering their defence efforts. In later years, Zurakowski's views on that period have changed, a recent interview revealing: 'In retrospect, Jan feels it probably saved many of their lives. Most of them were already considering means of continuing the battle from other countries, whereas, if fuel and ammunition had been more assured, they would have stayed and tried to fight on until the end, despite the overwhelming odds.'[7]

Zurakowski knew that the defenders' situation was increasingly desperate. After flying five missions in the P7 trainers early in 'Black September', he was at the controls of a Potez 25 that had been used as a target tug at Deblin. 'The Potez was so hopeless that I would have been immediately shot out of the sky. I tried to stay close to the ground when I flew, but if the Messerschmitts would have come, I would not have had a chance.' Zurakowski and other instructors at Deblin were given orders on 10 September to go to Romania in anticipation of a shipment of Fairey Battle bombers and Hawker Hurricane fighters from Britain. Two hundred pilots and ground crew had been assembled to take on this new role. Skeletal crews had, for some time, been gathering in the vicinity of the Romanian border to prepare bases for the reception of 111 British planes on their way by ship. Romania's main port, Constanza, was the shipping point. 'A railway, part of it single-track, joined

---

[7] Painter, 'Zura: Turning Cartwheels', 27.

Constanza with Cernauti on the Polish border and Stanislawow in Poland.'[8] The pilots assembling close to the Romanian border were awaiting the promised shipments in vain.

The first ship, the SS *Lassell*, had been sent in early September through the Mediterranean and the Black Sea to Constanza. Its cargo consisted of ten Hurricane fighters, one Spitfire and seven Fairey Battle bombers, the latter, among others, destined to equip II Wing/2nd Air Regiment of the Bomber Brigade. The cargo also included 6,000 tons of bombs, 112 Browning machine guns and 2,750,000 rounds of ammunition. The next two ships, the SS *Clan Menzies* and SS *Robur VIII*, had later embarkation dates of 17 September and 20 September respectively, which made their precious cargoes completely redundant since the Soviet attack on 17 September prevented these deliveries.

The morning of 17 September 1939 saw the Red Air Force launch surprise attacks on the airfields of Dubno, Luck and Kowel, where they destroyed seven fighters along with three bombers destroyed on the ground. The Polish planes of the Pursuit Brigade that managed to get off the ground fought back with a vengeance, shooting down two SB-2 bombers and five I-16 fighters.

The Soviet Union invaded eastern Poland on 17 September, occupying the bordering provinces of western Belorussia and western Ukraine, as agreed with Germany in a secret annex to the Hitler-Stalin Pact. The first advances into Polish territory had been virtually unopposed as there was great confusion over the Soviet motives for entering the conflict. 'The Russians, as they crossed the Polish border, spread the news that they were coming to help Poland.'[9] The Polish Air Force only saw limited combat against the Red Air Force. When the Red Army struck, the remnants of the PAF (more specifically, the Bomber and Pursuit Brigades and the Army 'Karpaty' Air Force) moved to the air bases at Dubno, Luck and Kowel in the region of Polissia, from where they were to support the building of the planned bridgehead in south-eastern Poland.

During the short Polish air campaign, an estimated 230 enemy aircraft were destroyed in action, primarily by Polish fighter aircraft

[8] Nicholas Bethell, *The War Hitler Won: The Fall of Poland, September 1939* (New York: Holt, Rinehart and Winston, 1972), 167.
[9] Walter Zebrowski, *In Search of Freedom:Tales of World War Two* (Whistler, British Columbia: Whistler Ventures Inc, 1995), 29.

(which the Luftwaffe grudgingly acknowledged as fearsome 'wasps') and anti-aircraft artillery. Though greatly outnumbered, the valiant Polish flyers managed to down more than 100 German aircraft, including the deadly Messerschmitt Bf 109, and a handful of Soviet aircraft. According to the wartime research by a PAF special commission, the Polish Air Force scored 126 confirmed kills.

Escape

On 17 September 1939, after the surprise Soviet attack from the East, General W Kalkus, the Commander-in-Chief of the PAF, seeing the futility of the situation, acted quickly to preserve his defensive forces. He ordered all surviving Polish aircraft that were in flying condition to fly to Cernauti in neutral Romania. During the next two days, ninety-eight planes from combat units escaped from Poland. The total included forty-three P7 and P11 fighters from the Pursuit Brigade, eleven Karas bombers from the Bomber Brigade, and seven P7 and P11 fighters, together with eleven Karas reconnaissance bombers, eighteen Lublin R-XIII and eight RWD 14 Czapla observation monoplanes of the army air forces.

More than 150 planes from other units, including forty to fifty Los and Karas bombers from training and fitting-out units and some sixty civilian trainers and private aircraft, also managed to escape to Romania. Two cadets flew the two remaining P7 Deblin 'defenders' to Jassy in Romania. The aircraft, together with their startled aircrews, were immediately interned. In the final account, ten air force planes were unaccounted for, although some are known to have landed in Hungary. The Los and Karas bombers were handed over to the Romanian Air Force and used against the USSR from 1941. By that time, however, Poland and the USSR had become allies. In the north, about forty trainers and light aircraft of the 5th Air Regiment and the Wilno/Vilna/Vilnius Aero Club made it to Latvia, where they were interned, to be taken over by the Soviets when they invaded that country in 1940. A number of civilian Polish airliners flew to Sweden for safe haven.

On news of the Soviet attack, Zurakowski and other pilots in his unit were hastily assembled at the border areas of Romania, at Kuty near the River Czeremosz. The flyers were crammed into any available cars and trucks, which that same night crossed the border in this mountainous region. 'I can't remember this tragic moment very well; I can recall only the unending rows of vehicles and dimmed lights. The road was winding, and so, at moments, it appeared to be a slowly slithering snake glimmering with a violet light, and this image seemed to be completely unreal.'[10] Escape had meant that Zurakowski had to leave behind his family and loved ones. He and Anna had planned to meet in the first weeks of September. He sent her a postcard with the sardonic message, 'I am sorry I could not come because of Hitler.'

After the Soviet attack, numerous Polish government officials, soldiers, pilots and naval units managed to escape the swift Nazi and Soviet advances. Hundreds of thousands of military and civilian personnel, mainly from eastern Poland, made their way through the Carpathian Mountains. Enduring horrific forced marches under attack, thousands of Polish troops reached the border areas, only to be captured within sight of freedom; many more made it to their destinations. While the Polish airplanes had been flown to friendly airfields, the surplus air personnel and ground crews also initiated their own forced marches to reach Romania. Many did make it to havens in Romania, Hungary, Latvia and Lithuania and ,like the pilots that had preceded them, were interned.

Many escaping soldiers and airmen found their route to Romania blocked by the Soviet occupation of that southern sector. Smuggling themselves singly and in small groups across unguarded stretches of the Romanian and Hungarian borders, the escapees resorted to countless unusual schemes. Many pilots simply packed aircrew and ground personnel into any available aircraft and flew across the border. A number of Polish troops skied through the high Tatra and Carpathian Mountains to safety. South was the only safe passage; north to Latvia or Lithuania meant immediate detention by the conquering Soviet forces. Romania became a refuge for most of the surviving Polish military because the majority of the populace was sympathetic to the Polish cause. Even though the land was rugged and the locals had suffered from poverty, as Zurakowski and his comrades drove through small frontier villages Romanian women came out to give them bread and milk.

At the Romanian frontier post of Zaleszczyki, where the border was closed, thousands of Polish refugees and fleeing military forces were crammed together in a massive traffic jam. On the evening of

[10] Marek Kusiba, *J. Zurakowski: From Avro Arrow to Arrow Drive* (Toronto: Adres Press Ltd, 2003), 26.

16 September the barriers were suddenly lifted, allowing the Poles to enter Romania. The scene was recounted by a senior Air Force officer. 'It was a horrible moment. I don't know whether I shall ever manage to eradicate it from my memory. We all had tears in our eyes. Some kissed the white-and-red barrier, others kissed the ground or even the border guard's sentry-box. Some of the men were sobbing loudly, some were on their knees praying. Almost everyone scooped up a lump of earth or a pebble, or picked a flower or leaf as a last memento of their homeland... From time to time, a shot would be heard, as someone who found the shame of defeat unbearable and the future too horrible to contemplate took his own life.'[11]

Although both of Poland's southern neighbours had declared an official neutral status in 1939, the Romanian and Hungarian authorities were largely under the influence of Germany. The Nazis placed a price on every Pole who had escaped, and subsequently officials in both nations confiscated aircraft, weapons and equipment from the Polish escapees. Zurakowski surrendered his sidearm and joined his countrymen in a large detention camp. These internment camps were crowded and disease-ridden; an outbreak of malaria was later to cripple numerous Poles. Rather than finding freedom, the Polish military men now had to effect escapes from these camps. The easiest means was simple bribery, with the largest group of 2,000 or more aircrew being secreted out of the camps by the Polish ambassador to board a train in Bucharest in October 1939. The planner of the mass exodus had arranged a 'black-out' exercise in the capital to disguise the escape. The airmen proceeded to a railway station in silence, boarded a blacked-out train at a special siding and were whisked to Constanza, under the noses of the Germans. From this port, ships took the men to Marseilles, and the organiser dutifully collected a £5 bounty for each rescued airman from the Polish embassy.

Zurakowski had not been part of the first group of 'swallows' who had made their way out of Romania. He had been held briefly at a detention camp, but most of his time in confinement was passed by essentially being 'billeted out' in south-eastern Romania with the Nistors, a family sympathetic to the Poles. The head of the family was a municipal official in Tulczy province. Using his background in French, Zurakowski managed to communicate with the family and established a close relationship.

[11] Zebrowski, *In Search of Freedom*, 33.

Meanwhile the situation in his homeland was increasingly grim. From the Polish Command at Focsani, Romania, Zurakowski and other surviving Poles heard the devastating news that their capital had fallen. The people of Warsaw had resisted gallantly until 27 September, but were finally forced to surrender. Stanislaw Mikolajczyk, the leader of the Polish Peasant Party, described the final days of the fighting as 'a bitter rout ... which became an endless succession of bombings, retreats, sickening sights of broken cities and strafing and blasting of roads clogged with defenceless people.'[12]

The Polish campaign had ended with the encirclement of the main Polish armies and, although individual unit actions had valiantly defended territories and even caused great causalities in the German forces, it was a hopeless struggle. The Germans lost approximately 45,000 soldiers, 697 aircraft, 993 tanks and armoured cars, 370 guns and mortars and 11,000 military vehicles. Polish losses were appreciably greater, with 60,000 killed and 140,000 wounded – and the loss of their independence.

On 28 September Germany and the Soviet Union signed a treaty in Moscow, dividing Poland between them. Two weeks later the northern and western parts of Poland, with the cities of Danzig, Poznan, Lodz and Katowice, were incorporated into Germany. The Polish inhabitants of these areas were soon to suffer the fate of the vanquished and were either driven out of their homes or turned into slave labourers for the Nazi war machine. The central and southern regions, which included Warsaw, Krakow and Lublin, were renamed the General-Gouvernment and were administered by the Germans from Krakow. The partitioned territory of the far south, including the cities of Lwow and Wilno, was ruled as part of the Soviet Union.

On the heels of the German soldiers came the Nazi terror squads of the SS, whose ruthless and brutal treatment of the Poles began with numerous executions of members of the intellectual and professional classes. In diminishing the elite of Poland, the Nazis aimed to create a cowed, subjugated people. In Hitler's own words, 'the Polish gentry must cease to exist... All representatives of the Polish intelligentsia are to be exterminated.'[13] The general

[12] R F Leslie, ed, *The History of Poland since 1863* (Cambridge: Cambridge University Press, 1980), 212.
[13] William L Shirer, *A Native's Return: 1945-1988* (Boston: Little, Brown and Company, 1990), 254.

population of Poland, considered 'subhuman' by the Nazis, was under great strain from the use of indiscriminate violence and the murder of anyone suspected of being an enemy of the state. By withholding food, the Nazis attempted to reduce the ordinary citizen to a state of near starvation. Segregation of the diverse Polish populace led to the Jewish ghetto communities. Soon Hitler's designs for the Jews would be known far too well.

The Soviet regime was as savage and oppressive as the Germans, and Poles found that they were being repaid for their effrontery in defeating the Soviets in 1920. The NKVD (People's Commissariat of Internal Affairs), the Soviet state security organisation, was dispatched to Poland to conduct a campaign to eliminate 'undesirables'. Not only were all the Soviet's political foes eliminated, but vast numbers of students, police officers, government officials, members of humanitarian organisations such as the Red Cross, and members of the clergy and the professional/business class were rounded up and shipped to the Gulag Archipelago. Polish military personnel were especially targeted for annihilation. More than one and a half million Poles were eventually to die at the hands of the Soviets.

A call to arms

The Polish government refused to surrender, and individual ground units continued to fight until 5 October, although organised resistance had virtually ceased after 18 September 1939. The Polish Prime Minister, Ignacy Moscicki, called on all able-bodied Poles to head south into Romania, then on to France to continue the fight.

Over time, with the help of Polish embassies and consulates and tacit but unofficial Romanian and Hungarian approval, tens of thousands of Polish soldiers and airmen 'escaped' to the west. With remarkable foresight, members of the Polish diplomatic corps and government ministries had established offices in Bucharest, mere days after the beginning of hostilities. An advance contingent had made its way to Kuty on the Polish-Romanian border on 5 September. A Polish government-in-exile was formed in Romania but transferred on 30 September to Paris, France, with Ladislaw Raczkiewicz appointed as its President. The main imperative of the government was to continue Polish resistance.

Heeding the call of General Wladyslaw Sikorski, Commander-in-Chief of the Polish Armed Forces, the newly relocated diplomats in Bucharest provided ex-Polish military men with false documentation and bribe money. Elaborate ruses led to the creation of 'Sikorski's tourists', when large numbers of young Poles began travelling in Romania in a variety of ruses as tourists, artists, teachers and businessmen. Realising that he might be forced to stay in detention in Romania and that there would soon be few opportunities to flee, Zurakowski laid out plans to escape. Like other Poles who struck out for the west, overland and by sea, he attempted to slip out of Romania, to secure passage on a ship leaving the war zone and eventually head for France.

From the Polish Command in Focsani, which had become a staging base for the Poles, Zurakowski received instructions and a small amount of money (300 zloty). A female Polish courier, Barbara Wojtulanis, had flown from Bucharest at the beginning of October with a falsified passport for him. As women were not subject to internment in Romania, the Polish High Command utilised three female pilots as couriers. The three women were constantly detained but continued to undertake their hazardous missions throughout the autumn. Zurakowski's new-found friends, the Nistors, arranged for a tailor to produce a suitable change of clothing. Having abandoned his military uniform, Zurakowski now could pass as a civilian. One by one, other Polish military men disappeared from the camps, until virtually no Poles were left in detention. At one camp, when a Romanian guard attempted to collect the reward from German authorities for turning in a Polish internee, only one prisoner remained.

In making his escape, Zurakowski had again found that many ordinary Romanians were supportive of the Poles. When he arrived at the nearest small railway station, a middle-aged railway conductor immediately recognised who he was and placed a railway ticket in his hand. Equipped with false identification papers that indicated that he was a forester (prophetically to be echoed in a future life), he possessed a change of clothing, pocket money and little else. Making his way to the Black Sea port of Balcic, Zurakowski joined a large group of nearly 200 Polish pilots and 600 aircraft mechanics, technicians and other military staff.

Although there was a strict prohibition on travel for the Poles and a threat of arrest, most of the residents in Balcic turned a blind eye as Zurakowski and the other military men, dressed in a variety of tattered and dishevelled civilian dress, gathered in the small port.

Janusz Zurakowski in the guise of a forester in his 1940 passport. (*Zurakowski collection*)

Securing lodgings in a number of hostels and hotels, the young escapees waited fretfully for days before a boat arrived. Zurakowski spent his time exploring the steep escarpments overlooking the town. From these vantage points, he could see storks arrive; he imagined that they were Polish storks that were about to set out to sea, just like he soon would.

With sufficient bribes to the harbourmaster and the Romanian police, on 14 October 1939 the Poles were allowed to board the *Saint Nicholas*, an old Greek tramp steamer. Screening of Polish airmen was arbitrary as some documentation was refused. One officer produced papers showing he was a student, was refused, came back later in the guise of a priest and was again turned away. Just before embarkation, he appeared again with an official-looking document that was really his driver's licence, and was waved on board. A large group of approximately 100 airmen who had been denied passage waited till the steamer eased away from the dock, bribed the station commander and jumped into the harbour, clambering aboard the ship as it slowly cast off.

The freighter was embarking for the French protectorates in the Middle East. The League of Nations had given France a mandate over Syria in 1922 and the Lebanese Republic in 1926. French officials and other sympathisers would at least help the Poles reach France if they made it to French-controlled territory. The cargo vessel, normally loaded down with an assortment of goods including livestock, was rumoured to deal in smuggling illegal immigrants to Palestine. The unbearable smells on board the vessel, which now carried a tightly packed hold of Poles and other refugees, contributed to a miserable voyage. To accommodate the large number of passengers, all the men below decks had to lie on old mattresses that were crammed one next to the other in the hold. Conditions were made more difficult as the passengers faced meagre rations consisting mainly of cheese and bread. Another concern was the small supply of drinking water. The Poles resorted to 'cat-licking' themselves clean and maintaining a sense of humour despite their ordeal. Zurakowski once commented on the trip, 'As the dirty little steamer reached open water, I took out my true documentation and papers and threw them over the side. My fate was now sealed.'

During the slow journey south, the first hurdle was in clearing the Straits of Bosporus, which were controlled by the Turks. A Turkish boarding party undertook a cursory examination of the boat which culminated in the acceptance of a suitable bribe. As the *Saint Nicholas* entered the Aegean Sea, the captain of the steamer raised a quarantine flag. This flag indicated disease on board and guaranteed the passengers' safety even if they were stopped in their passage through the Dardanelles to Beirut, the first port of call on a long voyage to freedom.

The week-long voyage was favoured by good weather and smooth seas. Reaching Beirut, Lebanon, on 21 October, in the midst of an oppressive heat wave, Zurakowski noted that the trade centre was prosperous and bustling. The arrival of the Poles was greeted warmly by a French military band. After the arduous sea journey, the spirits of the group were further raised when their hosts provided a sumptuous dinner that evening at the French Legion's barracks. After a week of poor rations, the Poles finally were able to satisfy their appetites in an evening of food, drink and merriment. Even the teetotallers in the group, like Zurakowski, were moved to partake in the champagne that was served.

The next day, Zurakowski and other Polish airmen boarded the luxury liner *Ville de Strasbourg*. Accommodation on the liner was very different from their previous transport. Their rooms were clean and spacious, and appetising food was available in ornate dining rooms. The dangerous Mediterranean passage was marked by poor weather and zigzagging around suspected Italian submarine routes. The pitching and heaving ship managed to make everyone seasick before it finally reached Marseilles at daybreak on 30 October.

The battle for France

Upon disembarking at Marseilles, the airmen were greeted by the mayor of the city who hosted a grand banquet. After the formal reception, with a flourish of Polish and French national anthems played by a military band, the group embarked in a convoy of buses. The non-commissioned officers were sent to Air Base 125 at Istres, a L'Armée de l'air training base. The regular officers, including Zurakowski and the other pilots, were dispatched to Air Base 701 Salon (Salon de Provence), about fifty kilometres north of Marseilles. At the time Salon was the home base for a squadron flying Potez 63 medium reconnaissance/bombers.

Zurakowski's first impressions of France were troubling. The serene countryside of villages and vineyards seemed idyllic and peaceful. The French went about their business as if nothing were amiss. He thought to himself, *'Can this be wartime France?'* The consensus amongst the Polish flyers was that the French were too complacent and unprepared for the struggle to come. Hurried military preparations had been made over the winter and spring of 1939-1940 in the 'Phoney War' period, for an anticipated German attack along France's eastern borders. British General Lord Gort commanded the British Expeditionary Force sent to France in 1939. By May 1940 it had consisted of ten infantry divisions, one tank brigade, and a Royal Air Force (RAF) element of 500 fighters and light bombers. This force was spread thinly along the French border facing Germany and added to the military units that were being mobilised by the French. The main French defences had 104 divisions available, but the numbers were deceiving. Antiquated equipment and poorly thought-out strategy were to doom the French.

The one great bulwark of the French defences was the 'impregnable' Maginot Line of fortresses and underground tunnels. The Maginot Line was built between 1929 and 1940 to defend the traditional invasion routes across France's eastern frontier. The belief in the strength of a static defensive zone was rooted in First World War experiences when massive armies had faced each other scant metres apart, dug down in trenches. The onslaught to come would overwhelm the French defences in a slashing, searing assault that bypassed the Maginot Line and struck through the undefended Ardennes forest into the heart of Belgium, the Low Countries and France.

For Zurakowski, France was more than a refuge. He was fluent in the French language and was able to easily communicate with the villagers living near the air base. Even the scenery and landmarks appeared familiar, and he realised that he recognised them from his studies. As he settled into his new surroundings at Salon, a postcard arrived from his cousin, Dr Maria Boczkowska, who worked at an agricultural station in Versailles. 'Manusia', as she was familiarly known, was a welcome connection to his family, which he would not see again in the war years and for many years to come. His cousin brought news from home and information about the war. Her efforts in locating both Janusz and Bronislaw had been successful. Janusz's brother had been employed in research and development at the Doswiadczalne Warsztaty Lotnicze, which produced the famous RWD series of aircraft. When the war broke out, he flew an RWD 21 out of the factory to Stanislawow via Swidnik, near Lublin. Despite not having a pilot's licence, Bronislaw had been a qualified glider pilot. After reaching Romania, he then made his way back to Warsaw on foot. All seemed well with his mother, father and sisters. She wrote that a new Polish government-in-exile had made its way through Sweden to France.

By November 1939 another contingent of evacuated Polish airmen had arrived in Salon. A freezing winter followed the pleasant autumn, making the crowded conditions more uncomfortable as the chill permeated the thin barrack walls. Word soon came from Paris that a newly formed Polish-British-French commission had met to direct future Polish operations. A decision to move the Polish flyers northward at the beginning of December led to the detachment at Salon setting out cross-country to a new base at Lyon-Bron.

The surviving Polish Army, from a staging point in Bessière, in the northern suburbs of Paris, emerged as a newly constituted Polish Army Legion. Approximately 43,000 Polish army officers and enlisted men re-formed in France under the command of General Wladyslaw Sikorski. This army was joined by 40,000 recruits from the Polish community in France, forming a semi-independent army. The French military greeted the new Polish troops with some reservation, as the Poles who had escaped Romania had arrived without any fighting gear and virtually penniless. The emotions in this group ran high because the Poles were spoiling for a fight and the French were concerned about their apparent lack of discipline.

As units began to train and supplies of equipment, weapons and uniforms were obtained, the French authorities soon realised that they had misjudged the qualities of the Polish fighting man. One advantage to the French forces was that more than half of the ordinary soldiers and almost all of the new Polish officers were able to speak French. Taught as a second language in schools and used as the language of the intelligentsia, French was widely used by the officer class of the Polish Army and Air Force. The Polish forces in France consisted of the 1st Grenadier Division, 2nd Rifleman Division, Independent Podhale Rifleman Brigade, Light Mechanised Brigade, units of two French infantry divisions and seven Air Force wings.

Like the Polish Legion, Polish flyers also emerged as a fighting force, with more than 8,000 survivors staging at Lyon-Bron. There, shortly after their arrival on 17 December and following a preliminary screening by senior members of the PAF, the fighter pilots were reorganised into two detachments. A thousand of the flyers (approximately half of the fighter pilots) were to go to England as part of a training and advance party. Zurakowski was ordered to report to England as part of this group, to join the RAF Volunteer Reserve. Before his departure, he received word from Versailles that Manusia wanted him to spend Christmas with her in Paris. She also invited three of Bronislaw's friends who were stationed in Coetquidan, the Polish base in Brittany. The three young men were all graduates of the Warsaw Institute of Technology as well as being glider enthusiasts like Janusz and Bronislaw. When he arrived on Christmas Eve, Zurakowski found the capital bathed in an eerie cascade of faint street lanterns and dimmed automobile lights. It gave Paris a beautiful but melancholy hue.

That evening Zurakowski, together with his brother's friends, shared a meal with his cousin at a quiet restaurant in Versailles. When an older French gentleman overheard their dinner conversation in Polish, he commiserated with the group over the loss of Poland and ordered them a bottle of wine. The young people enjoyed their time together, but soon after, Zurakowski was to leave for England with the first detachment of Polish combat airmen.

The other Polish pilots were to continue their fight in France in a special fighter unit, Squadron 1/145, known as the 'Warsaw Group', composed almost exclusively of Polish pilots. Although they were training on the Morane 406 and Bloch 151, the Polish pilots flew the Caudron C 714 Cyclone, a lightweight fighter derived from earlier racing aircraft. In 1940, as the Battle of France began, all available fighters were needed and the Caudron C 714 was thrown into battle.

In April 1940 a brigade from the new Polish Army in France had its first engagement near Narvik in the abortive Norway campaign before being evacuated back to France. As the detachment was being disembarked on 10 May 1940, the Germans struck at Belgium. With the swiftness of the blitzkrieg tactics honed in Poland, the Luftwaffe delivered the first blows to airfields on the perimeter of the battlefront and, in a daring use of gliders, overwhelmed the Belgian fortress of Eben Emael, thereby opening up the northern front. Quickly securing bridgeheads on the River Meuse, the panzer units leaped into the fray. A sudden five-day campaign, punctuated by the indiscriminate bombing of Rotterdam, then took Holland out of the war. As British and French forces redeployed to the north to shore up the front in Belgium and the Low Countries, a slashing assault by the German Army Group A through the Ardennes forest caused an immediate withdrawal of the Allied troops to France. The retreating armies ran headlong into the panicked civilian populace that clogged all the roads to the south. Allied infantry and armoured units fought desperate holding actions, but the Allies realised that German advances were too rapid for effective counter-attacks to be launched.

During the Battle of France, most Polish Army units were stationed in the south of France and escaped the brunt of the blitzkrieg attack. 'The Grenadier Division fought in the Saar, on the Marna-Rhein Canal and in the defence at Lagarde.'[14] The swift end of the battle forced another retreat by the Poles. Salvaging any of the Allied forces now became a matter of urgency.

Squadron 1/145 became the most successful Allied air combat unit in French skies during the campaign. The Polish pilots used the marginal Caudron C 714 fighter with great success over the Roeun-Dreux area in June 1940. Other Polish pilots were attached to standard Armée de l'air units or in sections or flights, sometimes referred to as 'stacks'. However, these arrangements were not looked upon with favour by the Poles who wanted to fight the Germans as integral units. The Polish flights assigned to the local defence of cities and industrial production centres were known as 'Chimney Flights'. Notably, the Bloch factory defence unit at Chateauroux-Déols in the region of Bourges was made up of Poles, flying the production Bloch MB-152 fighters and MB-155 prototypes.

Other Polish units under the Patrouilles de Protection flew a mixed collection of Morane-Saulnier 406, Dewoitine D-520 and Koolhoven FK 58 fighter planes. This last fighter type was a Dutch design that was part of the re-equipment programme for both the

[14] Margaret Brodniewicz-Stawicki, *For Your Freedom and Ours* (St Catharines: Vanwell Publishing Ltd, 1999), 68.

Netherlands and France. Notable air engagements, including the air support protecting the evacuation of the Armée de l'air personnel from Rochefort, were also undertaken by Polish fighter pilots. During the French campaign of 1940, for a second time the Polish flyers fought bravely in a losing cause, with fifteen pilots killed but with sixty-nine victories scored against the Germans.

The military rout that enveloped the Allies included the largest Polish Army contingent under General Sikorski, which fought its way to the Bay of Biscay and English Channel ports. In these embattled harbours, the Poles joined the Allied forces that were waiting for evacuation to Britain. After sustaining heavy losses during the French and Belgian campaigns of 1940, the battered remnants of the BEF were given an astonishing reprieve of twenty-four hours when the German attack in the north was halted. The delay allowed the British Admiralty the time to devise a rescue from Dunkirk, 'Operation Dynamo'. The remaining French forces in the region fought desperately to keep open a narrow breech in the front lines. Leaving much of their equipment behind, 300,000 Allied troops were evacuated by a flotilla of military and private vessels from 26 May to 3 June 1940.

The Dunkirk survivors included the main elements of the BEF and a mix of French, Belgian, Dutch and Polish troops. A group of 22,500 Polish survivors, including army, naval and air force personnel, joined the exodus from Dunkirk and other Channel ports and were able to be evacuated by ships to England. The remaining Polish forces in France were faced with a dilemma when the main body of the French Army capitulated on 25 June 1940. Fighting a holding action in July in Champagne, some 13,000 Polish troops were forced to retreat to the border of neutral Switzerland and later crossed into that country to seek refuge. All the surviving Polish forces vowed to continue the fight against Germany.

The defeat suffered in September 1939, and later in France, had not stopped the remarkable saga of the Polish resistance. A Polish government-in-exile was formed in Britain. Recognised by the Allied powers and based in London, the new government had Wladyslaw Raczkiewicz as President, while General Sikorski became the first Prime Minister. The Armia Krajowa (Home Army), operating underground, was formed in Poland and used the weapons of intelligence, subversion and propaganda to prepare for armed resistance and an eventual challenge to the invaders. At its peak in

1944, the Home Army numbered some 350,000 soldiers. General Stefan Rowecki-Grot was the Commander-in-Chief of the Home Army until the time of his arrest on 30 June 1943, when he was replaced by General Tadeusz Komorowski-Bor. Other military units were formed, such as the National Armed Forces (NSZ), which recognised the Polish government-in-exile but did not come under the Home Army command.

The Home Army was essentially the military arm of an underground state. Some relief for the general populace was provided through soup kitchens and rudimentary medical stations operated by the Red Cross and other charitable organisations that were tolerated by the occupying powers. The resistance movement, loosely patterned after the Resistance of 1863, clandestinely maintained the fundamental elements of a civil government. More importantly, a school system for primary to university training was secretly established for an estimated one million students. Although Anna Danielski had completed her education in pre-war Poland, she continued some studies through the underground schools. The penalty exacted by the Nazis for both teachers and pupils who were discovered was death.

Britain had now been considered the 'last-hope island' by the embattled Poles. The relationship between these two allies was unnecessarily strained by the desperation of the fighting in 1939-1940. Recently the Polish Foreign Minister, Mr. Wladyslaw Bartoszewski, has noted the paradoxical perceptions of the time. 'I well remember the euphoria we experienced upon learning that Great Britain had joined the defensive war waged against Nazi aggression by Poland from 1 September 1939. We were convinced that Britain's entry on our side meant the end of the war and a speedy victory. The prolonged struggle of victory that ensued was therefore difficult to accept. And it was all the more painful to realise that the opportunity to share the pride and joy of victory was not tantamount to enjoying the most priceless fruit of victory – freedom.'[15]

---

[15] Wladyslaw Bartoszewski, conversation with the author, 2001.

Chapter Four

Battle of Britain

Zurakowski and many of his comrades had escaped the disaster in France by chance. In Paris a decision had been made in late 1939 to keep half of the Polish fighter pilots in France as part of the defences and to dispatch the second group to England. A number of pilots were to receive further training by the RAF, while the others would form the nucleus of a future combat unit. The RAF Commission that had arrived at Lyon-Bron recruited mainly former bomber and army cooperation crews. Additionally, fighter pilots were recruited to serve in the Bomber Command, since at that time the RAF had not intended to utilise Polish fighter pilots. At first, Zurakowski was reluctant to leave France and thought that the selection of pilots to embark for England was too arbitrary. 'I spoke French, so naturally I was sent to England,'[1] he recalled with an ironic smile.

Poles had started to arrive in Britain soon after the fall of Warsaw. Many members of the leading government, scientific and professional classes had joined the military exodus. One amazing gift that a number of Polish mathematicians had brought would contribute to unveiling the secrets of the Nazi's 'Enigma' coding machines. Communication with submarines, surface ships, and armies on all war fronts was conducted through Enigma messages, and Polish mathematicians delivered a working model of their code-breaking machine to England in July 1939. The Polish Enigma device helped the British cryptographers at Bletchley Park finally break the sophisticated German secret codes and possibly shorten the war.

Following a British agreement made in the previous month to accept a contingent of Polish aircrew and naval personnel, the first Polish pilots reached England in December 1939. Zurakowski was part of a larger Polish Air Force group made up of 2,000 mechanics and technical staff and 300 fighter pilots who were subsequently assembled. After making their way by rail to the port of Dunkirk, this group crossed the English Channel by boat, landing in England in January 1940.

---

[1] Bernard S Shaw, 'Jan Zurakowski', *The Country Connection*, No 21, Spring 1994, 31.

There was initial resistance to accepting foreign pilots into the RAF Zurakowski was told, 'Only English pilots protect the homeland.'[2] Reflecting later, he pondered whether it was because of pride that the English would not allow foreigners to defend their country. As the war situation worsened in continental Europe, a change in this resistance swiftly took place. In view of the imminent collapse of all defences on the continent, the British Air Ministry agreed to form two Polish bomber squadrons as part of the Royal Air Force Voluntary Reserve.

Air Chief Marshal Sir Hugh C T 'Stuffy' Dowding, head of the RAF Fighter Command, strongly opposed forming the Polish fighter squadrons for which the Polish government-in-exile had pressed so strenuously. Dowding had gained his unflattering nickname from fellow airmen due to his stubborn yet persistent manner. It was ultimately his resolve, as well as his skilful tactical deployment of resources, that would be called upon to save Britain. Due to the rapidly deteriorating military situation and to Britain's very survival being dependent on the few fighter pilots it could muster, an agreement to form Polish fighter squadrons was finally reached on 5 August 1940.

On that date a Polish-British military pact was signed, establishing Polish military forces on British territory and in the Middle East. The 1st Polish Army Corps was organised in Scotland. As part of the agreement, four bomber squadrons (300 Masovian, 301 Pomeranian, 304 Slaski, and 305 Ziemia Wielkopolska) and two fighter squadrons (302 City of Poznan and 303 Kosciuszko) would be formed in Britain in 1940. The airmen in these squadrons would be drawn from the second group of Poles who had escaped from France shortly before its capitulation. These would formally constitute an independent air force; operationally, however, the Poles would be under British command. Unlike the rigid army structure under which the Polish Air Force had operated in Poland, the new Polish Air Force was to be a separate part of the Polish Armed Forces, entitled 'Polskie Sily Powietrzne' – literally 'Polish Air Force'.

Zurakowski and the first group of Polish fighter pilots who had already landed in England were integrated into existing RAF fighter squadrons in time to join the upcoming Battle of Britain. He recalled,

[2] Bill Topham, 'Remembering the Arrow's first flight', *Brighton Independent*, 6 October 1998.

P/O Zurakowski in 1940. *(Zurakowski collection)*

'The spirit of our Polish pilots was very good… We were furious about what the Germans had done to Poland. We had already experienced German domination, so that's why we were anxious to fight.'[3]

Preparation for battle

With Britain preparing for the German invasion, it was clear to Winston Churchill and the RAF that Hitler's first operational need would be to establish air superiority over southern England. The Luftwaffe amassed nearly 3,300 aircraft in northern France and Scandinavia in preparation for the assault on Britain.

[3] 'Polish Air Force in the Battle of Britain', *The Ottawa Citizen*, 20 September 1999.

As Air Chief Marshal Dowding's RAF Fighter Command was constituted on the eve of the battle, there were four groups. These were organised into larger sector stations, supporting satellite stations and forward air bases, many of which were rudimentary and consisting of basic facilities and grass fields. The 11 Group commanded by Air Vice-Marshal Keith Park included the Tangmere, Biggin Hill, Hornchurch, North Weald, Debden and Northolt sector stations. Air Vice-Marshal (AVM) Trafford Leigh-Mallory was in charge of 12 Group and controlled the airspace north of London from sector stations such as Duxford. The largest area (Scotland, Northumberland and North Yorkshire) was patrolled by 13 Group led by AVM Richard Saul at Newcastle Fighter Station. The 10 Group, established late in July 1939 under AVM Quintin Brand, protected Southampton and the South West from bases such as Middle Wallop and St Eval.

The squadrons were identified in three categories: 'Category A', which indicated an experienced, frontline unit maintained at full strength in terms of numbers of pilots and aircraft; 'Category B', reserve squadrons; and 'Category C', training squadrons. In the heat of battle, two of the Category B squadrons were pressed into service to relieve decimated operational squadrons, and even Category C squadrons saw action.

A vital component of the air defence of England was the untried early detection systems based on ground observers, sound detectors and the revolutionary RDF (Radio Detection Finder) or radar stations. A chain of twenty antenna tower and receiver units stretched along the coastline from the Shetland Islands to the Isle of Wight. Although in operational tests the radar 'plots' had detected aircraft at altitude, the 'Chain Home' stations would only provide a precious six to ten minutes of warning. The ground observers would provide confirmation by the time the raids had crossed the Channel, but radio messages would already have alerted the fighter command and sector stations.

At command level, air officers directed an overall interception strategy but allowed the sector station commanders to have broad control over operational tactics. The control of interceptions was largely directed by radio messages from sector stations or individual fighter bases. Due to the limited number of fighters available, Hurricanes and Spitfires had to be in the air at precisely the right moment.

By the summer of 1940, when Lord Beaverbrook was appointed Minister for Aircraft Production, the programme shifted its emphasis to fighter production. Creating organisations such as the 'saucepans to Spitfires' aluminium collections and the Civilian Repair Organisation (CRO), and harnessing the production capabilities of Canadian and other foreign aircraft factories, Beaverbrook supplied the crucial number of fighters the RAF needed. The total number of fighters in service amounted to about 660 and, more importantly, there were only about 1,300 pilots. In the heat of battle, aircraft could be replaced; pilots could not.

The RAF's Fighter Command consisted of a total of fifty-five operational fighter squadrons. Of these, there were twenty-six squadrons of Hawker Hurricanes and only nineteen squadrons of Supermarine Spitfires, the most modern fighters available. The other fighter squadrons flew a diverse number of types including the biplane Gloster Gladiator, 'turret-gun' Boulton-Paul Defiant and twin-engined Bristol Blenheim. Fighter Command maintained its strength through a series of far-seeing initiatives. In pre-war years 'shadow factories' had been created, under the direction of big industrialists such as Lord Nuffield, in readiness to build combat aircraft when hostilities began.

Each sector of Fighter Command consisted of two to four individual fighter squadrons that were controlled by an independent operations room. The fighter squadron was typically sixteen aircraft, which included twelve operational fighters and reserve aircraft. The squadron was divided into 'A' and 'B' flights, which were further subdivided into sections of three aircraft, known by a colour code. Each aircraft had an engine fitter and an airframe rigger assigned to it, while a larger group of specialists – armourers and wireless, electrical and instrument mechanics – were attached to the flights. The squadron complement would stand at approximately twenty pilots, who were led by a squadron commander, flight commanders and section leaders. Although the position of 'fighter formation leader' could sometimes be assigned to another pilot, the commanding officer normally assumed that role.

Foreign nationals were initially posted to RAF squadrons if they were qualified aircrew. At first, Czech and Polish personnel were not well received and the resistance in the RAF to the Polish flyers especially was based partly on the mistaken belief that they were a defeated and demoralised group. While Polish fighter pilots had already been involved in two losing campaigns in Poland and France, their actions in the subsequent battle proved that their passion for battle and, notably, retribution on the Germans was undiminished. 'None fought in the air with greater single-minded ferocity than the Poles and Czechs, many of whom had lost families as well as homes and had witnessed the depraved barbarism of the German invaders.'[4]

A more fundamental reason for the initial reluctance to employ the Polish flyers as fighter pilots was that valuable aircraft and instruction time would be tied up in training. A lack of knowledge about Polish air training had also led to the belief that the new pilots would be inferior or substandard airmen. Johnny Kent, the Canadian 303 Squadron Commander, had initial misapprehensions about the abilities of the pilots under his charge. He treated them harshly until he realised that not only were they magnificent flyers but that they also had a combat creed that had been instilled right from their earliest training. Although there were some hurdles to overcome, the Poles acquitted themselves memorably in training.

Shortly after he arrived in England, Zurakowski joined the Royal Air Force and was inducted into the RAF Volunteer Reserve at RAF Eastchurch as RAF No 76715, with the rank of Pilot Officer (Plt Off). The Volunteer Reserve organisation was utilised to provide a pool of pilots necessary for the increased demands of fighter squadrons. Many volunteer reservists were transferred from other RAF commands and, although only provided with rudimentary instruction on Hurricanes and Spitfires, they offered a temporary relief to the beleaguered frontline squadrons. On the other hand, the availability of experienced Czech, Polish and later French pilots changed the operational picture substantially.

Eastchurch was designated officially as a Ground Training School and served as a transition centre for the Polish inductees. This base was commanded by Group Captain A Davidson, who had previously been head of the British aerial mission in Poland. A Polish command was also established at Eastchurch with Colonel Boleslaw Stachon in charge.

The RAF orientation involved both instructional courses and military training such as marching and drilling. An introduction to English culture was also provided, as the RAF pilots invited Zurakowski and other Poles to partake of traditional rites such as

[4] Richard Hough and Denis Richards, *Battle of Britain* (London: Hodder and Stoughton, 1989), 186.

afternoon tea and pub visits. He quickly became accustomed to the camaraderie of a combat unit, although he felt at a disadvantage. 'I was twenty-six at the time, and that was older than the average. If a guy was thirty, he was an old man. My English was not good then, and I had a hard time because of it.'[5]

Pilot Officer Zurakowski's preparation at Eastchurch from January to May 1940 involved ground school courses as well as a crash course in the English language. While the newcomers learned the squadron operational systems, they also had to acquire enough mastery of the English language to be effective in the standard radio procedure required in combat. Radio communication was especially difficult because all exchanges were in English. The radio/telephone (R/T) messages relied on simplified terms, and once 'key code-words (such as 'Angels', 'Vector' and 'Buster') and numerals were memorised and understood, the Poles could at least pick up the gist of the controllers' instructions.'[6] Language instruction was intense but could be confusing and even border on the bizarre. At RAF Station Uxbridge in Middlesex, Polish pilots equipped with a rudimentary R/T, a compass and a speedometer were mounted on children's tricycles. Pilots wore a 'blinker' to limit their vision as they trundled around a track while receiving signals from a controller.

The R/T in the aircraft was adjusted manually to a level loud enough to hear ground control over the noise of the engine. Zurakowski's memories of that period were related recently: 'I would be flying along, with the volume turned up, trying to figure out whatever was being said from the ground. Because the volume was up, another pilot breaking radio silence was like an explosion in my ears. But even though I generally could not tell what was being said, I knew that when the voices sounded excited, the Germans were near. Then I just switched the radio off and got ready.'[7] For Zurakowski, like many other pilots, years of loud radios and roaring engines eventually contributed to his loss of hearing.

In May 1940 Plt Off Zurakowski was sent to the Polish Detachment at Manston before reporting to 3 (Polish) Wing at the seaside resort of Blackpool. At this RAF station each British officer

---

[5] Melady, *Pilots*, 106.
[6] Anthony Robinson, *RAF Fighter Squadrons in the Battle of Britain* (London: Brockhampton Press, 1999), 249.
[7] Melady, *Pilots*, 106.

was assigned a Polish 'understudy'. In addition, each instructor had a Polish interpreter who eventually replaced the original British staff. At the height of the Blackpool operation, more than 1,000 pupils were accommodated at the base. For the young Poles, the initial duties were regarded as tedious and quite demeaning. Construction of prisoner of war camps was often the closest action many saw in the early months of the war.

There were still some problems in training during the period the British called the 'Phoney War'. Zurakowski recalled: 'I became platoon commander, with the platoon composed of some one hundred soldiers and junior officers. I was officially responsible for their behaviour, which wasn't an easy task. The whole company was somewhat demoralised by a long wait and, absent temporarily from camp discipline, started to act up, fighting amongst themselves, having romances with hostesses of billets and chatting up local beauties. I was running around trying to pacify everybody, swearing to myself, 'We are at war, France is collapsing and here I am, like an old governess, dragging my half-baked charges to lectures, to beaches and looking after their virtue.''

Zurakowski had previously left his logbook behind in Poland, but now that he was about to go back to flying, he dutifully noted his previous hours in a new logbook issued by the RAF This logbook would stay with him for life. 'It was a panicky time, everyone running around and no proper training. There was a lack of instructors and training facilities. I called it 'patching up' training.' Once, when Zurakowski wasn't sure of the starting procedure on an aircraft, he found he had to rely on another Polish Sergeant Pilot for help. The pilot indicated the button marked 'fire', which was actually the fire extinguisher. Yet the Polish pilots made rapid strides in training during the spring, acquiring the basic operating procedures and checking out on primary and intermediate trainers before moving on to the operational Hurricane and Spitfire fighters. Plt Off Zurakowski was posted to the Army Cooperation School at Old Sarum, where he would be evaluated.

One of the difficulties for the Polish flyers in moving up to a modern fighter was to remember to activate the retractable undercarriage. Another crucial difference was that the throttle operation in a British aircraft acted in reverse to normal Polish practice. Pulling the throttle back in PZL fighters advanced the throttle. Trying that in a Hurricane or Spitfire would lead to disaster as the Poles would be slowing the engine just as they needed full throttle. Forgetting to retract the undercarriage never caught out Zurakowski, but his use of throttle controls nearly did. In his first flight in a de Havilland Tiger Moth on an orientation flight at the Army Cooperation School, he taxied the light training aircraft to get a 'feel for the controls'. As he pushed the throttle forward, the sprightly bi-plane was launched into the sky. He never made that mistake again.

Another inadvertent take-off marked his time at the school. In transitioning to new aircraft, Plt Off Zurakowski was checked out on an old Hawker Hector trainer, which reminded him of the Potez 25 he had last flown in Poland – old and slow but still suitable for a familiarisation flight. Still unsure of the routine expected, he waited until the instructor pilot had the plane in the air before he spoke into the speaking tube that connected the two cockpits. As the barely audible message gave him the command to begin some gentle manoeuvres, he took over the controls and flew as exactly as he could to demonstrate each manoeuvre. With the noise of the engine and the wind rushing through the open cockpits, he wasn't sure that he had picked up all the instructions but nevertheless tried to fly carefully and precisely. 'Communication was hopeless as the Flight Lieutenant was shouting in the tube in English.' Following the landing, the British instructor commented that the flight had been smooth and sure except for the steep climb on take-off. Zurakowski laughed as he tried to explain that he hadn't even placed his hands on the controls and thought that the instructor had taken the plane off the ground. It appeared that the solid and steadfast Hector had flown itself.

After months away from the controls of an aircraft, Zurakowski found it exhilarating to be back in the air. He was soon demonstrating a proficiency in flying that was noted by his instructors. When he completed a short four-day stint with the Army Cooperation School, carrying out thirteen flights in an almost continuous series, Plt Off Zurakowski was then transferred to fighters. This change coincided with the RAF decision to utilise experienced Polish fighter pilots as replacements in fighter squadrons rather than training them as bomber pilots. At No 5 Operational Training Unit (OTU), at Aston Down in Gloucestershire, he joined other Polish pilots including Pilot Officer Zbigniew Olenski, Flying Officer Piotr Ostoja-Ostaszewski and Captain Stanislaw Brezina, all of whom he had known formerly as pilots in Poland. Brezina and Ostoja-Ostaszewski had also been instructors at Deblin, while Olenski, the other experienced pilot in the group and one of the 'old men' at 31, had been an engineer and test pilot in Poland prior to hostilities. While they trained together at No 5 OTU, a mutual interest in flying and engineering would lead to a bond between Olenski and Zurakowski and they became fast friends. Their friendship and parallel pursuits would continue for many years to come.

Operational training involved flying the North American Aviation Harvard 1 and the Miles Master advanced trainers prior to moving on to fighters. The Harvard, also called the AT-6 Texan in the USA, was the standard advanced trainer in many Allied air forces, while the docile Master provided an easy transition to operational fighters in the RAF This low-wing training aircraft with its moderate power and wide-set retractable undercarriage was, despite its mediocre top speed, being considered in those desperate days as a stop-gap fighter; a number were armed and prepared as emergency replacements for the Hurricane and Spitfire fighters that made up the frontline squadrons. When Zurakowski remembers that frantic period, he notes, 'A few flights in the Master was all that was given. I asked the instructor, 'What will be the signals?' The Flight Lieutenant said, 'Just follow me.' We learned in Poland just to stick to another plane. I was following him all over the sky. He said, 'Enough of that.'' Zurakowski subsequently found out that the instructor had about thirty hours of flying time while Zurakowski had already accumulated approximately 550 hours on many different types of aircraft in Poland.

Supermarine Spitfire

After four solo flights in the Master, Zurakowski began a transition to the Supermarine Spitfire, which was a complete departure from the trainers he had just flown. As he squeezed into the narrow cockpit and stared out over the long engine cowling, he was finally in a first-class fighting machine. His memories of this training still remain clear: 'My first Spitfire flight was at No 5 Operational Training Unit at Aston Down, on 24 July 1940. On the second flight, I was instructed and authorised to do 'acrobatic'... One problem with aerobatics on the Spitfire was in spinning. The proper technique for spin recovery was described in the Pilot's Notes, though spinning was not recommended. I determined that it was not possible to stop a spin in exactly the required direction. Training did not improve the situation. I was disappointed because on the old Polish PZL 11 fighter I could stop, after any number of spin turns, in the exact desired direction.'[8]

Throughout his RAF war service, Zurakowski was associated with the beautiful but deadly Spitfire fighter, made famous in the Battle of Britain, and he remembered the aircraft fondly. 'I gained a lot of experience on Spitfires. I made over one thousand flights in fifteen different marks, from the Mark I to the Mark 24 (with the Mark 22, the number system was employed for the types), while I was in the RAF and the Polish Air Force in England.'[9]

The Spitfire had sprung from the design desk of R J Mitchell, whose Schneider Cup Trophy racers could be considered part of the Spitfire's lineage. His Type 300 combined the potent new Rolls-Royce (RR) Merlin V-12 engine within a compact design marked by graceful lines. From the outset, the speed, climb rate and manoeuvrability of the Spitfire made it a potent interceptor. Continual development throughout the war led to the Spitfire emerging as a larger and heavier, but much more lethal, weapon. Various changes in the design of the wings, variations in armament (the original armament of eight .303 Browning machine guns was supplemented by 20mm Hispano cannons, HVAR rockets and bombs), and the engine change to the more powerful RR Griffon dictated its many identities.

By war's end the Spitfire had flown in every theatre of combat and had evolved from a land-based defensive fighter to an offensive fighter, fighter-bomber and photo-reconnaissance aircraft, and had been converted into a naval fighter, the Seafire. Today, the Spitfire continues to be revered as one of the most significant fighter aircraft ever built.

First posting

After completing an operational training course on the Spitfire, which amounted to sixteen flights, Zurakowski and Olenski received their first postings to 152 (Hyderabad) Squadron at RAF Warmwell Satellite Station on 5 August 1940. (Other Polish fighter pilots joined RAF squadrons as follows: four in July, forty-six in August and eighty-five by November 1940.) As Plt Off Zurakowski began

[8] Robert Bracken, *Spitfire: The Canadians* (Erin: The Boston Mills Press, 1995), 13.
[9] Ibid, 14.

squadron service, his first posting was nearly jeopardised by his exuberance. 'I was posted to an operational squadron. After my first flight there, with a bit of aerobatics over our airfield, I was called to the station commander, who furiously explained to me that to do aerobatics on a Spitfire one needed fifty hours' experience on the type plus a written permission from the station commander. My poor English (Polish was my first language) and the evidence in my logbook that I was cleared for aerobatics saved my skin.'[10]

Completing a period of defensive patrols in the North East, the Spitfire squadron shifted its attention to the Portsmouth area to help defend southern England against attacks from the Luftwaffe forces, which were now based in northern France. On 12 August 1940, just as the Battle of Britain was beginning in earnest, Zurakowski was transferred to 234 Squadron, which was operating at the time from St Eval near Newquay in Cornwall and flying Spitfire Mark Is.

234 Squadron

234 (Madras Presidency) Squadron re-formed in November 1939 as a bomber squadron, having been first established as part of the coastal defences in the First World War. Squadron Leader W A J Satchell, its first commanding officer, was injured in a car accident the day after the squadron was established, and was replaced by Squadron Leader R 'Dick' Barnett.

The squadron converted to a fighter unit on 11 March 1940, receiving the first shipment of Spitfire Mark Is three days later. The B Flight commander, Flight Lieutenant Paterson Clarence 'Pat' Hughes, led the transition to the potent new fighter. One of the original members, Pilot Officer R F T 'Bob' Doe, remembered the first Spitfire coming to the squadron: 'This beautiful thing arrived. We walked around it, stroked it. We took turns sitting in it. After you'd flown it once, you realised you weren't flying an aeroplane any more; you just strapped wings on your back and you flew.'[11]

234 Squadron, operating temporarily out of RAF Leconfield, began patrols three or more times during the day and night over Portsmouth and, under Hughes's direction, quickly came up to operational readiness by 8 May 1940. The squadron then shifted to Coastal Command Station St Eval – where conditions were primitive

[10] Ibid, 13.
[11] John Willis, *Churchill's Few* (London: Michael Joseph, 1985), 30-31.

– sharing the base with a bomber squadron. Compared to many other RAF fighter squadrons, 234 included a number of experienced pilots who had as much as 400 hours on fighters. The squadron's four months of training contrasted greatly with the training provided in later stages of the battle when replacement pilots joined the squadron with only limited instruction on Hurricanes or Spitfires. Their training was so basic at the Operational Training Units that the new pilots were only able to take-off, hold formation and land. Aerial gunnery and tactics would have to wait until later or come from experienced pilots such as Zurakowski. These young pilots would suffer great casualties during the forthcoming battle.

Each RAF fighter squadron was allotted two or more Polish pilots from the first group of Polish evacuees. Zurakowski joined other Polish pilots at 234 Squadron, including the newly arrived Sergeant Pilots Zigmund Klein and Joseph Szlagowski. The latter had also been an instructor at Deblin where, on 8 September 1939, he had been caught in a bombing attack on the school. With his mechanic, he barely managed his escape from Poland in a lumbering RWD 8 observation plane. Like Zurakowski, Szlagowski escaped to Romania and followed the standard escape route to France by ship, via Beirut, disembarking at Marseilles where he eventually joined a fighter squadron. Since he lacked combat experience, he and seventeen other Polish pilots were sent to England for specialised training in March 1940, just prior to the Battle of France. It was a lucky break for Szlagowski and for Zurakowski – it was good to see a familiar face. A few days later Zurakowski was cheered by the arrival of Zbigniew Olenski, who had also been transferred from 152 Squadron.

Szlagowski, Klein, Olenski and Zurakowski soon gained nicknames from the British pilots in the squadron, who struggled with the unpronounceable (to them) Polish names. Szlagowski was soon known as 'Slug', and Zigmund Klein as 'Klug'; Zbigniew became 'Big Enough', or simply 'Bee', while 'Zurakowski' was shortened to 'Zura'.

The battle begins

Operation Sealion, the first stage of a German campaign to invade the British Isles, saw the Luftwaffe launch a series of attacks on coastal shipping in the English Channel in July 1940. After moving back to St Eval, 234 Squadron had its first victory on 7 July – a Ju 88 damaged – and on the following day another Ju 88 was destroyed

234 Squadron, Summer 1940. *(234 Squadron archives)*

over a convoy in the North Sea. Although skirmishes like this were taking place early that summer as the initial phase of the Luftwaffe assault, the first major clashes with the RAF in the aerial conflict (soon to be known as the Battle of Britain) took place on 8 August 1940. By the middle of August, the Luftwaffe was raiding England daily, leaving the skies of southern England marked by a myriad of contrails. The fierce, searing air battles of the early days of August had already cost frontline RAF squadrons a toll. Many of the units of 10 Group and 11 Group were already reeling.

By 13 August three of the most ravaged fighter squadrons were moved back and replaced by other fighter squadrons, including 234. Air Vice-Marshal Brand, the Commanding Officer of 10 Group, had visited St Eval two days earlier. Although Brand recognised the value of moving this proficient and experienced squadron closer to the fighting, a decision was also made about its leadership. Squadron Leader Barnett relinquished his command, and temporarily Flight Lieutenant 'Pat' Hughes was appointed as the acting Commanding Officer. Not only was Hughes a popular officer but he also had already been accepted as a natural leader. Szlagowski recalled, 'He knew a lot and taught us all how to fight.'[12] According to Flight Lieutenant Keith A Lawrence, 'He was an inspiration to us all... Quite different from other leaders, he rather suggested than told you and that put everyone at ease, and with his leadership the squadron

[12] Ibid, 103.

ran exceptionally smoothly… 'Pat' always wore his Australian RAAF uniform rather than wear the traditional RAF uniform. He was very smart, as the RAAF uniform was a darker shade than ours and it emphasised the gold braiding on the sleeves.'[13]

While air operations switched from escort and convoy duty to interception, the RAF began to encounter heavier formations of Luftwaffe raiders. Even though St Eval was not considered a forward air station, it was bombed and strafed during the August raids on RAF airbases. On 13 August the attacks on the Detling and Rochford airfields in the South East, on Southampton, and on Middle Wallop airfield in Hampshire, in the Portsmouth-Southampton sector, caught the advance party of 234 Squadron that was being relocated to Middle Wallop. The base was the home of 604 (County of Middlesex) Squadron, which was flying Bristol Blenheim Mark IF night fighters, commanded by Squadron Leader M Anderson, and a Spitfire squadron, 609 (West Riding), led by Squadron Leader Horace S 'George' Darley. This sector station had been newly constructed and more than 300 workers were still completing the hangar and dispersal buildings.

That morning, the armourers, mechanics, fitters and mixed trades who formed the advance group of 234 Squadron had been bundled up in two old Bristol Bombay transports. Spitfires of the squadron took off later but caught up to the transports and landed ahead of them at Middle Wallop. After an hour and a half's flight, the transports were coming in for a landing at their new base when suddenly the airfield came under attack. One of the Bombay transports, after making two valiant attempts to land during the bombing, was diverted to the nearby Boscombe Down airfield. After being notified of an 'all-clear' at Middle Wallop, the 234 Squadron's ground crews were flown back to the base and immediately began refuelling and rearming their squadron's Spitfires.

The following day, the remainder of the 234 Squadron aircraft completed the move to Middle Wallop. Zurakowski had only flown once with his squadron before relocating to Middle Wallop. The transfer was a near disaster as the squadron that morning flew in a massed formation directly into a fog bank. Pilot Officer W H 'Bill' Hornby was terrified during the flight, remembering that 'dark

---

[13] 'Ramrod Books Book Launch of Kaleidoscope III', [online] cited on 2 September 2000: http://www.battleofbritain.net/ramrodbooks/booklaunch.html.

shapes loomed everywhere and it was a miracle that there were no collisions'.[14] The overcast conditions that were prevalent in England were to be a constant danger to pilots throughout the battle. Later in the autumn, four pilots from 302 Squadron encountered a thick fog and were to die in an attempt to let down over Sandown Park racecourse.

While the newly arrived 234 Squadron Spitfires were being refuelled, the enemy again struck Middle Wallop. Beginning at 1645 hours, three He 111 Ps from KG 55 Bomber Wing together with a lone Ju 88A-1 from LG 1 (Demonstration Wing) dropped from the overcast to attack the field. The Ju 88 dropped a stick of four 500kg bombs directly on Hangar No 5. When the alarm sounded, a maintenance party of four airmen had been desperately trying to close the giant steel-plated door of the hangar. The crew was still hand-cranking the door mechanism when a blast tore the thirteen-ton door off its guide rails and on top of them, killing three of the group outright. The deaths of these ground crew were soon avenged by a 609 Squadron Spitfire flown by Sergeant Alan Feary, which had, amazingly, been one of four Spitfires that had been able to take-off in the midst of the attack. Feary chased the raider and brought down the Ju 88 in a fiery pyre. Sergeant M C Boddington from 234 Squadron had also managed to reach the fight but not before the Ju 88 was shot down. Two other Spitfires from 609 Squadron caught two of the Heinkels, with Flying Officer John C Dundas finishing off one of the bombers that had been hit by Pilot Officer David Crook. The pair downed the lead bomber of the formation in which the KG 55 navigation specialist had directed the attack. The remainder of the enemy bombers were unable to formate properly and inadvertently attacked Netheravon, an old non-operational airfield twelve miles north-west of Middle Wallop.

As the smoke cleared, the damage was assessed as serious. Middle Wallop would experience another attack the next day and again on 21 August, gaining it the accolade of 'centre-punch', but none of the raids would be more deadly than that of 14 August. Three more fatalities had occurred when civilian workers in a construction crew had been caught in the attack, while scores of wounded were discovered at the barracks and the bombed-out hangar. Hangar No 5 had collapsed, crushing three 604 Squadron

[14] Willis, *Churchill's Few*, 103.

Blenheim night fighters and two 609 Squadron Spitfires that were under repair. However, more importantly, no pilots were hurt in the attack. It had nearly been a disaster for Zurakowski's squadron, as many pilots from 234 were caught in open ground, being picked up by lorries or walking across from the dispersal area to the Mess just 400 yards away. Joseph Szlagowski ran into a wood near the field only to find that the ammunition dump hidden in Knock Wood erupted in a huge fireball as an incendiary hit it. Bob Doe, together with other pilots from 234, had been in a lorry that careened across the field, driving at breakneck speed across the road.

Victory

On Thursday 15 August the weather conditions had cloud covering much of the South and South East during the morning, dispersing before noon when a ridge of high pressure right across Britain would ensure a fine and warm day. A large enemy formation, estimated as being more than thirty aircraft, was detected crossing the English Channel to the south of Portland at 1700 hours. The raiders were in fact a formation of forty Ju 87 dive-bombers from I Stukageschwader 1, accompanied by a massive escort of sixty Bf 109s of Jagdgeschwaders 27 and 53, and twenty-five Bf 110s from I Zerstörergeschwader 76. 10 Group Command dispatched five Hurricanes from 87 (United Provinces) Squadron and 213 (Ceylon) Squadron, and two Hurricanes from RAF Exeter in the Filton Sector to intercept the enemy. Other squadrons along the coast were scrambled, including 234 and 609 Squadrons at Middle Wallop, which was under attack. Zurakowski took off in the midst of the bombing to join up with the twelve Spitfires led by Hughes.

The small force of British fighters, although vastly outnumbered, forced the Luftwaffe raid to retreat during the epic battle. Zura, flying Spitfire Mark I X4016, code-marked 'AZ', climbed up into the swirling mêlée at 10,000 feet a few miles south of the base. As they were being attacked, seven large Messerschmitt Bf 110 twin-engined German fighters attempted to form a defensive circle that the RAF had called 'the circle of death'. Zurakowski latched on to the last Bf 110C-2 (marked 'M8+BP') flown by *Feldwebel* Jakob Birndorfer and gunner *Unteroffizier* Max Guschewski, which abruptly broke from a group of fighters and turned roughly south in a shallow dive.

At treetop level, Zura carried out three stern attacks and repeatedly hit the streaking Messerschmitt, noting that 'the top of the fuselage of the Me-110 looked like somebody had hacked on it with an axe.' As Zura broke away after the last attack, a lone Spitfire of a fellow Polish pilot, Pilot Officer Ostaszewski-Ostoja of 609 Squadron, joined the pursuit. The pair of Spitfires followed the stricken German fighter through the barrage balloons over Southampton, and as the other Spitfire broke off, Zurakowski finished off the Bf 110. In his combat report, Zurakowski briefly described the attack: 'I attacked circle of Me-110 from above and behind the last aircraft; enemy dived down to the ground. The rear gunner ceased to fire. On the way down a second Spitfire from 609 Squadron attacked, but when it broke away, I engaged five more times; e/a eventually crashed in Isle of Wight.'[15] His bursts in his final quarter-beam attacks damaged the Bf 110, which flew slowly, propellers still turning. The Messerschmitt flew low across the Solent and over the Isle of Wight, force-landing on Ashey Road in North Ashey Down.

Ten-year-old Ron Morton lived at Whippingham in Coburg Cottage and remembered the battle overhead in these words: 'A twin-engined German aircraft was circling. The Whippingham guns were blasting away, and shrapnel was falling on the cottage. Mother became very frightened, and we were worried that as the plane circled lower, the anti-aircraft shells would take the cottage roof off. We huddled in the porch. Eventually the plane was lost from view heading inland towards Wootton.'[16] The Black Watch Regiment stationed at Havenstreet had indeed joined the battle, with Private John Heasfield, who was perched at the shrine on the top of hill, emptying a complete magazine from his Bren gun into the stricken enemy fighter. He recalled that behind the Messerschmitt Bf 110 a 'Spitfire waggled its wings to thank him and departed hot on its tail'.[17]

At 1806 hours the Messerschmitt skidded across a gravel lane below a quarry near West Ashey Farm to come to rest in the grass a few hundred yards from the sea. The wreckage was immediately surrounded by fifteen to twenty members of the Jersey Militia who were billeted nearby. The pilot was killed upon landing, while the gunner, who had been wounded earlier in the combat, lay unconscious in the rear of the aircraft. Zura flew back in company

---

[15] Robert Gretzyngier, *Poles in Defence of Britain* (London: Grub Street, 2001), 25.

[16] John Howard Worsley, Notes for art print 'Incident at Ashey', 21 June 2002.

[17] Ibid.

with Ostoja-Ostaszewski. Each pilot made a claim for the victory; it was awarded to Zurakowski, although they both probably shared in bringing down the enemy plane.

In 1987 Gunner Guschewski described Zurakowski's first victory: 'From Le Mans, we moved our Bf 110s to Rennes; this was Gruppes I and II Our Gruppe was III/ZG76. Preparations were made for the attack on England. Our 110s were fitted with long-range tanks. August 15, 1940. Soon after 1600 we took off, heading for our assembly point at Guernsey, where we were to escort 40 Ju 88 bombers, but owing to so many losses, only 18 came. We flew over Cherbourg for England at 200 metres. As we flew over the Channel, we climbed to 1200 metres. Our target was an airfield at Salisbury. As we neared the English coast, the skies were clear, not a cloud to be seen between Portland and the Isle of Wight. Only the condensation trails streaming behind our aeroplane's engines.

'We looked down and saw Spitfires climbing up to meet us. We reached Salisbury and prepared to attack the airfield. It was then the battle commenced. Spitfires appeared to be everywhere. We flew away from the target, but the bombers had not released their bombs, so we returned again. They dropped them, but not all fell on the target. We turned to fly back to our base. Our right motor was hit, then our left one was hit and the propeller on it stopped. When I was hit by a machine-gun bullet, I went unconscious. I came to as we landed in a field and again I went unconscious for a few minutes. Soldiers of a Scottish infantry regiment arrived. I could not get out, so the soldiers lifted me out. I still had my parachute on, which was of British design, and the release buckle was jammed. I tried to stand but could not because my left side was paralysed. An officer of the Scottish infantry came and he tried to interrogate me.'[18] Although the accounts of Pilot Birndorfer's death varied wildly as rumours flew through the Isle of Wight, he had been unfortunate to resist at the time of capture. Apparently his spirit still inhabits this small hamlet: locals relate that the ghost of a young German pilot appears at windows, and his last flight was recently recounted in a vision by a woman in Ryde. In her apparition, a ghostly German plane, chased by a Spitfire, flew over her and crashed into a field.

[18] Winston Ramsey, ed, *Blitz Then and Now, Volume 1* (London: Battle of Britain Prints International Ltd, 1987), 217.

Three Bf 110s had been brought down that afternoon; however, the British had suffered greatly. Three of the five Hurricanes from 87 Squadron were shot down with two fatalities, including their Commanding Officer, Squadron Leader Lovell-Gregg, while one pilot was seriously injured in a forced landing near Bridport. Of the thirteen 234 Squadron Spitfires that were scrambled that day, five aircraft were shot down and three pilots were lost. Pilot Officer Cecil H Hight, leader of the Yellow Section, was mortally wounded over Bournemouth, yet brought his Spitfire back to base, only to die shortly after in the arms of the intelligence officer. Pilot Officer V 'Bush' Parker ditched in the Channel, while Pilot Officer Richard Hardy, leader of the Red Section, was forced down at Cherbourg, France. Both of these pilots were taken prisoner by the Germans. Two pilots, including Sergeant Klein, were shot down but survived by taking to parachutes. Klein returned to the unit shortly after.

The enemy fighters

Zurakowski's first victory had been over the Messerschmitt Bf 110 Zerstörer (Destroyer) twin engine fighter, one of twenty-seven that fell that day. The Bf 110 was used as an escort fighter to cut a path for the bombers through defending aircraft. The large two-seater boasted a relatively high speed and long range but it could not dogfight effectively with single-seat fighters.

Limited numbers of the Bf 110 were used in the Polish campaign as fighter-bomber and ground-attack machines, but its real baptism of fire against modern fighters came in 1940 over the Low Countries and France. Eight Gruppen of Bf 110s were committed to daylight operations over Britain where Hurricanes and Spitfires of the RAF decimated them. By the end of the year, the German High Command had been forced to remove the Zerstörer as an offensive fighter and to concentrate on the single-engine Bf 109E

In the Messerschmitt Bf 109E, the RAF faced a much more lethal opponent. The 'Emil', the Luftwaffe's standard single-seat fighter from the commencement of hostilities in Poland, was unquestionably one of the world's finest single-seat, single-engine fighters. Until the Battle of Britain the Bf 109 had not faced serious opposition and had amassed an extraordinary score of victories. The first encounters with the RAF proved that the Bf 109 was a potent foe – it could dive and climb better than any RAF fighter due to its Daimler Benz fuel-injected engine, and its cannons were effective at ranges where the RAF's rifle-calibre machine guns were useless.

The other clear advantage of the Bf 109s was the superior wingman-leader tactic, which could prove decisive in a mêlée. In this scenario, Spitfires operating independently or in the outmoded 'vic' formation would face a coordinated attack where the Bf 109 pilots would stick together and help each other. Once the Spitfire was in the Bf 109's gunsights, the twin cannon could 'shred a Spit' in a well-placed snapshot. This was partially nullified by the mere seven seconds of cannon fire available, but a disciplined shooter could be quite lethal.

Although the '109' was faster, it could be easily outmanoeuvred by the sturdy Hurricane. Fractionally slower than the Spitfire at most heights, the 'Emil' could meet its match in a well-flown Spitfire. In a one-to-one battle, once the Bf 109E was above 15,000 feet its better altitude performance started to help; below that height, the Spitfire Mark I was as fast, and could out-accelerate, out-turn and climb almost as well.

On the downside was the difficulty in flying the Bf 109 due to restricted vision through a heavily framed and cramped cockpit, heavy control loads at speed, a 'grabbing' of the automatic wing slats, and wicked landing characteristics. The Bf 109's most serious deficiency in the Battle of Britain was its limited range; even though long-range fuel tanks were available, they were rarely fitted. Pilots only had about fifteen to twenty minutes of combat time over the target and often returned with their red fuel lights flashing. This shortcoming proved to be detrimental during the Battle because the Bf 109 could not function effectively in a bomber escort role.

The thin margin of victory that the RAF exploited was based on the tactical and logistical advantages inherent to the defender. The Bf 109s were operating at a disadvantage in the Battle, having only a limited endurance to spend over Britain in combat with British pilots. The RAF also had the added advantage of an early warning system based on a complex of ground observer stations, radar tracking and sector stations that used radio communication to guide intercepts. The benefits of being able to recover damaged aircraft, as well as aircrew, led to the Luftwaffe fighting a battle of attrition that heavily favoured the RAF Being shot down over friendly ground or in the English Channel where RAF pilots could be picked up by rescue launches gave the RAF a chance to continually regroup its precious human defenders. X4016, the Spitfire that Zurakowski had flown on 15 August, was lost the very next day when its pilot, Flying Officer F H P Conner, was forced to bail out after being attacked by a Bf 109 over Southampton. In two days, 234 Squadron had lost six Spitfires, but Conner was back on operations the next day and the Spitfire was soon replaced.

In the Battle of Britain, compared with the British Hurricane and Spitfire, the Bf 109 was equal to the task, and historians will argue for years to come which was the best aircraft. A Luftwaffe strategic decision late in the autumn of 1940, to tie the Bf 109s to a close escort role with the savaged bomber formations, probably tipped the balance in favour of the RAF Without the ability to range ahead or utilise its high speed, the Bf 109 went on the defensive and allowed the Spitfires to select fighter opponents while the Hurricanes tore into the bombers in a deadly one-two punch. Overall, of the three, the Spitfire was possibly the best fighter in the Battle of Britain. Had Germany made the necessary technical improvements to the Bf 109 and reverted to earlier, more effective tactics, the outcome of 1940 may well have been different.

Desperate times

Now Zurakowski was in the thick of the action, sometimes flying two or three missions per day during that desperate time. Zura noted in his records: 'I was with Stew Young (Pilot Officer J S 'Stew' Young) in 234 Squadron. At that time, I was a pilot officer, and so I flew any aircraft that was available. According to my logbook, I carried out eight sorties on Spitfire Mark I No 4182 (X4182) and thirteen sorties on No 3191 (N3191).'[19] 'Some of the discomforts of squadron life during this time included having to keep pilots sitting in their aircraft at standby for long periods, and, during the colder nights, having to run up the engines at intervals to keep them warm. The squadron was at standby generally from 0300 hours until 1900 hours, and often throughout the whole twenty-four-hour period.'[20]

Air Chief Marshal Dowding's instructions on 27 July had mandated that all fighter pilots would have a minimum of eight hours off duty in each twenty-four-hour period and at least one complete day off each week. In those hectic and trying days, it was uncertain if

[19] Bracken, *Spitfire*, 13.
[20] Ray Stebbings, *A Short History of No 234 Squadron, Royal Air Force, 1917-1955*, c1969.

these orders were fully carried out. The ground crew were under a similar strain. Airman Stan Waterson added, 'We started the routine of sleeping under canvas at dispersal point every other night, and some mornings were up so early that it was still dark, but had to wait till first light before starting up the engines in case we attracted some Germans returning from a late-night raid.'[21] During the long readiness cycles, the pilots would sometimes sneak one of the two squadron mascots – a kitten and a small puppy – into the cockpit with them for company. It was rumoured that the mascots had taken part in combats, as they were unceremoniously tucked behind the seats when a scramble was announced.

The squadron mechanics performed real miracles in the Battle, often salvaging damaged and shot-up planes (which the pilots had expected had breathed their last) and making them ready for the next day's start. 'So that's why, when we enjoyed a short night's rest, the workshop and field teemed with frantic activity. After all those years, Zbigniew Olenski always recalled a young mechanic, face smeared with grease, asking after each mission, 'Did you win today, Sir?" That young country boy was in awe of the Poles, whom he somehow imagined had come from the 'North Pole', as he had no concept of where Poland was located.

Unlike some of the young British pilots with their casual attitude, Zura began to get a reputation for his grim determination to get at the enemy. A fellow pilot remarked, 'Zurakowski was quite another cup of tea. His experiences getting out of Poland didn't bear relating but it happened to a man who didn't forget and lived with him every waking hour.'[22] Bill Hornby remembered, 'Zurakowski was a different mould, purposeful and just a bit dangerous-looking.'[23] Even the new Commanding Officer, Squadron Leader Joseph S 'Spike' O'Brien, who had arrived on 16 August, noticed that Zura was constantly flying, resulting in O'Brien trying to get him to stand down and take a normal rotation. It was to no avail. Other pilots who counted the scrambled Spitfires began to notice that the thirteenth aircraft was invariably Zurakowski's. While a full complement of the squadron's

[21] Frank H Ziegler, *The Story of 609 Squadron: Under the White Rose* (London: Crécy Books, 1993), 100.
[22] Stebbings, *No 234 Squadron*.
[23] Ibid.

twelve planes was launched, a 'ready' machine was always warmed up and available in case one of the Spitfires faltered. When O'Brien questioned him, Zura typically replied with 'No understanding' and a suitably perplexed countenance. The inevitable difficulties in language and the differences in age (he considered himself a bit 'old' at twenty-six) meant that he was seen as an intense and distant figure by many of the young English pilots. However, when Zurakowski and Olenski, the other Polish veteran of the squadron, shared some quiet moments, Zura was more himself, joking and sociable.

Downed but alive

On Saturday 24 August, nine days after his first victory, while flying Spitfire Mark I N3239, Zurakowski was himself shot down over the Isle of Wight by a Bf 109E flown by either *Oberstleutnant* Hans-Karl Mayer of I Lehrgeschwader 53 (operating from Rennes, Le Touquet) or *Leutnant* A Zeis of Staffel Jagdgeschwader 53, or a combination of both pilots' attacks.

A major shift in Luftwaffe tactics had taken place on that date with the introduction of 'stepped' raids, using successive formations of aircraft at different altitudes, from low-level fighter-bomber groups to high-level bombers at 24,000 feet. When one formation set off, another group assembled behind Calais. As the armada swept over England, the raiders split off into feint attacks, making interception most difficult at all levels and positions. The late-afternoon German raid over Portsmouth had been intercepted by twelve Spitfires, including all four Polish pilots of 234 Squadron and aircraft from 609 Squadron.

Encountering ten Junkers Ju 88s in a bombing run of Southampton harbour, Zura swung into an attack but met their formidable escort of Messerschmitt Bf 109s and Bf 110s. In trying to climb back to the squadron, his Spitfire shuddered from cannon strikes. With its tail badly damaged and no aileron or rudder control, Zurakowski was faced with a dilemma. 'My Spitfire then went slowly into a turn, stalled, and ended up in a flat spin. Because I could not control the plane, I bailed out. At about 18,000 feet, I slid open the canopy, climbed out of the cabin, and jumped. I soon found I was descending faster than the Spitfire, which was spinning above my head. I was afraid to pull the rip cord to open the chute because that would have slowed me down, risking a collision with my spinning Spitfire. The ground was approaching fast, and when I could distinguish a man standing in a field with a gun, I decided to pull the rip cord. It was now or never!'[24]

With a jarring tug the parachute opened, pulling Zurakowski out of the way of his Spitfire, which impacted nearby. 'A Spitfire's vertical speed in a flat spin is fairly low, so the damage to my Spitfire on impact with the ground was not severe. The main engine mounting failed and there was evidence of two gunshots (probably 20mm calibre) in the rear fuselage tail junction and one in the port wing.'[25] The aircraft did not catch fire, and as he landed he saw an old farmer approaching with a shotgun. The man was likely a member of the Home Guard, the Local Defence Volunteers, which had been formed earlier that year. The old gentleman demanded identification. Badly shaken by the crash, Zura slowly gathered up his parachute and deliberated whether his broken English would suffice in proving he was not a German. 'Since my English was poor, I decided to remain quiet. I tried to show him my RAF identity card, but his hands were shaking so violently that he could not take it. I decided to start packing my chute, and a British army officer arrived and cleared the situation.'[26]

Zura was driven back to the Army Officers' Mess, but the local policeman who escorted him back decided to show off the airman to the locals. As he stopped in one house after another, each housewife had 'a lovely cup of tea' ready. Zura recalled that he was nearly awash with tea after the third house and, to this day, he is not fond of the drink.

He eventually made it back to Middle Wallop the next day, but by his own account, however, he received a shock: 'Next morning I returned to my squadron. I was flying again, but learned from my friends in London that I had been officially killed. I had to send a report to the effect that I was very sorry, but that since the date of the crash, I had carried out six operational sorties in August, so I was obviously alive. Shortly afterward, I received two letters addressed to me, marked 'Killed in Action' on the envelope. I kept those letters as souvenirs.'[27] The mistaken account of Zurakowski's 'death' survives in many records, and is even mentioned in a recent book on the Battle of Britain.

[24] Bracken, *Spitfire*, 13.
[25] Ibid, 14.
[26] Ibid, 13.
[27] Ibid, 14.

Back in action

Although he had missed an intercept the day before, Zurakowski wanted to get back into battle. Led by Squadron Leader O'Brien, 234 had scored a record fourteen Bf 110s and one Do 17 destroyed for only one damaged, its best day yet. In three weeks, the squadron had become the highest scoring unit in 10 Group. On Thursday 5 September 1940 at 1538 hours, flying Spitfire Mark I N3279, Zura shot down a Messerschmitt Bf 109E-1 off the Isle of Sheppey. This machine (Werk No 6252) from 9 Jagdgeschwader 53 'Pik As' was flown by *Feldwebel* A Oschenkuhn. 234 Squadron had been flying a loose formation when Zura had picked out two aircraft low on the horizon, flying south on a slight zigzag course.

The dive down to confirm their identity had fogged up the windscreen, but as it cleared, Zurakowski identified them as Bf 109s streaking for home. He fired a short burst that served to alert the enemy to their danger. One Messerschmitt turned sharply and dived away, but the other pilot chose to loop upwards right into his sights. Zurakowski's report, made out immediately after landing, describes the battle but reveals none of the excitement or elation that might have been expected after a combat victory.

'I was Blue 2,' wrote Zura, 'and we were flying at 22,000 feet. I went down to investigate two machines and then saw a Me-109 flying south at 14,000 feet. I approached from astern and as he turned, gave a short burst from 100 yards. He half rolled and dived and flew low due south. I stayed on his tail and fired one burst at 140 yards and then the rest of my ammunition from very close. After my first attack he was smoking slightly and, later, heavily. The enemy pilot opened his hood as he crash-landed on the sea. The pilot got out and two minutes later the machine sank. The Me-109 out-dived me, but I overtook him easily flying straight and level.'[28]

The German pilot had nearly been able to make his escape because his aircraft had been so low that it had been difficult to aim at it without closing in at times to thirty metres. Momentarily, in his side window Zurakowski had caught the outline of the Bf 109 silhouetted in the sky as it crested a hill. He closed in immediately and began to score heavily. The combat had ended at almost

---

[28] Geoffrey Norris, 'Impossible – of Course!', *RAF Flying Review*, XIV, 8 (April 1959), 29.

housetop level over Hastings, and later Zura was troubled that he had expended the last of his ammunition over the city in his furious attack. The Bf 109 ditched in the sea only twelve miles from the coast. As Zurakowski swept over the wreckage, he observed the German pilot swimming away. Oschenkuhn was subsequently rescued, unhurt, by the Hastings lifeboat, *Cyril and Lilian Bishop*.

The next day, Friday 6 September at 0940 hours, the squadron was vectored into an early morning intercept over Dover of fifteen Bf 110s acting as fighter-bombers, escorted by twenty-five Bf 109s. The German fighter escort quickly turned towards their attackers with the combat reverting to individual battles. The 234 Squadron's fighter formation leader, Flight Lieutenant 'Pat' Hughes, had a weaving Bf 109 in his sights, one that had been escorting a damaged Bf 110 at the rear of the formation. He fired a long burst, which damaged the Bf 109's oil tanks, spraying Hughes with oil over his windscreen and tailplane. Almost immediately he was forced to disengage as he had no more ammunition and was under fire from three other Bf 109s in a beam attack.

Again at the controls of Spitfire Mark I N3279, Zura pounced on the first Bf 109, engaging him in a head-on attack. After the initial exchange of fire, the enemy aircraft spiralled away with Zurakowski on its tail. With an opportunity for a long burst from his favourable shooting position, he was able to shoot down the Bf 109E-1 (Werk No 3877, '5+1') from 7 Jagdgeschwader 26 'Schlageter'. The attack had ended at low altitude, and as Zura clawed his way back to the fight, he was 'bounced' by three Bf 109s. Taking hits and with no chance to run, Zurakowski spun, corkscrewing to the ground, pretending to be shot down. Limping home, his badly damaged Spitfire barely made it back to base at Middle Wallop, where he was able to crash-land.

His dispassionate account after the combat nevertheless captured the essence of the battle: 'I was Blue 2. Saw Blue 1 attack and reformed with Blue 1 (Hughes). Saw formation of Do 17 with Me-109s. Attacked a Me-109 in front of the bombers from the front and from a beam. He holed my wing. He went over on his back, dived and I followed him. He climbed and went on his back again; fired second burst, and third burst and he crashed. Three Me-109s attacked me at 3,000 ft. Saw close formation of Me-109s in southerly direction, far away. Returned to base and my machine overturned in landing.'[29]

[29] Gretzyngier, *Poles in Defence of Britain*, 29.

The Messerschmitt that Zurakowski had hit attempted to land but crashed heavily and caught on fire at Swamp Farm, Old Romney. The pilot was trapped in the burning aircraft and was probably already grievously wounded when a detachment of local soldiers appeared on the scene. Unable to get closer to the aircraft due to the heat of the inferno, they fired into the cockpit and killed the pilot to prevent more unnecessary suffering. His remains were later interred at the Folkestone New Cemetery, Hawkinge, in a grave marked only by the inscription 'Unknown German Airman'. Two Luftwaffe pilots were unaccounted for on this date and it appears to be likely that *Gefreiter* Karl Bieker or *Gefreiter* Peter Holzapfel of 7 Jagdgeschwader 26 met their demise that day.

Zurakowski's Spitfire was shot up over Beachy Head, receiving heavy damage to its underside and wings. When Zura selected the undercarriage, he found that it would not lower itself fully nor would it go back up. He was forced to land with it half-extended, resulting in the Spitfire digging in on contact with the ground and turning on its back. After releasing his seat belts, Zura dropped down on his head; luckily, as he later described it, his 'thick' helmet and 'thick' head absorbed the impact and, amazingly, he walked away from the crash slightly woozy but otherwise unhurt. After the ground crew inspected the damage to the undercarriage from cannon shells and small-calibre weapon holes in the wings, his Spitfire was repaired and was soon back in the air.

That autumn the tide of the battle was changing as the Luftwaffe altered its strategy from Channel and airfield raids to a concentration on English cities, especially the capital. While London increasingly became the target, the beleaguered fighter stations gained an unexpected reprieve. For 234 Squadron, whose motto was 'We spit fire and death', the constant fighting had taken a heavy toll. When Zurakowski was rested for two days, the squadron lost nine out of twelve pilots, including its two highest scorers and its new commanding officer. On 7 September Squadron Leader O'Brien was killed when he was shot down by enemy aircraft and crashed near Biggin Hill. During the same mission Flight Lieutenant Hughes, the squadron's leading ace with fourteen confirmed victories up to that point, died during combat when he crashed into exploding debris after he destroyed a Do 17 bomber. As his wingman, Olenski, watched in horror, one of the bomber's wings struck the Spitfire that Hughes was flying. The tumbling wreckage fell to the ground in Kent.

Zurakowski mourned 'the losses of so many good men, especially Hughes who was not only a skilled pilot but a great leader whom everyone respected.' The day before his death, Hughes had complained of eye problems but refused to ask to be relieved. Both O'Brien and Hughes were awarded the Distinguished Flying Cross (Hughes received his award posthumously in 1942). They had gallantly led the squadron through the fierce battles of the summer, but now there was no one to take over. Squadron Adjutant 'Bish' Owens had to write to two grieving widows that day; Hughes had only been married thirty-eight days.

Supermarine had stencilled each Spitfire's serial number on the interior frame of the aircraft. At the height of the fighting, Zurakowski noted that replacement squadron aircraft invariably carried serial numbers indicating that they were recently constructed. Intuitively he realised that the RAF had nearly run out of fighters. The aircraft strength of 234 Squadron had fluctuated from sixteen to nine serviceable Spitfires during this period, but more aircraft were becoming available from the stepped-up production lines of Supermarine and Hawkers as well as their subsidiaries. However, the loss in pilots could not be that easily made up.

Bloodied

By 11 September 1940, the pilot fatalities of 234 Squadron were so catastrophic, particularly the loss of leaders (including both flight commanders and the squadron commander), that Fighter Command was forced to withdraw the squadron. Fifteen of twenty-two pilots had been lost in just two weeks, and despite replacements being sent, only ten pilots, including Zurakowski, were left. Of the original squadron pilots who had been present in November 1939 when the squadron had been formed, only three survived. Flying Officer E B M 'Mortimer' Rose, in charge of A Flight, and Flying Officer Keith S Dewhurst, leader of B Flight, temporarily took charge of the squadron.

The squadron was moved back to St Eval in Cornwall to 'lick its wounds'. Zura attributed the large number of fatalities in part to the relentless punishment of high-altitude skirmishes and to the inevitable fatigue that had set in with the constant sorties. It was this last factor that led to the deaths of many pilots. 'It was estimated in the summer of the Battle that every pilot kept in action for more than six months would be shot down because he was exhausted or stale, or even because he had lost the will to fight. In terms of flying hours, the fighter pilot's life expectancy could be measured at eighty-seven.'[30] The RAF's dogged reliance on outmoded tactics of fighter interception, such as the 'vic' formations and line-astern attacks, also led to many needless deaths, according to Zura.

On 29 September, towards the end of the Battle of Britain, Zurakowski, while flying Spitfire Mark I N3191, engaged and probably destroyed a Messerschmitt Bf 110c approximately five miles south of Exmouth at 1345 hours. His account is taken from the time. 'I was Blue 2 ordered to Falmouth. I saw anti-aircraft bursts but no aircraft. I proceeded to Plymouth. Again saw anti-aircraft burst and the enemy aircraft in front proceeding north-east. I chased it and attacked from starboard beam and fired one burst of five seconds, I then broke away and enemy aircraft turned south-east. I followed it, joined Blue 1 (Plt Off Dewhurst) and two minutes later Blue 1 attacked from astern and I attacked afterwards from starboard rear, I saw both engines smoking then enemy aircraft disappeared into clouds.'[31] Only one Bf 110 was lost that day, when an aircraft from II Zerstörergeschwader 26 crashed at St Aubin aerodrome in France. This combat, listed as a 'probable' and claimed by both pilots, was the last of Zura's Battle of Britain victory claims.

234 Squadron, now commanded by Squadron Leader Mindon Vaughn 'Mindy' Blake, had earlier been moved to Warmwell, one of the forward airfields in the sector, but was 'relaxed' to St Eval. The squadron was exchanged for 238 Squadron, which was flying Hurricanes. In one move, 234 Squadron was no longer rated as a Category A squadron and had been placed in the rear as a Category C unit, suitable only for training. This move did not suit Zura very well and, together with Flying Officer Olenski, he requested a transfer to an 11 Group squadron actively involved in the fighting.

An attempt was made to re-form 234 Squadron in Cornwall using the surviving members of the squadron. However, after recent transfers (Doe went to 238 Squadron), there were only six pilots left including Zurakowski, just barely the minimum requirement for a fighting unit. On 6 October 1940 both Zurakowski and Olenski were posted to 609 Squadron. Szlagowski and Klein, the Polish Sergeant

[30] Derek Wood and Derek Dempster, *The Narrow Margin: The Dramatic Story of the Battle of Britain and the Rise of Air Power, 1930-1940* (New York: Paperback Library, 1969), 393.

[31] Gretzyngier, *Poles in Defence of Britain*, 119-120.

Pilots, were transferred to 152 Squadron. One of Zura's wartime reports at the time noted: 'In October, I was posted back to the Middle Wallop RAF station and joined 609 Squadron, where Ogi (Keith Ogilvie, or 'Ogi' as we called him), was my section leader.'[32]

609 Squadron

Led by Squadron Leader Michael Lister Robinson, 609 Squadron was the other Spitfire squadron operating from Middle Wallop. Two Polish pilots were already there: Flying Officer 'Osti' (or 'Post') Ostoja-Ostaszewski and Flying Officer Tadeusz 'Novi' (or 'Novo') Nowierski, who like many Polish pilots already bore English nicknames. Nowierski had also recently gained fame as 'The Terror of the Henhouse', receiving this accolade after he was forced to abandon his Spitfire when his landing gear malfunctioned. He ended up having to take to his parachute and landed in the middle of a hen run on a nearby farm at Chisenbury, Wiltshire. His wingman and fellow pilots rushed to his rescue, being afraid, as in Zurakowski's earlier bail-out, that the farmers descending on the flurry of feathers would mistake Novi for a German.

No 609 (West Riding) Squadron was formed in 1936 at Yeadon as a day bomber unit of the Auxiliary Air Force; the squadron was redesignated a fighter unit on 8 December 1938. After defensive duties in the north, the squadron moved to South East England in May 1940 and flew patrols over Dunkirk to cover the evacuation of the BEF Stationed in Middle Wallop throughout the Battle of Britain, 609 became the first Spitfire squadron to destroy 100 enemy aircraft. Its squadron motto was, fittingly, 'Tally Ho'.

By the time that Zurakowski's transfer to 609 came through, the Battle of Britain was coming to an end. On 7 October, during the mid-afternoon, more than fifty German bombers, mostly Ju 88s, headed towards Yeovil and the Westland Aircraft Works. Spitfires from 152 Squadron and Hurricanes from 238 and 601 Squadrons joined the 609 Squadron Spitfires to engage the bombers over Portland. Some of the Ju 88s managed to get through, and a number of bombs were dropped, causing damage and thereby delaying work at the factory. In the early evening, a series of separate raids crossed the coast at Dungeness, Beachy Head and Selsey. These were some of the last daylight bombing raids for Fighter Command. The intensity of the day's

---

[32] Bracken, *Spitfire*, 14.

fighting was reflected in the number of aircraft shot down on both sides. There were still deadly aerial battles over England in the autumn of 1940, and during one of Zurakowski's combat missions on 28 November 1940 he was on the receiving end of an attack.

The squadron had been in preparation for an imminent move to Warmwell and was in the process of 'standing down'. That day, a tour of 150 cadets and staff officers from Sandhurst was under way at the station, complete with rugby, football and field-hockey matches laid on. In the midst of the visit, two scrambles of the squadron took place. The second scramble in the late afternoon found 609 and 152 Squadrons in a dogfight with the Bf 109s of Major Helmut Wick's Jagdeschwader 2 Richtofen Squadron. At the time, Wick was the highest scoring Luftwaffe ace in the Battle of Britain, with fifty-five kills. On his second mission of the day, a *Freie Jagd* (free hunt), Wick shot down a Spitfire. His fifty-sixth victory was Pilot Officer Paul A Baillon from 609 Squadron, whose Spitfire was hit in the first strike through the ascending Spitfires.

The battle that afternoon over the Needles, three chalk pinnacles that once joined the Isle of Wight to the English mainland, had taken place at high altitude, around 3,000 metres. The Spitfires were bounced from above by the Messerschmitts, with many individual

F/L John Bisdee taxiing 609 Squadron Spitfire Mk 1a PR-O in 1940. *(IWM collection)*

combats taking place. It had been difficult for the Spitfires to engage a sole Bf 109 without encountering a swarm of wingmen, as the enemy, low on fuel, savagely fought their way through to the Channel. As Zurakowski wheeled around, suddenly a cannon shell, possibly from Wick himself, tore through the port wing of his Spitfire (X4165, bearing the squadron code 'PR'). Zura coaxed the aircraft home, landing at 1525 hours.

He was lucky. His old wing mate at 234 Squadron, Sergeant Klein, now flying with 152 Squadron, had been shot down into the sea and killed after shooting down a Messerschmitt. Wick had also been brought down in the fight, possibly by Klein, Pilot Officer Eric Marrs of Klein's squadron, or ace Flight Lieutenant John Dundas of 609 Squadron. Like Klein and Baillon, Dundas did not return from this bloody encounter, being immediately dispatched by Wick's number two, *Oberleutnant* Rudi Pflanz. Wick was seen to bail out over the Channel, but despite intensive air and sea searches, he was never found.

The next day 609 Squadron moved from Middle Wallop to Warmwell and was immediately scrambled. That action turned out to be inconsequential and typified the next three months at this forward base. The squadron operated under canvas in sordid, swamp-like conditions. In one storm, all the tents including the operations tent were blown down, requiring the airmen to retrieve telephones from the sodden wreckage to maintain even a semblance of operational capability. The still-standing airmen's marquee was the only refuge after the storm.

The enemy attacks had now shifted to a nightly blitz of London and other English cities over the late autumn and winter of 1940/41. These raids marked a departure in tactics as the Nazi High Command had abandoned the possibility of an invasion of the British Isles. With fewer daylight interceptions taking place, 609 Squadron was ordered to relocate to the larger base of Biggin Hill as part of 11 Group on 22 February 1941. Zurakowski commented at one time: 'In 1940, RAF fighters saved Britain from Hitler's invasion. Without air superiority the Germans could not succeed, even with the colossal strength of their armies.'[33] During the Battle of Britain, Zura had flown fifty-four missions by the last days of October. It is appropriate to look back at Winston Churchill's famous declaration about those who fought in

---

[33] Ibid.

the Battle of Britain: 'Never in the field of human conflict has so much been owed by so many to so few.'

Zurakowski is one of those 'few' who changed the course of history. Near the bottom of a blackout board at the White Hart Inn near Biggin Hill, you can still see his signature with those of other Battle of Britain pilots.

Signatures of Battle of Britain pilots on the black-out board at the White Hart Inn. Zurakowski's name is in the bottom left. *(Michael Harvey)*

Chapter Five

'For God, Honour and Country'

In the RAF, 3,080 aircrew are officially listed as having taken part in the Battle of Britain, with 520 casualties. More than eighty per cent were British-born, the remainder including Poles, Czechs, Canadians, Americans and others from many nations. However, the bare figures conceal the full extent of the Allied contribution to Fighter Command. Almost all these volunteers had come to Britain at their own expense or after extraordinary escapes and adventures, and had brought a fierce, sometimes savage, determination to the struggle.

Left to right: P/O Wladysalw Gnys, F/L Zurakowski and F/L Julian Kowalski at Northolt, 1943. *(Zurakowski collection)*

Poles in the Battle of Britain

Polish fighter pilots had formed a substantial element of the defensive forces in the British Isles, with sixty-six pilots serving in two Polish squadrons and seventy-five in other RAF squadrons. In total, six per cent of the fighter pilots in the Battle of Britain were ex-Polish Air Force, the single largest group of foreigners in the RAF. The most successful fighter squadron of the Battle was 303 (Polish) 'Kosciuszko' Squadron, with more than twelve per cent of all fighter claims being made by Polish fighter pilots. Twenty-nine pilots were killed in the Battle, a relatively small loss rate considering the decimation suffered by some squadrons.

Undaunted by earlier reverses in Poland and France, Polish fighter pilots fought with a grim resolve. The Poles deeply resented the canard that their air force had been wiped out in the first hours of the German invasion in September 1939, for some of them had flown and fought until the bitter end. They were much more highly trained than most British pilots of the period, although they had no experience of high-performance monoplanes. From the beginning, their scores were phenomenal, for Polish pilots were also remarkable marksmen. In addition, their tactical and operational innovations gradually changed the regimented RAF procedures. In 609 Squadron, a spread-out arrow-shaped formation derived from Polish formations was a complete departure from the pre-war RAF 'vic' or line-astern sections. The squadron employed two aircraft as 'weavers' at the extreme ends of the formation. These weavers invariably were Polish pilots like Zurakowski, who maintained a higher position and constantly checked the rear of the flight. The lead aircraft directed the sections, and a simple 'cross-over' of the sections was used to complete a change of direction. The efficiency of this formation led to its adoption by first the Czech squadrons, then other RAF units and even the Americans. Zura fondly remembered that the 'Polish weavers were so integral to its success that if any of us were rested or unavailable, the squadron was reluctant to fly.'

Some obstacles had to be overcome. Most Polish pilots were not able to speak fluent English and were given British squadron and flight commanders to lead them alongside their own officers. The Polish squadrons were not allowed to become fully operational until late August 1940. In those desperate days, the claims made by Polish pilots had led to great consternation at 11 Group. Group Captain Stanley Vincent, the Station Commander of Northolt Airfield, was not prepared to accept the victory totals of 303 Squadron without verification. On 5 September Vincent flew along as an observer with Squadron Leader Ronald Kellett. 'What Vincent saw, at 21,000 feet over Thameshaven, astern of the Poles and 1,000 feet below them, was a spectacle that he was to recall with awe a quarter of a century later. He saw Poles crash-diving into space with near-suicidal impact, and a mighty horde of glinting Dorniers breaking formation like dolphins fleeing before a shark. Pole after Pole was holding his fire until twenty yards distant, accepting with grim equanimity the risk that the last great explosion would equally claim his own life. Planes and parachutes were fluttering like charred paper across the sky, yet even in this mass slaughter, Poles were angrily nosing Vincent's Hurricane aside, grudging him so much as a shot.'[1]

There was never again any question about the claims made by the Poles. In September, 303 (Polish) Squadron achieved the highest 'kill' rate in Fighter Command and, together with one other Polish squadron, No 302, contributed seven and a half per cent of the entire total of enemy aircraft destroyed by Fighter Command in the Battle. Their squadrons 'swung into the fight with a dash and enthusiasm which is beyond praise,' wrote Dowding. 'They were inspired by a burning hatred of the Germans, which made them deadly opponents.'

Polish pilots were often glamorised as wild and impetuous loners, but the official documentation of the Battle belies these claims. From the regulations of 303 (Polish) 'Kosciuszko' Squadron that were in place during the war, and typical of many Polish squadrons' practices, it was evident that a code of honour was imperative to wartime Polish flyers:

> The following regulations apply to all the members of the squadron:
>
> First and foremost, be an adult. Be respectful to those around you, your squad mates as well as your opponents. Any fighting, 'unfriendly' name calling, and any other childish behaviour will not be tolerated.
>
> Teamwork – You will be assigned a wingman. Your first and the most important priority during squadron flight is safety of your wingman. We don't leave anyone behind, we don't use each other for bait. You will be expected to have a good 'flying' relationship with your wingman.
>
> If you have any ideas for a mission or about squadron organisation, please voice them. We use rank

[1] Philip Kaplan and Richard Collier, *Their Finest Hour* (New York: Abbeville Press, 1989), 180.

structure to get things organised, once everyone is in
place, everyone is even.

Personal standards – Remember that you represent
RAF 303 every time you enter the arena. That applies
to the time you fly as well as everywhere else. People
will notice your association with a squadron and build
an impression based on that. Many great pilots and
squadrons have a good opinion of RAF 303. Don't let
your actions dishonour the squadron.[2]

The Polish Republic's Minister of Defence, General Florian Siwicki,
in describing the Polish contribution to the RAF, said, 'The success
of Polish pilots in the battle to save the British Isles has always been
a source of national pride. Today, they are a part of military legend.
With Poland under the Nazi occupation, our pilots' successes were
an inspiration for many Poles to continue the fight.'[3]

Flight instructor again

In February 1941 Zurakowski, while still a member of 609
Squadron, was awarded the Polish Cross of Valour with Bar in
recognition of his Battle of Britain combat flying. He had been
credited with the destruction of a Bf 110, two Bf 109s, and another
Bf 110 shared as a probable. By the end of February, all the Polish
pilots in the squadron had received new postings; coupled with five
other transfers, the squadron was nearly decimated in terms of
experienced flyers. The transfers of the Polish pilots were held up by
request of the squadron commander until the new squadron
replacements were adequately trained.

Zura's skill in the air was now widely recognised, and with his
combat background he joined other valued Battle of Britain veterans
in training the RAF's growing number of replacement pilots. After
his promotion to Flying Officer on 1 March 1941, Zurakowski was
posted as a flight instructor to 57 Operational Training Unit at
Hawarden on 21 March 1941. He was still flying Spitfires but, this
time, tutoring younger pilots. He found it curious that instead of the
Polish system of providing operational training to the pilots with the

---

[2] 303 Squadron (Polish) 'Kosciuszko' RAF – Regulations (cited on 21
October 2001).
[3] Graham Christian Garnett, *Against All Odds* (London: The Rocco Group,
1990), 187.

least hours but the greatest ability, here he was 'seeing the reverse. The pilots I was sent were not fully trained due to the lack of instructors and proper training methods, which hampered any significant progress. The Spits were not dual control. Some pilots were quite happy to take up an aircraft without dual instruments; for other pilots, solo in a Spitfire was terror.' Zurakowski's patient tutelage made the difference for many young pilots.

Zura's lessons of combat flying

Respected as a battle-hardened pilot who had seen action prior to the Battle of Britain, Zura was also known for his ability to use the lessons he learned. He had begun to theorise about tactics and share some of his combat experiences with his fellow pilots. One example was an unorthodox use of a combat manoeuvre.

> During the Battle of Britain, I often used spins to save my life. I can think of at least four times when the simple but dramatic manoeuvre of pretending to be shot down came in handy. I used it when I was attacked by German fighters and had no chance to fight successfully. I usually started with a snap roll, which culminated in a vertical stabilised spin. I would quickly close and open the throttle, producing black smoke from the engine exhaust.
>
> To German pilots, a spin was an indication that the Spitfire was out of control. Black smoke confirmed that the aircraft had been shot down. Why follow and confirm the crash if it meant losing height over enemy territory? Better to claim one Spitfire shot down!
>
> Evidence after the war indicates that German fighters claimed the destruction of three times more RAF aircraft than actual RAF losses in combat. So I was spinning happily, recovering at 5,000 feet or so, and if there was enough gas and ammunition, I would climb again in search of better fighting opportunities.
>
> One might wonder why anyone would use this manoeuvre. There were situations, especially in the Battle of Britain, where we were so outnumbered that the Spitfire had no chance. The manoeuvrability of the Spitfire was so superior to the Me-109 that in a dogfight I considered two or even three Me-109s equal

opponents. A section of four Me-109s normally had a smart leader and would generally decline a dogfight. Instead, they would spread widely in all directions, and I would immediately be in good position to open fire on any enemy. However, another Me-109 would also be in a good position to open fire on me, and then I would have to break the engagement.

Above 5,000 feet I could not out-dive or out-climb the Me-109, so if my Spitfire's superior manoeuvrability could not be used, pretending to be shot down was a good strategy, saving both the Spitfire and me for the next fight. At low altitudes, with emergency engine boost, the Spitfire allowed for three minutes of extra power and was definitely better all-round in performance than the Me-109.[4]

A theory of intercept that Zura had proposed was adopted in the RAF's publication *Fighting Talk No 5* under the heading of "The Tizzy Angle': An interview with 'Zura' (F/O Zurakowski)'. This term for an interception plot was derived from Sir Henry Tizard, the Chairman of the Committee for the Scientific Survey of Air Defence in the pre-war years. The Bawdsey Radar Station evolved the streamlined plotting technique that was to become known as 'the Tizzy Angle'. Successful use of this technique in the field, however, fell to the combat pilot. The author of the booklet described Zurakowski as a 'practical man ... [who] has thought this matter out and now offers a simple tip for judging correctly the distance to steer ahead in order to effect an interception at the earliest possible moment.'[5] Zurakowski contended that maintaining a constant angle ('the Tizzy Angle') between the line of flight of your aircraft and the enemy would bring you to an ideal intercept.

In the illustrated booklet, Zura is quoted: 'Fly towards him in what you believe to be the correct direction. Fly steadily for a moment – hold your head stationary and note in which direction he appears to travel along your windscreen. If he appears to move forward, steer further ahead and hold that course. Check again and continue to steer further ahead until he appears stationary.

[4] Bracken, *Spitfire*, 14.
[5] *Fighting Talk No 5*, 1942.

'If he appears to move backward in your windscreen, then turn more towards him and repeat this process until he appears stationary. You will then be flying on the shortest route to intercept him. Check from time to time as you fly along this line for he may increase or decrease his speed.'[6] One further bit of advice was that if the aircraft seemed to get bigger in the windscreen as you got nearer, Zura cautioned, 'This is the time to avoid a collision.'[7] The RAF continued to issue the notes throughout the war years, with continual updates to Zurakowski's rank. The last printing indicated that they were Squadron Leader Zurakowski's guidelines to interception, reflecting his final rank in the RAF.

Several other postings for Zura as a flight instructor to a bewildering succession of OTUs followed in 1941 and 1942. He was sent to 55 OTU at RAF Usworth on 15 April 1941, followed by a posting to 56 OTU at Sutton Bridge the next day, before returning later that month to 55 OTU on 22 April. At that time a special squadron was formed at the training unit to train fighter pilots who were already qualified on Hurricane fighters. Zura was posted to 61 OTU at Heston in August, before ending up in 58 OTU at RAF Grangemouth in Scotland in September that year. Many of the pilots whom Zurakowski trained were Poles, for Grangemouth had a Polish section. He knew the work he was doing was important but he longed for action again. Although Zura felt that the most important lessons to teach young pilots were some of the combat tactics successfully employed in the Battle, he often had to deal with more mundane flight instruction tasks.

Some of his trainees at Grangemouth were naval personnel and other flyers drawn from a variety of non-operational units, who found the transition to Spitfires daunting. 'It was common to see a Spit coming in for a landing with no undercarriage down. You could send up a red Very flare but we needed to train these new pilots in carefully doing their cockpit checks.' The trainees were confronted by the inevitable memorisation of cockpit checks, but Zurakowski thought, '*I must do something more. What if you set the gear indicator for landing and a light would go on to show you what you did?*' He began to experiment with a visual warning system, so that as each operation was completed, a light would flash as a signal,

[6] Ibid.
[7] Ibid.

alerting the pilot that he could continue the checks needed for take-off or landing. Rigging up a power source and a series of lights, Zurakowski came up with an apparatus, a rough model of his system. When he proposed the design to his superiors, the proposal was directed to the Air Ministry where some 'boffin' (research scientist) turned it down as too complex for fighter aircraft. (Years later when Zurakowski bought a small Chevrolet Chevette, he was amused to find that the car employed a warning light system very similar to the one he had proposed in 1941.)

Combat training was the main area in which Zurakowski and other veteran instructors specialised. The instructors instilled into their pupils that survival depended on basic tenets of combat. 'In a dogfight, get right in the thick of it. The pilot who hangs around the edge of a scrap stands a good chance of being singled out and shot down.'[8] Zurakowski chafed in the role of flight instructor as he still looked for a chance to get back 'in the thick of it'. An opportunity to return to operational flying and to fight with his countrymen soon presented itself.

Into the fight

In June 1941 Hitler had suddenly launched Operation Barbarossa, an attack against his former ally, the Soviet Union. The Soviet forces fought heroically but suffered staggering losses, and it was only America's entrance into the war on 8 December 1941, the day after the Pearl Harbor attack by the Japanese, that brought hope to beleaguered Europe and finally turned the tide of war. Under some pressure from the Allied powers, the Polish government-in-exile formed an uneasy partnership with the Soviet Union, which continued throughout the war. A further military treaty was signed by Sikorski with the Soviet government in London on 30 July 1941.

This treaty led to the formation of the First Polish Corps under General Wladyslaw Anders, drawn from surviving servicemen and refugees in Russia. Where previously hundreds of thousands of Polish citizens had been deported to Siberia, Stalin now endorsed the creation of a Polish Army. Anders moved his troops to the Middle East to join British and American forces fighting in the African theatre, where they especially proved their worth during the siege of

[8] Hugh Halliday, *The Tumbling Sky* (Stittsville, Ontario: Canada's Wings, 1978), 132.

the fortress city of Tobruk. Eventually General Wladyslaw Sikorski, Commander-in-Chief of the Polish Army, convinced the Soviet Union to create another Polish military unit, which proceeded to fight the Germans alongside the Soviet Army. During 1942 Polish units were also formed within the Soviet Air Force, and these operated in support of units fighting on the eastern front.

In England, after the Battle of Britain, additional Polish bomber and fighter squadrons were established. Skilled and experienced fighter pilots were still in short supply, and consequently Polish pilots were heavily engaged in the RAF's offensive operations carried out over France. Pilot Officer Witold Herbst wrote: 'The RAF went on the offensive in the spring of 1941, attacking targets in France, Belgium and Holland, and the tasks imposed on fighter pilots became very much more complex and difficult. The primary duty of our fighters was no longer to shoot down Luftwaffe fighters but to prevent them from shooting down our bombers. This was not easy, particularly in the early stages, ie. in 1941 and 1942. Our fighters no longer had freedom of movement, being tied to their bombers like hounds on a leash. Their line astern formations became more vulnerable particularly for the 'arse men'.

'Mention therefore should be made of the fighter leader who introduced the line-abreast squadron formation of three sections flying in a finger four formation. Major Pisarek invented it and put it into practice while leading 308 Squadron in the summer of 1941. This guaranteed not only tactical advantage for the fighters but also better protection for the escorted bombers. No wonder the 308 was the top scoring squadron of the RAF in 1941, which was otherwise a very difficult year for our fighters. And no wonder that this fighter formation was eventually adopted by all the Allied fighter squadrons.'[9]

On 16 July 1941 a symbolic ceremony took place when the Polish Air Force standard arrived in England. The PAF did not have an official ensign in its pre-war history (although Zurakowski's Officers' Training School in Deblin had its own standard). In order to exemplify the unity between the Polish Air Force in exile and the motherland, a PAF officer arranged with a priest in Wilno to complete a unique, embroidered ensign. The standard had been smuggled from occupied Poland and now was paraded in elaborate

[9] Postowicz, 'Polish Aviation History Page'.

ceremonies for each of the newly formed squadrons. This symbol of the homeland occupied a place of honour and was passed from squadron to squadron for three-month periods. The standard bore the traditional four red-and-white fields with religious symbols, the Virgin Mary and St Teresa of Lisieux. Below the Virgin Mary was the inscription 'For God, Honour and Country'. The standard in England served to signal the rebirth of the PAF and, even after the war, it remained in London until its final return to Poland in 1992.

The Polish squadrons

On 8 December 1941 Pilot Officer Zurakowski was posted to 315 (Polish-Deblinski) Squadron, commanded by Squadron Leader (Major) Stefan Janus, based at Northolt. This was the first time that Zura flew directly with his Polish comrades. All the other units in which he had flown since arriving in England were British, although other Poles had flown with him in RAF squadrons. He now exchanged the 'VR' insignia worn on his collar with the miniature Polish rank insignia that marked PAF personnel. His Polish rank equivalent was Second Lieutenant. (Polish rank insignia were each worn with buttons, cap badge and pilots' wings exclusively Polish).

The Polish squadrons were based on the group of flyers who had escaped from France after June 1940, but as more pilots received combat experience, new pilots were incorporated. During the period 1940-1941, the initial group of fighter pilots who had served in RAF squadrons were transferred to the Polish squadrons. Due to the limited numbers of trained personnel and to the combat losses, the PAF rotated squadrons to the north for rest periods and constantly introduced new trainees. Zurakowski was acutely aware of these circumstances. 'Especially in the Polish situation, we tried to train not only operationally and to have quite good combat pilots and then remove them so that we can have new ones. So, in the case that we expected that maybe we would need them after the war, we would have a high number of qualified pilots ready.

'After France collapsed, we had a supply of pilot candidates of the Army from Soviet-occupied Poland. We had lots of volunteers from different countries: United States Argentina, South Africa and France. Yet we were still running short of not fighter pilots but aircrew so we got some from the Navy. The problem still remained that we could not expand, and some of the Polish units, Coastal Command and Bomber Command, had more and more pilots from other countries.'

No 315 Squadron was equipped with Spitfire IIs. This latest Mark was a development of the initial Spitfire Mark I and had a 1,175hp Merlin XII engine matched to a Rotol three-blade propeller. Reflecting on combat experience, 73lb of armour protection was added, but this variant was otherwise similar to the Spitfire I Deliveries commenced in 1940, as the Spitfire II became the first major production variant to be delivered from Castle Bromwich.

Zura was promoted to Flight Lieutenant (Captain) on 11 April 1942 and was posted as a Flight Commander to 306 (Polish-Torunski) Squadron, part of the first Polish Fighter Wing, based at Church Stanton. The squadron at the time was equipped with the Spitfire Mark VB, a further development of the aircraft with a slightly more powerful Merlin engine and armed with both cannon and machine guns. Shortly after Zurakowski's arrival, Squadron Commander Major H Wczelik and the Wing Leader, Flying Officer (First Lieutenant) Jankowski, were killed during a mission escorting English bombers attacking German cruisers in French ports. With no other senior officers available, Zurakowski was temporarily appointed Commanding Officer. Flight Lieutenant (Captain) Tadeusz Czerwinski became the new CO on 14 April 1942.

306 Squadron had been devastated by many losses and, having an inadequate standard of freshly trained officers, the squadron was sent north on 3 May 1942, to Kirton in Lindsey, for further training in an effort to foster squadron cohesion. While serving with the squadron, Zura became friends with Wladyslaw 'Spud' Potocki, who had joined the squadron early in January 1942 as a Sergeant Pilot. Zura recalled that Potocki stood out at that time over the other Polish pilots. Not only was he a proficient pilot, but he also had a unique personality. His effusive nature, matched with a sense of fun, was remembered by many of the squadron. He acquired the ungainly nickname due to his large nose, which was nearly always offset by a huge smile and twinkling eyes.

On 6 June 1942 Zurakowski was promoted to Squadron Leader (Major) and appointed as Commander of 316 (Polish-Warszawski) Fighter Squadron, operating from RAF Station Heston (later from Croydon and Hutton Cranswick) as part of the No 2 Polish Fighter Wing. This promotion was typical of the Polish squadrons' use of pilots with combat experience in leadership positions, although sometimes the young flyers were better fighter pilots than administrators. In his first official command Zura was fortunate to have the assistance of an experienced adjutant, Captain Benek Krupa. The much older officer had been the adjutant of the Cracow Regiment in the pre-war period. Zurakowski found that he could rely on Krupa to unravel all the administrative and personnel problems of the squadron, leaving Zura a free hand to carry out operational and training flights. He remarked at one time on finding a treasure like Krupa: 'As an adjutant with good organisation knowledge, he was worth his weight in gold.'

Zurakowski flew a dozen combat missions as the Commanding Officer of 316 Squadron. The Squadron was equipped with the Spitfire Mark IX, a further progression in the fighter series specifically designed to deal with the more powerful Messerschmitt Bf 109F and Bf 109G, and especially the potent new Focke-Wulf Fw-190 fighter. 316 Squadron tallied eighteen enemy aircraft destroyed, seventeen probables and twelve damaged in 1942. Zurakowski's role as Commanding Officer continued until 29 December 1942.

In January 1943 Squadron Leader Zurakowski was posted as Sector Gunnery Instructor (retaining his squadron leader rank, which was not often the case in RAF transfers) to RAF Station Northolt. Northolt airfield was considered the cradle of the Polish Air Force in England, where the first Polish fighter squadrons and wings were stationed. The base steadily became more and more Polish in character. The mess hall, which was often the scene of lively parties, sported a sign 'English Spoken'. In February 1943 Zurakowski received a second bar to the Polish Cross of Valour in recognition of his operational service and combat flying.

During this period the flying and gunnery of the Polish squadrons was outstanding. Zura explained that '11 Group realised that there was something special about the Poles when they conducted a competition over the Channel. Every squadron sent representatives and used a different colour of ammunition. When the target sleeves were brought back, three Polish squadrons had placed first to third. The fourth was a Czech squadron.'

The aerial gunnery competition was staged on 11 April 1942. Three Polish squadrons – 303, 316 and 315 – took the first three places (out of twenty-two squadrons) with scores of 808, 432 and 193. The best British squadron came fifth, with 150. These high standards were sustained throughout the war, by pilots from combat units on rest from operational duties and taking part in the training of rookie pilots. It is no wonder that the Polish pilots were to be considered the best-trained pilots in the RAF, especially when compared with ordinary RAF or even Luftwaffe pilots. The combat record of Polish pilots, with a consistently high ratio of victories to losses, also confirmed their capabilities.

To keep 'in practice', Zura took part in some fighter sweeps or intruder raids over France. On 17 May 1943, during one of these raids (also known as 'Mosquito' sorties) Zurakowski, flying Spitfire Mark IX BS456, damaged a Messerschmitt Bf 109G over Abbeville-Amiens, France. The combat nearly turned deadly, as Zurakowski recalls. During the mission he had spotted five enemy fighters below and quickly dived into the fight. Realising he had almost overrun the first Messerschmitt below him, he had just enough time for a quick shot, observing strikes on its port wing. Zura vividly remembers that he wanted to put on a good show as he was the gunnery instructor for Northolt and did not want to pass up this opportunity to show his compatriots how to make a proper interception. 'I was over the Messerschmitt but I wanted to make sure, so I closed to 150 yards. As I fired, I entered some turbulence from being too close. I was making some strikes then rolled inverted to see what had happened.' As he stared down at the enemy, his Spitfire shuddered. Quickly reversing himself, Zura checked the controls and noticed a sluggishness. He rejoined his flight but carefully 'nursed' his plane home.

After he had landed, one of the ground crew pointed out damage to the tail. There was the unmistakable evidence that he had been hit. 'I suspected some German shells had hit me but no, it was our .303 bullets that made the holes.' Just then, Zurakowski was joined by another pilot who described his combat with an enemy fighter with rounded wingtips and how he had put some rounds into the rolling and inverted Messerschmitt. As that pilot continued his account, Zura realised that the fool had nearly shot him down: 'That 'Messerschmitt' was me!'

In July 1943 Squadron Leader Zurakowski was given the role of Deputy Wing Leader of the Polish No 1 Fighter Wing stationed at Northolt, leading the Wing in forty-six combat sorties. These consisted mainly of flying fighter sweeps and 'rodeos' (escorted bomber missions intended to draw out enemy response) over occupied Europe. The escort missions included shepherding the USAAF (US Army Air Force) bombers on their daylight raids on

Germany. The Polish flyers had only enough range in their Spitfires to bring the bombers to the Low Countries and the borders of Germany before returning to their home base. The escort fighters would land and catch up with the bombers (savagely mauled by German fighters) as the Americans headed back to England.

RAF wings provided escort on inbound and outbound USAAF bombing missions but proved to be of little use, for they provided top cover and rear protection only and left the bombers vulnerable to frontal and 'belly' attacks. The Poles in the Northolt Fighter Wing developed a unique 'close-cover' formation that effectively protected the bomber armadas. One fighter squadron was stationed directly above, one behind and below, and a third squadron flew ahead and above the bomber fleet. This protective formation was found to be the most effective means of forcing enemy interceptors to have to deal with the fighter escorts first. Eventually the USAAF requested that all RAF wings adopt this escort formation. Zurakowski's record of escorting bombers and protecting his squadron mates was one he still recalls with pride: 'As wing leader, my aim was to keep the wing in one place and losses negligible... On forty sorties we lost two pilots and then only because of a collision.' The sight of the battered American bomber fleets remains with Zura to this day: 'There were some horrible sights ... bombers that were all shot up, just hanging in the air.'

His last posting saw Zurakowski transferred to Fighter Command Headquarters at Stanmore on 30 October 1943. Until March 1944 he was in charge of tactics and training. His memories revealed: 'In a duty they called 'Squadron Leader-Tactician Training', which was partly organisation, a bit of personnel work but mainly trying to raise the level of tactical and gunnery preparation.' One area that he railed against was the RAF's reliance on outdated combat tactics including line-astern formations and cumbersome three-aircraft 'vics'. The pre-war Polish strategy was to fly in a two-plane team where you could see either side of the aircraft and be constantly 'weaving'. More aircraft could be added to this team to spread out sideways. Zura ruminated that, 'The three-ship vic was behind us, losing a lot of pilots. The end aircraft was shot down without anyone knowing what was happening.' Gradually a change in tactics was effected, but Squadron Leader Zurakowski's last wartime posting saw him more deskbound than in the air, and he longed for a return to operational flying.

Zurakowski was awarded Poland's highest order, the Virtuti Militari (sometimes called the Polish Victoria Cross), Silver Cross Class (No 08488), on 20 December 1943. This medal, presented in five classes (Grand Cross, Commander, Knight, Gold Cross and Silver Cross), is only granted for the most outstanding acts or services in time of war. The Order was revived from the original Order in 1919 and was re-established in 1940-1941 by the Polish government-in-exile. Today it continues to be Poland's highest decoration.

1943 awards ceremony at Northolt, General Izycki presiding (S/Ldr Zurakowski is third from the left). *(Zurakowski collection)*

The Polish Cross of Valour, Krzyz Walecznych, with two Bars, was also awarded to Zurakowski by General Sikorski, Commander-in-Chief of the Polish Armed Forces. He received the Cross of Valour and Bar (KW) on 12 January 1941, and the Second Bar to the KW on 20 February 1943. The Cross of Valour is awarded for outstanding acts of military valour and may be awarded multiple times. It was re-established by the Exile Government of 1940 and People's Republic of Poland (Polska Rzeczpospolita Ludowa or PRL) in 1943. Re-established in 1990 by III Republic of Poland (RP), it is now awarded mainly to UN peacekeepers.

From 1940 to 1944, Zurakowski's operational flying included more than 150 operational flights with RAF Polish squadrons alone. In Zura's explanation of his combat record he says, 'The operational tours that were established by the Polish were similar to those of the Americans, with about six months in a combat unit. When there were very heavy losses like there were initially on the Fairey Battle, pilots sometimes were rotated after a short number of missions to give them a rest. Later they increased the number to thirty or forty flights before they moved to a less active unit. Some of the pilots stayed in for a very long time, two tours or more.' He had flown 209 missions, of which more than half had involved combat in enemy territory or in visible range of the enemy. Although Zura had survived the many combats, he had several close calls, with his Spitfires being shot up on five separate occasions.

Zura's use of a parachute had qualified him for membership in the 'Caterpillar Club'. This unique organisation was established in the early 1920s and was named after the silkworm that produces the material used to make parachutes. By the end of the Second World War more than 34,000 thousand club members had 'hit the silk', saving their lives, and today the club continues to add new members.

On three occasions, in March 1941, June 1942 and June 1945, Squadron Leader Zurakowski was mentioned in despatches for distinguished wartime service. He also later received the King's Commendation for Valuable Service in the Air in February 1948. His air victories consisted of three destroyed, one probably destroyed (shared) and three damaged (one in Poland). A confusion in these claims has often resulted in his being credited with six victories or more, but Zura officially is not considered an 'ace' (a pilot with five aerial victories). The number of victories that he scored may be quite different from the official record, he explained: 'Combat was fast and sometimes head-to-head; you could be shooting down the enemy but one never knew.' Other pilots asserted that Zura never put in all of his claims and even assigned some of his victories to his wing mates.

His wartime experiences are indelibly etched into his memory, yet Zurakowski rarely speaks about them in his later life. Years later, fellow test pilot and friend Peter Cope remembers that 'he would never speak about those days.'[10]

[10] *The Ottawa Citizen*, 9 January 1997.

Chapter Six

Test Pilot

As Zurakowski faced the inevitable postings to desk jobs, a new chapter in his life began. He recalled, 'Close to the end of the war, when victory was only a question of time and my superiors were trying to push me from operational flying into a staff job in London, I discovered that there was a place for one Polish pilot in the Empire Test Pilots School.'[1] His friend Zbigniew Olenski had already become a test pilot in the RAF During Olenski's stint at 609 Squadron, 'he had prepared an extensive report on good and weak points of the Spitfire and filed it to RAF authorities, which resulted in his immediate posting to RAE Farnborough.'[2] The report highlighted concerns about visibility in the Spitfire and was highly valued because it had come from an operational pilot. Zura stated, 'Olenski had determined how much visibility was obstructed, and at first it was a hopeless situation in the small Spitfire cockpit. The vision rearward was poor, but bubble canopies and streamlined canopies were a great improvement. One story about how experts saw things: when Olenski had approached a high-ranking officer before the report was published, the expert's comment was, 'Why are you worrying about visibility to the back when you fly to the front?' Olenski was transferred from 609 Squadron to the test establishment at the Royal Aircraft Establishment, Farnborough, on 23 March 1941.

For test pilots in Britain there had been few opportunities to learn the trade prior to the war, but the demands of wartime production, together with the necessity to test the newest designs, led to the development of a dedicated training centre at Boscombe Down, which continues to this day. Today's test pilot is usually a qualified engineer with above-average flying skills who can understand the scientific background of the airplane being tested. The majority are experienced military, or former military, pilots, although some manufacturers pay for their own civilian pilots to attend a test pilot school. There are a limited number of other

---

[1] Greig Stewart, *Shutting Down the National Dream* (Scarborough: McGraw-Hill Ryerson, 1997), 226.
[2] Gretzyngier, *Poles in Defence of Britain*, photo captions.

comparable schools including the United States Air Force Test Pilot School at the Edwards Air Force Base in California, the Patuxent River Naval Test Center in Maryland, and privately run training centres in Europe and North America.

On 15 March 1944 Zura began his career as a test pilot, being accepted into the prestigious training programme for test pilots at the Empire Test Pilots School. The stringent aircraft testing requirements that arose from the Second World War led to the need to train a specialised group of test pilots. In 1943 a test pilots' school was established at Boscombe Down with the first candidates recruited from among RAF ranks. The school provided trainees with a proper technical background, as well as honing the flying skills necessary for this demanding job. The first course was considered a success, although the programme had not been fully developed.

As the second and first full course was organised, Americans, Canadians, Chinese, Norwegians, New Zealanders and South Africans joined pilots from Great Britain, producing a total of thirty-seven pilots. Course work consisted of technical lectures and flying up to twelve different types of aircraft. Zura's background had been mainly in small fighter aircraft but he found that flying bombers would be his first assignment. The transition to heavy bombers actually came 'relatively easy. All planes fly the same way.'[3] The air training was rigorous and dangerous; one of the Canadians, Squadron Leader Roger Mace, was killed on the course.

Zurakowski recalled that his time at the Empire Test Pilots School was a pleasant experience. He enjoyed meeting pilots from other nations and found that his fellow students had many commonalities regardless of education, experience, nationality or race. As was customary in RAF transfers of this nature, Zurakowski accepted a reduction in rank to Flight Lieutenant, but within three months he was again a Squadron Leader. During the nine months of training, Zura ranked third in the course after preliminary examinations and quickly established himself as one of the more proficient flyers.

He recently evaluated his training: 'In comparison, the best training was in Germany. There the Germans had an engineering degree and were made into pilots. No test pilots in England had an engineering degree. Boscombe Down gave pilots engineering knowledge so that they could talk to designers in their own

[3] Zurakowski, *The Toronto Telegram*, 7 May 1959.

language. The engineers tried to show what was going on in flight by using only maths formulas. I was flying with a young engineer when he noticed the speed was only sixty knots and we were still in the air. He could not understand that speed was different in steady flight, believing too strongly in formula calculations.' Zura showed that pilots could teach engineers something. When he graduated from Course No 2 at the Test Pilots' School on 5 January 1945, the certificate he received indicated that he had 'carried out all the flying and technical exercises required for the performance testing and handling of all classes of landplanes'.

1945 Course No 2 Empire Test Pilots' School (Zurakowski is fourth from the left in the middle row). *(Zurakowski collection)*

The Polish question

The year 1945 marked the end of the war, and for some Polish expatriates like Zurakowski a difficult decision had to be made. 'Poles serving in the Polish military forces in the West had two goals: the destruction of Hitler's Germany and to return to a free Poland. The first was achieved on 4 May 1945 when the German armies that were gathered on the western shore of the Laba River capitulated. The realisation of the second goal looked less and less possible each day.'[4] Polish frontiers had undergone a major shift after the Allied conference in Potsdam, Germany, in 1945. The

[4] Zebrowski, *In Search of Freedom*, 217.

Soviet Union retained control of the territories that it had invaded in 1939, while Poland gained large areas of former German territory in the west, including the industrial region of Upper Silesia, the ports of Gdansk and Szczecin, and a long Baltic coastline. Poles from the Soviet-occupied areas were resettled on lands that had expelled Germans in the west. Communist control was intensified with the removal of the more liberal political leaders in Poland. A bitter struggle ensued between Poles and their new Soviet-controlled government, which led to near chaos. Many returning Polish military found the situation untenable. 'Zurakowski would have liked to return to Poland but he could not reconcile himself politically with the new regime in that country.'[5]

After the cessation of hostilities in the Second World War, more than 250,000 Poles were in uniform, but the Polish forces that fought under Allied command were scattered throughout Europe. The Polish Air Force was based in England, but the Polish armies were still on the front lines. The 1st Polish Armoured Division was stationed at Oldenburg, Hanover and Munster in Germany, while the 2nd Corps under General Anders was located mainly in Brindisi, Barletta and Triani near the Pau River in Italy, and in the Middle East. Many of the Polish veterans under General Anders's command were unwilling to be repatriated to Communist-controlled Poland and were transported back to Britain for gradual demobilisation. More than two-thirds of the Polish soldiers chose to stay in Britain, with approximately 36,000 remaining in Scotland. The following year the Polish Resettlement Corps (PRC) was formed to help integrate Poles into British society. Professional training and assistance for those seeking a new life in a Commonwealth country was the goal of the PRC The returning veterans were joined by soldiers' dependants (including wives and families), Polish government dependants, wartime Polish refugees, and post-war 'Displaced Persons' (DPs) mainly made up of people deported from occupied Poland.

For Poles in England, 1945 was a strange time. In 1940 they had been seen as the plucky survivors, willing to stand shoulder-to-shoulder with the only European country as yet undefeated. Their pilots had been lionised, with the exploits of 303 Squadron, in particular, being used in huge propaganda offensives against the Germans. At the beginning of 1941 there was a fully-fledged yet

---

[5] Norris, 'Impossible', 29.

semi-autonomous Polish Air Force operating within the RAF, and the PAF was larger than the combined air forces of all the Free French, Dutch, Belgians and other European Allies operating from Britain. By the end of the war, 17,000 Polish pilots and ground crew members in fourteen bomber and fighter squadrons had served in every war zone in both Europe and Africa. Polish fighter squadrons destroyed 957 enemy aircraft, with another 175 unconfirmed, destroyed a further 25 on the ground and damaged 259. PAF bomber squadrons flew a total of 102,486 sorties, notching up 290,895 operational flying hours, dropping thousands of bombs and laying hundreds of mines. The PAF won 342 British gallantry awards as well as 15 American awards, achieved at a cost of 1,973 killed and 1,388 wounded. But in 1945, especially with the new Labour government of Clement Atlee in place in England, the Poles started to have a difficult time. Atlee was unwilling to antagonise Stalin with demands on the Poles' behalf, yet, with the vast majority of the Polish military forces in Britain choosing to remain, the British government was all but forced to give permanent shelter to those Poles who did not wish to return to a Soviet-controlled homeland.

The 'Polish Question' was largely unsettled in post-war Britain, and the British government was faced with an increasingly difficult dilemma. Despite Churchill's wartime promise of a home for all Poles who had served the Allied cause, trade unions and socialist members of Parliament (anxious, apparently, about absorbing so many foreigners who would take the jobs of returning Englishmen) actively campaigned for their immediate repatriation.

Perceived resentment about the resettled Poles in Britain was fuelled by a post-war labour crisis, as well as propaganda from Poland and the Soviet Union that characterised the Polish veterans as 'fascist'. Atlee and other supporters of the new Labour government were concerned about upsetting the Soviet Union and, on Stalin's insistence, Polish soldiers were not allowed to take part in the Victory Parade staged in London on 8 May 1946. The day before the parade, General Anders was asked to provide a delegation to replace an army contingent that was unable to fly from Poland to England on time. He indignantly refused, following the earlier example of the Polish flyers. Although the British authorities had belatedly recognised the contributions of the Polish Air Force and asked for a token representation, the airmen had quietly declined.

There were many voices raised in the Poles' defence. Public

subscription in Britain led to the dedication of the Polish Air Force Memorial in 1948, commemorating the contributions made by Polish flyers in the defence of Great Britain. Of notable significance were the more than 150 schools of all types set up in Britain, the Middle East, Africa and liberated Europe to enable Polish children to carry on their education. These included three university departments: Architecture (Liverpool), Medicine (Edinburgh) and Law (Oxford). Meanwhile, since the British government no longer recognised the Polish Armed Forces stationed in England as legitimate, Polish servicemen were moved from the now disbanded military units to the Polish Resettlement Corps.

In the Polish elections of 1947 the outcome was decidedly in favour of the pro-Communist parties, although Anna Danielski commented that 'everyone in Poland knew from the beginning that the elections were one big fake'. Accordingly, Britain and the USA recognised the Soviet-led government in Poland. Years later it was determined that the true results had shown a victory for the democratic parties opposing the Soviets in Poland. Only after Stalin's refusal to hold free elections in Poland did the British government feel obliged, in early 1947, to pass the Polish Resettlement Act, which offered a haven to all Poles in Britain.

Any anti-Polish sentiment in Britain was eventually mollified by the post-war labour shortage in the country. By April 1948 almost all the quarter-million Poles in military service had been brought to Britain. Of these, only 105,000 returned to Poland. The remainder enlisted in the PRC, which had been extended to gradually integrate all the Poles who were in Britain into the British way of life. The Polish government-in-exile remained in London until 1990 in order to oppose the Communist takeover of the government.

The Polish Question resurfaced in 2000 with the formation of a British-Polish Joint Historical Commission in charge of clearing up fallacies and misconceptions about the two countries' wartime roles. A new generation of Brits was finally told of the true nature of the contributions made by the Polish armed forces to the victory in Europe. Not only were military contributions such as the Polish role in the Battle of Britain, the conflict at Monte Cassino and the assault on Arnhem recognised, but also the true history of the Poles in breaking the cipher of the German 'Enigma' coding machines was acknowledged. Presenting a copy of the Enigma machine to Polish Prime Minister Jerzy Buzek, Prince Andrew declared: 'The Enigma codes would not have been broken if it were not for the knowledge of Polish mathematicians... It was a remarkable gift that you gave us in July 1939, to hand over to us working models of the Enigma machine, and without it, we would never have been able to bring forward the Allied victory.'[6] This belated recognition of the Poles was in marked contrast to the situation in 1945.

Another dramatic and largely undisclosed example of the role of the Polish underground in the Second World War was the Poles' involvement in the campaign against the German V weapons. The V-1 and V-2 Vergeltungswaffe (Vengeance) weapons were ground-to-ground missiles used by the Germans towards the end of the war. In 1941 Polish underground intelligence had revealed that the Nazis were embarking on design and production of weapons of mass destruction. The Poles even managed to steal a V-1 and have it shipped to England. The ramjet-powered V-1 'buzz bombs[' were launched against targets in England and later in Antwerp, Belgium, during 1944. Due to their relatively slow speed – 550km/h (350mph) – and low altitude – 3000 feet – more than half of the V-1s launched were shot down by fighter planes and anti-aircraft fire or were brought down by barrage balloons. Although they were directed at mainly civilian targets, and caused 6,000 fatalities (plus 40,000 wounded) and a great deal of property damage, the Allies considered them no more than 'nuisance' raids. Nevertheless, Zurakowski personally witnessed the terrifying effect of the attacks. 'Those buzz bombs scared me a few times. One day I was walking along Oxford Street in London when a V-1 dived about a hundred yards away. The top three floors of the house there disappeared.'

Polish reports and maps delivered to British intelligence in 1942 and 1943 identified Peenemunde on the Baltic Sea as a research centre for a new form of ballistic missile. A British bombing raid on the base in 1943 necessitated moving the production facilities for the new weapon to the Harz mountain region of Germany. When additional testing took place in Poland in early 1944, Polish intelligence officers in concert with the Polish underground Home Army operation called 'Trzeci Most' (Third Bridge), located a V-2 rocket. The intact test example was embedded in a marsh close to the bank of the River Bug near the village of Sarnaki, some eighty miles

---

[6] Robert Jobson, 'Prince ends Enigma of Poles' role in bringing war to end', [online], cited on 19 September 2000: http://www.lineone.net.

east of Warsaw. Under the noses of the German patrols, the Polish underground fighters pulled the V-2 out of the mud and disassembled it. A young Polish teen, Jerzy Jasinski, was assigned the dangerous job of 'whistle-blower', stationed on the river bank. He recalled years later how afraid he was that the whole mission would be doomed.

On 25 July 1944 a British C-47 Dakota piloted by Flight Lieutenant Culliford and Pilot Officer Szrajer made a hazardous rough field landing in occupied Poland, and had the disassembled rocket, together with five passengers important to the defence of Poland, loaded aboard when braking problems compounded by a sodden field halted the operation. Polish underground fighters managed to free the transport but the precarious flight back to Allied territory was accomplished with a disabled landing gear. The vital components of the V-2 were examined in England and alerted the Allies to the new threat.

On 8 September 1944 a huge explosion rocked quiet Staverley Road in Chiswick, West London, destroying six homes, killing three people and seriously injuring seventeen others. 'The Staverley Road explosion, the first salvo in the German V-2 ballistic missile offensive, marked a turning point in the history of warfare. The V-2 offensive against London continued until March 27, 1945, representing the first and still the heaviest military attacks by ballistic missiles on a city. During it, some 518 V-2s hit London, causing 21,380 civilian casualties (2,511 deaths, 5,869 serious and some 13,000 light injuries). Moreover, these V-2 attacks destroyed 20,000 houses and damaged some 580,000 others.'[7] Only after the launch sites were captured by advancing Allied armies did the V-2 menace end.

The Zurakowski family

One factor made Zurakowski's decision to stay in Britain a difficult one: his family was still in Poland. All three of Janusz's sisters had survived the war, although one died soon after. During the conflict he had lost many relatives, including two of his brothers-in-law, but most tragically, in September 1941, Zurakowski's father had been killed in an accident. 'Bronek' (Bronislaw) had written to his brother during the war about their father's death, but he couldn't write about the circumstances of the accident until after the war. Zura then

---

[7] Center for Defence & International Security Studies: 'Ballistic Missile Threats' [online], cited on 9 April 2002: http://www.cdiss.org/v2.htm.

learned what happened on that day. Since the late autumn of 1939, Dr Zurakowski had been helping in one of the health centres in Lublin. He usually bicycled back to a small house outside town, which became a shelter for the Zurakowski family during the war. As his family related the story, 'Dr Zurakowski's path led through the long Bychawska Street, and that day, even though he kept close to the kerb, he was hit from behind by a speeding German ambulance. Eyewitnesses maintained that the driver, with premeditation, swerved to the side in the empty street and hit Father... I have later learned that Father's funeral became a demonstration of sorts in Lublin; masses of people followed the coffin through a kilometres-long route, leading from our house to the cemetery at Lipowa Street.'

Bronislaw, Zura's older brother, had married in 1940. Following the Second World War he became an aeronautical engineer and first worked on improving the performance of glider aircraft at the Aviation Institute in Warsaw. He then began research in vertical flight for the restructured PZL works. From 1947 onwards the nationalised industry WSK (Wytwornia Sprzetu Komunikacyjnego or Transport Manufacturing Works) emerged as the overall identity for separate subsidiaries that carried the old name PZL (Panstwowe Zaklady Lotnicze). Design and manufacture of helicopters was established in a separate subsidiary known as PZL-Swidnik (WSK Pulawski Works).

Bronislaw was the principal designer of the BZ-1 'Gil' helicopter ('BZ' was derived from Bronislaw Zurakowski), the first of a series of experimental helicopter designs in the 1950s. Leading a team of engineers, including Dr Brzoska and T Chylinski, Bronislaw calculated and designed the complex sub-assemblies such as the rotor and the control system, which were described in contemporary sources: 'Particularly noteworthy is the resonance-type vibration damper on the head of the rotor. This device was designed by [B] Zurakowski in 1952 and successfully test-flown long before such a device appeared in other countries.'[8]

Powered by a 100hp Hirth 504 piston engine, the two-seat light helicopter featured an enclosed fuselage, open cockpit and fixed tricycle undercarriage. The orthodox helicopter design incorporated a two-bladed rotor mounted on a universal joint, with a small ancillary

[8] Ryszard Witkowski, 'Rotorcraft in Poland's Civil Aviation History', *Aerospace*, January 1981, 14.

rotor and servo blades located above the engine to regulate cyclic pitch, and to ensure stability in the main rotor. The anti-torque tail rotor was placed at the end of a monocoque boom made of plywood.

Bronislaw had acted as test pilot during the early trials and completed the first flight of the prototype SP-GIL on 4 April 1950. Although the helicopter proved stable and showed an adequate performance, it never entered series production. In 1953 a further development led to the BZ-4 'Zuk' ('bug' in Polish), a four-seat helicopter with a single main rotor, main fuselage/cabin section, open-frame rear boom structure, fixed four-wheel undercarriage and one 300hp Narkiewicz WN-4 piston engine located behind the cabin. Work progressed slowly on the project, with ground tests beginning at the end of 1956 and the first flight taking place on 10 February 1959. Eventually the project wound down and the two BZ-4 Zuk prototypes that had been built were retained for testing. The innovative design of the Zuk was not followed up, for a decision was made to undertake large-scale production of a Russian helicopter, the Mi-1, and, later, the Mi-2.

Zurakowski continued to follow his brother's work from England. All the news coming from Poland indicated that the situation in the country under Communist rule was unfavourable and especially perilous for members of the Polish military from the West who decided to return to their homeland. Janusz understood that because of these conditions no one in his family, not even his mother, asked him to come back. Zurakowski never considered a return to his native land till many years later.

During the war years Janusz had corresponded with his family through an elaborate scheme devised by his cousin. Postcards (often crammed with tiny notes written by his mother, to get the most into each space) were channelled through mutual friends in Switzerland but had to pass through both British and German hands. The messages had become a sort of code, as each party was sure that wartime censors would not allow them to correspond freely. Zurakowski became 'little Zura' in the letters. The ruse of talking about a little boy seemed to work, for none of the correspondence was ever stopped.

There had been someone else in Poland whom Zurakowski missed, and notes had also come from Anna Danielski during the war. Janusz remembered belatedly his promise to see her in 1939, and he began to write to her in earnest after the war.

During the war Anna found employment in the offices of the

Municipal Utility Power Station in Lublin. This position, together with an orange identification card, gave her some immunity from periodic sweeps, called *lapanka* or 'catching', carried out by the Germans. At the same time Anna was working with the Polish underground and performed many tasks. One of her assignments was to teach mathematics to a young boy who, she recalled, 'had lost his leg in the fighting in 1939 but never his spirit'. She worked with the underground in many other ways including passing out leaflets and keeping communication flowing between the families and the 'boys' in the Polish underground. At a factory owned by a bakery chain, bread was distributed in carts that brought sacks of flour from the country and, underneath, mail from the Polish Home Army fighters. The owner's daughters sorted the letters and answered requests. Anna related, 'During the winter, one of the most common was for warm underwear but also for books and even poetry.'

Life in wartime Poland under German occupation was stressful and perilous for everyone. Later in the war Anna's job at the power station placed her in jeopardy when the power was inadvertently shut off to a Gestapo officer's residence. He stormed into the office and placed a loaded Luger at her temple. Her cool and calm demeanour pacified the angry German, but it was a near tragedy.

After two days of fighting in July 1944, Lublin was occupied by the Soviet Army and became the seat of a provisional government, rivalling the Polish government-in-exile in London. During the fighting Anna's family was caught in the crossfire. They had taken refuge in the cellar of an old convent building where the Sisters ran an orphanage. When a fire bomb hit the roof, setting off an inferno, the people who had taken refuge in the cellar formed a bucket brigade, utilising the well in the courtyard. The orphanage was saved. The Sisters of the convent said that it was providence that they had sheltered so many people in the cellar, for without them the orphanage and the convent would have been lost.

Anna's father was working in the Polish underground government during the war. After the Soviet occupation of Poland, he was taken to Russia and the family faced persecution. Eventually her father was able to come home after a prolonged internment. At the war's end Anna moved to Gdansk, finding a job at Radio Gdansk where she began as a reporter but also filled in as an announcer. Early in life she had developed an interest in writing and was now able to work in this field. All the programmes were 'live' and included very patriotic messages that often drew the attention of Central Government censors.

Her work in broadcasting lasted one and a half years, 'then the letters from Janusz started to arrive, and with the decision to join him, all [her] plans and [her] life changed...' In those days it was very difficult in Poland to obtain a passport. Anna enrolled at the University of Warsaw, spending a year studying French literature. These courses opened up possibilities of continuing her studies in Paris.

Boscombe Down

From 1945 to 1947 Zurakowski became a test pilot with the Aeroplane and Armament Experimental Establishment (A&AEE) at Boscombe Down, England, where he joined a number of other Polish pilots including Flight Lieutenant Leszek 'Midzi' Miedzybrodzki, who became one of his best friends. Zura had, by this point, become an accomplished test pilot, as he had all the necessary attributes required at Boscombe Down. Not only was he an exacting pilot, but he had developed a critical approach in identifying problems, establishing limits and developing techniques, many of them unique to himself. On one occasion his rapid completion of the stability tests on an aircraft had drawn the attention of military and industry experts. Three wing commanders from various squadrons descended on Boscombe Down, accompanied by E T Jones, Chief Technical Officer of the A&AEE, to determine how Zurakowski was able to complete the required tests so effectively. The technical department was not able to plot his data properly, so at first 'fixing the results' was thought to be occurring, but Zurakowski was able to obtain the actual data plots to show that his testing was accurate.

The real job of a test pilot is often more routine than romantic. 'He or she must make every new airplane as easy as possible to fly and as safe as possible to fly. Whether it is a fighter or an airliner, the plane must perform to exacting standards.'[9] Rather than showing bravado, and unlike the Hollywood stereotypes, a test pilot does not take unnecessary risks with the aircraft or with his or her life. Small steps are taken toward expanding the flight envelope, which marks the limits of speed and height to which an aircraft can be flown. These steps lead toward a larger objective: developing a safe aircraft that is able to fulfil

[9] Mike Gething, *Test Pilots* (Vero Beach: Rourke Enterprise, 1988), 12.

its task, whether it be as a military bomber or as a civilian airliner.

Test pilot Peter Cope emphasised also that the physical requirements of the job were extremely high. 'Test pilots are examined for heart function, blood pressure, vision and hearing... A test pilot has to be able to meet the demands of high altitude, which entails considerably reduced atmospheric pressures, combined with the need for continuous oxygen usage, and excessive bodily pressures encountered during high-speed manoeuvres.'[10]

Test pilots are responsible for evaluating an aircraft's performance and flight characteristics, which involve the handling qualities such as stability and control as well as the functioning of equipment, systems and services. Performance throughout the flight envelope is determined first by a test pilot 'wringing out' up to but not exceeding the design limits of the airframe. 'One cannot be certain that the calculations and reserves of strength are adequate in every corner of the flight envelope. Especially is this true of high-speed, when kinetic heating and aero-elasticity enter the picture. In service, fatigue is a prominent consideration. The task of the test pilot is to seek reasonable levels of assurance, proving by demonstration, looking for snags and traps for the unwary.'[11]

Zurakowski's engineering and technical background had been broadened, so he could communicate easily in the language of the scientists and engineers and discuss problems on a near-equal basis. In written reports he remained accurate, measured and factual, a characteristic that all good test pilots establish. However, till the end of his career his idiosyncratic use of English was a feature unique to Zurakowski.

Test flying encompasses a number of unique types of testing. The experimental test pilot would be trained to provide the data necessary to 'prove that a new or modified airplane is safe, and that it meets all customer or government requirements.'[12] Another area involving experimental test flying is in the purely research context, where new techniques or standards are established. This type of experimental flying is normally done at facilities such as NASA, Canada's National Research Centre (NRC) or other government

[10] Ken Lamb, ed, 'Wit matches speed at 650mph', *Shell News* 7, 3 (March 1954), 3-4.
[11] Darrol Stinton, 'Test Pilot', *Airforces Monthly* (August 1988), 52.
[12] Lorne Ursel, conversation with the author, 2001.

agency. Test flying also involves the more mundane work of company production testing wherein the aircraft is tested to provide evidence that customer requirements for safety, performance and quality have been met. Acceptance test flights can also be undertaken by the customer or client pilots prior to introduction of a new or modified aircraft.

S/Ldr Zurakowski (far right in back row) in 1945. *(Zurakowski collection)*

The Aeroplane and Armament Experimental Establishment was charged with determining that the flying characteristics of all aircraft produced for British service were suitable for their intended purpose. To that end, the organisation provided both experimental and research functions. The A&AEE was subdivided into four squadrons, with A Squadron testing fighter aircraft, B Squadron testing bomber aircraft, C Squadron testing Fleet Air Arm aircraft for the Royal Navy, and D Squadron testing non-military aircraft. Initially Squadron Leader Zurakowski was assigned to C Squadron, where he became involved in testing both British and American naval aircraft. The Air Ministry wanted to investigate the possibility of converting all possible RAF fighters for naval use.

Even though Zurakowski was test flying naval aircraft, he had not yet landed on an aircraft carrier and could not easily evaluate this aspect of their performance. To remedy this, he was sent off for a quick course in carrier deck landing, or ADDL (Aerodrome Dummy Deck Landing). These simulated carrier landings were carried out at Naval Air Station East Haven near Arbroath, Scotland, which operated a deck landing school. There, over a three-day period, Zura carried out five practice landings in a Seafire III, a navalised version of a Spitfire V, with an arrestor hook and folding wings. The Seafire had a notorious record for deck landing accidents, attributable to its poor visibility over the nose and narrow-track undercarriage. Zura was guided down to the deck by the hand signals of a Deck Landing Control Officer, or 'Batsman', on a 'carrier deck' painted on the runway.

On completion of this training, Zurakowski flew the Seafire successfully in his carrier qualification on HMS *Ravager*, the British training carrier operating in the North Sea off the Scottish coast. Zura was such an experienced Spitfire pilot that he completed four sets of landings and take-offs without incident on 29 November 1945. He is certainly one of the very few Polish pilots to have ever landed on a British aircraft carrier. His first real deck landing came aboard an escort carrier with a flight deck measuring less than 500 feet. The *Ravager* was one of thirty-seven escort carriers converted from merchant ship hulls with a small wooden flight deck mounted on top. They had been built in the United States and transferred to Britain under lend-lease.

Later Zurakowski was assigned to A Squadron and flew most of the contemporary British fighter aircraft designs that were being evaluated at the time. He gained a reputation for serious analysis as he strenuously put aircraft through their paces. In his own words, he 'killed a few airplanes and was not very popular with aircraft companies. If an aircraft had faults, it was no use going on with its production. One of the worst examples was the Spiteful, designed to fight the Focke-Wulf threat, which I revealed to my boss at Boscombe Down, 'Summy' Wroth, as 'hopeless'. The latest Spitfires from the same company were better airplanes.' One distressing fault of the Spiteful showed up when taxiing any distance over rough ground – the tailwheel invariably collapsed. In wartime poorly designed aircraft would be rushed into service, but Zura reasoned that there was no need to jeopardise safety during peacetime. His insistence on redesigns and modifications eventually led to improvements in a number of British aircraft, including two de Havilland designs, the Vampire and the Hornet.

de Havilland Hornet. *(Zurakowski collection)*

Aerobatics

The new de Havilland Hornet intrigued Zurakowski. 'In April 1945 we got, for testing, the latest de Havilland product, the beautiful looking Hornet fighter. Very clean aerodynamically with two powerful Merlin engines, it looked like the Mosquito but had much more power and was smaller. At that time, we had, for all sorts of test programmes, up to six Hornets.'[13]

While test flying the de Havilland Hornet twin-engined fighter, Zura began to experiment with a new aerobatic routine. In the 'Hornet File' Lewis G Cooper noted: 'Zurakowski (Zura) never let an opportunity pass by without giving the staff a display which usually included single-engine aerobatics.' Zurakowski recalled:

> As the war ended, I think an effort was made to sell some aircraft abroad, and we were called upon to demonstrate the latest aircraft in flight. I demonstrated the Hornet a few times, but being really a Spitfire pilot, a single engine was good enough for me! After high-speed runs, I was switching off one engine, feathering the propeller and completing the show looping and rolling on one engine. As long as I kept my speed above 170 knots, the Hornet was really a good single-engine fighter.
>
> I should mention that before the war, in Poland, I was flying quite a lot on gliders and learned a bit of aerobatics. So I thought, Why not to try a loop on the Hornet as on a

[13] Janusz Zurakowski, 'Zurabatic Cartwheel in a Meteor', *Wingspan* (1986), 4.

glider, both engines switched off? First I tried a few times at a safe altitude. I needed about 400 knots for a fairly round loop with recovery above the starting point. One day I demonstrated this 'no engines' loop, quite successfully, for some VIPs at Boscombe Down. It was considered not safe because unfeathering the propellers to start the engines again was electrically-operated. What if the battery fails? My argument was that I asked for a new battery to be put in the aircraft before each flight, and even if I were unable to restart the engines, I would have enough height or speed to land power-off. Boscombe Down airfield was quite large and the runway was one of the longest in the UK, being about 3,400 yards long. Gliders always land with power off. But you cannot win with 'authority'.

The Hornet, on one engine, had a problem. It was a small aircraft with powerful engines, probably with more power than a Wellington or Dakota, but they were nearly twice as large. There simply was not enough aerodynamic rudder force to counteract the asymmetric power thrust.

In evaluating this problem, I was instructed to assess the aircraft in an engine-cut case at take-off: to simulate an inexperienced pilot, cut one engine in take-off configuration with the undercarriage up and wait three seconds before taking correcting action. In initial tests it was obvious that, at lower speeds, live engine power had to be decreased quickly, otherwise, even with full opposite rudder, keeping direction was not possible and the test was not safe at low altitude. I repeated this test at 10,000 feet at 140 knots full twin-engined power, at one engine cut, and waited three seconds before taking control.

The test was easy, but it was difficult to describe or to put on the pilot's pad what was the behaviour of this aircraft. I think it was a bit like a flick roll followed by an erratic spin. Control was regained but not before live engine power was reduced to idling and a few thousand feet were lost in recovery. Other test pilots watching my flight could not describe what the aircraft was doing and did not believe me that it was just a test of 'single-engine cut case at take-off!'[14]

It was on the Hornet, which had two powerful Merlin engines mounted quite far apart, that Zura made his first attempt at a cartwheel. He relates: 'Later I made a few attempts to make a horizontal 360 flat rotation by cutting the power of one engine (the other at full power), but even at stalling speed the asymmetric power was not enough to overcome the drag of the fin and rudder. The only way to do a cartwheel was to reduce speed to about half-stalling speed. This was not possible in horizontal flight but possible in vertical flight.'[15] 'In the meantime new aircraft arrived for testing at Boscombe Down, among them the Meteor, Vampire and Spiteful, and I did not think any more about the Hornet.'[16]

It was at Boscombe Down that Zurakowski started to earn his reputation as an extraordinary aerobatic pilot. It fell to both wartime RAF ace Squadron Leader Neville Duke and Zurakowski to do aerial demonstrations for the many visitors who came to the base. In the air Zura and Duke were a matched pair; yet while Duke was quiet and intense, flying was his only interest. Zura was different. He spent his leisure time restoring an old car behind the Officers' Mess at Boscombe Down. He had located an old Austin 7 and devoted his spare time to not only getting it running but also making it as 'spiffy' as possible. His natural ability with engineering and equipment continued to be employed profitably.

During this period Zurakowski gained jet experience in testing Britain's first jet fighters, the de Havilland Vampire and the Gloster Meteor. 'Duke and Zura demonstrated the Meteor and Vampire brilliantly.'[17] On one occasion, however, Zura outdid himself. While flying the Vampire F 1 TG274 for a visiting Russian delegation (the British called them 'snooping trips' and resented the intrusions), he thrilled them until the end of his display. Easing in on a low-speed approach with flaps and air brakes out, his engine suddenly failed. With no room to manoeuvre, Zura stalled the aircraft right on top of the Russians. As he 'pancaked' in with a cloud of dust and debris,

[14] Ibid, 4-5.
[15] Bill Bialkowski, conversation with the author, 2001.
[16] Zurakowski, 'Zurabatic Cartwheel in a Meteor', 6.
[17] Tom Neil, 'Boscombe Down Memories: Reflection of an A&AEE test pilot', *Air Enthusiast* 54 (Summer 1994), 36.

the visitors beat a hasty departure but took the incident in their stride and laughed at their narrow escape. However, Zurakowski's inadvertent drama served to send the unwanted guests on their way.

In 1945 the A&AEE put on a public display in which there were a number of demonstrations of aircraft and weaponry. An Avro Lancaster Mark III dropped a live 12,000lb 'Tallboy' high-explosive bomb, while other aircraft made live rocket-firing passes at a target located to one side of the public viewing area. Zura was one of the stars of the show as he 'wrung out' a Vampire F 1 in:

> ...the most brilliant exhibition of high-speed aerobatics probably ever seen... Words like 'fast' and 'slow' as applied to aircraft mean nothing when a Vampire comes down to about 100 feet, 'handsomely exceeding' 500mph and then turns up vertically and continues to go up vertically until it disappears into the blue.
>
> A moment later, it could be seen coming down with a faint whistle, vapour trails coming from the jetpipe at some altitudes. Then there is only the briefest glimpse of a smooth nose and two intakes, and a sharp crack of a whip as it flashes past, followed by a shrill scream as the aeroplane goes up vertically, slowly rolling out of sight into the blue. Perhaps the most astonishing way of gaining altitude was when Zurakowski came down flat and then, from just above the tents, went up into a tight half-loop followed by a half-roll, and so on until the aeroplane was lost to sight. He ended by giving a series of loops and rolls until it was hard to tell which way he was. He exploded the myth that dogfights are not possible at nearly Mach 0.8.[18]

In his Boscombe Down period Zurakowski made test flights in more than thirty types of aircraft. The list of types he flew spanned the range of British fighters, bombers, fighter-bombers, trainers and utility aircraft; Canadian training and utility aircraft; as well as American bombers and fighters available during wartime and in the immediate post-war period. His logbook identifies the following aircraft:

> Airspeed A S10 Oxford
> Auster VI

---

[18] *Aeroplane*, 1945.

Avro Lancaster I
Blackburn B-37 Firebrand III
Boulton Paul P82 Defiant
Chance-Vought Corsair IV
de Havilland DH 98 Mosquito II, 32, 34
de Havilland DH 100 Vampire
de Havilland DH 103 Hornet I
de Havilland Canada DHC 1 Chipmunk
Fairey Barracuda
Fairey Firefly
Fairey Swordfish
Gloster Meteor I
Grumman Avenger I
Grumman Hellcat
Grumman Tigercat
Grumman Wildcat
Handley-Page Halifax II
Hawker Fury I
Hawker Sea Fury
Hawker Tempest II, V
Hawker Typhoon
Martin B-26 Marauder
Martin-Baker MB5
Noorduyn Norseman
North American B-25 Mitchell II
North American F-86 Sabre
North American P-51 II and IV Mustang
Percival Prentice
Reid & Sigrist RS 3 Desford
Republic P-47 D Thunderbolt
Supermarine Attacker
Supermarine Seafire III and XV
Supermarine Spiteful
Supermarine Spitfire, ten different marks
Vickers Wellington III
Westland Welkin

One of the more unusual aircraft flown by Zura during this period was a Canadian aircraft – the de Havilland Canada Chipmunk, designed by Polish expatriate W 'Jaki' Jakimiuk. He was the same

designer responsible for the majority of the PZL line of fighters that
Zurakowski had flown in Poland. 'I was testing fighter aircraft for the
Royal Air Force's Aeroplane and Armament Experimental
Establishment at Boscombe Down in England. On 15 April 1947, my
commanding officer, Wing Commander J Baldwin, asked me to fly
an unknown, Canadian-designed, light aircraft bearing the strange
name 'Chipmunk' to see if it would be any good as an initial trainer.

'I was surprised by its excellent flying characteristics and
simplicity of design. All the other pilots in A Squadron who tested it
confirmed my enthusiastic opinion. This aircraft was the de Havilland
Canada Chipmunk CF-DIO-X, an original prototype.'[19] The
Chipmunk was later adopted as the basic trainer for the RAF and
RCAF as well as for many other air forces worldwide. Jakimiuk later
designed the world-famous Beaver and Otter for de Havilland Canada.

Martin-Baker MB 5

The Martin-Baker MB 5, one of Britain's most advanced piston-
engined fighters of the Second World War, was another aircraft test-
flown by Zurakowski, and it became one of his favourites. Zura had
been assigned this aircraft and he soon found that James Martin's
creation was a superb machine. 'Every fitting, every component,
seemed to be just perfectly placed. The ease of maintenance that
resulted was vastly different from the current fighters we had,
notably the Spitfire. All of this was accomplished with a small,
dedicated team. It really showed what could be done when things
were done logically.' The testing of the Martin-Baker aircraft went
smoothly and was completed in only three weeks, rather than the
lengthy process endured by most other types.

Zurakowski's report pointed out that the MB 5 was 'excellent and
infinitely better, from the engineering and maintenance aspect, than
any other similar type of aircraft... The layout of the cockpit might be
very well made a standard for normal piston-engined fighters and the
engine installation might, with great advantage, be applied to other
aircraft.'[20] In the air the MB 5 was a magnificent performer; it just
came too late in the war to have any future in a jet-powered age.

In June 1946 the air display of the Society of British Aircraft
Constructors (SBAC) that year was the final hurrah for the MB 5.

[19] WCAM Aviation Review, 1998.
[20] 'Mr Martin's Memorable MB 5', *Air International* (February 1979), 80.

Martin-Baker MB 5. *(Martin-Baker Company)*

'Zurakowski flew the MB 5 in a big display at RAE Farnborough in such a way that none who saw it will ever forget. It was, perhaps, the most impressive display ever performed by a piston-engined fighter.'[21] *Aeroplane* reported that 'Zurakowski can do almost anything with the Martin-Baker 5. He has an extraordinary act of flicking the aeroplane about at very slow speeds and so reproducing the 'old falling leaf' act. The aeroplane suddenly seems to tilt up sideways and is only saved from a spin because he puts the nose down just at the right moment as he does it. One cannot see him put the nose down, but after half a dozen of these manoeuvres he has lost 1,000 feet or so of height and he is only some 500 feet above the ground.'[22] His display clearly demonstrated that Zura was a superlative show pilot.

He recalled that Martin had personally asked him to do the demonstration and that his pay was his first 'civilian pay cheque which amounted to twenty-five pounds for four three-minute demonstrations'. This association with Martin would continue for many years, as the Martin-Baker Company began to dominate in the production of ejection seats for the military. After his success as a demonstration pilot was established, Zurakowski related,

[21] RAF662 CFSG (Royal Air Force 662 Combat Flight Sim Group) [online], cited on 23 September 2001: http://www.dyno-tech.com/bravo/fighters34.html.
[22] *Air International*, 80.

'Jimmy' Martin (later Sir James Martin, knighted in 1965) continued to ask him to fly for the Martin-Baker Company at an SBAC display. His idea was for Zura 'to 'come roaring down the field and then eject right in front of the grandstand'. I laughed and humoured him but he was quite serious, I think.'

Fellow test pilot Peter Cope recalled, 'Everyone in England considered Jan to be one of the very best test pilots in the business, a very, very conscientious flier and a brilliant pilot.'[23] Gloster's chief test pilot at the time was Eric Greenwood, who was impressed with the high technical skills and superb flying of Zurakowski. On visits to Boscombe Down to discuss the latest Gloster Meteor developments, Greenwood began to talk about a possible position for Zura after demobilisation.

[23] *The Ottawa Citizen*, 9 January 1997.

Chapter Seven

The Gloster Years

With the dissolving of the Polish Air Force in Britain, Zurakowski retired from the Polish Air Force and the Royal Air Force as a Squadron Leader in June 1947. After flying north to a resettlement centre at Lincoln Lodge, he was quickly whisked through the paperwork. He joked that he was 'on a bicycle, came in with a military uniform, got a 'bit too small' civilian jacket, went back as a civilian pilot'. He then joined the Gloster Aircraft Company as a test pilot. His first assignment consisted of development-flying of the Meteor twin-jet fighter. It was a marvellous opportunity to continue his career in an aircraft that was not only entering squadron service but also receiving worldwide attention. Zura was active in bringing this important jet fighter through its development stages and, as an experimental pilot, he brought it through the F 4, F 8 and T7 series. He was also part of the later Gloster E1/44 and Javelin test programmes.

Gloster had begun as the Gloucestershire Aircraft Company, founded by George Holt Thomas in 1912 at Brockworth Aerodrome, Gloucester. As the demands of wartime resulted in orders for the de Havilland DH 2 fighter, BE2C and Farman bombers, the company took in the H H Martyn & Co facility, known for its skilled woodwork. In 1917 the Gloucestershire Aircraft Company relocated to Hucclecote, east of Gloucester. Renamed Gloster Aircraft Company Limited in 1926, it began to specialise mainly in the production of high-performance military and racing aircraft.

During the early 1930s the Gloucester and Cheltenham Councils established a proper airfield at Staverton, Gloster's new home. The many successful types developed and built by the company, including the Grebe, Gamecock, Gauntlet and Gladiator, were responsible for the steady expansion of the works' organisation in the inter-war years. The Air Ministry requisitioned Staverton at the start of the Second World War and laid three tarmac runways. After production of the Gladiator ceased, the company was employed in the licence production of 2,730 Hawker Hurricanes and 3,330 Typhoon fighters, with a production rate of 24 aircraft a week achieved before December 1945. Through the war years Gloster was associated with Frank Whittle's jet engine research and built a flying prototype, the E 28/39 Pioneer, also known as the Gloster Whittle. Gloster later became one of the first jet aircraft manufacturers, producing the successful Meteor and Javelin jet aircraft series.

Reunion

During his Gloster years, Zurakowski was reunited with Anna Danielski. In those times it was not easy to leave Poland. Two earlier, abortive attempts at escape had ended with Anna's arrest and imprisonment. Upon her release Anna and Zura devised a new plan. While enrolled in university at Warsaw, Anna applied to study French literature abroad, obtaining permission from the authorities in 1948 to study at the Sorbonne in Paris. She began the lengthy journey to the West by train. Leaving Poland, she had to travel through Czechoslovakia and cross the occupation zones in Germany before entering France. The journey was a difficult and anxious one, as she did not know who else was aboard the train. One stranger who attempted to ingratiate himself with her mysteriously vanished as Jan's cousin approached on the station platform in Paris. Anna then settled in Paris and made contact with Janusz in England. Finally Anna and Janusz were to be together.

Obtaining a two-week holiday leave from Gloster in 1948 and wearing his only suit, which he described as 'a good brown cloth suit that had to serve for all occasions', Zurakowski went to France.

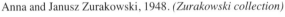

Anna and Janusz Zurakowski, 1948. *(Zurakowski collection)*

Anna warmly remembered her first glimpse of him in Paris: 'It was the first time that I had seen him in civilian clothes and not in a uniform. He still cut a dashing figure.' After a skirmish with the French civil authorities that lasted ten days, they received the proper documentation and were married in Paris in a civil service on 13 May, and later in a Polish church. The next step became a battle of paperwork and wills. For Anna to come to England as Janusz's wife required a 'mountain of forms' and the slow process of registration. After six weeks Zura finally received the necessary entry visa to allow Anna to join him in Cheltenham, near where he was now based. Their first home was a furnished flat in the town, but later a tiny house complete with garden was found. A year later their first child, George, was born. 'Midzi' served as the godfather. In the same year Zura became a naturalised British subject. By then Anna had grown accustomed to England, but there was not much opportunity for her to continue her career as a writer and journalist.

'Zuraisms'

When Zura joined Gloster, he was already well known in the close-knit circle of test pilots as an outstanding development pilot and an extraordinary aerobatic performer. Many test pilots at the time were household names, such as John Derry at de Havilland, Neville Duke at Hawker and Roland Beamont at English Electric. Some cut dashing figures – the kind of square-cut jaws and swept-back locks that Hollywood movies had portrayed. Zura looked nothing like this. His small, slight, spare frame, receding hairline and quiet demeanour were, however, deceptive.

When younger and more aggressive pilots misjudged Zurakowski, it was mainly because he didn't look the type – but were they ever put in their place if they ever flew with him! 'When the younger test pilots began putting on the pace and making faster and lower passes over the airfield, Zura proved he could dice with the best of them.'[1]

Zurakowski soon established himself as a unique personality: he was slightly older, a family man, and more experienced than his contemporaries in both wartime and test flying, with more than 2,000 flying hours by 1950. He definitely did not fit the mould. To begin with, his Polish-English dialect was peppered with his own

[1] Norris, 'Impossible', 30.

'Zuraisms'. 'What the time is?' or 'What the story is, little man?' 'What a weather it is?'[2] was his way of slyly tweaking people's noses. Zura found a way to end irritating conversations quickly. As he began to speak, the Zuraisms became more frequent, according to Geoff Worrall, one of the test pilots at Gloster (later to become the chief test pilot). After attempting to explain the argument more clearly, the speaker would be faced with a quizzical look and a 'What is?' interjection that led to an eventual abandoning of the conversation. If the retreating speaker would have stopped to look at Zura, he would have noticed the twinkle in his eyes and know that he had been 'had'.

Worrall fondly related his first encounter with Zura:

I had landed at MV [Moreton Valence] in an old Meteor Mark III to pick up some spares for No 610 RAF Squadron on summer camp detachment at West Malling, Kent. Zura was walking from the service aircraft repairs and refurbishing hangar and smiled a greeting. 'What a day!' I said, looking at the lowering cloud base. 'Yes!' Zura agreed, 'what a weather!' Getting into my old Mark III, I cracked, 'Ah, they don't make 'em like this any more!' In the style of a vintage car owner, 'No,' he said, 'We have much better ones now.'

As I started up, taxied out and took off, I had observed and felt his professionally critical, yet kindly eye upon my various actions and manoeuvres. Shortly after Rodney Dryland's sad death in a Meteor PR Mark IX prototype, I had the very real pleasure and privilege of getting to know Zura better.[3]

Language difficulties would come to Zura's aid when bad weather threatened to stop flying and a call was sent to all aircraft to return. His English would almost desert him on these occasions. After answering the call by repeating three times very clearly 'Allo! Repeat again your message please,' there would be a loud click as Zura switched off his radio. Some time later, when he had completed his flying to his own satisfaction, his Meteor would loom up out of the murk

---

[2] Ibid.
[3] Geoff Worrall, conversation with the author, 2001.

and a quiet little voice would say: 'Allo, Pinkpill
Control. Permission to land?'[4]

Zura was well liked by his fellow pilots and was sociable although
not a drinker. 'He will go along to the local with his colleagues and
become quite as merry with his glass of orangeade as they do with
their pints.'[5] Zurakowski loved talking about flying and once
listeners cued into his unique English dialect, they realised that Zura
was 'of a modest and very retiring nature, but he has technical
abilities that are not always apparent except when he is discussing
aircraft and flying; it is then that he is seen as the master of his art,
sound in his theories and skilled in his explanation.'[6]

A sense of fun was also part of Zura's personality. Geoff Worrall
related this incident: 'We had no canteen, so lunch-time
arrangements were somewhat impromptu, but Zura made good use

Gloster test pilots in 1952. Left to right: Brian Smith, Michael Kilburn, Eric
Greenwood, Ray Julyan, S/Ldr Bill Waterton, Janusz Zurakowski, Miss MJ
Robinson (control tower worker) and Geoff Worrall. *(Zurakowski collection)*

[4] Norris, 'Impossible', 30.
[5] Ibid.
[6] 'Canada's Gain is Britain's Loss', *Flight* (25 April 1952), 487.

of these short breaks. He had ingeniously contrived an electrically-driven portable air compressor out of a surplus B-17 and with this he very professionally resprayed his elderly car (1937 Ford Prefect) an impressive Meteor silver. At that time, Lord and Lady Docker, of paint-manufacturing fame, were disporting themselves in a gold-embellished Daimler when not aboard their yacht *Shemara*. Zura proudly drove out his resplendent car from his 'spray shop' next to the Moreton Valence Air Traffic Control Building and responded to admiring comments with, 'Ah, but now I have my Docker Ford.' We craftily stuck a paper Daimler logo over the radiator's Ford badge, but I think it came off in the rain. Pity.'[7] Later, when one car after another that belonged to the test pilots broke down at the airfield, even the Docker Ford wasn't immune. Zura said he would not park close to the other cars any more or he would catch their 'virus'.

Zurakowski was a force to be reckoned with, as noted by Squadron Leader Bill Waterton, his last chief test pilot at Gloster. 'He didn't suffer fools gladly, and there were times that I could see he disapproved of something I had done. He wouldn't always say it out loud, but you knew it if you had displeased him.'[8] He had what his fellow test pilot at Avro, Spud Potocki, called 'iron in the blood'[9], the ability to dig in one's heels and stand one's ground. Behind his seemingly calm personality Zura had a backbone of steel. In his work at Gloster he would need that trait at times.

The one aspect of his personality that most affected his flying was the methodical and scientific approach he took to all of his work. 'He would visualise a situation and then sit down and consult his numerous homemade graphs and tables, get out his slide rule, jot down figures, and then jot down some more. Often this would go on for days.'[10] On one occasion, another Gloster test pilot, Jim Cooksey, head of the production test pilot office, asked him what he was working out. At the time, the Bristol Aircraft Company was designing the Brabazon, which was to be the largest aircraft ever built in Britain, in nearby Bristol. They were lengthening the runway at Filton Airport to allow this gigantic airliner to take-off, and in the process they were levelling the neighbouring village of Filton.

---

[7] Worrall, 2001.
[8] Bill Waterton, conversation with the author, September 2001.
[9] Stinton, 'Test Pilot', 53.
[10] Bialkowski, 2001.

Zurakowski at Gloster Aircraft Company, 1948. *(Zurakowski collection)*

'I cannot understand,' replied Zura, 'why they are knocking down the village of Filton so that the Bristol runway can be extended for the Brabazon to take-off. That aeroplane, when it makes its first flight, will take-off in 400 yards.'[11] A year later the Brabazon made its maiden flight and took off in 400 yards! Although later Zurakowski was not able to recall this incident, it appears to be indicative of his method of thinking. He added, 'It stands to reason that on its maiden flight the Brabazon would be lightly loaded, perhaps thirty per cent under gross weight, and would have a very short take-off run.'[12]

The value of test flying was apparent to Zurakowski, but he often questioned the way the Gloster design office seemed to be at odds with the experimental test pilots' group. 'An experimental test pilot is not a popular person in a design department. Most of the designers are highly optimistic about their own design, and it is not a pleasant task after a flight to explain or to prove that their optimism is not justified. Quite often the reaction of a designer is to say that everything is excellent, that the pilots are simply too 'fussy' or that they want to have their own way or that they have the 'prima donna complex'.

'But if everything was so excellent, why then, for example, did such a successful aircraft as the Meteor require more than fifteen hundred airframe modifications during its development and more than five hundred engine modifications of which about thirty per cent had to be developed and proved in flight? Maybe because of the continuous effort to improve the Meteor and its engines, the speed and ceiling of the aircraft was increased by more than twenty per cent, range and armament doubled, with continuous improvement of reliability. Four Gloster Aircraft Company pilots lost their lives on this work.'[13] Being able to understand the engineering and design issues inherent in a new design provided Zurakowski with a definite advantage.

When one problem in the air puzzled him, he recalled that Gloster's engineers could not help him. 'I went to an aerodynamicist expert but I wasn't sure what he was doing. He scribbled down a formula, which didn't make sense, and then he scribbled down more formulas. It still didn't make sense, but that was the expert's reliance

---

[11] Norris, 'Impossible', 30.
[12] Bialkowski, 2001.
[13] Jan Zurakowski, 'Test Flying the Arrow and Other High Speed Jet Aircraft', *The CAHS Journal* 17, No 4 (Winter 1979), 101.

on formulas.' Zurakowski regarded Fred Saunders, a highly respected engineer appointed by the Hawker Siddeley Group to run the troubled operation, in a much different light. Zura considered him 'a gifted engineer, perhaps the best in business in England'.

Acting Chief Test Pilot

In 1949 Sir Roy Dobson of A V Roe Limited had asked Bill Waterton to come to Canada to test-fly the XC-100. It was another example of the talent in the Hawker Siddeley Group being utilised. A member of the RAF's first jet-powered World Air Speed Record team (the Gloster Meteor flown by Group Captain Teddy Donaldson had set a speed of 616mph on 7 September 1946), and subsequent holder of the Paris-London speed record in 1946, Waterton was already a well-known name. He brought with him not only a great deal of jet fighter experience but also a reputation as a stellar test pilot. Although a Canadian by birth, Waterton had served in the RAF as a member of 242 Squadron (mainly composed of Canadians), at one time led by the famous British legless ace, Wing Commander Douglas Bader. Shortly before the Battle of Britain, Waterton became a flight instructor at No 6 Operational Training Unit, where he trained more than 600 students by 1942. He rose through the ranks to become a squadron leader and later, as a member of the Air Fighting Development Squadron of the Central Fighter Establishment, was heavily involved in developmental work.

While Waterton was away, Zurakowski was appointed Acting Chief Test Pilot, taking over much of the experimental work. As an experimental pilot Zurakowski undertook a number of the first flights of Meteor developments. On 12 October 1948 at Moreton Valence he carried out the maiden flight of VT150, a modified F 4 that served as the prototype F 8. Zura was also the pilot of VZ438, the first production day-fighter Meteor F 8 on 21 December 1948. The prototype Meteor photo-reconnaissance versions, the FR9 (VW360) on 22 March 1950 and PR10 (VS968) on 24 May 1950 were also first flown by Zurakowski. By the end of this time with Gloster, Zura had carried out more than 1,000 flights on the Meteor.

Zura also flew a special-purpose Meteor F 4 (RA490), which was a flying test bed with a strengthened centre section used to test the Metropolitan-Vickers F 2/4 Beryl axial-flow turbojets. These engines were originally intended to be used in the Saunders-Roe SRA-1 flying boat fighter, and at 3,850lb thrust they were slightly more powerful than the standard Derwents. He demonstrated the spectacular rate of climb of this hybrid at the 1948 SBAC Display and continued to test-fly this Meteor. When the press reports finally revealed its climb-to-altitude capabilities in January 1949, the newspaper headlines proclaimed '7½ miles up in 7½ minutes, by an unnamed Polish pilot'.[14] All the news reports ended with the note that the flights had been conducted by an unknown Polish pilot. This description, which Zura thought was amusing, was indicative of the times. Zura's next assignments would certainly link his name and that of the Meteor in the headlines.

In 1950, when Zura was asked to fly the most powerful special-purpose Meteor version built, he was intrigued by the prospect. The WA620 was an experimental F 8 that had strengthened fuselage, wings and tail to allow two 7,600lb-thrust Armstrong-Siddeley Sapphire turbojets to be fitted. A quick calculation showed that the heavily modified aircraft would have an outstanding 1:1 thrust/weight ratio. In checking his tables and charts, Zura immediately determined that pulling it off the runway at full power at approximately 120 knots would launch the fighter vertically. Zura realised that there was a risk that an engine failure in the critical seconds of take-off might spin the aircraft. The risk was acceptable but until he had worked out a cartwheel manoeuvre on paper, the thought remained with him that the spinning moment had great possibilities.

Meteor with Sapphire engines, 1950. *(Zurakowski collection)*

[14] Ibid.

Zurakowski would often resort to mathematical calculations to explain his theories, but when he tried to show Jim Heyworth, Chief Test Pilot for Rolls-Royce, that he had come up with something different, Heyworth was baffled. 'Zura said that he discovered a new aerobatic manoeuvre and demonstrated the theory of it on paper.'[15] As the complex formulae were laid out in a series of notes in Zura's Hucclecote office, the Rolls-Royce pilot couldn't grasp the idea of the tumbling flight path. Knowing that Zurakowski was a very competent engineer, Heyworth believed that there could possibly be something there. He had little idea that he was being shown the beginnings of the 'Zurabatic cartwheel'.

The basis of the new manoeuvre would be the widely set-apart engines and the sturdiness of the Meteor fighter. The special-purpose Sapphire-engined version, WA620, was flown exactly as planned, and the spectacular take-offs proved that the Meteor was a potent airframe indeed, especially in Zura's hands.

Janusz with 'Sapphire-engined' Meteor test-bed, 1951.
(Gloster Aircraft Company via Zurakowski)

[15] Don Middleton, *Test Pilots: The Story of British Test Flying 1903-1984* (London: Collins Willow, 1985), 34.

Gloster Meteor

The early story of the Gloster Meteor is intertwined with British efforts to develop turbojet engines. In 1929 RAF Flying Officer Frank Whittle designed a gas turbine engine and by 1936 had set up a small firm named Power Jets Limited to pursue his ideas. The first working model, the 'Whittle Unit', impressed the Air Ministry, which ordered a flight-worthy engine, the W1, from Power Jets. In September 1939 the Air Ministry asked Gloster to design an aircraft, the E 28/39, in order to test-fly the engine. In the meantime, Frank Whittle was hearing rumours that the Germans were also working on 'turbojet' engines, as they came to be known.

With the success of this first prototype, in 1940 the Air Ministry issued F 9/40, a specification for an operational turbojet-powered fighter. Gloster's Chief Engineer, George Carter, proposed a twin-engine aircraft with the company designation 'G 41', which became the Meteor.

The jet engine development effort by both Power Jets and Rover struggled until 1942 when Rolls-Royce's Ernest Hives took Rover's S B Wilks out to lunch. As the story has it, Hives proposed a deal to Wilks: 'Give us this jet job and we'll give you our tank-engine factory in Nottingham.' Rolls-Royce then began its long history of jet engine development. The first of its projects was the simple, cheap and reliable centrifugal-flow RB 41 Nene, which was bench-tested in October 1944 and provided 2,270kg (5,000lb) of thrust. By July 1945 the Nene was powering the American Lockheed YP-80A Shooting Star. At the time, the Nene was the world's most powerful jet engine and was made in large numbers, with versions being made in Canada, Australia, France, the US, and the USSR Although other engines were tried, eventually a scaled-down version of the Nene, known as the Derwent V, powered the Meteor.

The first Meteors entered RAF squadron service with No 616 Squadron, beginning in July 1944. The Meteor I was no faster than contemporary piston-engine fighters at high altitude but, unlike them, it retained its speed at low altitude and consequently was pressed into service to intercept low-flying German V-1 bombs that summer. Meteor pilots knocked down thirteen buzz bombs by cannon and by 'tipping', a dangerous tactic in which the pilot unbalanced the V-1 by moving the Meteor's wing under the missile's wing and, using air pressure, tipped its gyroscope, causing a crash. With the success of the V-1 intercepts, Meteors were established as a frontline fighter.

The initial production Meteors were crude and suffered from a number of 'teething problems' including a lack of power, heavy controls, a poor view to the sides and rear, and jams in the cannons, but the type had considerable potential as was proven by the first full-scale production version, Meteor III This new version featured a stronger airframe, higher thrust engines, greater internal fuel capacity, a rear-sliding canopy and problem-free cannons. Some hurdles proved to be more difficult to solve, including a balance problem, heaviness of the ailerons, poor manoeuvrability in the rolling plane, and a tendency to 'snake', which limited the Meteor's usefulness as a gun platform.

Continual development led to the Meteor F 4, which went into production in 1947. It featured Derwent V engines and clipped wings, a stronger airframe, fully pressurised cockpit, lighter ailerons to improve manoeuvrability, and rudder trim adjustments to reduce snaking. The F 4 could also be fitted with a drop tank under each wing, and experiments were performed with the carriage of underwing weapons stores such as rockets and bombs. The new version even briefly set world speed records of 975km/h (606mph) and 991km/h (616mph).

The Meteor was finally a success with not only production status in England and service with the RAF, but also international sales to Argentina, Belgium, Denmark, Egypt, France and the Netherlands.

Gloster decided to undertake a significant redesign of the F 4 to keep it up to date while retaining as much of the manufacturing tooling of the F 4 as possible. The result was the Meteor F 8 (G-41K), first flown in 1948 by Zurakowski. This type became the principal version that saw combat in the Middle East and in Korea (flown by Australians). Additional sales were made to Australia, Brazil, Egypt, Israel, the Netherlands, South Africa and Syria.

Although it was in frontline service with the RAF from 1950 to 1955, the Meteor F 8 was obsolete by that time as a day-fighter. Subsequent development by Gloster and its subcontractor, Armstrong Whitworth, centred on photo-reconnaissance, night-fighter and trainer variants, which remained in service until the 1970s. Other countries continued to fly the Meteor for a similar period, but most Meteors were retired from operational use in the 1960s. Today a few examples continue to take to the skies as flying memorials to the first Allied jet fighters.

Photographer's model

During test flights one observation made by Zura was that considerable distortion of the Meteor's rear fuselage panels was evident at high speed. The design team had demanded evidence before proceeding with modifications. Having the availability of a Meteor T7 trainer, he enlisted the aid of Russell Adams, the chief Gloster photographer. Adams recalled:

> Some years ago when the Meteor 7 two-seater was introduced, both Bill Waterton and Jan Zurakowski quickly foresaw its use as a photographic machine to observe other Meteors during high-speed flight.
>
> Our test pilots would often tell of what they had seen when flying alongside another aircraft, but they had no photographs to convey the story to the design staff. So I asked for the chance to use my camera to bring back the answers, and 'Zura' soon arranged my first assignment and piloted me whilst I photographed another Meteor at close quarters and at top speed. The results were very convincing and proved useful to the design staff.[16]

The first photographic flight was made late in the evening one day over the Severn Estuary, and the T7 was flown alongside a Meteor fighter at low altitude. Both aircraft were 'flat out' as Adams snapped off a large number of shots. As soon as they landed, 'Zura insisted that the films be processed immediately and then Zura dashed off with the prints to the home of the Chief Designer that same evening to prove his point.'[17]

Adams continued:

> 'Zura' shared my enthusiasm and a series of similar flights soon followed. The equally keen cooperation of Chief Production Test Pilot Jim Cooksey made the scheme completely successful. Technical air-to-air photography at Gloster was thus well established and, of course, we were in a position to turn out the 'pretty' pictures too, thus ensuring a constant flow of new photographs to the technical press. These covered every

[16] 'Canada's Gain is Britain's Loss', 487.
[17] Gerald J Green, 'Readers' Letters', *Aeroplane*, 30, No 10, Issue 354 (October 2002), 21.

phase of air activity at Gloster and showed the development of the Mk 8 in almost every respect. Credit for taking the lead in this work must go to 'Zura' who, although hard-pressed with experimental and development flying (Bill Waterton was then in Canada), always made time for me to get the pictures. His very equable temperament and willingness to cooperate made my job easy. Nothing was too much trouble; he would never procrastinate and disliked red tape immensely. No less enthusiastic was Jim Cooksey, who always managed somehow to provide a Mk 7 just at the right moment.[18]

Zura and the Meteor were featured prominently in many press and promotional features. Although not one to seek out publicity, he managed to continue being profiled because of his extraordinary skill with various marks of the Meteor. A succession of press photographs showed the Meteor upside down, going vertical or at odd angles; invariably it was Zurakowski at the controls. The most famous photograph of the Meteor came from Zurakowski's imagination. One day Adams asked Zura if they could do something a bit different. 'He grinned and replied: 'Of course, what about this?' He used his hands to represent his own and the photographic aircraft, and I quickly gathered his proposal was a vertical dive. The picture was duly secured at the first attempt and *Flight* kindly gave it great prominence. But little did I realise the worldwide publicity which it was to receive, particularly in the USA, where it was published in 198 periodicals.'[19]

Record-setter

Two events prominently marked Zura's time with Gloster. The first took place on 4 April 1950 when, as Acting Chief Test Pilot, he set a series of international speed records between London and Copenhagen with a Meteor F 8, VZ468. Using a standard production aircraft complete with all normal military equipment including cannon armament and a ventral fuel tank, the record flight was a public demonstration of the standard Meteor's performance.

[18] 'Canada's Gain is Britain's Loss', 487.
[19] Ibid.

Taking off from Northolt, Zurakowski flew the first stage of 604.17 miles (972.32km) from London to Copenhagen in 1hr 5min 54.9sec at 541mph. His arrival at Kastrup Airport, Copenhagen, was carefully timed. 'Zura taxied straight towards the two waiting Esso kerosene bowsers, free-wheeling the last few yards with 'Derwents' stopped, so that the refuelling crew could get to work immediately.'[20] The refuelling was facilitated by Royal Danish Navy personnel who had been involved in the planning and operation of the refuelling procedure. They rapidly completed the fuelling process in four and a half minutes, and Zurakowski was in the air again four minutes later, streaking back to London.

After setting a speed record in a Meteor Mark 8. (*Zurakowski collection*)

The second record run, from Copenhagen to London, took 1hr 11min 16.6sec at 500.7mph. The total London-Copenhagen-London round trip (including time on the ground) took 2hr 29min 8.5sec at 480.29mph. Most of the flight had been made in clear but hazy

[20] 'There and Back to see how near it is!' *Hawker Siddeley Review* 3, 4 (December 1950).

conditions at an average height of 34,000 feet. These record flights shattered the previous records that had been recently made by the de Havilland Comet airliner. Military officials in Denmark were suitably impressed, and the Danish Air Force became the third European customer to buy the F 8. Ironically, its small order of twenty machines became the last order for frontline Meteor day fighters for service in Europe. They continued to be used until the late 1950s.

Zurakowski became famous as a record-breaker and acted as a consultant when the RAF's 600 Squadron was vying for its second consecutive win in the 1951 RAF Cooper Trophy, a closed-circuit 'round the pylons' handicap race. Wing Commander Jack Meadows, the pilot who was to fly the course, was advised not to fly a direct course over the three corners (which seemed odd) but to take an outer circle that would result in a faster speed overall. Meadows practised the tactic and found that Zurakowski was right: 'Carefully judged rate-four turns would just clip the actual turning points. The extra distance over the ground was more than made up by less loss of speed from steeper turns.'[21] In the Cooper Trophy, Meadows flew a standard Meteor F 4 (VZ429), winning the event by following Zura's instructions.

Zurabatic cartwheel

The second climactic event in the Gloster years involved Zurakowski at the Farnborough Air Show, where he devised a manoeuvre in which a Meteor could be 'cartwheeled' in a vertical climb using asymmetric thrust. Farnborough is Britain's largest aviation event and is attended by thousands of people. The displays there of the Society of British Aircraft Constructors in the 1950s were 'what might be considered the great days of British aviation following the Second World War. We had not yet learnt to be safety conscious, and the test pilots of the day literally 'flew by the seat of their pants'.' Bill Waterton of Gloster was to claim that untried aircraft were pushed into unknown territory, the important thing being to thrill the spectators, commercial and public, and impress foreign buyers.

'Such were the feats of the pilots both at SBAC and elsewhere that in the fifties they were all household names, which in a number of instances still live on today, and you will still come across press references to Peter Twiss and the airspeed record of 1,132mph

[21] Jack Meadows, 'The Auxiliary Tradition', *Aeroplane Monthly* (June 1987), 285.

achieved in the Fairey Delta 2; 'Cat's Eyes' Cunningham and the flight of the de Havilland Comet, the world's first jet airliner; and Neville Duke and his exploits with the Hawker Hunter... Superb flying with what were really very mundane aircraft, Jan Zurakowski climbing a Meteor 8 vertically until it stalled, then doing a cartwheel.'[22] Zura was not a Farnborough newcomer as he had demonstrated the Martin-Baker MB 5 in 1946. At Gloster he had been called upon to display RA-490, the Metropolitan-Vickers F 2/4 Beryl-powered Meteor F 4 in 1948, a production F 8 in 1949, and WA620, the Sapphire Meteor F 8 in 1950 at the SBAC Displays. Zura recalled that during that period, 'I missed one year because the Meteor was demonstrated by somebody else that day.'

Typical of Zurakowski's aerobatic displays was the 1949 show. *Aeroplane* described his performance that year in the following way. 'Zurakowski, in the Meteor 8, gave one of his perfect demos. Anyone who has watched him at the armament demonstrations will recognise his pattern of flying. The whole show is planned to the second. Several of his upward sweeps carry him to 6,000 feet and at this height he did several turns of a horizontal spin. He then plummets down vertically and leaves the pull-out to the last possible moment, clearing the runway at 40 feet.'[23] All of his flight routines were impressive, but Zura's 1951 appearance would go down in history as the most memorable flying display ever at Farnborough.

His friend and fellow test pilot Peter Cope later disclosed, 'The idea for the Zurabatic cartwheel had been in Jan's mind for several years before he was finally able to try it.'[24] The origin of the cartwheel manoeuvre was related to Zura's aerobatics on the DH Hornet in 1945 and his recent work with the Sapphire-powered Meteor. This aircraft had its powerful twin engines located quite far out along the wings like the DH Hornet. The Hornet would never quite cartwheel but it was on the Meteor that Zura perfected the cartwheel manoeuvre for which he became famous. Zura had once mentioned to a reporter that he had performed the cartwheel in 1950: 'I had been thinking about it for some time, I had worked it all out and was sure that it was theoretically possible, so one day I thought I

---

[22] 'Farnborough Air Science Trust Newsletter', No 14 (December 1998) [online], cited 2001: http://www.fasta.freeserve.co.uk/ fasta.htm.
[23] 'Farnborough.: The Opening Phases', *Flight* (September 1951).
[24] Peter R Cope, 'The Zurabatic Cartwheel', *Flying* (May 1956), 69.

Zura striaght down. *(Russell Adams)*

would see if it was practical.'[25] After performing the manoeuvre, Zurokowski felt he had proved it was possible and didn't do it again. However, fate intervened when, 'early in 1951, pilots from the Empire Test Pilots School at Farnborough were visiting Gloster. In the evening at the bar, some discussion took place about aerobatics, and I mentioned that a cartwheel was easy on the Meteor. I had an empty glass in my hand because I do not drink.

'They were sure that I was shooting a line and they started pulling my leg that I was drunk. 'Cartwheel is not possible' – that was the verdict. This forced me to prove my words at the first opportunity. Gloster Aircraft was competing with the de Havilland Co. The Ministry of Supply and the RAF considered that the Venom fighter should be used as a ground-attack fighter and the Meteor as a high-altitude interceptor. Engine characteristics of the Venom at high altitude were much superior to the Derwent engines of Meteors, but the Meteor was better at low altitude and its load-carrying was much higher than the Venom's.'[26]

Eric Greenwood, by then the company's Technical Sales Manager, had proposed a tactical fighter concept in 1949. In 1951 Gloster's private venture prototype, the Gloster Meteor G-AMCJ known as the G 44 F 4 GAF (Ground-Attack Fighter), provided Zurakowski with the possibilities of making a cartwheel work. The GAF had acquired a more official sobriquet, the 'Reaper', taken from the company's list of aircraft names submitted to the Ministry of Supply in 1941. It was not a standard Meteor, being built with a strengthened wing and numerous hardpoints for tip-tank, underwing and fuselage stores. The GAF was a formidable weapons package with twenty-four rockets or bombs supplementing the normal cannon armament. Wingtip fuel tanks and modifications to accommodate 1,000 gallons of fuel brought its military gross weight up to 22,000lb. During 1951 G-AMCJ was flown extensively with various combinations of external loads. At the end of July it was painted silver and registered 'G-7-1' in accordance with a new Air Ministry Class B civil markings scheme. These markings were in red, with similarly coloured rocket projectiles (RPs) and 'wingtip tanks painted red to draw attention to its heavily laden condition.'[27]

[25] 'Zurabatic Cartwheel', *Hawker Siddeley Review* 4, No 4 (December 1951).
[26] Zurakowski, 'Zurabatic Cartwheel', 6.
[27] 'Farnborough: The Opening Phases', 344.

In preparation for his memorable display at Farnborough the following month, Zurakowski flew G-7-1 again on 9 August 1951. As he recalled, 'Gloster management was keen for a ground-attack Meteor, but failed to interest the 'High Brass' about the logic of this idea. The last chance was to demonstrate aircraft suitability at the Farnborough Show. I had to demonstrate that the Meteor ground-attack fighter loaded with twenty-four rockets plus normal armament of four 20mm guns and two 100-gallon wingtip tanks did not lose much of performance in short take-off, had a good rate of climb, high speed and manoeuvrability.

'In 1951 many new modern designs like the Hawker P1052 or Supermarine 508 were demonstrated, and the Meteor, which was flying in all shows since the war, was unlikely to attract attention. I had to do something to pull the officials out of the tents to watch the old Meteor fly. Cartwheeling the Meteor did the trick, but my show did not convince the 'High Brass' that the Meteor could be a good ground-attack aircraft, and so further development was directed into night fighter and all-weather fighter roles.'[28]

Zurakowski, as usual, had first worked out this cartwheel manoeuvre with a slide rule and graphs. To test the manoeuvre, his special Meteor flew with twenty-four 90lb rockets slung under the wings and fuselage and two 100-gallon tip-tanks, giving it extra rotational inertia (although the tip-tanks were empty for the Farnborough exhibitions). 'One day at the end of a routine development test flight, he stood the prototype on its tail at 10,000 feet and commenced a vertical climb under full power. Speed decreased steadily from the entry speed of 350 knots, and finally with the airspeed needle coming down to the 70-knot mark, Jan cut one engine, leaving the other at full power. As he expected, the airplane started a wingover in the direction of the dead engine, and a clean entry into the cartwheel.'[29] The dizzying twist 'surprised even Zura'.[30] After perfecting the complicated gyration in secret practices, Zura performed it for the first time publicly over the Gloster's home airfield at Hucclecote. Starting from a low-level flypast, he streaked up to 6,000 feet in a vertical climb before astonishing onlookers with the cartwheel. Zura was now ready for the 1951 Farnborough Air Show.

[28] Peter R. Cope, 'The Zurabatic Cartwheel,' 69.
[29] Ibid.
[30] Norris, 'Impossible', 42.

Janusz Zurakowski at Farnborough in 1951, entering the 'cartwheel'.
(Geoff Worrall)

Sunday 16 September, the first public day of Farnborough, saw more than 140,000 spectators. The day was cloudy, but the low cloud base was better than the dark and stormy conditions of the previous day. A number of the air show's first performances were spectacular, including the STOL take-offs of N J Capper's impressive Scottish Aviation Pioneer light transport and the multiple spins of R G Wheadon's Percival Provost trainer. Then Zura started his routine, with the Reaper leaping into the air and instantly beginning a high-speed run over the runway. 'The first run would have been fast and low enough to vex the keenest AA guns.'[31] If the audience thought that the Meteor was only going to do the traditional 'flash and zoom' show, they were startled when Zurakowski put the Meteor into a vertical climb with full power on both Derwent V engines. Then, at slow speed he cut one engine and slammed full rudder at the same time. The resulting cartwheel was prolonged to one and a half turns by the flywheel motion of the rockets.

Announcers at the Farnborough Air Show exclaimed that Zurakowski had just demonstrated a new aerobatic. Major Oliver Stewart, the editor of *Aeronautics* and the official commentator during the trade days of the exhibition, declared that it was 'the first entirely new manoeuvre to be developed during at least the last twenty years'[32] (the only other new aerobatic was the Lomcevak). It became variously known as the 'Fin Sling' (Zura's private term for it), 'Catherine wheel', 'Zurabatic Cartwheel', 'Zurabatics' or simply 'Zuras'.

Zura elaborated further:

> Coming back to the cartwheel, I tried it on the Meteor by zooming at full power until I reached a vertical climb and when my speed dropped to about eighty knots I cut the power of one engine. When the aircraft started cartwheeling (rotation in the yawing plane), I would cut power of the other engine after one turn. Rotation would slow down, and in half a turn, vertical down speed was increased enough to stop the aircraft rotation. In the vertical position speed was building rapidly and at about 250 knots I was pulling out of the dive.
>
> It sounds fairly simple but there were three factors involved. First, in vertical climb assessment of vertical

[31] 'Farnborough: The Opening Phases', 344.
[32] 'Zurabatic Cartwheel', December 1951.

position is difficult. By looking ahead at the blue sky or on the clouds there is no reference point of vertical flight. You have to look right and left to be sure that the wings are level and at right angles to the horizon. Second, rotation of aircraft with one engine running at full power introduces a gyroscopic moment tending to change the attitude of the aircraft to alter zero air flow required to keep rotating in the vertical plane. And third, no-lift incidence of the wings during rotation is controlled at the beginning of the cartwheel by the elevators and close to the end. Halfway through the cartwheel only rotational speed is present in practice. There is no vertical speed and negligible aerodynamic loads. If the airflow over the wing is at high angles a normal or inverted spin can start.

At the end of the cartwheel the Meteor flicked into a spin; I put it intentionally into two turns of a spin to lose excess altitude. If the cartwheel was badly executed it could spin, but properly executed it stopped even without any oscillation at the end. The manoeuvre was a bit of fun but not of combat value, so I was not interested much about it any more.[33]

The cartwheel was especially difficult to achieve perfectly, even by Zura. The commentators at Farnborough had noticed, 'That the manoeuvre is tricky can be judged by the fact that on one occasion (at Farnborough) it did not come off and the Meteor fell away into a spin.'[34] The Farnborough feat astonished even the professionals; one test pilot was heard to speculate, 'I wonder how many people are going to risk their necks trying to do the same thing.'[35] The aerobatic manoeuvre that the military flyers had dubbed 'Zuras' resulted in some dangerous situations in the RAF squadrons that were flying the Meteor. Zura related, 'In the RAF, some pilots were successful in cartwheeling the Meteor and Flying Officer Bacon demonstrated it at a Battle of Britain display and sent me an instruction, 'Aerobatic Cartwheeling of Meteor Aircraft', but the manoeuvre was prohibited later. I understand

[33] Zurakowski, 'Zurabatic Cartwheel', 6.
[34] James Hay Stevens, 'Farnborough '51', *Pictorial and Air Reserve Gazette* (September 1951), 313.
[35] 'Zurabatic Cartwheel', December 1951.

that in one squadron of the Danish Air Force all pilots flying the Meteor F8 were good at cartwheels.'[36]

Zurakowski himself performed the cartwheel on the Meteor (including standard production Meteors with no weapons stores) an estimated sixty to seventy times in a variety of configurations. He never considered it a dangerous manoeuvre since the speed entering the cartwheel was an estimated 60-70 knots (110-130km/h) and the spin only reached approximately 100 knots (185 km/h). The cartwheel required an altitude of 3,000-4,000 feet to ensure safe recovery, but Zura described it as 'easy to do; the aircraft is quiet and steady.'[37] There was very little strain on the airframe throughout the low-speed manoeuvre. Zura even remarked, 'I didn't expect that I would be flying according to the recommendation of my mother: 'fly low and slow'.'

Worrall reflected recently: 'At our flight test airfield, Moreton Valence, some six miles south of Gloucester, we had many Meteor-equipped RAF airfields within easy reach. Following Zura's famous 'Zurabatic' pinwheel manoeuvre, it was not uncommon to see, as we went about our test flights, Meteors tumbling about in a variety of unsuccessful attempts by squadron pilots to emulate his unique aerobatic. 'I saw three 'autumn leaves' [a Gloster's nickname for the manoeuvre] this morning, Zura,' I said. 'What is problem? Turbulence, you think?' responded Zura slyly.'[38]

Pilots in 600 RAF Auxiliary Squadron were attempting the manoeuvre in private. Their commanding officer, Wing Commander Meadows, was sure that 'Zurakowski's apparent semi-inverted upward spin in a Meteor at Farnborough the previous year had, without anything being said, fired some imaginations. Its secret was to shut one engine at the critical stage. I had an idea that Jack Jagger and Keith (Hazelwood) and Mike (Oliver) were trying it.

'One day, a very shaken Jack appeared back in the office and I asked him what had happened. His 'Zura' attempt had become a full inverted spin at 12,000 feet and he could not recover. Nor, because of the Meteor's violent gyrations, could he manage to jettison the hood and bail out (Meteor 4s did not have ejection seats). He had given up hope when, at 3,000 feet, he went through a cloud layer with enough

[36] Zurakowski, 'Zurabatic Cartwheel', 6.
[37] 'Zurabatic Cartwheel,' December 1951.
[38] Worrall, 2001.

turbulence to upset the airflow and knock the Meteor into an inverted dive from which he just managed to roll out in time. It was clearly necessary to tell our enthusiasts to cool it. Zuras were banned.'[39]

The GAF had garnered publicity but no orders from the RAF or abroad, although India had expressed interest in it as a long-range fighter in 1953. For years, the private venture Meteor languished in obscurity as a factory development machine used in the development of spring-tab ailerons, before a remarkable transformation changed it into a T7 trainer demonstrator. With a two-seat cockpit grafted on and a new type of tip-tank with stabilising fins fitted fore and aft, it appeared at the 1954 Farnborough Show, painted a larkspur blue with ivory civilian markings 'G-ANSO'. In this guise the aircraft was sold to Sweden, and after many years of service it is now resident at Svedino's Automobile and Aviation Museum. A restoration of G-ANSO is currently under way.

Gloster Javelin

Inevitably Gloster began to look at a follow-up to the Meteor, leading to the E 1/44 single-engine (Rolls-Royce Nene) design. Construction of the E 1/44 prototype, SM809, started in late 1944 and was completed in July 1947. However, when the prototype was being delivered by road to Boscombe Down for testing, the transport vehicle jack-knifed and the first prototype was damaged beyond repair. Work was speeded up on the second airframe, TX145, which took to the air on 9 March 1948. A third prototype, TX148, flew in 1949 and was still under development in 1951. The whole programme was stopped at that point, because the Meteor proved to have more development potential. Zurakowski carried out fifty flights on the E 1/44 before the project was abandoned.

When Gloster undertook its next fighter design, the GA 5 Javelin, it was more revolutionary. The sleek two-seat interceptor, powered by two powerful AS Sapphire engines housed in a thick delta wing, featured a powerful radar set housed in its large nose radome. Initially two 30mm Aden cannon were fitted, and the Firestreak AAM (anti-aircraft missile) was adopted as armament in later versions. Problems relating to the conventional T-tail slowed development, but the Javelin went on to become an effective all-weather interceptor with 436 being built. The Javelin served with the RAF until 1967.

[39] Meadows, 'The Auxiliary Tradition', 287.

Gloster Javelin prototype, 1952 *(Avro News magazine)*

Several Gloster pilots joined Chief Test Pilot Waterton, who had returned from Canada, in the Javelin's development programme. Zurakowski, Brian Smith, Geoff Worrall and Peter Lawrence, in addition to Squadron Leader Peter Scott, RAF Project Liaison Pilot, logged time in WD808, one of the prototype series. Zura flew the new Gloster Javelin aircraft on 6 February 1952 in the first of fourteen test flights he completed. There were many problems associated with the development of the new Javelin, which, when first tested, was a vicious aircraft. The maiden flight was made by Waterton, who later barely escaped death in the first prototype, WD804, when part of the tail section broke off during a high-speed run. Both Waterton and Zurakowski had identified serious deficiencies in handling and had fought for modifications, yet the design office steadfastly refused to rectify the problems. 'To the design staff ... the Javelin was their baby, and like doting parents, they blinded themselves to its faults, and took most unkindly to anything which might reflect on their parentage.'[40]

Zurakowski was furious with the design office.

> On the evidence of wind tunnel tests it became obvious to me, more than two years before the first flight, that longitudinal instability was present in the Javelin at lower speeds. I was faced with a difficult problem. Urgent modifications were required, but control of the flight test programme was in the hands of the design office, which did not want to face the facts. The stability flight test programme therefore called for stability measurement only within the stable range of speeds. During one of the flights, I decided to check the low-speed range. It did not look safe, so I climbed to 30,000 feet and slowly started reducing speed. I reached a condition when, with the tailplane setting fully up and elevator fully down (both controls in diving position), the aircraft was still climbing, and finally stalled and went into a spin. Spin recovery was satisfactory.
>
> Of course, after this experience, I made it clear to the design office that stability of the aircraft was unsatisfactory as proven by the flight recorder.

[40] W A Waterton, *The Quick and the Dead* (London: Frederick Mueller, 1958), 197-198.

Unfortunately, the design office had the authority to issue the final flight report. Not all the evidence from the recorder was included, and the only comments were, if I remember correctly, 'Pilot investigated the stalling characteristics of the aircraft, and height lost in recovery was recorded.' There was no mention of extreme instability or spin... In a production department, the experimental pilot again is not a popular person. Nearly every production manager would like to set up his assembly line, set up a schedule and run the production smoothly without any interruption. He is furious when every week five or more modifications have to be incorporated somewhere on the assembly line and, in the worst case, when the aircraft is ready for acceptance flight. Who is to blame? Of course, the test pilot. Why did he not discover the trouble before? Is the modification really necessary? Why did it take so long to prove the modification in flight? And so on... This report convinced me that I was wasting my time at Gloster, and the conclusion accelerated my move to Canada.[41]

Zurakowski had served as Acting Chief Test Pilot Experimental while Waterton was away in Canada testing the Avro CF-100. At the time, the flight test operation at Gloster consisted of Jim Cooksey, Chief Test Pilot Production, Mike Kilburn, Brian Smith and Geoff Worrall. Frits Vyzelaar was added to the team as the Dutch Air Force Liaison Pilot. Worrall regarded that period as being busy but productive. 'Despite a significant workload with Meteor 8 development and the Javelin prototype GA 5 preparation, Zura always made time to be readily available for discussion and resolution of day-to-day problems and varying commitments. He was both lucid and cryptic!'[42]

Time for a change

On Waterton's return, things weren't right between Zura and his superior. 'Bill Waterton was my boss at Gloster, and I was Acting Chief Test Pilot. I never really wanted to be Chief Test Pilot because

[41] Zurakowski, 'Test Flying the Arrow', 101.
[42] Worrall, 2001.

Gloster Javelin in RAF squadron service. *(Geoff Worrall)*

I didn't like the bureaucracy and all the sales stuff – I was quite happy doing experimental things – but eventually Waterton felt I was trying to take his job and started acting against me.'[43] Zura never considered there to be ill feelings or a feud, he just wasn't the type. He did try to explain the tenuous relationship this way. 'He was my boss, but Waterton had some quirks that could drive people mad. He could be very emotional. An incident involved a 'hot' landing where the engine was a prototype Metro Vickers and was ruined in the flight. Waterton stormed into the flight test office and demanded who had set the brakes at such a low pressure.' Jan had dismissed the incident as just too hot a landing, but it seemed typical of the differences in personalities and styles between the two men.

Before too long, Zurakowski began to realise that the time was right for a change. Waterton felt uncomfortable about their relationship but also related that Zurakowski and his family had not really been happy in their adopted home; he ventured the belief that fear of the Soviets attacking England in the 1950s was also a factor in the Zurakowskis' departure. The coolness between the two men was perceptible. Zurakowski recalled, 'I didn't want to fight about it, and since my wife was unhappy in England, I sent letters to de Havilland and A V Roe in Canada, and Roe accepted.'[44]

Encouraged by reports from Peter Cope, who was already

---

[43] Stewart, *Shutting Down the National Dream*, 227.
[44] Ibid.

employed at A V Roe Canada as a test pilot, Zura had began to seriously consider a new move. Peter Cope explained, 'Knowing Jan from my time at the Empire Test Pilots School and, of course, I had a lot to do with Gloster and Zura when we both flew Meteors... I was with Armstrong Whitworth as a test pilot and we found that Jan shared a great deal of information with us; I told him to come.'[45]

In April 1952, after the factory and the flight test office found out about his intentions, they planned a huge going-away ceremony. Zurakowski typically shied away from those kinds of displays and it ended up as a semi-formal but low-key reception held outdoors in front of a Javelin prototype. Zura received a gift and made a few remarks, later shaking hands with his fellow test pilots, crew and factory workers, who made it evident that he would be missed at Gloster. Worrall's comments reflected the thoughts of many at the firm. 'We were all very saddened. We had lost a true friend and unassuming leader. It had been a privilege to work with him and enjoy his company. I was proud to call him my friend.'[46]

Zurakowski had decided to leave the Gloster Aircraft Company to work for Avro Aircraft Limited of Toronto, Ontario, as an experimental or development test pilot. His new job would be to test the CF-100, the first jet interceptor aircraft designed and built in Canada. Zura summed up his life at Gloster simply: 'After doing flight-test work in Britain for a few years, my wife Anna and I and our two young sons, George and Mark, moved to Canada in 1952 where I commenced testing aircraft for Avro.' Both children had been born in England, with Mark Ian being born in 1951. A new adventure was soon to begin for Zura and his family.

[45] Peter R Cope, conversation with the author, 2001.
[46] Worrall, 2001.

Chapter Eight

Avro Canada

A V Roe Canada, the fledgling Canadian company Janusz Zurakowski was about to join, was, like Gloster, also a member of the Hawker Siddeley Group. Its origins stemmed from industrial expansion in the war years when Victory Aircraft of Malton, Ontario (owned by the federal government), rose to become one of the most important aviation companies in Canada. Victory had turned out a large number of aircraft for the RAF and the RCAF including the Avro Anson twin-engined bomber/trainer and the famous four-engined Avro Lancaster bomber (430 aircraft were built), which was used extensively in the European theatre of operations. Sir Roy Dobson, the Managing Director of A V Roe Limited in the Hawker Siddeley Group, made personal visits to Victory during the war and had been impressed by the Canadian operation. Following the cessation of hostilities, he offered to purchase the company and its sprawling plant, a massive factory of more than 800,000 square feet. Dobson's offer seemed to be either an audacious or foolhardy move. C D Howe, the shrewd Minister of Reconstruction in Canada's government, who was brokering the deal, remarked that 'Dobson had more guts than brains.'[1]

Dubbed 'Dobson's Folly', the decision to set up a new aircraft company in a foreign country, especially in the precarious post-war economy, seemed doomed. Yet on 2 November 1945 an agreement was signed between the Canadian government and the Hawker Siddeley Group that would lead to the formation of A V Roe Canada Limited. As part of the deal, Dobson was able to acquire another Crown corporation, Turbo Research Limited, which had been involved in turbojet research and development and had produced by the war's end an experimental engine known as the 'Chinook'. Existing Turbo Research staff and equipment were transferred to an expanded facility on the Malton site, across from the main A V Roe Canada plant. Called the Gas Turbine Division, it came under the direction of P B Dillworth as Manager and Chief Engineer. The

[1] Gilbert D S Garrett, ed, 'Aircraft Development in the Commonwealth', *Hawker Siddeley Review*, 3, No 2 (June, 1950), 11.

Hawker Siddeley Group's new subsidiary was now able to design and manufacture both airframes and engines, making it one of the few aviation manufacturers to combine both operations.

The provisions of the agreement included a requirement that the new company be involved in design and development and that it be essentially a Canadian concern with a Canadian president. The first employee of the new company was Fred Smye, former Assistant General Manager of Federal Aircraft in Montreal, who took on the role of General Manager. Mr Dobson and A V Roe Canada management made great plans for the company.

A nucleus of 300 workers from the former Victory Aircraft operation continued on as the first employees of A V Roe Canada, which was more familiarly known as Avro Canada. To keep the massive plant going, the initial contracts that A V Roe Canada received were for 'forms for plastic hairbrushes and fenders for Wilson trucks, to design and test oil burners, and to make the occasional part for Cockshutt tractors.'[2] The first government contracts, likely influenced by C D Howe himself, were for modifications of the wartime Lancaster bomber and for overhaul and maintenance of RCAF and RCN (Royal Canadian Navy) aircraft.

The future role of A V Roe Canada would not be merely as a subcontractor. Smye, together with a select group of English designers, including W H Lindsay (Armstrong Siddeley Gas Turbines), W G Carter and W W Downing (Gloster Aircraft) and S D 'Stu' Davies (A V Roe), planned a number of progressive and far-reaching projects. In a series of meetings in Canada late in 1945, they proposed that the new company undertake the design of a jet engine, jet fighter and jet airliner.

A V Roe Canada assembled a very talented design team. Many key personnel, such as Stan Cyma, Jack Millie, Mario Pesando and Bryan Wood, were part of the former Victory Aircraft Company, but others came from many different sources. Canadian James A Chamberlin from Noorduyn Aircraft joined the team as Chief Aerodynamicist. There were also many English engineers. Edgar H Atkin, Chief Engineer, and James C 'Jim' Floyd, designer, came from A V Roe Limited (Manchester). John C M Frost was recruited from de Havilland (United Kingdom) and arrived later. Polish expatriate designer Waclaw Czerwinski, arriving in 1946, and

[2] Stewart, *Shutting Down the National Dream*, 50.

Avro Aircraft Limited factory site in 1956. *(Avro Aircraft Ltd)*

Robert N 'Bob' Lindley, an engineer from A V Roe Limited, added in 1949, were to later complete the exceptional group.

Their first project was a pure jet airliner, the first of its kind in the world, designed with one customer in mind – TCA (Trans-Canada Air Lines, now Air Canada). The basis for the new jet transport was originally part of a feasibility study in England undertaken by Jim Floyd, but the specifications and blueprints (along with Floyd) were then transferred to A V Roe Canada. After review of the Avro proposal, '30-seater Transport Aircraft for TCA – Issue Number Two – March 5, 1946', a letter of intent was signed between TCA and A V Roe Canada. The TCA President, H J Symington, framed the conditions carefully for a further contract. A V Roe Canada had to specify costs, performance and delivery dates after detailed specifications were provided by TCA. One of the crucial aspects of the TCA specifications that were submitted was that advanced Rolls-Royce AJ65 axial-flow engines would be utilised. Preliminary negotiations with Rolls-Royce revealed that the AJ65 was still undergoing development, leading to the redesign of the original twin-engined airliner (now known as the C102) into a four-engined version, powered by the proven RR Derwent centrifugal flow engine. The new centre-wing section would accommodate four jet engines in a semi-podded arrangement that was to allow for fitting a shorter, sturdier main undercarriage unit. The final blueprints showed a conventional straight-winged, high-tail arrangement with sleek, purposeful lines that hinted of the future. Avro Canada named it the C102 'Jetliner'.

While deliberations for the civil jet transport had been taking place, A V Roe Canada had been negotiating with the RCAF in order to meet the Air Force's operational proposal 'Air-7-Issue 2', which called for a Canadian-designed, twin-jet engined, all-weather interceptor to defend Canada's northern frontier. By October 1946 the company had signed a contract to construct one static test airframe and two prototype aircraft, to be known as XC-100.

The jet engine programme of A V Roe Canada had been one of the elements that were vital to the company's future developments. It was linked to an earlier research programme that had led to the design of the Chinook engine. Development of the Chinook continued throughout 1946 as a means to confirm design and development objectives, as well as to help set up production standards for manufacturing jet engines. A facility near Parry Sound – the Nobel Test Establishment (a former wartime explosives plant) – provided the basis of a plant for testing compressors, combustion chambers and turbines. Much of the testing equipment already designed by Turbo Research was manufactured in the A V Roe shops. By April 1947 the Engine Division had its first contract for the TR-5 Orenda 1 jet engine, with Chief Designer Winnett Boyd heading up the project. He had created a ten-stage axial compressor with six combustion chambers and a single-stage turbine. Along with this new jet engine technology, having a military jet fighter contract in hand and the prospect of a TCA order to come, A V Roe Canada looked secure for a future as a manufacturer of both military and civilian aircraft.

The XC-100, Avro Canada's other aircraft project, had entered an extremely precarious stage in its development. Chief Engineer Edgar Atkin had been instrumental in the original design, but on 14 June 1947 John C M Frost, the de Havilland (UK) designer, had been assigned as the new Project Engineer of the XC-100, which was now in the mock-up stage. Frost set out to change the design subtly, basically 'cleaning up' the fuselage. The choice of a semi-podded, engine-fuselage location allowed for ease of maintenance and eventual change or substitution of engines, although it created a large drag-producing section. Stubby straight-wing and tailplane surfaces contributed to limiting the airframe to a subsonic performance range.

While Frost was in England conferring with Avro engineers at Manchester, Chief Aerodynamicist Jim Chamberlin, with approval from Chief Engineer Edgar Atkin, moved the engines back, after wind tunnel tests had shown that the centre of lift was too far forward. He had to alter the wing spar by 'notching' it, to accommodate the engines, leading to a flexible structure where there was heavy stress. This deadly flaw was to cripple the development of the new fighter.

In 1947 the design office, amounting to more than 200 staff, issued production drawings for the first Jetliner prototype. At this point TCA advanced a series of technical issues that were to jeopardise the project. Protracted development of instrument landing systems at Canadian airports had resulted in a new set of specifications requiring increased fuel allowances, higher cruising speeds, and 'stacking' times. The most crucial element of the arrangement with TCA was that company's insistence on a fixed price per unit, which led to an impasse between the airline and A V Roe Canada. TCA approached C D Howe and the government for support in being released from the contractual arrangements of its letter of intent, which TCA received.

With more than one-third of the Jetliner prototype complete, the entire project was in peril. Howe also recognised that the loss of the C102 Jetliner programme would be disastrous not only to the company but also to the political fortunes of its primary backer. He found $1.5 million 'seed money' for the jet transport programme in order to keep the company afloat. In late 1948 Sir Roy Dobson and senior management reviewed the work to date and concluded that the jet transport had faced initial difficulties, which were to be expected when breaking new technological barriers, but that the C102 was still a viable design. Dobson gave it the go-ahead.

Although the first C102 prototype was nearing completion in the factory, TCA no longer had official interest in the Jetliner project. With both aircraft projects in trouble, Avro Canada entered a crucial year in 1949. Throughout the spring and summer, CF-EJD-X, the Avro C102 Jetliner prototype, underwent a long period of testing and preparation in order to deal with a number of minor problems. James 'Jimmy' Orrell, Chief Test Pilot for Avro (UK), was asked to take over the first flight and the preliminary trials, with A V Roe Canada's Chief Test Pilot, Don Rogers, serving as his co-pilot. Although A V Roe Canada and Orrell were understandably cautious with their 'hand-built' prototype, the prestige of being the first into the air with a jet airliner was not missed by the company. Last-minute delays in dealing with skin deformation around the engine nacelles, together with taxi trials held up by runway construction at Malton Airport, led to the first flight taking place on 10 August 1949. The Jetliner just missed its chance for immortality – the de Havilland Comet had flown in a 'test hop' just thirteen days earlier.

All of the development programmes of A V Roe Canada now seemed to come together at the same time. The Jetliner had flown, the Orenda jet engine was installed in a Lancaster test bed that was being readied for the engine's first air test (two jet engines replaced the outboard Merlin piston engines in this test aircraft), and the XC-100 was approaching its maiden flight. Powered by derated Rolls-Royce Avon RA2s, No 18101, the first CF-100 Mark I prototype, took to the air on 19 January 1950. Bill Waterton, Chief Test Pilot at Gloster, on loan to Avro Canada, was at the controls. During testing, the weakened centre section of the wing spar would lead to a series of near disasters, including a cracked spar during a flight demonstration at the Canadian National Exhibition in Toronto.

While the CF-100 programme struggled along, the Jetliner looked to be a success. Even after an emergency belly-landing on its second flight, which would be the only mishap in more than 500 hours of test flying, a series of Jetliner demonstration flights brought worldwide attention to Avro Canada. 'The flight programme went unbelievably well. Airline flight times were halved by the Jetliner on intercity flights all over the US and Canada; many US airline executives were carried on these flights and without exception were enthusiastic about the aircraft.'[3] Unfortunately, the Avro Jetliner would never see production, because C D Howe had stepped into the picture again. In the wake of Cold War tensions resulting from the Korean conflict, he considered that the fighter project should be the main priority for Avro Canada. He instructed the company to close down the Jetliner programme (irrespective of the interest shown by Howard Hughes from Trans World Airlines, National Airlines, and the United States Air Force) and divert all of the company's resources to getting the troubled CF-100 into production.

Test pilot Peter Cope, now assigned to the CF-100 experimental programme, had found, like Waterton, that the CF-100 needed an urgent wing-spar redesign. He anxiously reported, 'I cracked the secondary structure on the main spar while doing structural integrity work at 4.5g. This resulted in major rework on all main spars.'[4] As a result of an engineering 'blitz', eventually the weakened spar was corrected by a 'fix' designed by Waclaw Czerwinski, the group leader in the A V Roe Canada Stress Office (and another member of the 'Polish connection' at Avro). A pin-joint at the intersection of the wing and the engine nacelle was a simple retrofit that was incorporated in the preproduction batch of RCAF CF-100s.

After successful flight testing of the Orenda jet engine in 1950 in a Lancaster test bed, another engine conversion was undertaken and had long-term results when the Orenda was successfully tested in an F-86A Sabre in October of the same year. The North American F-86 had been chosen as the RCAF's day fighter, to be built under licence by Canadair Limited of Cartierville, Quebec, as the CL-13 Sabre. The Orenda-powered Sabre was a much improved variant, and after the prototype was flown at the North American Aviation plant in California, the Orenda series was used in the remainder of the Canadair Sabre production line. The Mark 2 Orenda powered the first flight of the CF-100 Mark 2 in 1951, and from then on the Orenda, in various versions, was also the engine used in the Avro CF-100 series.

[3] James C Floyd, 'The Avro Story', *Canadian Aviation* (June 1978), 58.
[4] Cope, 2001.

In 1951, in the midst of teething problems in the CF-100 programme, A V Roe Canada Limited acquired a new and dynamic Canadian Chief Executive Officer. Dobson, now Chairman of the Hawker Siddeley Group, appointed Crawford Gordon Jr to oversee the troubled operation as its President. Gordon was well known in Canada as a successful industrialist with a long history with C D Howe, stemming from his role as one of 'Howe's boys' in wartime. He was born in Winnipeg on 26 December 1914 and Gordon's star rose meteorically in the worlds of finance and industry. By the age of twenty-one he was the Comptroller of Finance at Canadian General Electric; at the age of twenty-eight he was the boy wonder at the Ministry of Munitions and Supply; and at the age of thirty-two Gordon was President of the English Electric Company in Canada. He brought a completely new management style to A V Roe Canada. Immediately he put his stamp on the company; loyal to a fault, stubborn and dogmatic, he was also decisive and charismatic. Gordon would bring fame to the company as well as playing a part in bringing it and himself to an ignoble end.

Reacting to the criticism levelled at A V Roe Canada by the Canadian government and indirectly by the RCAF, Gordon enacted momentous changes in the management and engineering teams in 1952. After reviewing reports from Stuart Davies, Chief Engineer at A V Roe in England and a trusted Dobson man, and from Fred Smye, General Manager, Aircraft Division, he began to act. Chief Designer Atkin was reassigned to the position of Technical Director. Later in August 1952 Atkin left to take a position at Grumman Aviation in the United States. In the restructuring of the design office, Jim Floyd became Chief Engineer early in 1952, replacing Atkin's position of Chief Designer and assuming responsibility for what Floyd termed 'the executive management of the aircraft engineering division of Avro'.[5] Frost was also removed as Project Engineer of the CF-100 to head the new Special Projects Group. Shortly after these changes, Gordon divided the operation into two separate organisations, the Aircraft Division, with Smye as General Manager, and the Gas Turbine Division, with Tom McCrae as Smye's counterpart.

As Chief Engineer, Jim Floyd took over responsibility for the main aviation programmes – the C102 Jetliner and the CF-100 fighter. Production and continued development of new versions of

[5] Floyd, 'The Avro Story', 110-11.

the CF-100 all-weather fighter became the main priority of the company, with the C102 Jetliner relegated to the role of a camera platform (which continued until 1956 when the prototype was scrapped). Floyd and many others at Avro were devastated by the loss of the Jetliner. The C102 was regarded not only as the proving ground for jet operations in North America but also as the learning tool for the engineering and design staff who would later create the Arrow. To this day, he considers that 'the abandonment of the Jetliner project was an even greater tragedy for Canada than the cancellation of the Arrow.'[6]

In order to effectively deal with the increased demands for testing, together with Flight Test Engineering, a Flight Operations Office was set up, providing for both production and developmental test flying. Janusz Zurakowski would become one of the developmental test pilots, joining his friend Peter Cope and, ironically, eventually taking over the role that Bill Waterton had established, that of Chief Developmental Test Pilot.

Horizons unlimited

Coming to Canada meant a great challenge for Zurakowski and his family. He also recognised it as a great opportunity. Writing for the Avro house magazine soon after his arrival, in an article he entitled 'Horizons Unlimited', he said: 'There is obviously a great future for Canadian aviation. (As a matter of fact, that is one of the reasons I came to Canada and to Avro Canada particularly.) This country is now at the beginning of tremendous developments in the field. We have all the basic requirements for an aircraft industry – hydroelectric power, such raw materials as aluminium, and we are close to the US Development, tooling and mass production methods are on hand. Provided Canada plans on producing for world markets, there are splendid sales opportunities for our aviation products. The success of the industry, however, basically depends on the intense enthusiasm Canadians have for flying. Of that enthusiasm, undoubtedly, the horizon is unlimited.'[7]

Mike Cooper-Slipper, an A V Roe Canada test pilot who had already worked on the CF-100 and the Jetliner, wrote recently that Zurakowski's arrival was a much-anticipated event at Avro. 'I was flying back to Canada on the same plane as Jan. I was astonished

[6] Floyd, 2001.
[7] Jan Zurakowski, 'Horizons Unlimited', *Jet Age* (Summer 1952), 11.

that he had a greeting party when he landed at the airport. Everyone in the industry knew about him but as soon as he arrived, it seemed that he and his family were swept up by members of the Polish community. I don't think I saw him much in the first weeks.'[8] A letter to the Polish Combatants' Association had resulted in a small delegation being dispatched by Jan Falkowski, a wartime pilot. The group had even arranged an apartment for the family.

The Zurakowski family's trip was a memorable experience for everyone. The young boys (George was three years old and Mark only nine months old) had handled the long flight on a Boeing Stratocruiser well. Anna recalled that their first stop was Shannon, Ireland, then calling at Reykjavik, Iceland, before reaching Gander, Newfoundland. At Dorval, Quebec, they transferred to a smaller plane for the final leg of the journey. Zura remembered his arrival differently, and his quick start in the company was what stuck in his memory. 'On 21 April 1952 I landed in Canada and the next day I started as experimental pilot for A V Roe at Malton.'[9] That certainly matched the way J R 'Roy' Combley, an Avro Canada flight engineer, remembered that time. 'Zura's reputation certainly preceded him. My first contact with Zura was when I got to drive him to work. The company (Avro) had kept him so busy on his arrival that he hadn't had time to buy a car!'[10] Later, Peter Cope became his chauffeur before Zurakowski obtained his own vehicle.

A V Roe Canada featured its famous new test pilot in a press conference two days after his arrival. Never really comfortable with the media's preconceptions of the dashing test pilot, Zura took pains to explain that his fame had come primarily from his ability to perform aerobatics. The reporters were provided with a detailed explanation of his Zurabatic cartwheel, which he described as a difficult manoeuvre that he had worked out in advance on a slide-rule. Although there was some strain on the airframe, the cartwheel was not really dangerous, Zurakowski said. 'The danger is that the plane's parts won't be able to stand the unconventional stresses and strains caused by the unusual manoeuvre.'[11] He jokingly added, 'If I

[8] Mike Cooper-Slipper, conversation with the author, 2001.
[9] Stewart, *Shutting Down the National Dream*, 226.
[10] F R Combley, conversation with the author, 2002.
[11] Derm Dunwoody, 'Inventor of Zurobatic (sic) Cartwheel joins Avro as Test Pilot', *Toronto Telegram*, 24 April 1952.

said it wasn't dangerous, they'd probably cut my pay ... but (he'd) be happy to demonstrate his cartwheel to Canadians.'[12] The press conference ended with Zurakowski analysing the latest developments in high-performance jet fighters, including the Avro Canada CF-100.

CF-100 Canuck

Avro Aircraft Limited's main production in the 1950s was based on the CF-100 Canuck, the first military jet aircraft wholly designed and built in Canada. It was destined to be the only Avro Canada aircraft to go into full production and to enter active service. The official name, Canuck, chosen by the RCAF, was considered inappropriate at the time for a fighter, as the editor of *Canadian Aviation* noted in 1951. Unofficially pilots called it the 'Clunk' and the 'Lead Sled', together with other less tasteful names. Pilot Officer Garth Turner laughed in recalling that everyone in the RCAF called it 'the Clunk, because it was the sound of the undercarriage coming up and banging into place.'[13]

The CF-100 Canuck became operational in April 1953 and served for ten years as an all-weather long-range interceptor for the RCAF It was equipped with two Orenda jet engines designed and built by Avro Canada; the first two examples, the Mark I prototypes, used Rolls-Royce Avon 56 engines. The preproduction series Mark 2, fitted with the Avro Orenda 2, were mainly assigned to operational training units and many examples were equipped with dual controls. The CF-100 Mark 3 was a more refined variant with the higher-powered Orenda 8 and armed with eight .50 calibre machine guns in a ventral pack. This version was the first series of production aircraft assigned to frontline fighter squadrons.

The definitive CF-100 Mark 4 emerged with up-rated Orenda 9 engines and a powerful radar scanner matched to a Hughes MG-2 fire control system mounted in a longer, blunt but rounded nose. Zurakowski undertook the first flight of the Mark 4 prototype on 11 October 1952. The first Mark 4 was No 18112, a rebuilt Mark 2 airframe that served as the workhorse for the Development Section for years. Both the CF-100 Mark 4 and the later Mark 5 versions were deployed to RCAF NORAD and NATO squadrons.

The CF-100 Mark 5 was an evolution of the Avro HAV (High Altitude Version) research programme carried out in 1953-1954. Its

[12] Ibid.
[13] Garth Turner, conversation with the author, 2001.

principal differences included extensions to the outer wings and tailplanes and reliance on an all-rocket armament. Additional changes were more subtle, with more than 500lb removed in the form of eliminating the machine-gun armament and a host of redundant equipment. Zurakowski conducted the first test of the prototype Mark 5, No 18516 (a modified Mark 4), on 12 October 1955. The main improvement in performance was in the operational ceiling – the Mark 5 was able to operate up to 53,000 feet.

While the CF-100 was not as fast as contemporary fighters, Zura would fly the CF-100 through the sound barrier in a dive, one of the first straight-winged jet aircraft to accomplish this feat. The CF-100's good climb rate, excellent radar, twin-engined reliability and all-weather capability made it suitable for defence in the extreme conditions of the Canadian north, and later in NATO service in Europe. Eventually, 692 CF-100 Canucks were built, with fifty-three sold to Belgium. After a long service career, which included a final change in role during the 1970s and 1980s to that of an ECM (Electronic Counter Measures) aircraft, the Canuck was ultimately retired in 1981 by the CAF (the RCAF was formally incorporated into the single Canadian Armed Forces [CAF] in February 1968).

The Avro Canada test pilots

The testing of the Avro CF-100 and the C102 Jetliner was undertaken by the Flight Operations Department headed by Chief Test Pilot Don Rogers and the Flight Test Engineering Department of Avro Aircraft Limited directed by Mario Pesando. Zurakowski regarded Pesando as 'a very experienced engineer, with a clear, practical approach to any problem.'[14] Although his main responsibility was engineering, Pesando maintained a close working relationship with the test pilots. He recalled his association with Zurakowski with fondness. 'Janusz Zurakowski is a true gentleman and was above company politics. We worked as a team; quite the opposite to Bill Waterton who was a prima donna and whom I hold responsible for many of the delays and improvements that should have been accomplished during the fifteen months that he was at Avro Canada. Needless, we didn't get along and he misled the company about the max speed of the CF-100... Unlike the relationship between flight test and engineering at Gloster, I had a

[14] Zurakowski, 'Test Flying the Arrow', 101.

CF-100 in a dive. *(Russell Adams via John F Painter)*

excellent rapport with my staff (we had spent several years on the design of the Jetliner and the Canuck) so we were able to carry out the necessary improvements whether or not they came from engineering.'[15]

Pesando played a crucial role as the Chief Flight Test Engineer, but he had the qualifications to match. He modestly described his two

[15] Mario Pesando, conversation with the author, 2001.

and half years as Flight Test Liaison Engineer at Victory Aircraft on the Lancaster, 'where I was able to solve a number of problems without any help (there was no true aircraft designer in the whole plant). The credit for turning out about 400 Lancasters belongs to the tool engineers, contracting and energetic shop personnel. When the war ended, I was asked to stay and for about three years I was an aerodynamicist working for Jim Chamberlin. I then was sent to A V Roe in England for several months for flight test training and, upon return, I set up and ran Flight Test for about seven years.'[16] Flight Test Engineering eventually came under the direct control of Design Engineering, under Floyd. 'The engineers in Experimental Flight Test, who occupied a bullpen area with rows of desks adjacent to the executive offices, were divided into two groups, Aerodynamics and Equipment. The Aerodynamics group did all flight tests related to performance, and the Equipment group did all others.'[17]

Zurakowski flying in a Douglas DC-3 Dakota to a meeting in Ottawa about the Avro Arrow. *(Zurakowski collection)*

[16] Ibid.
[17] Robert D Cockfield, conversation with the author, 2002.

In Flight Operations, Zura became part of a unique band of test pilots led by Don Rogers. Rogers eventually directed all the flight test programmes of the C102 Jetliner, CF-100 Canuck and later CF-105 Arrow. Flight Operations was not directly connected to the Engineering Department; it maintained an independent organisation and reported directly to top management. The test pilots all had executive offices in the main building. Two separate flight test divisions, production and development (experimental), were operated under Rogers's direction.

In Rogers the test pilots had not only an exceptional leader but also an experienced pilot. He had joined National Steel Car as a test pilot and stayed on at Victory Aircraft as the Chief Development Pilot of the Avro Lancaster X bomber, Lancaster XPP transport (similar to the Avro Lancastrian) and Lancaster-Orenda test bed for Orenda Engines. He logged thousands of hours in ferry missions and flight testing during the war years. After joining the new A V Roe Canada, Rogers became its Chief Test Pilot in 1946. He assumed the leadership of the Jetliner flight-test programme from Jimmy Orrell, the Avro (UK) Chief Test Pilot. After sixteen flights Orrell returned to England and Rogers continued the Jetliner test programme with company test pilot Thomas Paul 'Mike' Cooper-Slipper as his second-in-command. Rogers also was the main pilot in the CF-100 programme that followed.

Cooper-Slipper DFC was a decorated RAF wartime pilot who had become famous at the height of the Battle of Britain, while flying Hurricane fighters in 605 Squadron, for 'ramming' a Dornier bomber and surviving. His final victory total of nine aircraft destroyed ranked him near the top of the Battle of Britain aces. In 1941 he had flown out one of the last three Hurricanes as Singapore was overrun by the Japanese. Over Burma, Cooper-Slipper ran out of fuel and bailed out in a jungle region. Weeks later he emerged from the jungle, sick with malaria but miraculously still alive. During the war years he had also been a test pilot in England. Cooper-Slipper had started at A V Roe Canada in 1947, assigned to the Chinook engine project where his first job was 'filing jet blades for the Chinook at $2.50 an hour'.[18]

Taken on as a test pilot, Cooper-Slipper began flying overhauled Mitchell trainers and Lancaster bombers before being assigned to the

[18] Jason Eldridge, conversation with the author, 2001.

Avro Canada test pilots. Left to right: Peter Cope, Chris Pike, Janusz Zurakowski,
Mike Cooper-Slipper, Don Rogers, Stan Haswell and Glen Hynes.
(Zurakowski collection)

Jetliner and CF-100 programmes. Later he became Orenda Engines'
Chief Test Pilot, flying the Lancaster-Orenda test bed, the Sabre and
CF-100 before becoming the Pilot-in-Command on the B-47 test bed
fitted with the Orenda Iroquois engine. In the CF-100 programme,
Cooper-Slipper worked mainly in developmental testing. As Orenda
Engines' Chief Test Pilot, Mike Cooper-Slipper undertook the
engine development programme of the Canadair Sabre series, right
up to the Mark 6, which included 'dozens of shut-downs and
relights, which was quite exciting in a single-engine aeroplane'.[19]
The Orenda proved to be the right engine for the Sabre and the Mark
6 was considered the 'best' of the Sabres built. By the mid-1950s,
when the Canadair Sabre Mark 6 was flown by RCAF squadrons
both in Canada and in NATO, it was 'acknowledged as the top
fighter in Europe'.[20] The Orenda test pilot staff also included Len
Hobbs, another former wartime flier with RAF Bomber Command
and Transport Command experience, who in post-war years had
worked for Vickers-Armstrong as a test pilot. At Avro Orenda,
Hobbs served as a co-pilot on the B-47-Iroquois test bed.

[19] Cooper-Slipper, 2001.
[20] Ibid.

The first tests of the CF-100 had been undertaken by Gloster's Chief Test Pilot, Squadron Leader Bill Waterton, who was on loan to A V Roe Canada from December 1949 to February 1951. Working closely with the Flight Test office and the Chief Engineer of the CF-100, John Frost, Waterton brought the first CF-100, No 18101, to flight-ready status. After the first test flight, Waterton continued on with Avro Canada, helping sort out teething problems with the airframe and related systems of the CF-100.

Unlike other test pilots at Avro Canada, such as Zurakowski, who were quiet and reserved, Waterton was a boisterous and controversial figure. He looked and acted the part of the daring test pilot with a flamboyant handlebar moustache and a gregarious and outgoing personality to match. He certainly made an impression on everyone who met him. Waterton exasperated some people at the company, but he had firm supporters in other quarters. Don Rogers considered him a skilled pilot and valued his contributions to the CF-100 development, while Peter Cope dismissed him as 'just a blowhard showman pilot'.[21] Zura did recall, 'When the Gloster flight personnel heard that Waterton was assigned by Sir Roy Dobson to go to Canada to perform the initial flight tests on the CF-100 and could be gone for a year, the entire Gloster's flight test group cheered.'[22] Regardless of the emotions stirred by Waterton, he was acknowledged as one of the most experienced test pilots around, and his Gloster work had demonstrated a flair for showmanship.

After the initial test flight, Waterton enthusiastically took over the role of 'chief salesman' of the CF-100. He extensively demonstrated the new jet fighter to the RCAF and another potential customer, the US Early flights showed the great potential of the CF-100 Mark I (the designation eventually borne by both flying prototypes, Nos 18101 and 18102), but also showed that the flaw in the spar was a serious problem. During one flight at the air display of the Canadian National Exhibition in Toronto, Waterton heard a 'violent crack: a sharp thunderclap of sound clearly audible above the engine and wind noise'.[23] Gingerly putting the CF-100 prototype on the ground, the pilot and the technicians discovered that the crack had been a rupture of the skin at the junction of the wing and centre section.

[21] Cope, 2001.
[22] Pesando, 2001.
[23] Waterton, *The Quick and the Dead*, 177.

On the eighth flight of the first prototype, scheduled for a cross-country trip to Ottawa and back, Waterton flew with Frost in the second seat. To the test pilot, this was a revelation: he found that the young designer was 'very much the keen English public-schoolboy type. Here was another delightful contrast to England, where I was never able to find a designer with spare time enough to fly in his own creation.'[24] The troubles with the CF-100, however, were to weigh heavily on Frost; the reason for his coming on board was to see for himself the extent of the flexing on the wing. Despite their efforts, Frost and Waterton were not able to weather the storms in the Engineering and Flight Test offices. Although he had wanted to stay on with the experimental programme, Waterton was informed that his time with A V Roe Canada was at an end. When Flight Lieutenant Warren, an RCAF pilot seconded to the company in 1951, was appointed as the new Chief Test Pilot for the CF-100 programme, Waterton returned to Gloster Aircraft.

Bruce Warren was an acclaimed wartime pilot and graduate of the 1949 Empire Test Pilots School. His term was intended to be two years. However, soon after his appointment, Warren and his observer, Robert Ostrander, died in a crash on 5 April 1951, while flying the second prototype CF-100 Mark I The aircraft had been carrying out a cruise-climb fuel-consumption test with long-range ferry tanks at high altitude when the accident occurred. The probable cause was a faulty oxygen system in Warren's helmet, that may have incapacitated him. The crash led to the cancellation of the CF-100 debut that year at the SBAC Air Display in Farnborough, England, and it was not to make its Farnborough appearance until Zurakowski demonstrated the aircraft there in 1955. After Warren's death, Rogers and Cooper-Slipper continued with most of the experimental CF-100 test flying until British test pilot Peter Cope, in May 1951, and, later, Zurakowski joined the team.

Cope had been a war veteran, serving with the RAF but also being attached to the United States Army Air Corps as well as liaising with the Egyptian and Portuguese Air Forces. He had first met Zurakowski at the Empire Test Pilots School in 1945. After completing the test pilots' course (in two separate years), he went to Armstrong Whitworth to fly Avro Lincolns and Gloster Meteors. With his extensive background in jet fighters, Cope was recruited to test the CF-100 in

Canada. After Warren's death, Cope took over the experimental programme on the fighter but found that the prototypes were woefully inadequate. He was despondent after his initial experience with the CF-100. 'I was extremely disappointed in both the performance and handling, which in no way compared to the Meteor Mark 8.'[25] More importantly, he considered the aircraft 'dangerous'.

'I had a major discrepancy write-up on the airplane that brought out some nineteen points which would not be acceptable for an operational airplane. As this report was read by the RCAF before our top management had reviewed it, it created quite an uproar, resulting in a high-level meeting where Avro's chief designer in England came over. He backed me up on eighteen of the nineteen points I had made, which made many of the Avro engineers unhappy.'[26]

Experimental testing of the CF-100 and, later, the CF-105 was carried out by Cope, Zurakowski and Spud Potocki. Wladyslaw O Potocki was another member of the 'Polish connection' at Avro Canada, and whose wartime career had mirrored that of Zurakowski. He had fled occupied Poland and made his way to England to join the RAF in 1942 as a Sergeant Pilot for 306 Squadron, where he had met Zurakowski. An excellent pilot, he is often listed as an ace although his combat record is officially recorded at 4.75 kills. He began test flying with an aircraft development unit, the Intensive Flying Development Flight at RAF High Point, which evaluated Spitfire variants. While a Flight Lieutenant (Captain), Potocki gained fame as one of the two Polish test pilots who evaluated the 'clipped' Spitfires between November 1942 and February 1943. These Spitfire Mark XIIs had the long curved wing tips modified into shorter-span wings that improved low-altitude speed and handling. The modification came at a crucial time and helped the Spitfires to fight against new potent enemy fighters. Reaching the rank of Squadron Leader (Major), Potocki became the Commanding Officer of 315 Squadron from April 1945 until February 1946. He was awarded the Distinguished Flying Cross, the Victory Medal and the Cross of Valour with three bars. After the war Potocki also continued as a test pilot, graduating in 1951 from the tenth course at the British Empire Test Pilots School in Boscombe Down. He was a skilled experimental test pilot at RAE Farnborough and had joined

[25] Cope, 2001.
[26] Ibid.

Zura's old friend Zbigniew Olenski in the A V Roe (UK) Flight Test Department to fly the Avro Vulcan.

'While an RAE test pilot flying the Avro Vulcan prototype (designed by Stuart Davies, who had been project manager on Sydney Camm's Hurricane fighter ... very important fellow to the Avro story), Spud had saved the aircraft when an airborne emergency occurred. Zura said Spud's coolness and quick reactions saved the aircraft, and perhaps as a result, the Vulcan programme... Zura also told me that he helped raise the pay of test pilots by insisting on better wages than RAF test pilots, (which he was earning) before coming to Avro Canada ... thereby doing that class of pilots a favour, since they were earning, if I recall correctly, less than a TCA DC-3 pilot up to that time.'[27] Potocki was considered a top prospect for the Avro Canada Flight Test Department, but it took a lot of persuasion by the Personnel Department for him to leave a fairly comfortable life in England to migrate to Canada. He was offered a suitable salary, but undoubtedly one of the enticements was an opportunity to be reunited with Zura. When Zurakowski retired from active test flying, Potocki would go on to become his replacement in the Avro Arrow programme.

Part of the Avro CF-100 flight test programme was based on production test flying with Stanley M Haswell and Christopher Pike, who had joined in 1952. Both pilots were wartime flyers, with Pike (the 'youngster' in the group) being an experienced former RCAF and RAF 'fighter jock'. He assumed the position of Chief Production Pilot. Haswell's prior time was mainly in multi-engine transports, and before he was hired as a test pilot with Avro Canada he flew as a flight observer in the Flight Test Engineering Department. Haswell's first encounter with Zurakowski in November 1952 was a harrowing experience because their flight ended with an engine flame-out and a landing back at base with one engine. 'I was his flight test observer, taking down readings, telling him what was going on from the back seat.'[28] Haswell still fondly recalls the flight in the Avro CF-100 Mark 2 No 18106 with Zurakowski: 'I got five dollars an hour for the privilege.'[29]

Glen Lynes joined the production test pilots group later in 1953.

[27] Randall Whitcomb, conversation with the author, 2001.
[28] Stan Haswell, 'Test Flying the CF-100', *CAHS Journal* (Fall 1983), 87.
[29] Stanley M Haswell, conversation with the author, 2001.

Lynes was a former RAF test pilot who had carried out development flying on the Vampire and participated in the flight testing of the Meteor F 8 at Boscombe Down. After Lynes died while testing a CF-100, other test pilots took up the production test flying responsibilities until his replacement, Lorne Ursel, came to Avro in 1957. Ursel had been an RCAF CF-100 pilot who had done a lot of acceptance flying with Avro Canada. The production test pilots group was ultimately responsible for all acceptance and production test flying, ending up flying nearly all of the CF-100s. Production flying could sometimes involve experimental work when equipment was installed in production-line aircraft before the experimental group had a chance to approve it. Haswell recalled, 'An example of that was the Honeywell auto-pilot, which gave us some hairy rides in some of the initial testing, but it proved that the procedure could be done successfully with a good engineering team.'[30]

Later in 1953 Flight Lieutenant Jack Woodman joined the flight test team as the acceptance pilot in the RCAF detachment at the Avro plant, first commanded by Squadron Leader Ken Owen. Woodman was a trained test pilot who had graduated in 1952 from the Empire Test Pilots School, and for two years was attached to the Avro Flight Test Office. He left in 1956 for a specialised course on supersonic fighters at Elgin Air Force Base, where he was part of the United States Air Force Phase VII team evaluating the Convair F-102 Delta Dagger. In 1957 he became the Chief Test Pilot at the RCAF's Central Experimental and Proving Establishment and returned to Avro Aircraft Limited as the RCAF Project Pilot on the CF-105 Arrow. Two other RCAF pilots were part of the same unit, Flight Lieutenant Reg Kersey and Flight Lieutenant N 'Norm' Ronaasen. In 1978 Woodman reflected on his time at Avro: 'Flying with Don Rogers and the Avro team was an honour for me, and I thoroughly enjoyed the four years I spent at Avro. I mentioned Zurakowski being the best test pilot I have ever known; the rest of the team, and all the Avro troops, were of the same calibre.'[31]

Zurakowski was the ideal test pilot for the experimental phase; he had come to Avro Canada with a wealth of experience – more than 2,500 hours on fifty-four types. 'These years of experimental

[30] Haswell, 'Test Flying the CF-100', 87.
[31] Jack Woodman, 'Flying the Avro Arrow', Canadian Aeronautics and Space Institute Symposium, Winnipeg, 16 May 1978.

testing of aircraft taught Zurakowski not to accept much at its face value, to doubt nearly everything until proven, and to respect evidence and the importance of collecting flight test information by special instrumentation.'[32]

In 1952, when asked to describe his experiences as a test pilot for the house organ *Jet Age*, Zurakowski reflected on his test flying. 'Most pilots, particularly experimental pilots, are keen on flying because it provides an ever-new challenge, ever-new flight problems. Test pilots are particularly fortunate because they are helping in the development of new aircraft and they are the first to see how, flight by flight, they are progressing.'[33] The testing of any new aircraft design, whether military or commercial, is undertaken by test pilots whose flying includes experimental or developmental tests, and test pilots also engage in production or acceptance work.

The Zurakowski touch

Commentators continued to marvel that Zurakowski was a unique individual who didn't fit public preconceptions of what a test pilot should be. The media described him as 'publicity-shy and very reticent. He was small and balding and it was said that he looked like anything but a test pilot.'[34] A V Roe Canada's publicist, John Grace, had once described him as 'a small, quiet man with an alert face and strong, capable hands. He has the manner of a fine Alpine guide.'[35] His other qualities included 'the sharp and agile brain of a test pilot, and a sense of humour'.[36] The public perception of a test pilot could sometimes have amusing consequences. When Zurakowski began to receive some notice in the press, word got back to Avro that a barber was talking about his 'inside knowledge' of the company's famed test pilot. Peter Cope, ever a joker, realised immediately that Zura would not be frequenting a barbershop on a regular basis, but he decided to have some fun with the barber. When he casually inquired about Zurakowski, he was told that the man was tall and had a head of curly hair. The story was brought

[32] Alice Gibson Sutherland, *Canada's Aviation Pioneers* (Toronto: McGraw-Hill Ryerson, 1978), 249.

[33] Zurakowski, 'Horizons Unlimited', 11.

[34] Sutherland, *Canada's Aviation Pioneers,* 249.

[35] 'I shot an Arrow...', *Hawker Siddeley Review* (June 1958), 36.

[36] Sutherland, *Canada's Aviation Pioneers,* 249.

back to the company, where Zura had a chuckle. 'Management, however, wasn't impressed and sent security to have the man stop spreading rumours.'

Other compatriots commented that Zurakowski was a special kind of test pilot who knew how to use a slide rule and mathematical calculations for development purposes. His careful appraisal of aerodynamics led to an unusual ability to diagnose problems. When one CF-100 continually dropped a wing in stall tests, and none of the other test pilots including Don Rogers could find the reason for the puzzling flight characteristics, Zura joined Rogers and Chris Pike, the head of production flying, as they studied the wing. He looked at the wing for a while, then produced a straight-edge metal ruler. He placed the ruler on the leading edge of the starboard wing and pointed out a dip in the surface. When the imperfection was filled, the wing reacted normally. The other pilots were simply amazed. Pike recalled: 'That's only one example of his intense understanding of problems... I'd think to myself, 'Why didn't I think of that? Why didn't one of the other pilots think of that?' Here's a guy that did think of it.'[37]

Engineer-pilot Zurakowski often worked out solutions on his slide rule.
(Zurakowski collection)

[37] Sean Rossiter, *The Chosen Ones* (Vancouver: Douglas & McIntyre, 2002), 118.

Britain's leading test pilot of the 1950s, Neville Duke, described Zurakowski in this way in *Test Pilot*: 'Zura is one of the finest examples of test pilot-technician; he often calculates or reduces his own test results, sometimes causing the boffins a headache.'[38] Robert D Cockfield from the Avro Flight Test Engineering Department assessed Zura from a different perspective: 'His ideas were intuitive and empirical and not always based on sound engineering principles... As spectacular an aerobatic pilot as Zurakowski was, I don't think he was as capable an engineer as he was reputed to be. He is pictured as calculating with his slide rule the flight path to reach sonic speed in the CF-100, but the analysis could not have been made without help from the Aerodynamics Department. His ideas for adding fairings to streamline the junction between the nacelles and the wings of the CF-100 were somewhat naive.'[39] However, when asked for his comments, Duke simply called Zurakowski 'the best test pilot in the world'.[40]

Roy Combley logged a lot of flight time with Zurakowski and recalled, 'I flew with Zura on approximately fifty flights and during my 315 hours in the back seat of CF-100s as a test observer at Malton and later as a radar operator on Project K armament testing at Cold Lake, Alberta, I have never flown with a smoother pilot. Zura was very quiet during test flights, concentrating on the job in hand, with no small talk. During a production check, one of the requirements was to check the manual reversion mode of the flight controls. When the power controls were re-engaged, the ailerons were locked. Zura landed with no problem, although I was somewhat apprehensive of what would have happened if we had encountered a wing drop close to the ground.'[41]

The one aspect of the flight that the ground crew always watched for was the typical Zurakowski 'beat-up' of the field. If he flew by upside down, it was a sure indicator that some parts had been loose in the cockpit and someone would hear about it. It was rumoured that he would go inverted and let small FOD (foreign object debris) fall on to the canopy. The parts were known to jam controls, and pilots were especially cautious about leaving anything loose in the

[38] Neville Duke, *Test Pilot* (London: Grub Street, 1997), 164.
[39] Cockfield, 2002.
[40] Neville Duke, conversation with the author, 2002.
[41] Combley, 2002.

cockpit. He confessed later that he had a far simpler method; he 'merely created some negative G in a shallow dive and snagged objects in the air as they floated upward.' (This method of checking on the mechanics' work in wartime France had been common practice by Polish fighter pilots.)

The Zurakowski 'walk-around' inspection sometimes involved the uncanny. Avro's Chief Production Test Pilot, Chris Pike, related the story that one check Zura performed turned up a threaded hole in the recesses of the landing gear area. 'Not a rivet hole, but a machined receptacle for a set-screw that was structurally important. 'I'll bet you,' Pike said recently, 'the rest of us wouldn't have found it.'[42] 'After each flight, Zura would list the 'snags' for the benefit of the ground crew and inspectors and always end up with 'Otherwise Perfect'.'[43] Flight Test Engineer Fred Matthews remembered, 'More often the only entry on a Zura snag sheet were the cryptic initials 'NNS', meaning 'no new snags' – a gentle hint to the ground crew to fix any outstanding old ones.'[44]

Robert Cockfield, one of Avro Aircraft's Flight Test Engineers, explained the close relationship of flight test engineering and the test pilots. 'The role of the Flight Test Engineer was to plan the test flights, usually to satisfy a specific request from the Design Department. That involved selecting the type of instrumentation and writing the test procedure. Many of our tests were simple enough that the instruments could be read by an engineer sitting in the back seat rather than by installing a strip recorder. The test plan was always reviewed and approved by the pilot assigned to the test. As a new engineer, I was just learning such routines as converting the requested flight data (often expressed in Mach number) to IAS (Indicated Air Speed) at various altitudes. Zurakowski once corrected my faulty calculations and said, 'If you want me to fly at a constant Mach number, then just say so.'[45] The precision with which Zurakowski flew was the mark of a true professional.

Zurakowski tested his experimental aircraft to their limits, often in his own way. The unique approach he utilised was that of 'a rare combination of skilled engineer, painstaking test pilot and

[42] Rossiter, *The Chosen Ones*, 117.
[43] Combley, 2002.
[44] Fred Matthews, conversation with the author, 2002.
[45] Cockfield, 2002.

unparalleled display pilot'.[46] In the RAF *Flying Review*, Geoffrey Norris noted how, on occasions, he would find himself ahead of the company programme. 'It was not long after he had left Gloster to join Avro Canada that he was seen performing, of all unlikely manoeuvres, tail-slides in the CF-100. He pointed the nose up, cut the power, let the aircraft come to a standstill and then slide backwards for a short way before putting the nose down to fly in the right direction once again. He said nothing about this when he landed, and the Avro team were left wondering. Then, a short time later, the Research Department decided that a few tail-slides would clear up a technical point. Zura listened impassively and then pronounced solemnly: 'Tail-slide in this aircraft no good. Can't do.' 'But,' explained one of the exasperated research team, 'we know it can be done. We saw you doing tail-slides only the other week!' 'Aha!' Zura explained politely, 'That was for me. For you, tail-slides no good.'[47] Zurakowski disputed this incident strongly with the assertion that he knew that tail-slides were not dangerous, but that attempting one in the CF-100 required an experienced and competent pilot.

At one point the CF-100 test programme was experiencing a little trouble with the fuel-flow measurements.

The engineers were under pressure from Zura to investigate the readings from the electronic counting circuits which were apparently faulty. The engineers did not have too much success although they did everything they could to justify their readings. Still the gauges did not agree with the actual amount of fuel left in the aircraft. All this time, Zura had been quietly checking the pilot's fuel gauges with the weight of fuel left after each flight. Then one day, after landing, he sauntered over to the engineers, his helmet still under his arm. 'You want to know how much it weighs?' he asked them. The engineers had had no luck with their calculations. They waited for Zura's pronouncement. 'It weighs 30,400 pounds,' he said and then walked off. As Zura made this pronouncement the weights engineer was just finishing adding up the figures obtained through weighing the aircraft.'[48]

Don Rogers recalled, 'I bent over the weights engineer's board as

---

[46] Derek N James, *Gloster Aircraft since 1917* (London: Putnam Aeronautical Books, 1971), 425.

[47] Norris, 'Impossible', 42.

[48] Ibid.

he was adding up the figures; 30,400 pounds it was, exactly. Jan walked away and we were left just a little dazed. The weights engineer turned to me and said, 'If that isn't designed to give a man a swelled head, I don't know what is.' But it never did, as nothing ever would. Only those who have worked with him in the engineering sphere can really understand.[49]

A story that Zurakowski relates about the test pilots' concerns begins with a bit of a prank. When something had gone wrong, he had indicated to his boss, Don Rogers, that he intended to resign from experimental flying. He had a secretary make up a resignation letter and left it on Rogers' desk. 'Rogers knew Zura wasn't serious about quitting, so he just turned the letter over and went on with his paperwork. Zura had another letter prepared, and again Rogers just turned it over (Zura watched all this through a window between Rogers's office and the outer office). Zura had a third letter prepared, this one with the same letter typed on both sides of the page. He said the look on Rogers's face when turning it over to find the same letter on the other side was priceless!'[50]

Supersonic

Zurakowski's skills and instincts were honed not only by experience at Boscombe Down and Gloster – he had also acquired an innate ability to pinpoint problem areas in an aircraft. This characteristic meant that he was not always popular with the design engineers. Zura wanted to work closely with the engineers in the Design Office in the CF-100 programme as part of a team effort, but that was not to be. 'We, in the Flight Test Section, hoped that we would be part of the team and participate in the solution of problems which we would have to face sooner or later.

'There was a rumour that the directional stability of our new aircraft was poor. At this time, a number of American fighters disintegrated in the air, and some designs were quickly modified to provide a bigger fin area. We asked the Design Office for aerodynamic reports. We met with refusal because there could be a wrong interpretation of the reports by the pilots.'[51]

[49] 'Zurakowski's Retirement', *The Aeroplane* (10 October 1958), 548.
[50] Tim McShane, 'In the Loop', e-mail correspondence to R. C. Hangar, 16 February 2000.
[51] Stewart, *Shutting Down the National Dream*, 227.

Problems came to a head when Zurakowski inquired about the relatively low limiting speed of the CF-100; it had a maximum design speed of 0.85 Mach, or about eighty-five per cent of the speed of sound, but its level speed at high altitude was slightly faster. 'When Zura once asked Jim Chamberlin what would happen if a pilot accidentally exceeded this speed, he was told that wind tunnel tests indicated that the aircraft could be uncontrollable, and that, besides, the pilot's notes clearly showed Mach 0.85 to be the limiting speed.'[52] That answer didn't resolve Zura's questions. 'For me, this answer was not satisfactory. The CF-100 was an all-weather and night interceptor, and if the pilot was not careful, he could be past aircraft limitations in no time. I considered it my duty to investigate behaviour of the aircraft at higher speeds and, if dangers were discovered, to recommend some action. With instrumented aircraft, I ran a series of dives at high altitude, checking recorded results between flights.'[53]

Throughout early December 1952, Zurakowski carried out a number of preliminary flights in No 18112, the CF-100 Mark 4 prototype, testing the aircraft's limits. His first dive to supersonic speeds had indicated Mach 1 on the Machmeter but the combination of a lack of observers or of a specially calibrated instrument meant that the flight was not officially recognised. On 16 December an accompanying Canadair Sabre with a correctly calibrated Machmeter failed to keep station in a dive, leaving Zura with another unofficial record. He told Pesando that the next flight would be successful.

Pesando recently recalled the supersonic flight on 18 December 1952.

> When Janusz went supersonic for the benefit of engineering – I suspect that he did so several times, when he would fly to some quiet area and perform this feat without telling anyone. (I know that he did the spin trials before we were able to hold up our end.) Coming back to the 'breaking of the sound barrier' incident, Jan and I conspired to pull this off. The scenario was like this. Jim Floyd had notified his senior staff who were involved with the CF-100, and me, to meet in his office at a given time to discuss the possibility that the CF-100

---

[52] Ibid, 228.
[53] Ibid.

was capable of supersonic flight (with the aid of gravity) with no loss of control and recovery by the pilot.

Engineering flatly stated that this was impossible as the aircraft would become uncontrollable, leading to a catastrophe! Jim Floyd's office was equipped with a radio link to the aircraft and, at my cue, Jan had already positioned himself over the plant at 45,000 feet. He rolled the aircraft to an inverted position and thus was able to select the proper dive angle without losing much altitude, as we wanted the aircraft to do its thing and be fully recovered above 25,000 feet so that it would not be exposed to high G loads. You know the rest of the story.[54]

Seconds later, a thunderclap rattled windows in Malton. Zura had done it. He casually reported, 'Finally, I reached 1.08 Mach Number indicated in a dive at full power. A sonic boom on the ground confirmed surpassing the speed of sound. Behaviour of the aircraft was satisfactory. The Flight Test Department, company management, and the Air Force were delighted, but to the Design Office, I discovered, I was enemy number one.'[55]

Zurakowski is credited with being the first to fly beyond the speed of sound in a straight-winged production aircraft. This was a notable achievement for the CF-100, an all-weather jet interceptor not originally designed for supersonic flight. In 1996 this event was commemorated by the Canadian Mint issuing a special-edition twenty-dollar silver piece, 'which depicts a gold cameo of Janusz, as part of a series of coins commemorating powered flight in Canada since World War II'.[56]

In the Design Office, the achievement was not heralded, as it put them in an awkward position. 'Previously, without the knowledge of either the flight test section or the pilots, the Design Office had prepared a proposal for the RCAF recommending extensive redesign of the CF-100 by decreasing the thickness of the wings, sweeping them slightly back, and increasing their area – all this mainly to obtain a maximum diving speed of 0.95 Mach.'[57] The abortive swept-wing

[54] Pesando, 2002.

[55] Stewart, *Shutting Down the National Dream*, 228.

[56] 'SETP' [online], cited 2001: http://www.setp.org/contactingsetp.htm.

[57] Zurakowski, 'Test Flying the Arrow', 103.

CF-103, cancelled in December 1951, had no chance now of being resurrected; the wooden mock-up of the aircraft that had been built at the back of the plant was quietly removed and broken up.

Testing at supersonic speeds may have been spectacular, but Zurakowski's work was likely to forestall any deliberate attempts by service pilots to duplicate the feat. It was conjectured at the Flight Test Office that a number of unofficial efforts to break the sound barrier had taken place. At Avro, Peter Cope duplicated Zura's Mach 1 dive on at least one occasion. Avro attempted to record Zurakowski in a supersonic dive on a later flight, but when he pulled out, the technicians waited for several seconds then switched off the recording equipment. Immediately after, the sonic boom shattered the silence. The incensed engineers had apparently forgotten to calculate that it would take thirty seconds for the sound to reach the ground.

With all the publicity surrounding the supersonic flight, some media reports made it look like a dangerous stunt. There was nothing farther from the truth. Zurakowski never did anything dangerous; he always had a well-thought-out plan before he proceeded with any phase of experimental tests. The insistence that the spin chutes on the CF-100 series functioned properly was just such an example of his cautious approach to the job. 'All new aircraft must be equipped with a small spin-recovery chute prior to commencing spin trials. We installed the chute with engineering help, or vice versa, but we couldn't get it to deploy properly. Jan flatly stated that the device must work properly before he would perform spin trials.'[58]

In another example, Zurakowski had worried about the climate controls of the CF-100 and again used an unorthodox method of showing the problem to the Design Office.

> A heating and air conditioning system was designed for the CF-100. A specification was raised for the manufacture of a unit delivering a specified amount of air per minute at a specified temperature and engine speed. The aircraft was instrumented to check this system, and flight tests were carried out according to the Design Office programme. Their technical observer was very happy: the system delivered everything as designed, and, in spite of my objections, the results were considered as satisfactory.

[58] Pesando, 2002.

From my own experience, I was sure that the system was poor. The cockpit heating and air conditioning system was designed for maximum cruising power (very close to maximum power) at the highest altitude, but at the most economical cruising speed, engine power was so low that the temperature in the cockpit was around the freezing point.

I managed to squeeze in one more test. Before the night, however, I secretly put on two sweaters and two pairs of thermal underwear, without saying anything to my satisfied observer. After a one-hour cruise, my observer, George Shaw (Fern Gard flew as the observer on the majority of the air conditioning system tests), was so stiff from cold that upon landing, he had to be pulled out of the cockpit. After a half-hour defrosting, he agreed that the system required considerable improvement.[59]

Life in Canada

By 1954 the Zurakowski family had become accustomed to their new home. They had found that adapting to the customs and way of life in Canada had been eased by their close association with the Polish community in Toronto. Anna had started to write again, contributing articles for the local Polish newspapers; her interest in painting and ceramics was also revived. The youngsters had found the transition the easiest. Although the Polish language was used predominantly at home, both boys fluidly picked up English from their friends in the neighbourhood. After beginning elementary school, George and Mark excelled at their studies and found that they never had problems with language at school.

From a small apartment downtown on Concord Avenue, the family had moved to a house on Westhead Road, a new subdivision of Etobicoke. They eventually found a much larger, older home on Indian Road that suited their growing boys. High Park nearby was a place for the family to enjoy nature trails, playgrounds, picnic areas and swimming and wading pools in the summer, and a skating rink in the winter. Both boys were enrolled at St Vincent de Paul Catholic School on Fermanagh Avenue, with George beginning to show an

---

[59] Zurakowski, 'Test Flying the Arrow', 101-102.

interest in mathematics and science even at an early age.

One of the family's favourite pursuits was taking holidays in northern Ontario. They spent two summers in the popular lake region of Muskoka, and during the third summer they discovered the beautiful, picturesque Wadsworth Lake in a region called the Canadian Kaszuby, 200 kilometres west of Ottawa, close to Algonquin Park. The rugged beauty of the forests, hills, lakes and rivers had reminded its first Polish settlers of the northern region of their homeland. At once, both Anna and Janusz felt at peace in this area. Anna reflected that 'at the time we did not realise that this would become our future and permanent home.'

Father Rafal Grzondziel, a former Chaplain of the 2nd Polish Army in Italy, was the tireless patron of the area. This dedicated priest contributed considerable time, energy and heart to the building of a chapel and home base for the Franciscan Order. At this time the Polish Scouts formed in Canada, and decided to build their summer campsites in this area. In 1955, when the government, acting through Father Grzondziel, began to sell property in the Wadsworth Lake area, Zurakowski bought land to create a summer home. He bought two plots, with the intention of selling one piece of land to another Polish family. This was soon realised when Henry Malinowski and his brother-in-law, Kazik Szrajer, purchased the second parcel of land, becoming the Zurakowskis' neighbours. Malinowski was an aeronautical engineer at Avro Canada and had known Janusz since before the war when he had lodged with the Zurakowski family in Lublin; at that time he was an intern with Zura's brother Bronek at the Plage & Laskiewicz Mechanical Plant (renamed the Lublin Aircraft Factory in 1936). Szrajer was a bomber pilot in a Polish (RAF) squadron during the war (he had been involved in the V-2 retrieval operation) and worked as a pilot for one of the Canadian airlines.

One of the conditions of sale at Wadsworth Lake was that the purchaser had to construct a cottage or residence within one year of the purchase. The Zurakowskis resorted to a prefabricated structure offered by a building company. Due to the pressures of work Janusz had to remain at Avro, but Anna and the boys, over a summer, travelled out to the lake and Anna quite efficiently supervised the construction project. The simple wooden-frame cottage surprisingly served for years as a sturdy summer house. Whenever time permitted over the next few years, the Zurakowski family travelled to the cottage and spent many a weekend and summer holiday enjoying fishing and boating, often in company with the Malinowski and Szrajer families. The boys loved the outdoor life, and at times both Mark and George could barely be persuaded to come out of the water. They became great swimmers but, like all mothers, Anna fretted over the boys. Being natural athletes, both excelled at water sports and skiing on the slopes of nearby hills in the winter. Later, Mark would call on his athletic prowess to become a ski instructor. At the cottage, Zurakowski loved to 'work with his hands' and recalled, 'Through my years at Avro, I have built sailboats as a hobby, so that every one of us has a boat of my design and make.'[60]

In the evenings the family took part in the Scout bonfires. This became a special time that took Anna and Janusz back to their younger years when, together with friends, they would sit, sing and socialise around a bonfire. Every Sunday many people would gather in Father Rafal's chapel and, over the coming years, more and more people attended the church. Eventually Father Rafal ordered a huge tapestry with the painting of Mother Mary of Czestochowa and hung it in a forest clearing. There the community constructed wooden benches that formed the basic shape of a forest church. This became a popular place known to its parishioners as the 'Cathedral in the Pines'. For the Poles who now began to come to this region, the summer homes became more than a retreat, and a number of families planned to have permanent residences. For Zurakowski, the tranquil and idyllic time he spent at the cottage would contrast with the deadly serious work of test flying in which he was engaged.

Staring death in the face

One of the most dangerous problems that Zurakowski faced on the CF-100 nearly cost him his life. In an attempt to sort out the engineering of an experimental ventral rocket pack, Zura and Peter Cope had flown the CF-100 Mark 4 prototype, No 18112, through a protracted programme of test firings. This was the same machine that Zura had earlier flown supersonically. The retractable rocket pack housed forty-eight unguided FFAR (folding-fin aircraft rockets) in a flush-mounted, mid-fuselage belly housing just behind the standard .50 calibre gun pack. The unit was designed to be

[60] *The Toronto Telegram*, 14 May 1959.

deployed in flight by being lowered into position with a hydraulic jack. The operation of the rocket pack involved rapid deployment and a firing and retraction sequence that lasted less than a second.

Ground tests had shown electrical and spent-cartridge FOD problems, but aerodynamic buffeting when the rocket pack was deployed at speed could only be sorted out in a flight test. The Design Office anticipated that the sudden rocket-pack deployment would lead to an air braking and pitch-up condition that would have to be corrected. Initial tests with an extended empty pack confirmed that the problem existed, and test firings of salvos of six, twelve, thirty and forty-eight rockets revealed a pitching phenomenon that would affect the rockets' accuracy. An automatic pitch-correction system to counteract the high-speed buffeting and pitching encountered when the rocket pack was extended was intended for production CF-100s.

On 23 August 1954, Zurakowski flew with twenty-eight-year-old engineer John Hiebert as his observer to test the firing sequence and obtain data on the change of trim that occurred with the rocket pack extended. Near Ajax, Ontario, when Zura retracted the lowered rocket pack at 5,000 feet, a sudden explosion in the rear rocked the aircraft. The CF-100 began a steep dive, crippled with frozen controls. Zurakowski immediately gave the order to eject. 'I yelled to John to prepare to bail out ... wait a few seconds and jettison the canopy. I then jettisoned the rocket pack and prepared to abandon the aircraft.'[61]

The aircraft was rocked by a second explosion. 'A few seconds after jettisoning the canopy, I heard a bang and assumed my observer had ejected; I was a bit surprised he had already gone.'[62] Hiebert had ejected, Zurakowski thought; he then proceeded to eject from the stricken fighter at 2,000 feet. 'In an attempt to force the aileron controls, I had forced my seat out slightly to the right, and during ejection, for a moment, my foot supported by the step was overloaded by my knee hitting the side windscreen which deflected the momentary sideload, but that was enough to fracture my ankle.' When his parachute opened at 300 feet, he knew almost immediately that his right ankle was broken. Descending rapidly from the tumbling fighter, Zura had only scant moments to prepare himself

[61] Stewart, *Shutting Down the National Dream*, 186-187.
[62] Ibid, 187.

for impact. 'I landed on my left foot on a hard field near Ajax.'[63] Only 500 yards away, the CF-100 disintegrated in a fiery crash.

After landing heavily on his one good leg at the Fleming farm off Highway No 2, Zurakowski was found sitting in the field by anxious bystanders, local farmers John Chubb of nearby Whitby and Desmond Kavanagh with his two-year-old daughter, Margaret. Although Zurakowski was in pain, his first thoughts were about his observer: 'How is the other fellow?'[64] Unknown to him, Hiebert had been pinned inside the CF-100 and had been unable to eject. The second explosion had possibly disabled the radio or Hiebert's cockpit area. Thousands of local residents had seen the doomed aircraft, with its rear fuselage ablaze, plunge to the earth. Moments after the crash, the scene was jammed with hundreds of onlookers who stopped beside the busy thoroughfare as flames engulfed the crashed fighter. Back in Toronto, George Zurakowski heard the news of his father's crash on the radio and rushed to tell his mother.

Desmond Kavanagh carried Zura to his car and, with a police escort, sped to the Oshawa hospital. Doctors determined that he had a broken right ankle and a damaged vertebra together with minor bruising, and they fitted him with a walking cast during his overnight stay. Zura had had a frightening experience, but it affected Anna and the family even more. During her hospital visit she tried to compose herself. Anna had always worried about her husband's work but confided recently, 'These were difficult years. When my husband was flying, there was a lot of anxiety.'[65]

While he was in the hospital, news stories proclaimed Zurakowski as the hero again. Speculation ran wild that the aircraft had been steered away from populated areas and that Hiebert had died due to his remaining on board to save top-secret equipment. Zura's ejection of the ventral pack may have prompted this version of the story. The rocket pack was found near Ajax and was dutifully guarded by Ontario Provincial Police Constable G C Partington. The Mayor of Ajax wrote to Zurakowski extending his sympathies for the loss of his observer and praising his courage. Zura could only sardonically reply that he had little control over the events following

[63] Stewart, *Shutting Down the National Dream,* 187.
[64] 'Jet Ace Hurt, Aide Killed but Save Homes from Crash', *Toronto Daily Star*, 24 August 1954.
[65] *The Ottawa Citizen*, 9 January 1997.

the explosion. 'Daily press stories that I was trying to save populated areas by directing the aircraft to open fields have no relation to facts. After the first explosion, I was unable to move the controls even a fraction of an inch.'[66]

The CF-100 accident report was inconclusive, but the cause of the explosions may have been related to a fuel line rupturing and being ignited by a spark due to the buffeting of the rocket pack. Zura's injury was traced to the pilot seat having two back plates improperly fitted, allowing the seat to twist sideways on its guide rail. When attempting to duplicate the conditions that the back-seater had faced, Avro engineers carried out a simulation on one of the CF-100s in the flight test hangar. With charges removed from the aircraft, a group of flight test engineers took it in turns to sit in the back seat, equipped with full flying gear and breathing oxygen, their helmets secured and face masks down.

The engineers went through an ejection drill, pulling the face blind above their heads to trip the sear or release mechanism of the seat. The first subject, Ron Page, immediately had problems and was unable to trip the sear. Other engineers were successful in deploying the escape mechanism, but it was noted that a number of the group had difficulty when the face shield was pulled out slightly to the side. When that occurred, the sear release cable would not trip. In relating the trials, Ron Page wrote, 'There were some thoughtful faces at the conclusion of our little exercise.'[67] In those last desperate moments, did John Hiebert also wildly pull down his face shield to find that he was trapped in a gyrating, doomed fighter?

The ventral rocket pack was abandoned in 1954 in favour of wingtip rockets, which performed far better as the aircraft wings were strong enough at the wingtips to support the rocket pods, and the rocket launchings showed none of the turbulent air buffeting of the belly station. In the same year, new handles, mounted lower in the cockpit, had been fitted to the ejection seats to allow aircrew to activate the escape mechanism of the latest production CF-100s.

Flight Test Engineer Robert Cockfield was assigned to replace John Hiebert. He viewed flying with Zura with a mixture of awe and anticipation. After six weeks of convalescence, Zurakowski was back

---

[66] Stewart, *Shutting Down the National Dream*, 187.
[67] Ron D Page, *CF-100 Canuck* (Erin: Boston Mills Press, 1981), 57.

in the air. Cockfield reported: 'My first flight with Zura was to investigate a problem that had been observed in service, that the rubber fueltank liners in the wings, which were supported from hooks in the wing structure, tended to come unhooked during rapid descent. We had several workhorse CF-100s of various vintages in our hangar and they had been modified so many times it was difficult to tell what mark they were originally, except by their serial numbers. One was rigged with altimeters in the back seat that showed the pressure in the wing compartment as well as ambient pressure.

> My job was to record the two readings during a rapid descent, the difference between the two readings intended to be a measure of the differential pressure that might be causing the fuel bladders to unhook. At about 40,000 feet, Zura popped the air brakes, which allowed the aircraft to descend almost vertically in a 'minimum time descent'. I had my head down to read the altimeters, which were mounted on a panel below and to the left of the normal instrument panel. When the 'outside' altimeter read 20,000 feet, I attempted to raise my head, thinking we were below the clouds and I could now see the ground. When I did get my head up to canopy level, there were trees and telephone poles on our wingtips. As I figured out later, there was a significant lag in the altimeter, and the difficulty I had in raising my head was due to G forces during pullout from the dive. Zura finished the flight with his customary low-altitude tour that I always assumed was to find the best fishing spots around Muskoka. I flew many times with Jan, but my first ride was the most memorable.[68] (Zurakowski strenuously disputes the rumour that he was checking out fishing grounds.)

A later flight nearly ended in tragedy, as Cockfield reported: 'On another occasion, we were doing a test of the cockpit heating and air conditioning system, and the test plan called for a 'cold soak', which meant a boring hour or two at high altitude. After a while, I had loosened my mask to be more comfortable where it was cutting into my cheek. Some time later, Zura cut short the flight time at high

---

[68] Cockfield, 2002.

altitude when he did not get an answer from me on the intercom. At lower altitude, I heard his call and answered that everything was 'OK'. In the post-flight log, he requested a check of the intercom that was 'not working at altitude'. It was a long time after the flight before I realised that as a result of the poor-fitting mask, I had passed out from anoxia and that Zura had probably saved my life by cutting the flight short.'[69]

Gremlins

In 1955 Zurakowski was involved in another accident. This time it involved an inadvertent undercarriage retraction on the CF-100. After a routine test flight, he reported: 'I realised during the landing run that the undercarriage was retracting. Since the engine speed was too low to get airborne again, I switched off the engines and the aircraft skidded to a stop, damaging the flaps badly. After an investigation had been carried out in the hangar, it was determined that everything was in perfect order... Conclusion: pilot error.'[70]

The foreman had tested the retraction numerous times and when Zurakowski was called in to check, the undercarriage seemed to be operating properly. He sat in the cockpit and set all the controls and switches to their positions in landing, and hit the undercarriage button. It went up smoothly a few times. As he was getting out of the cockpit, the foreman said, 'You see, that's a really good old aircraft,' and enthusiastically slapped the fuselage with his hand. That started it. All by itself, the undercarriage retracted.

'It was later established that somehow the wiring of the master auto-observer switch was mixed up with the undercarriage selector wiring and that a short caused by the vibration of the aircraft as it touched down caused the undercarriage to retract.'[71] At least in Canada, the problem was identified and fixed. Too often in England, Zurakowski remarked, the situation would be simply dismissed as 'too many gremlins'[72], after the wartime sprites that seemed to plague aircraft.

An example of Zurakowski's ability to identify potential problems involved a more serious issue: ejecting from a stricken aircraft. Problems related to the canopy and the singular conditions

[69] Ibid.
[70] Zurakowski, 'Test Flying the Arrow', 104.
[71] Ibid.
[72] Ibid.

present in a rear-seat ejection were inherent in the CF-100 design. 'One of my last flights at Gloster was for canopy jettison on the two-seater Meteor Mark 7. During jettison, a canopy, weighing about 160lb and more than six feet long, had to be lifted by the air stream, pivoting at the rear hinge, and after reaching about 30 degrees, be disengaged automatically to then pass clear over the tailplane. The test was recorded from another aircraft by cine camera.

> The CF-100 had a similar size and shape canopy, but to my surprise the hinge pin at the back of the canopy was a bolt of one-eighth inch or three-sixteenths inch thickness, whilst on the Meteor it was half an inch. Because the cabin of the CF-100 was pressurised, I expected loads to be much higher, so I suspected that something was wrong. I was assured that ground tests were satisfactory, but when a test report could not be produced, I requested a test.
>
> More than twenty ground jettison tests were carried out, but results were none too satisfactory. Somebody arrived at the conclusion that ground simulations of the air loads were not representative enough, so the only answer was to test the system in flight. I was sure that if something didn't work on the ground it was unlikely to work in the air, but we started jettison tests. I jettisoned more than ten canopies over Camp Borden. The system was modified step by step, but results were not satisfactory and it was considered too risky to try at higher speeds.[73]

'Another problem that Zurakowski had identified when the canopy rails were modified was that in the new design the rails were designed to fly off in a canopy separation and could prove a problem. He wanted to see the results of the ground test. When Ground Test reported a successful ejection, Zura quietly asked if the rails had posed a problem. The Ground Test group replied: 'No, we lashed the rails to the canopy so they wouldn't be a problem.' Oops, back to the drawing board and retest.'[74]

Zurakowski carried out a series of in-flight canopy ejection tests with No 18120, an earlier Mark 3, and No 18185, a CF-100 Mark 4. The tests were photographed from onboard cameras and from the

[73] Ibid.
[74] Matthews, 2002.

CF-100 canopy trials. *(Fred Matthews collection)*

Avro C102 Jetliner, which was used as a camera platform. In 1955 the first successful ejection from the back seat was made by Squadron Leader Fifield of Martin-Baker, at an altitude of eighty feet, with Zura 'driving'. He was still unhappy with the test results when, as he recalled, the decision was taken out of his hands. While he was in Los Angeles on a three-day course on missiles, the company presented a case for its canopy jettison trials to be accepted as satisfactory. The RCAF agreed, and Zura had lost his battle. 'Maybe these battles were useful. On the new design, the Arrow, the crew emergency-escape system was developed to a very high standard for a much wider range of speed. For cockpit air conditioning, a ground testing rig was built to develop and prove the system, and I had no serious problems in flight.'[75]

A more serious problem existed in the rear cockpit of the CF-100. Flight tests were conducted to determine whether the rear seat ejection blind could be pulled down when the canopy had separated. 'At low speeds it was possible, but at higher speeds (if I remember correctly, about 300 knots indicated air speed) it was impossible.'[76]

One flight test engineer, Geoff Grossmith, volunteered to fly with Peter Cope in a CF-100 that was fitted with only a front windscreen. As speeds reached 300 knots, Grossmith found his arms

[75] Zurakowski, 'Test Flying the Arrow', 104.
[76] Matthews, 2002.

were pinned outside the cockpit when he reached up to activate the ejection sequence. Only after the aircraft slowed was he able to move his arms. The ejection procedure was also modified to the right hand moving directly over the face, elbows in tight, left hand gripping the right wrist. Eventually Avro fitted a small, clear Plexiglas windscreen into all test aircraft to deflect the airstream after canopy separation. After proposing that this modification be retrofitted to all RCAF examples, Avro was amazed that the RCAF's first reaction was to demand that the rear windscreens be removed from all test aircraft. Upon hearing this decision, Avro Flight Test engineers refused to fly in the rear cockpit, which precipitated a re-examination by the RCAF of the problem and a swift approval for the rear windscreen to be adopted in all CF-100s.

The nature of the business

Zurakowski's concerns about ejecting from a CF-100 were realised tragically in the death of Avro Canada test pilot Glen Lynes on 20 October 1955. After his recent very successful aerial demonstration tour of RCAF bases in Europe, Lynes was back home flying CF-100 Mark 4B No 18514 over Malton on a routine test flight. The modified Mark 4 was fitted with the extended wings and horizontal tail of the Mark 5 and was known as 'the four and a half' in Flight Test Engineering. Since the stability flight tests had not been completed, Don Ridler in Flight Test Engineering had specifically instructed Lynes not to attempt any aerobatics. Stan Haswell recently confided:

> Jan had told us [the Avro test pilots] to be careful and not to overdo it with that CF-100. No aerobatics! Glen considered himself as good as anyone and confided that 'I'll show him.' When he was testing a CF-100 at low altitude, he got into trouble. The aeroplane was a 4DE and was still undergoing testing in flight test.
>
> The accident came about in an inverted spin. Lynes couldn't release the canopy and ejected right through it. He managed the ejection but the canopy had severed the drogue chute rope for the main parachute. He was still in the seat but he didn't undo his seat belt. It would automatically undo and let him out, but he now had to release the seat manually and then actuate the parachute manually. This all took time, and he was too low for the chute to open fully. Glen was a smallish fellow, and the

D-ring had moved toward the side. By the time he would
have pulled it, he was too close to the ground.[77]

Horrified, Stan Haswell and Chris Pike, who were next on the
runway, watched as the aircraft 'augured in'. They taxied back to the
plant and shut down to await the outcome. Fred Matthews had
revealed that Lynes had 'once said he wouldn't waste time
jettisoning the canopy; he would just punch through it with his seat,
even though there were no tests to establish this as a viable method
of ejecting.'[78] In post-accident examination it was determined that
Lynes didn't survive the impact of smashing into the canopy,
breaking his neck. Later CF-100 ejection seats were fitted with
special spikes to break through the canopy.

Lynes joined the ranks of another Avro test pilot and two 'back-
seaters' who had died during the testing of the CF-100. Flight
Lieutenant Bruce Warren, then Chief Test Pilot of the CF-100, and
his observer, Robert Ostrander, had mysteriously crashed in 1951,
and engineer John Hiebert had died in 1954 while flying with
Zurakowski. Most of the test pilots tried to blank out the memory of
the others who died, and chalked it up to 'the nature of the business',
but test flying was a dangerous business.

Zurabatics

Immediately after his arrival, Avro Canada recognised that
Zurakowski was not only a test pilot, but was also an extraordinary
aerobatic pilot who could demonstrate the potential of the
company's new fighter in a sensational way. 'The Department of
Technical Sales and Public Relations was usually the only
department which was not always cross with test pilots. But when
priority was given for an urgent development flight and not for
demonstration of an aircraft for some important or not so important
guests, relations were strained quickly.'[79] Soon after he began work
at A V Roe Canada, Zura was asked to demonstrate the CF-100 at
the official opening of the Orenda factory at Malton on 29
September 1952. Members of the Cabinet, including C D Howe,
who officiated, and Air Marshal W A Curtis, Chief of the Air Staff,
together with representatives of the RCAF, were present.

---

[77] Haswell, 2001.
[78] Matthews, 2002.
[79] Zurakowski, 'Test Flying the Arrow', 102.

This delegation was joined by media and Avro executives located in a special stand in front of the new Orenda factory. The Avro Lancaster-Orenda engine test bed trundled out to do its turn as an air show performer. Then Zura, in a CF-100 Mark 3, began his nearly twenty-minute display in a spectacular fashion, roaring over the podium area upside down. *The Toronto Star* had reported that the 'feature of the afternoon was the performance in a CF-100 by Jan Zurakowski. He put the 18-ton aircraft through a series of manoeuvres including slow rolls and a 'falling leaf'.' The Avro public address system boomed out an continual commentary on the spellbinding performance, and as Zura disappeared in the distance, the show appeared to be over.

The invited dignitaries were just beginning the usual round of handshakes and congratulations when 'suddenly there was a whooshing roar that sounded almost like an explosion right over their heads as the sneaky Zurakowski, having completed a circuit that probably took him miles out over Lake Ontario, came zooming past directly over the roof of the hangar. It was Zurakowski's final pass of the day and it was such a dandy that the assembled 'brass' almost leapfrogged over each other in their startled surprise.'[80] Zura's 500mph, 100-foot-altitude knife-edged pass over the roof of the new Orenda factory made the CF-100 the talk of the day both in the media and the military. His display was described by Fred Smye, General Manager, Aircraft Division, A V Roe Canada, in a private letter: 'Your outstanding achievement did more for the fighter than any other single event which has taken place.'[81]

In May 1953 Zurakowski recreated the spectacular aerial photographs that had highlighted his time at Gloster. Working with Hugh Mackechnie, who was responsible for most of the aerial photographs of Avro aircraft prior to delivery to the RCAF, Zura had contacted other test pilots about the possibility of staging aerial photographs to dramatise the CF-100's abilities. Mackechnie joined A V Roe Canada in 1947 and was a master in capturing aircraft in flight using a modified 4X5 Speed Graphic with a handmade body designed by Lou Wise. He was invaluable to the experimental group, often flying with Zurakowski.

Shortly after his arrival at Avro Aircraft, Zurakowski briefed his

[80] Bruce West, 'Zura Lands', *The Globe and Mail*, 1 December 1952.
[81] Fred Smye, correspondence with Janusz Zurakowski, 1952.

fellow pilots about the techniques required. They would use radar check flights when CF-100s flew in pairs as an ideal time to practice formation aerobatics. Zura, Chris Pike and, later, Flight Lieutenant Woodman would complete their check flights, then rehearse up to ten minutes of formation loops, with Mackechnie initially along just for the ride. The rigours of aerial photography were described by Mackechnie to a newspaper reporter. Flying aerobatics alongside a fighter aircraft meant entering a manoeuvre at 400mph, usually at 2,000 feet or higher. As a loop was begun, the speed would drop to 150-200mph at its apex, with each loop stretching up one and a half miles in diameter. In a forty-second period, the pilot and photographer would feel the pressure of two to four G (force of gravity) loads. 'To get even four photographs, the cameraman must be good ... try holding a camera that feels like twenty-four pounds under those conditions,'[82] Mackechnie remarked.

As the photographer grew accustomed to the forces and discomfort of aerobatics, he began to devise camera angles needed for future photographic assignments. Zura always flew as the photographer's camera mount, assuming the more difficult role of maintaining position with another CF-100. The 'target plane' could be flying upside down or going straight up, but Zura always kept station with extraordinary precision.

One of Mackechnie's trademark photographs was shot when Zurakowski flew side-by-side with Woodman as the two CF-100 Mark 3Bs climbed to the apex of a loop. The Avro Public Relations Department splashed the dramatic image of the fighter streaking into the sky in a vertical climb in their house publications and soon the photograph appeared in newspapers and magazines throughout North America, mirroring Zura's earlier success at Gloster.

Zurakowski become known for more than the photo flights. Among all the Avro Aircraft Limited test pilots, he was the acknowledged master of aerobatic demonstrations, appearing as the company's representative at the National Air Show in Toronto from 1952 until 1954. His electrifying solo demonstrations were often the showstopper; he was constantly in demand for air shows, even impromptu ones. When famed wartime leader Field Marshal Bernard Montgomery toured the Avro facilities on 20 April 1953, Zura did his customary knife-edged 'beat-up' of the factory, roaring past, scarcely

---

[82] 'Picturebatics Tough in CF-100', *Toronto Star*, c1955.

a dozen metres above the heads of the startled official party.

A demonstration flight by Zura was graphically described by Hugh Young, an Experimental Flight Test engineer at A V Roe Canada.

> Probably the most strenuous flight I had in my five years on the CF-100 was with Zura on No 18120, on Coronation Day, 2 June 1953. The Brampton Flying Club had organised an air show to mark the day, and the company had agreed to provide a CF-100. Coincidentally, I had some handling tests to do with Zura on 18120; these would be completed in time for Zura to get back and take the show in a production aircraft. We were no sooner airborne when Curly Ridley radioed that the production aircraft had a snag and could Zura do the show in 18120?

Zura insisted that he had too much fuel on board 120 for aerobatics. There was Curly on the ground sweating bullets, with Zura squeaking away into his mike apparently being awkward. I was in the back seat chuckling to myself because I knew what Curly didn't – Zura was burning off fuel just as fast as he could (100 per cent power at nought feet). I was in for the ride of my life.

CF-100 over Dover. *(Russell Adams)*

> I remember the first low pass towards a grass field, some airplanes visible on the ground, and then Zura rolled inverted, and I found myself hanging like a pendulum from the seat pan. (Heaven knows how you fly an airplane like that.) After that my world toppled. At one point, Brampton Flying Club was revolving slowly in the windscreen, dead ahead, and in plain view.

Zura did some tail slides ... and then a falling leaf. This was to be the one, and only, I was to experience in any aircraft. The air flow must have been mostly sideways across the canopy, because there was a very loud swooshing noise, which I had never heard before, or since. This flight was the closest I ever came to being airsick; but not quite. It was a blessed feeling to take a deep breath and blow my cheeks out when Zura opened up the canopy.[83]

Farnborough 1955

Appointed as the Senior Development Pilot of Avro Aircraft Limited in 1955, Zurakowski appeared at the Society of British Aircraft Constructors' Sixteenth Flying Display and Exhibition at Farnborough that year. It was the first time that a military jet aircraft not produced in the British Isles had appeared at the prestigious air show display. Zura attracted world attention once more by stealing the show when he put the CF-100 Mark 4 through a series of elaborate manoeuvres, including the falling leaf, thrilling the huge crowd estimated at more than 120,000 visitors.

Zurakowski at the 1955 Farnborough Air Display. *(Zurakowski collection)*

[83] Page, *CF-100 Canuck*, 55.

The CF-100 Mark 4Bs (Nos 18321 and 18322) that Zura flew at the Farnborough Air Show were two of three machines (Nos 18320 to 18322) that Avro had sent to Europe for evaluation by the RAF. They were not special aircraft, simply three machines pulled off the production run to represent standard examples of the type. In an operation called Random 12, the CF-100 fighters had overflown the Atlantic in the first long-range mission flown by the type, and were in England for an extended four-month evaluation by the RAF at the Central Flying Establishment at West Raynham. British test and service pilots had a chance to fly the aircraft and spoke highly of its 'almost no vices'[84] flight characteristics and its capability as a long-range interceptor. Of particular note was the excellent equipment on board, with state-of-the-art navigational equipment, automatic pilot, collision-interception radar and gun firing mechanism.

Joe Morley, Avro Aircraft Limited's Vice President of Sales, took every opportunity to display the CF-100 in Europe. Earlier, in June 1955, the RAF's trial CF-100s had made an impressive Spitfire-type formation landing at the Paris Salon in Le Bourget, prior to Farnborough. The three CF-100s, flown by RCAF pilots Flight Lieutenant Woodman, Flight Lieutenant Roy Bennett, Squadron Leader Phil Etienne and Avro test pilot Glen Lynes, went on to appearances in Europe.

Later in September at the week-long exposition that made up the Farnborough Air Show, a crew of maintenance and flying personnel was established by the company. John F Painter, the manager of the operation, recalled, 'We used two of the three aircraft the RAF had evaluated at the Central Fighter Establishment which had been put into storage at Langar in Nottinghamshire.'[85] Technicians in the crew included Bob Blaylock, Don Ludlow, Bill Morgan and Jack Smale from Avro Aircraft Limited

After months of storage, the two CF-100s that were being prepared for Farnborough were in need of maintenance, but Painter and the Avro support crew were enterprising in finding spares and getting the aircraft in a presentable state. The bare-metal CF-100s were buffed to a glistening finish and impressed visitors with the high standard of workmanship. During the week of display flying, 100 per cent serviceability was achieved, despite a number of close

[84] John Gale, 'Farnborough Newcomer', *Jet Age* (Autumn 1955), 2.
[85] John Painter, 'Showing Off the CF-100', *Aeroplane Monthly* (1998), 36.

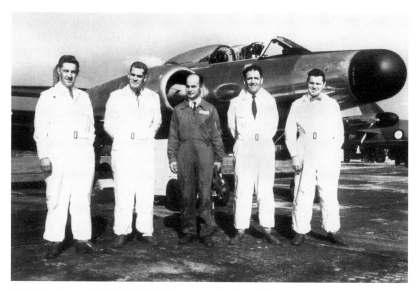

1955 Farnborough CF-100 exhibition team. Left to right: John Painter, Jack Smale, Janusz Zurakowski, Don Ludlow and Bill Morgan. *(Zurakowski collection)*

calls. Military representatives from Bolivia, France, Colombia, South Africa and the United States had a close look at the CF-100 in the Farnborough compound. The Belgian Air Attaché took a special interest in the display aircraft and later cornered Zurakowski for an off-the-record appraisal of the Avro fighter.

Zura reported: 'We made an attempt to sell the aircraft in Holland and Belgium. The Dutch Air Force had a rather poor fighter aircraft from the United States and needed a replacement, but they didn't want to upset their American friends... The Belgian Air Force had had bad experience with American aircraft.'[86] He gave the representative from the Belgian Air Force an honest assessment of the CF-100's strengths and alerted Morley to the interest shown in the aircraft. Avro arranged for Belgian pilots to test the aircraft in Canada during an RCAF exercise, 'Operation Banana Belt', at Cold Lake, Alberta, in November 1955. After further evaluations in Europe in the following year, the Belgian Air Force became the first and only foreign customer for the CF-100.

Going back to England was a joyous time for Zurakowski, as he renewed friendships at the Gloster firm and spent some time

[86] Zurakowski, 'Test Flying the Arrow', 110.

revisiting even his wartime haunts. In preparation for Farnborough, Zura 'wrung out' No 18322, one of the CF-100s stored at the RCAF's UK storage base at Langar. John Painter remembered, 'The level of flying skill was seldom witnessed around that airfield.'[87] After the first day's flying at the air display, Zura was once more reunited with an old friend, Gloster's photographer, Russell Adams, whose photographs appeared in many newspaper and magazine stories that accompanied the Farnborough visit. In a series of dramatic aerial photographs taken from a Fairchild C-82 'Packet' over the Gloucestershire countryside and further to the west off the south coast of the Isle of Wight, Adams precisely captured the aggressive look of the Avro CF-100 fighter. A striking head-on view of Zurakowski shot over the Isle of Wight evoked a modern version of the classic fighter intercept over Britain. It must have rekindled memories in Zura of a time when he had been in the air in his Spitfire, scanning the skies for the enemy.

On 5 September 1955, the first public day at Farnborough, Zura's routine began as soon as he took off. Holding the heavy fighter just above the runway, he rolled inverted and retracted the undercarriage before climbing away upside down. The next moments were described as 'so polished, so spectacular'[88] that the rest of the programme simply paled in comparison. 'He did a series of upward rolls, and having gained height, switched to the falling leaf in alternating directions. The fighter fell and floated about the sky like a piece of paper. The manoeuvre had sometimes been performed in the past with light aircraft; it was almost unbelievable to see it done with a modern fighter that, when fully loaded, weighs nearly 20 tons. Next, and with pause, Zurakowski went into a spin, pulling out with beautiful accuracy above the central runway. Many of the spectators on this opening day were, or had been, flyers; they could not have asked for anything better.'[89]

'Zura not only spun the CF-100 and did a falling leaf with it, but he also tail-slid it. This was an astonishing spectacle, for the CF-100 looks and is a big aircraft. Zura stood it on its tail and held it there until the speed had fallen away and nothing was reading on the clock. The aircraft then fell in a sharp stall and, on one occasion, did

[87] Painter, 'Showing Off the CF-100', 43.
[88] 'He did it.'
[89] Gale, 'Farnborough Newcomer', 2.

one turn of an inverted spin before being righted.'[90] 'Most startling of all was the Zura-Canuck method of landing. After the aerobatics, the airplane was brought down to circuit height, half-rolled to put the pilot on the outside and in this fashion, did a half-circuit, finally lowering the undercarriage before half-rolling right-way-in again. The final approach was made with free and easy S-turns that again emphasised good control.'[91]

These manoeuvres were in sharp contrast to what was expected from the heavy, long-range interceptor aircraft. 'If you mentioned the word 'impossible' in the pilot's tent at Farnborough that week, no doubt you would have received the reply, 'Of course it's impossible, it's Zurakowski.''[92] Most noteworthy was the fact that Zura had kept his routine within the confines of the airport during all his display flying, while many other performers had roared on and off stage. Zura later casually downplayed his performance by recalling that the falling leaf was an old manoeuvre that he had learned long ago while flying gliders and was nothing more than a set of incipient spins.

During Farnborough the leading European media as well as reporters from Canada had followed Zurakowski's exploits. A CBC crew filmed him in preparation and during the air display for a later broadcast. Although he was on hand for many interviews, Zura was typically ill at ease in playing the hero type. However, his aerial display did much to advance Canada's reputation in the field of aircraft design and manufacture, especially for Avro Canada. Fred Smye, Vice President and General Manager of Avro Aircraft Limited, wrote personally to Zura to thank him for what he described as a 'magnificent performance ... the highlight of the show and a demonstration of flying skill which will long be remembered by those who were fortunate enough to be present. This example of your outstanding ability and aerobatic artistry has brought widespread recognition to yourself, and to the company which you so ably represent.'[93]

[90] Oliver Stewart, 'News from Britain', *Canadian Aviation* (October 1955), 55.
[91] James Hay Stevens, 'Canada's CF-100s at Farnborough', *Aircraft* (November 1955), 17.
[92] Norris, 'Impossible', 28.
[93] Fred Smye, correspondence with Janusz Zurakowski, 1955.

The CF-100 was soon to become a fixture in European skies. By 1955 NATO realised that there was a shortage of all-weather interceptor capability and Canada responded by volunteering four CF-100 squadrons for service in Europe. One Sabre squadron per wing was stood down between October 1956 and August 1957 and replaced by a CF-100 squadron from Canada. Immediately after the SBAC show, a three-day tour of Canadian bases from 25 to 28 September 1955 was organised by the Avro Canada Armed Services representative, John Painter. Since Zura was needed back in Canada, Glen Lynes took over the demonstration flying with one of the Farnborough machines. The tour encompassed the four RCAF Wings in France and Germany as well as the Canadian Air Division Headquarters in Metz, France.

During Farnborough, Lynes had been the back-up to Zurakowski but he had not been called upon to fly. Painter had known Lynes from his days flying Meteor fighters at RAF Horsham St Faith in Norfolk, where he had been 'the 'usual' display pilot on the station when a show had to be put on for visiting dignitaries. 'Now he could demonstrate a CF-100 with equal panache. He was an impressive pilot, and I was sure he was quietly hoping the leading man (Zurakowski) would break a leg.'[94] Painter provided a lecture in the morning at each stop, then Lynes gave a demonstration flight in the afternoon. His flying was spectacular and even impressed the Sabre pilots who had privately expressed doubt about their new mount's capabilities.

In 1955 Avro Canada was seen as one of the world's most innovative and cutting-edge aviation manufacturers. Its next project, a supersonic jet interceptor code-named the C-105, was already on the drawing boards. At the same time, its designated test pilot, Janusz Zurakowski, would be destined to be forever linked with the new aircraft, soon to be named the Avro Arrow.

[94] Painter, 'Showing Off the CF-100', 48.

Chapter Nine

The Rise and Fall of the Avro Arrow

Given the length of time required for the design and development of a new aircraft, even before the CF-100 entered squadron service a replacement aircraft was being considered. Preliminary discussions between the RCAF, Defence Research Board (DRB) and National Aeronautics Establishment (NAE) in July 1949 had resulted in the publication of the NAE report 'Fighter Project Investigations', detailing estimates of military threats into 1956. At the same time, as a result of early Avro studies, a swept-wing redesign of the CF-100 had already been initiated. On 19 December 1949 Avro Aircraft Limited issued a preliminary brochure, titled 'Proposed Long-Range All-Weather Fighter', which outlined the company's vision for the future.

Genesis

The RCAF had formulated a detailed analysis of the increased air threat to North America posed by the Soviet Union, with the publication of RCAF Operational Requirement ORI/1-63 in November 1952. Subsequently Air Marshal Roy Slemon, Chief of the Air Staff, sent an evaluation team of senior RCAF officers led by Wing Commander Ray Foottit to the United States and Great Britain. The task of the 'All-Weather Interceptor Requirements Team' was to evaluate current flying fighter prototypes and aircraft projects in development in order to determine if the RCAF specifications could be met by available designs. Defence Minister Brooke Claxton stated, 'With the object of economy and to avoid unnecessary duplication, every effort has been made to determine whether future UK or US aircraft could meet our requirements.'[1]

The Convair F-102 Delta Dagger, McDonnell F-101 Voodoo and Gloster Javelin were among the contemporary designs reviewed before the Final Report of the All-Weather Interceptor Requirements Team was issued. Despite its promising concept, the delta-winged F-102 was unable to reach the required performance specifications until an extensive redesign turned it into a Mach 1-capable aircraft.

[1] Palmiro Campagna, *Storms of Controversy* (Toronto: Stoddart, 1992), 12.

A completely revised airframe and engine design led to a new version in 1955 known as the F-102B, renamed the F-106 Delta Dart. The limitations of its single-seat configuration, coupled with range concerns, seemed to be addressed in the new McDonnell project, the F-101.

Like the Convair fighter, the McDonnell F-101 Voodoo evolved from an earlier design, in this instance the 1948 McDonnell XF-88 all-weather interceptor. Originally conceived as a single-seat swept-wing supersonic fighter designed to escort bombers, the F-101 had a twin-jet-engined airframe that was able to be 'stretched' to fit requirements for a fighter bomber, a twin-seat all-weather interceptor and a photo-reconnaissance aircraft. However, the continual change in the anticipated role for the F-101, matched to a number of structural, propulsion, aerodynamic, and armament problems, plagued the programme. Although offering slightly higher performance than the Convair F-102, the Voodoo was unable to meet the RCAF's technical requirements, and likewise was eliminated as a candidate.

In Great Britain, the delta-winged Gloster Javelin, which Zurakowski had flown in prototype form, was in the midst of aerodynamic teething troubles similar to those experienced by the McDonnell F-101, coupled with a rudimentary performance envelope, leading to its outright elimination. After examining and rejecting all the current foreign designs, including 'paper' projects under consideration, the RCAF Air Staff issued Specification AIR 7-3, Design Studies of Prototype All-Weather Aircraft, in April 1953.

The AIR 7-3 supersonic all-weather interceptor aircraft specifications were:

- Operate from a 6,000-foot runway
- Have a range of 600 nautical miles
- Be capable of accelerating to Mach 1.5
- Have a crew of two, a pilot and a navigator
- Carry an advanced weapon system with an advanced targeting system capable of operating in Canada's harsh environment
- Manoeuvre at 50,000 feet while pulling 2G without loss of speed or altitude
- Have two engines[2]

[2] 'Design Study of Supersonic All-Weather Interceptor Aircraft in Accordance with RCAF Spec Air 7-3 Report No P/C- 105/1', A V Roe Canada Limited, May 1953.

The specifications outlined in AIR 7-3 were intended to initiate the selection of an aircraft design capable of meeting RCAF Operational Requirement ORI/1-63, Supersonic All-Weather Interceptor Aircraft. In the weeks after the specifications were drawn, an RCAF team met with Avro to determine if its design studies could meet the stringent requirements of AIR 7-3. The Avro Report P/105/1, which was submitted a month later, provided the basis for an advanced fighter interceptor designated the C-105, that would meet the original specifications. Specification AIR 7-3 was followed in July 1953 by a ministerial directive, Ministerial Direction ACDA-4, from the Department of Defence Production (DDP) to A V Roe Canada, authorising the design study of C-105 to meet Specification AIR 7-3. The company received authorisation of $200,000 to cover this design phase to 30 September 1953.

Avro C-105 design studies

As a designer, Jim Floyd had previously followed a design tenet in the C102 and CF-100 that was considered good practice in the aviation industry. In describing the C102's development, he had commented, 'In order to reduce the number of untried features to a minimum, which was obviously desirable both from the point of view of safety and rapid development, the aircraft was designed on reasonably conventional lines. It was felt that the incorporation of too many design features which had not been satisfactorily demonstrated on previous aircraft would entail considerable amount of laboratory testing and, at the same time, the development costs involved would be prohibitive.'[3] Now, the demands of the RCAF's technical specifications for a supersonic interceptor had dictated a radically new design, one that in no way could be considered conventional.

Early Avro proposals, project studies and tests to meet the RCAF's detailed technical specifications, which later resulted in the basic CF-105 design, were largely the responsibility of the Preliminary Design Office. Its new design originated from the innovative research and design studies carried out by the Long-Range Projects Group led by Jim Chamberlin from July 1948 to June 1952. This advanced project group had been directed to develop a swept-wing redesign of the CF-100.

[3] James C Floyd, 'Avro C-102 Jetliner', *SAE Quarterly Transactions* 5, No 2 (April 1951), 221.

The first Avro proposal in 1948 had been the C-100-S, powered by two Orenda TR9 turbojets, which incorporated a thirty-five-degree swept-low wing and a high-mounted fixed tailplane with swept surfaces. With DDP authorisation to continue with the project, by December 1950 the Avro design team submitted a new design, the C-103, which had gradually evolved from the earlier concept. The C-103 combined a longer fuselage, a larger wing with forty degrees forward sweep, a redesigned mid-set tailplane, as well as providing afterburning for the Orenda engines, to promise higher transonic performance. Renamed the CF-103, this design entered the mock-up stage in January 1951. Throughout the next months, as detailed design drawings and production tooling were under way, the design was evaluated at Cornell Laboratories in Buffalo, New York. The results of the high-speed wind tunnel tests were not promising. By December 1951 the swept-wing redesign of the CF-100 was 'dead', killed by the unexpected potential of the original CF-100 aircraft revealed in test flying and squadron service, and by the relentless advance of research into new designs.

On the Avro drawing boards was another series of concepts that had progressed from the C-100-S (which had spawned the CF-103 programme) to the more advanced design of a buried 'stacked' twin-jet concept known as the C-100-D A refinement of this design, designated the C-104, was re-drawn into a similar proposal utilising side-by-side twin jet engines. By 1951 the renamed Advanced Project Group explored more radical concepts, including delta wings and rocket engines powered by liquid oxygen-kerosene as the C-105 series. The C-104 and C-105 designs were developed simultaneously and were studied in a variety of configurations from single-seat, single-jet engines to twin-seat, twin-jet engines. The delta wings moved from a low to a shoulder-mounted position in the final studies.

Floyd described the supersonic fighter design process as a formidable challenge. 'As the analysis of the various possible configurations progressed, it became increasingly clear that it would be very difficult to meet the RCAF specification based on current technology, since in its desire to meet Canada's obligations as the 'first line of defence of North America' in a nuclear war, the Air Staff had asked for the moon. They required a two-place, twin-engined aircraft with all-weather reliability, long range, short-take-off-and-landing, an internal weapons compartment as large as the bomb bay of the B-29, and a supersonic manoeuvrability of 2G at

Mach 1.5 at 50,000 feet without any loss in speed or altitude – a requirement that has been met by few, if any, service aircraft even to this day. In addition, it was to be guided by the most sophisticated automatic flight and fire control system ever envisaged. It was small wonder that Foottit's team had failed to find any such aircraft on the drawing boards anywhere in the world.'[4]

Chamberlin and Floyd initially considered a single-seat C-104/2, Avro Orenda TR9-powered design. However, in May 1953 Avro submitted Report No P/C-105/1, 'Design Study of Supersonic All-Weather Interceptor Aircraft'. In it the C-105, a larger, more sophisticated two-seater version, powered by the new Rolls-Royce RB-106 engines, was proposed and 'exceeded' the RCAF specifications.

At this point in the design process, the work done by Avro was evaluated by the National Aeronautics Establishment (NAE), which acted as a scientific advisor for the Department of Defence Production and the RCAF. The first of a series of disagreements emerged as the NAE challenged the basic performance data provided by Avro. In November 1953 the NAE issued Report LP-87, 'Assessment of the Performance Characteristics of the Proposed Avro C-105/1200 All-Weather Supersonic Fighter Aircraft'. In the assessment, the crucial drag estimates by the NAE indicated that the design would not meet the RCAF's technical specifications. Jim Floyd was aghast; he recalled vividly, 'The project was stopped dead. I had hundreds of people idle as we had to go back over the figures and prove that the design was right.'[5] Only the intervention of the Director of the National Advisory Committee for Aeronautics (NACA), Hugh Dryden, who chaired a meeting with representatives from the RCAF, NAE, DRB, NACA and Avro Canada on 20 and 21 December 1954 at NACA Langley, ultimately allayed fears that the C-105 would not meet its design specifications.

The CF-105 design

Unlike its subsonic predecessor, the CF-100, the Avro C-105 (later designated Project Number CF-105) represented a significant technological achievement that would have surpassed the original RCAF design specifications. In order for Avro to meet all the design

---

[4] Floyd, 'The Avro Story', 126.
[5] Floyd, 2001.

requirements of a large weapons load and sufficient fuel for a considerable combat radius of action, a large aircraft had to be considered. The imposing, streamlined aircraft with high-mounted delta wing, powered by the advanced Rolls-Royce RB-106 jet engines, was an altogether audacious design. In the end, the design of the aircraft would only be restricted by the thermal limits of the aluminium alloy structure, the so-called 'thermal thicket'. The CF-105 Design Office, run by Jim Chamberlin as Chief of Technical Design under Jim Floyd, Chief Engineer and later Vice-President of Engineering, carried out the development of the aircraft. Robert Lindley later became Chief Engineer on the CF-105 with engineers Guest Hake and Ken Barnes, important additions to the team.

The performance characteristics of the airframe and wing required careful attention. Chamberlin and Floyd developed a complex aerodynamic design that featured area-rule modifications to the fuselage in order to achieve optimum supersonic capabilities. For minimum drag, the fuselage's cross-sectional shape at the wing junction was pronouncedly 'Coke bottle', or pinched. The fuselage was large and box-like; at its fore end the nose cone housing the radar and fire control system compartments tapered sharply. The heart of the avionics package aboard the CF-105 was a very sophisticated weapons control system specified by the RCAF, originally the American Hughes MG3/E9 and, later, the Hughes MX 1179 fire control system.

The fuselage incorporated a semi-pressurised cabin with provisions for two aircrew, in a pilot-navigator configuration. The navigator operated the radar and navigation systems (although the pilot also had a navigation console in the event of solo flights). Clamshell-type canopies were fitted, which opened on the top and had two side panels folding left and right. The tempered glass of the windscreens was one inch thick to withstand the heat generated by the Arrow's anticipated Mach 2 speeds. A streamlined V-shaped canopy and cockpit area was smoothly sculpted into a long dorsal tube that contained the elaborate air conditioning systems necessary for high-speed flight.

In the centre of the fuselage, engine intakes were rectangular, with large splitter plates to divert the boundary layer of air. The intakes were located ahead of the wing's leading edge and the engines; consequently a considerable fuselage volume was occupied by the intake ducting. Two fuel tanks were installed in the fuselage between the engine intakes. Provision for other fuel cells and external stores of fuel tanks was considered in later developments.

The armament bay installed below the intake ducts was larger than the bomb bays of a wartime Lancaster bomber, at 16ft 1in long, 9ft 6in wide and 3ft high. The armament was a mixture of air-to-air missiles and 2.75in air-to-air rockets housed in a retractable pod that was designed for quick reloading on the ground. The firing sequence would involve the opening of the bay's doors in 0.3 seconds, a rapid firing of the missiles/rockets and closing of the doors in less than a second. Two speed brakes were fitted below the fuselage, behind the weapons bay.

The two jet engines were installed at the extremities of the aft fuselage, with engine nozzles projecting beyond the wing trailing edge and the tail. The tail cone assembly, housing a landing parachute with operating mechanism, was a continuation of the rear fuselage section of the two engine tunnels. The engines could be removed by pulling them through the rear; a complete change of engines could be accomplished in thirty minutes. The original proposal to extract the engines by dropping them straight down for simplified overall maintenance access would have necessitated a shoulder-mounted or high position for the wing.

The thin delta wing, although outwardly conventional, incorporated subtle shapes: a leading edge droop, a semi-span 'dogtooth' notch and an outer wing chord extension along the leading edge with four degrees of anhedral. In plan view, the wing's leading edge was swept at sixty degrees and straight, apart from a notch at half-span, while the inboard panels had much less sweep. The notch and a wing extension controlled the spanwise flow of boundary layer air, preventing it from spilling towards the wingtips and leading to a separation of airflow over them. The wing's leading edge was drooped eight degrees at the inboard section and four degrees at the outboard section to prevent the airflow over the wing from breaking away at high angles of attack. This feature increased the 'aircraft's margins of manoeuvrability, allowing the pilot to maintain control during various manoeuvres, and increased the buffet boundary caused by early airflow separation.'[6]

Internally the spars of the outboard wing panel were swept at

[6] Stephen R Payne and A J Shortt, National Aviation Museum, Ottawa, 'Technical Aspects of the Avro CF-105 Arrow' [online], cited on 28 June 1999: http://exn.ca/FlightDeck/Arrow/words.cfm?ID=19990628-69.

almost the same angle as the leading edge, and this was reflected by the leading edges of the big control surfaces. The CF-105 had separate elevators and ailerons on its delta wing with a negative three-quarter-per-cent wing camber or curvature built into the bottom surface of the wing. Since there were no tail surfaces, extreme elevator travel would have to be applied in order to have effective control. The negative camber was a novel approach to building in elevator angle without creating excessive control surface drag.

The wing contained six integral fuel tanks in the inboard wing panel behind the landing gear compartment, in the wing roots, and a small tank in the part of the wing that was on top of the fuselage, inboard of the landing gear compartment. A prominent feature of the wing design was the four degrees of anhedral built into it. The anhedral provided a simple way to reduce the length required for the landing gear and provided no aerodynamic advantage.

One of the most crucial elements of the CF-105 design was the landing gear, supplied by Dowty Equipment. When a Dowty engineer bragged to him about the complexity of the system, Zurakowski remembered thinking, *'Too bad it wasn't the simplest.'*[7] The undercarriage was to fail in the two accidents that took place in test flying. As the CF-105 carried a shoulder-wing design, the main wheel legs were especially long. The Arrow also stood very high above the ground, with a nose wheel leg that was 3.65 metres long! The nose wheel leg, attached just behind the cockpit under the jet intakes, had its twin wheels side-by-side and retracted to the front in a conventional way. However, the main undercarriage legs, with two wheels set in tandem, had a more unusual retraction sequence. The main wheel legs compressed first, then retracted diagonally inwards and rotated to fit into the inboard wing panels. The main wheel legs were attached close to the leading edge, near the dogtooth extension at half-span. Powerful anti-lock brakes were provided as well as a braking parachute installed in the tail cone, between and just above the engines.

The Cook-Craigie plan

By December 1953, enthusiastic RCAF officers, defence scientists and defence industry officials had persuaded the Liberal government of Louis St Laurent to authorise two prototype airframes. It was anticipated that a production run of up to 600 aircraft was needed,

[7] Peter Zuuring, *The Arrow Scrapbook* (Ottawa: Arrow Alliance Press, 1999), 50.

each aircraft costing $2 million, with the interceptor scheduled to be operational by the RCAF in late 1961. Floyd now faced the daunting prospect of committing the company to a new airframe matched to a new engine. A very tight schedule was in place from the time of the initial design to the delivery to the RCAF for squadron use. After urging by Harvey R Smith, Head of Manufacturing, Avro studied a radical solution to the looming deadlines. In order to cut the inevitable lead time of developing and testing these new systems, Avro undertook an innovative approach known as the Cook-Craigie Plan. The Plan established production tooling from the outset, resulting in the first CF-105 being projected to reach completion status by October 1957. R K Anderson, the Assistant Industrial Engineering Manager of Avro's Aircraft Division, described the process in 1953: 'The real savings in cost are found in the lower labour cost of producing the first several production models. The cost of the first production aircraft will be reduced to the point where the cost will now be in the general area of fifteen to twenty man-hours per pound, whereas twenty-five to forty is more normal under previous methods. Take this difference over twenty tons of airframe, and a considerable savings have resulted.'[8]

The CF-105 was designed as a totally integrated weapons system, in which every factor affecting combat performance was to be coupled with every other item at the earliest possible stage of design. The decision to go with production tooling was not taken easily. Jim Floyd noted: 'We had to be dead right the first time. There was no flying the prototype, finding the problems on it and reflecting these back into the production drawings and issuing modifications. You had to be right, yet you had nothing to fall back on.'[9]

In the manufacture of the Arrow's components, the company employed advanced technologies. These included a large autoclave (a heated pressure vessel used in the metal-to-metal bonding process), a special heat-treat furnace, a giant skin-milling machine, and other heavy machining equipment. A 15,000-ton forming press (utilising rubber pads to form components), the largest of its kind in the world, was also in place. With more than 650 Canadian firms participating in the CF-105 programme, a significant number of

[8] R K Anderson, 'Production of an All Weather Long Range Fighter', A V Roe Canada Limited, 24 October 1954.
[9] *There Never Was an Arrow.*

sophisticated materials and processes were developed. Sperry Gyroscope, Dowty Equipment, the SKF Company, Canadian Honeywell Controls, Servo Mechanism Limited, Janitol, Aviation Electric, Canadian Steel Improvement Limited, Godfrey Engineering Company, Canadian Westinghouse, and Measurement Engineering were typical of the numerous firms, large and small, that contributed to the immense project by designing, manufacturing and testing individual components and systems.

In the example of one supplier, Jarry Hydraulics of Montreal had been the prime contractor for the CF-105's hydraulic systems. Jarry developed new high-pressure hydraulic fluids capable of operating at extreme temperatures, and the company would eventually provide hydraulic controls, the landing gear door jack, the armament door lock, the restrictor valves and the main gear-retractor jack, each a unique component design. In cooperation with its subsidiary, Weatherhead Company, it supplied more than 200 individual components for the hydraulic systems. Even though the parent company was an innovator and had pioneered a flareless fitting, off-the-shelf parts were unsuitable for the CF-105 project. Weatherhead developed a special environmental test chamber used to check hose assemblies, tube fittings or any fluid components under pressures as high as 15,000lb and at temperatures from -65 to 1000 degrees F. The pace of the overall programme was such that an outside contractor constructed the test chamber one week after receipt of a contract.

Engine troubles

The engine choice for the aircraft remained a concern even as the first wind tunnel tests of a series of configurations were made in September 1953. When Rolls-Royce stopped work on the ambitious RB-106 engine in the summer of 1954, the Curtiss-Wright J67 (a military development of the British Olympus 3/4 series) was substituted. The subsequent cancellation of the J67 in the following year left the CF-105 without an engine. The only suitable engine available was the Pratt and Whitney J75, although the dimensions of the engine required a further redesign of the fuselage.

During the same period Avro Orenda was developing a high-technology, private venture project for an engine with supersonic fighter and bomber applications, which came to be known as the PS-13 Iroquois jet engine. The dimensions of the Iroquois were close to those of the J75, and at an early stage the CF-105 Design Office planned for a more developed version of the CF-105 to fly with the new Orenda engine. The thrust and fuel consumption promised by the Iroquois would actually better the performance of the J75, which was subsequently considered an interim engine for the first series of aircraft, designated the CF-105 Mark I

The CF-105 Mark 2 was to be powered by two Orenda PS-13 Iroquois engines, development of which began in 1953. It was a twin-spool engine, designed to deliver 8,720kg dry thrust and 11,800kg with afterburner. The high-pressure spool had two compression and two turbine stages; the low-pressure spool had three compression stages and a single turbine stage. The then very scarce and expensive titanium was used for a number of parts, to keep the weight down. Of a total weight of about 2,000kg, titanium parts accounted for thirty per cent.

The PS-13 was run at full dry power during ground tests in 1955. In 1957 the RCAF received a B-47E Stratojet on loan from the USAF to test the Iroquois engine. The cooperation of the United States also extended to giving the Canadian crew of the aircraft a Strategic Air Command training course, and offering the facilities of the National Advisory Committee for Aeronautics to test the engine. In Project North Wind, Canadair installed the Iroquois engine at an angle on the right side of the B-47's tail, under the tailplane. In November 1957 Mike Cooper-Slipper made the first flight of the modified B-47, designated the Canadair CL-52.

Testing was not entirely without problems, including an in-flight failure of the turbine, luckily without any serious consequences for aircraft or crew. In general, however, the engine was progressing well. The Iroquois was the most powerful engine on the North American continent; it had a very good weight-to-thrust ratio and it was fuel-efficient. Development costs had not exceeded $90 million dollars – cheap, even for that time. However, the government reconsidered the use of the new interceptor by reserve units and consequently reduced its requirements to 100 aircraft, while unit costs of the programme rose.

The Achilles heel

While Avro was responsible for the airframe and engine development, the RCAF, as the 'customer', was in direct control of the procurement of other major systems. The electronics, guidance and weapons systems would also be new and unproven and would emerge as the greatest weaknesses of the CF-105 project. At the beginning of the project, Avro had wanted to use the Hughes MX 1179 fire control system to direct eight Hughes AIM-4 Falcon air-to-air missiles or unguided rockets that would be carried in a huge internal weapons bay. The Hughes avionics package and the Falcon missiles were available and, in principle, proven technology, although experience in the 1960s with air-to-air missiles would show the confidence of 1950s designers in their guided weapons to be somewhat misplaced.

A number of armament choices had been considered for the CF-105 including a Canadian design, the Velvet Glove missile. Originally designed in 1951 as an air-to-air guided missile for the CF-100 all-weather fighter, the Velvet Glove was developed by the Canadian Armament Research and Development Establishment (CARDE), a Defence Research Board laboratory at Valcartier, Quebec. The Velvet Glove was about 3 metres (10 feet) long and weighed about 200kg (500lb). The missile was powered by a solid rocket motor and equipped with a semi-active radar homing device. The radar transmitter was carried in the aircraft and the receiver in the missile, so the pilot had to keep the transmitter aimed at the target while the missile was in flight.

When management problems arose in the administration of the Velvet Glove programme, Canadair became more heavily involved and DRB asked it to assume control of the project. Aerial tests with Canadair Sabres and an experimental CF-100 took place during 1954 and 1955 and showed promise, but the missile did not offer any advantages over other contemporary examples. The Velvet Glove programme was terminated shortly thereafter due to lack of support from the RCAF

In 1955 the RCAF revised the technical requirements for the CF-105 weapon system and decided that it wanted new technology, in the form of the RCA-Victor Astra 1 radar and fire control system, and an advanced version of the Raytheon Sparrow, the Sparrow II (in addition to the eight Falcon missiles). This decision would have grave repercussions for the entire project as the development costs of these two programmes would ultimately prove to be prohibitive.

The Astra 1 design consisted of an integrated airborne system for electronic weapons navigation and communication. It provided automatic flight control, airborne radar, telecommunications and navigation, as well as special instrumentation and pilot displays, and could operate in either fully automatic, semi-automatic, or manual environments. This system was the prime responsibility of Radio Corporation of America in association with the Aeronautical Division of Minneapolis-Honeywell. The Canadian firms of RCA Victor Company of Canada, Honeywell Controls Limited, and Computing Devices of Canada received subcontracts for engineering services.

The all-missile armament of the new fighter was to be stored in an internal missile bay at the centre station of the fuselage, this belly location protecting the missiles from the elements and reducing drag. The shoulder-wing configuration that was adopted to reduce structural problems with the wing spars provided easy access to the missile bay, making maintenance easier. A quick-loading weapons pack provided rapid re-armament on the ground.

Although other armament was considered, the Arrow was always committed to an all-missile system, and the primary weapon chosen was based on the Douglas Sparrow Mark II Originally a US Navy project, the Sparrow 2D was considered a superior weapons system compared to the Hughes Falcon, but Douglas had lost its American contract, and only the RCAF's insistence that Avro continue with the missile as part of the Astra-Sparrow system kept the project alive.

Testing

By mid-1954 the first CF-105 production drawings were issued for manufacturing. The considerable aerodynamic advances represented by the aircraft required extensive wind tunnel assessment, particularly in the areas of stability and control. An extensive series of metal and plastic models of various scales from one-eightieth scale to full size was constructed, mainly at Avro. These models included complete aircraft as well as models of individual components such as intake areas. The tests were carried out in a number of test facilities in Canada and the United States. All aspects of the flight envelope were tested including high and low speed, stability and control, spin, flutter and even icing conditions. The first wind tunnel tests in 1953 took place at Cornell Aeronautical Laboratories in its 4ft by 5ft transonic 'throat of the wing' tunnel to determine longitudinal, lateral and directional stability and control. In the period 1954-1956 additional high-speed and low-speed testing took place at the NAE's 8ft by 10ft tunnel and new supersonic tunnel in Ottawa.

Later tests in 1955-1956 at the subsonic and supersonic wind tunnels of NACA Cleveland and NACA Langley established the final configuration of the CF-105. (Testing up to Mach 2.03 of a three-hundredth scale model built by Cornell Laboratories indicated no special concerns.) Specialised testing of the canopy and cockpit area involved water-tunnel testing at the NAE The Orenda engineering staff also tested a six-tenths scale engine duct model at the Orenda test cell. Sinclair Radio Laboratories, which was responsible for UHF-band and L-band antenna research, conducted a number of tests on small-scale metal (aluminium, copper and sheet metal) aircraft models and on full-scale fin and belly antenna models. All of these models were designed, manufactured and tested by Sinclair Radio Laboratories.

The wind tunnel testing and specialised water-tunnel testing were coupled with a unique series of free-flight tests that utilised rocket-powered test models to explore the upper ranges of the supersonic speeds (Mach 1.7 and above) that the CF-105 would encounter. Large one-eighth scale, 9-foot-long models were mounted on the top of converted Nike rockets. Nine of these free-flight models were tested over Lake Ontario from the CARDE Pt Petre missile test range from 1955 to 1957. Two additional tests were conducted at the NACA facility in Langley Field, Virginia, to take advantage of the 'facility's 'state-of-the-art' tracking and telemetry equipment'.[10] Each scale free-flight model had two FM transmitters that provided telemetry to a ground station. The test results verified the drag coefficients and the longitudinal and lateral stability, and confirmed that the aerodynamic design of the CF-105 would meet every expectation. (A hunt for these test models would later consume years of searching.)

Another critical aspect of testing was the extensive use of Avro ground test rigs before production drawings or tooling could be released. All rigs provided for evaluation of the compatibility, reliability and flexibility of systems and individual components, and the frequent diagnosis of faulty equipment stemmed from the use of the ground rigs. The models ranged from simple recreations to complex systems such as the fuel test rig. The prime contractor for the fuel system, Lucas Rotax, had developed a state-of-the-art system that provided a high rate of flow and flow variability as well as an electrical generating system unique to the CF-105. Avro engineers depicted this complicated system in a full-scale reconstruction of the fuselage tanks and the integral starboard wing

[10] Rich Thistle, 'Canada's Supersonic Fighter Fiasco', *Aviation History* (January 1998), 37.

fuel tanks. The fuel test rig was designed to simulate any flight situation and could measure fuel pressures and flow characteristics throughout an enormous range of conditions.

One of the unusual features of the integral fuel cells was that electrical and hydraulic components in the wings were incorporated in the 'wet' wing, necessitating a careful design of all fittings to ensure that the seals worked properly. The sealing problems were eventually solved when Avro obtained rights from an American firm for a process of injecting sealant along the channels of the wing joints.

Another important test rig was used to analyse the entire electrical system. In cooperation with Canadian Aviation Electronics, a firm charged with the design, development and production of CF-105 simulators, flight trainers, display systems, communication equipment, navigation instrumentation and radar systems, Engineering constructed a large full-scale control panel

Spud Potocki and Janusz Zurakowski in the Avro Arrow cockpit simulator, 1957. *(Zurakowski collection)*

complete with instruments and controls. The panel was the centrepiece of a group of panels that duplicated the entire electrical system of the aircraft. The device resembled a modern simulator complete with lights and warning indicators.

The complexity and cost of the CF-105 programme began to be scrutinised closely by the RCAF in 1955. In that year Air Marshal C Roy Slemon, Chief of the Air Staff, together with Dr Oman Solandt, Chairman of the Defence Research Board, requested that the US Air Force (USAF) provide an independent review of the CF-105 project. On 31 October and 1 November, an evaluation team from the senior members of the Air Research and Development Command (ARDC), together with representatives from the propulsion and fighter branches of USAF headquarters, toured Avro and Orenda. During the visit the Avro design team supplied technical data and provided first-hand background on all aspects of the design of the airframe and the engine. The RCAF request for a review had been broad enough to have the CF-105 design pitted against current and planned USAF interceptors. The extensive report that followed vindicated all areas of aerodynamic and propulsion concerns and even stated that the CF-105 would be the optimum choice as an interceptor for the early part of the 1960s (at least until the newest XF-103 and XF-108 would come into service). This curious 'mid-term' report should have raised alarm bells at Avro, yet it didn't. The main reaction in Malton was that the design was proven to be sound.

On 6 October 1956 the RCAF chose a new name for the CF-105, and by early 1957 the aircraft was officially named the Avro Arrow. Tests at Avro Aircraft indicated that, with the definitive engines, the CF-105 could well be the world's most capable interceptor. However, doubts continued to mount in the military high ranks and even in the company's greatest supporter in government, C D Howe, who now fretted over the role and costs of the Arrow. The Canadian government limited development of the CF-105 to eleven aircraft, subject to review after the first flight.

Avro's other projects

The CF-105 programme was not Avro's only innovative design project under way. A V Roe Canada also became involved in an incredible number of progressive designs that 'pushed the envelope' in many directions. It was estimated in the 1950s that seventy per cent of Canada's private research and development ventures were being carried out by the company and its subsidiaries. Most of these 'paper projects' were destined to remain only in the conceptual stage, although they did represent a unique vision of the future.

However, in the recesses of the factory, another aircraft project was beginning to come alive under the direction of John Frost and his Special Projects Group. The concept of a ground cushion was one that Frost had envisioned as being the basis for a vehicle that could have vertical take-off and landing (VTOL) capabilities and could still operate as an aircraft. His ideas revolved around a disk or saucer shape, a 'flying saucer'.

By July 1952 the concept was code-named Project Y, and the design group had not only completed a number of reports but had also constructed a wooden mock-up. After a meeting in England with members of the design group and Frost, Sir Roy Dobson was enthusiastic in his support. The project then gained both momentum and controversy. At Avro Canada, other designers, including Chamberlin and Floyd, were less than enthusiastic. There was also pressure from the Canadian government through Howe's office to concentrate on only the successful CF-100 and Orenda programmes and the future CF-105. Nevertheless, Frost continued to lobby for the project, now called the Y-2, and achieved an extraordinary breakthrough by demonstrating the project to the United States Air Force; with funding from the Americans, Frost could proceed with his design even without Avro Canada's support. From 1955 to 1959 the design team that Frost led concentrated on the VTOL programme, which spawned the VZ-9-AV Avrocar.

Throughout the 1950s A V Roe Canada began to grow, as the Hawker-Siddeley Group invested more in its Canadian subsidiary. In 1952 Crawford Gordon accelerated the build-up of the aircraft and engine facilities. A new engine-production plant had been opened at Malton and, with CF-100 tooling and production under way and now virtually filling the plant, an extension of facilities on the aircraft side was essential. 'It was estimated that more than 30,000 Canadians were now involved in the Malton programmes, in 400 different sub-contracting companies.'[11] By 1954 the company was undergoing an industrial expansion, diversifying into shipping, steel products, truck and bus transportation, iron and coal mining, railway rolling-stock, computers and electronics. On 29 July 1954 the Aircraft Division was incorporated as Avro Aircraft Limited and was commonly known as Avro Canada. The Gas Turbine Division became Orenda Engines Limited. The non-aviation subsidiary was

[11] Floyd, 'The Avro Story', 126.

Canadian Steel Improvement Limited, which was joined by Dosco, the Dominion Steel and Coal Corporation, in 1958. By this point A V Roe Canada was an industrial giant, in direct or majority control of more than forty-four companies, with total employee ranks of more than 50,000 and an annual sales figure of around $450 million. It now ranked behind only the CPR and Alcan as the most important corporation in Canada. Fittingly, the company motto that had been

Avro Aircraft Ltd factory. *(Ontario Provincial Archives)*

adopted in 1956 was 'The Next Big Step'.

In the mid-1950s the Avro and Orenda plants undertook a recruiting drive to find additional engineering and technical staff, swelling the combined ranks of these companies to a high of 15,000. William Dickie, in charge of Industrial Relations at Avro, supervised the recruiting drive. E J Silling, an Avro Aircraft Limited mechanical engineer, described the make-up of Engineering. 'The Design team was composed of Englishmen, Canadians, Poles and Americans. The Englishmen were in the majority, as Avro just completed their third annual recruiting drive through the British Isles. Canadians were local men, mostly in administrative positions. The Poles were recruited in Britain, and the Americans [were] contract workers, hired by Avro from a broker... The Poles were very good, mostly key men from the Polish aircraft industry. The most outstanding Pole was a mathematician whose capabilities in those days of slide rules and simple adding machines just bordered on sorcery. Among the Americans, one produced mind-boggling designs of sophisticated hydraulic components. Another worked on the drag chute, producing in the process several innovations patented by Avro.'[12] Elwy Yost recalls a number of trips to England where he would set up shop in the proximity of some of the great aviation firms of the day: Avro, Hawker, Supermarine and Gloster. The prospect of work on exciting projects and a chance to immigrate to Canada made the hiring of the workers relatively easy. These 'head-hunting' expeditions continued until 1958.

Learning to fly the Arrow

Zurakowski was always the first choice to fly the new Avro CF-105. Together with other test pilots at the company, he began to follow closely the progress of the project's testing and design. One of the first engineering mock-ups was a full-scale wooden model, completed late in 1955. It was originally unmarked but was later painted with RCAF roundels and in flashes as 'CF-201' as a weapons evaluation mock-up, then later marked as 'CF-206'. It featured a complete cockpit area that would help orient the test pilots to the new cockpit layout.

More importantly, a special cockpit and nose model was designed to be mounted on a modified Studebaker flatbed truck. 'A mock-up of the cockpit was built and tested by the test pilots to check visibility and instrument location under simulated flight conditions.' [13] The mock-up was mounted at the actual height and taxiing attitude of the Arrow. The pilots sat inside the structure and were driven down the runway to simulate taxi runs. At first this mock-up had only the cockpit enclosure mounted, but later a nose cone was added to more closely simulate the view forward of the cockpit. Peter Cope recalled: 'From the taxiing-out point of view, you had to be a bit careful at first, because you sat so far ahead of the gear that you had to make sure you didn't shortcut turns. Stick your nose well into the turn before you brought the rest of the aeroplane around. But that was no problem. It was a question of getting used to it after a shorter-gear aeroplane.'[14]

Zurakowski made some suggestions as to control and

[12] Murray Peden, *Fall of an Arrow* (Toronto: Stoddart, 1978), 28.
[13] Shaw, *There Never Was an Arrow*, 55.
[14] *The Chosen Ones*, 88.

instrument layout, but generally he was pleased with the cockpit, apart from the somewhat restricted view forward through the V-shaped windshield. Adoption of American-designed, slanted glass separators did much to improve forward visibility; however, as late as 1956 the RCAF still demanded changes in the size of windscreens, especially in the navigator's cockpit. Conceivably, altered windscreen designs could have been incorporated as a modification or retrofit after the trials were complete.

Wilf Farrance, the engineer directly involved in cockpit design, had tried to create an effective layout of controls and systems. One of the former Victory Aircraft engineers, Farrance had been appointed the Group Leader of Cockpit and Control (later known as Human Factors Engineering) by Edgar Atkin, who had placed him in command of twenty-two draftsmen and engineers during the CF-100 programme. Atkin advised him, 'You can copy, but don't forget to make it better.'[15] Farrance and his design staff carefully considered the ergonomics of the CF-105 cockpit environment. Pilot effectiveness was a primary concern of Farrance, and he ensured that the sophisticated cockpit would reflect this. Rather than settling for a customary arrangement of flight controls, instrumentation and panel layout, he sought out and valued the test pilots' opinions. One of his innovations was a slightly reclining seat that placed less stress on the pilot and aircrew.

Zura's concerns over the workload in the cockpit contributed to the placement and operation of gauges, panels and indicators. Not only were new instruments devised, such as a rectilinear Mach indicator that was easily read at a glance, but a series of warning indicators was used to alert the pilot to possible problems. (However, the use of an amber flashing light in bright sunlight was problematical because it was difficult to see. Peter Cope recommended a change to a brighter red light.) The test pilots had input into the cockpit design, as Cope remembered.

> We had a cockpit layout on the Arrow that was the best
> I have ever had in an aeroplane... There's always a
> great controversy between the pilots and engineers
> about what they want in the cockpit, and where it
> should be. Wilf Farrance was the intermediate man

[15] Wilf Farrance, conversation with the author, 2002.

between ourselves and the engineers for getting a good cockpit. Perfect gentleman, too. Very easy to work with. So we got a cockpit where we had a slightly reclining seat, so it was very comfortable. He worked with our engineers and ourselves, gave us the best cockpit, we thought, in the world.

The displays and controls were arranged as we wanted them, the main engine controls and gear controls were nicely sorted out. And then on the electronics, we had double banks each side. The most inboard bank was the stuff you used more frequently than the others, the outboard bank was the stuff [you used] on a secondary basis... But they were all there, a good layout. It was easy to be seen.[16]

When a USAF evaluation team was able to tour the Avro plant and observe the progress of the CF-105, General Caldara, the USAF Director of Flight Safety, was impressed with the cockpit, calling it 'unequivocally ... the best layout he had ever seen.'[17]

Farrance had specified Martin-Baker ejection seats from the outset and had travelled to England to confer with the company's owner, James Martin, who, in an irascible aside when he heard about the age of the engineer, remarked, 'Twenty-nine years old, a mere child!'[18]

When Farrance asked to see drawings of the Mark 4 ejection seat, Martin would not hear anything about business until his personal driver had chauffeured Farrance around the countryside for a week's vacation. At the end of the week, Martin unveiled the latest Martin-Baker C5 ejection-seat drawings. Ultimately, the CF-105 would be fitted with the C5 seat.

A full-scale steel mock-up of the Arrow followed in 1956, marked No 25000 and bearing the code 'WW-000', which was used extensively by the Engineering Department to check installation clearances for equipment. The most important areas were to ensure the proper fitting of the J75 engines and to evaluate the weapons pack, which was a primary function of the large armament bay of the

[16] *The Chosen Ones*, 87.
[17] *Storms of Controversy*, 56.
[18] Farrance, 2002.

CF-105. Both wooden and steel mock-ups were then modified to accommodate the Iroquois engine, which had slightly different dimensions. Additional equipment mock-ups were made in order to test systems and train the test pilots.

Zurakowski and other Avro test pilots continued to work with engineering teams in areas such as emergency features, hydraulics and electrical and fuel systems. The most complex system was a fly-by-wire control, which had never been used in production fighter aircraft of the time. The system was able to provide stability on all axes artificially. When the pilot moved the controls, a series of amplifiers and electronic relays activated the control servos, which in turn moved the control surfaces. In the event of a failure, the pilot could still maintain control through manual means. Although the system was unique and untried, the pilots quickly learned to deal with the complexity of the controls.

Danger signals

In 1955, in anticipation of the completion of the Mark 5 (the final production series of the CF-100), an improved high-altitude version was proposed to the RCAF to bridge the period up to the operational deployment of the CF-105. Together with equipment modifications and strengthened wings and airframe, the new Mark 6 was to incorporate the Orenda simplified reheat (afterburner) in the Orenda Mark 2 Series 6 engine in order to provide 11,000lb thrust – approximately fifteen per cent greater than the non-afterburner versions. Armament consisting of Douglas Sparrow or Hughes Falcon guided missiles would make the Mark 6 a more potent interceptor capable of operating at an operational ceiling more than 1,000 feet higher than that of the Mark 5. If the intruding aircraft was flying at a height of greater than 50,000 feet, the new CF-100 was intended to make a 'snap-up' acquiring of the target, to enable the missile guidance systems to lock on.

Research into the Mark 6 variant continued until October 1957 when the development programme was suddenly cancelled. The cancellation came from the new Minister of Defence, Hon George R Pearkes VC (as an Army officer who had won the Victoria Cross in the First World War), one of the recently appointed Cabinet ministers of the minority government of the Hon John George Diefenbaker, the newly elected Prime Minister of Canada. The unexpected election win on 10 June 1957 introduced an entirely different element into the story of Avro Canada. After years of Liberal governments, Diefenbaker's Progressive Conservative government reviewed its current commitments and was troubled by the previous Liberal government's support of the A V Roe company. Beyond his reluctance to deal with Bay Street types like Crawford Gordon (Bay Street was the heart of the Toronto, Ontario financial district), it was Diefenbaker's commitment to financial reform that signalled problems ahead for A V Roe Canada. The Hon Donald M Fleming, the new Minister of Finance, declared that the 'cupboards were bare', and looked upon Avro Canada as benefiting unduly from the previous government's largess.

The cancellation of the CF-100 Mark 6 arose from a recommendation of the Defence Committee, headed by General Charles Foulkes, who had been requested to reduce the overall defence budget. An immediate repercussion of the cancellation was the lay-off of up to 3,000 employees at Avro and Orenda. An uproar over this situation led to a meeting of the Minister of Finance and four other Cabinet members with officials of Avro and Orenda, in an effort to soften the blow to the companies. An order for twenty more Mark 5 fighters, together with some other contracts, allowed the firm to reduce the number of lay-offs until the CF-105 was in production. The continual six-month review of the programme was now in the hands of a decidedly wary Cabinet led by a prime minister who had no love for any project originating with the likes of C D Howe.

On 29 October 1957, following the advice of the Chiefs of Staff, the Cabinet approved a one-year extension to procure twenty-nine 'preproduction' Avro CF-105 aircraft, but served notice that the programme was under careful examination. Fleming characterised the Cabinet decision in this way: 'It was interim, it was costly and it was influenced by employment conditions as much as conditions of national defence.'[19] Thus the die was cast. The new Diefenbaker government had already made up its mind to cancel the Avro Arrow. Now events would transpire to reaffirm in the government's mind that it had made the right decision.

The first of these momentous events was soon at hand. The NORAD (North American Air Defence) Agreement, which had been

[19] Donald M Fleming, *So Very Near: The Political Memoirs of the Honourable Donald M Fleming, Volume One: The Rising Years* (Toronto: McClelland and Stewart, 1985), 416.

announced on 1 August 1957, integrated the air-defence forces of the United States and Canada under a joint command located at Colorado Springs, Colorado. (NORAD was renamed North American Aerospace Defence Command in 1981.) The Agreement had occasionally been a focus of controversy; however, Prime Minister Diefenbaker and his Minister of National Defence, George Pearkes, just installed in office, hastily accepted the advice of the Canadian military and agreed to integrate the RCAF with the USAF for the air defence of the continent.

As the implications of the Agreement began to sink in, the Diefenbaker Cabinet struggled with a new role in defending Canada against a nuclear attack. The recent advances in guided missile defences had led to the United States developing the Nike and Bomarc missiles to counter enemy bomber attacks. The IM-99 Bomarc (designed by Boeing in conjunction with the University of Michigan Aeronautical Research Center) was a ground based, rocket launched missile, powered by ramjets in flight to provide an area defence within a range of 250 miles. It operated in a semi-automated ground environment (SAGE) network where target acquisition and direction was acquired from ground controllers. On paper, the Bomarc seemed to be an effective defence against air attack over Canada.

Aggressive marketing of the IM-99 Bomarc was directed at the Canadian government. The US government on behalf of Boeing convinced Pearkes that not only was the Bomarc missile defence an adequate deterrent but it was also a cost-effective solution, although savings would only apply if the Bomarc support bases and the SAGE network were not factored in. The Diefenbaker government relied on a cost-sharing arrangement that would substantially reduce the overall cost of the Bomarc. Technical considerations such as the coordinated role of missiles and interceptor aircraft in the USAF or the effectiveness of this unproven system were not as readily considered.

In 1957 and 1958, the Diefenbaker Cabinet proposed that Bomarc missiles would be an alternative to the Avro Arrow programme. This premise was greatly resented by supporters of the CF-105 Avro Arrow. As Crawford Gordon launched a last-ditch effort to keep the Arrow project going, it was clear there was considerable resistance in the Diefenbaker government to continuing with its costly development. Even the shop-floor employees at Avro and Orenda realised that a crisis atmosphere had developed in the company. To knowledgeable people such as Zurakowski, the fears being expressed were inconsequential. He was sure that when the Avro Arrow eventually flew, everyone would see the tremendous potential of the aircraft.

Rollout

On 4 October 1957, the same day as Sputnik I was revealed to the world, another important event was taking place in Malton, Ontario, at the Avro Canada plant. After years of design and construction, RL-201 (No 25201), the first Avro Arrow CF-105, was ready for its public debut. The rollout took place on a bright and clear day – one of the few the programme would have.

The rollout ceremony took place in front of an estimated crowd of 12,000 people, which included more than 2,000 guests joining the Avro employees who had proudly built the aircraft. Representatives from the federal government and the Ottawa diplomatic corps, together with representatives from military organisations and the aviation industry in Canada and the United States, were present. Zurakowski was there that day, but was not a part of the elaborate ceremonies. Other test pilots were involved in a flypast of four Avro CF-100 aircraft, including a special development aircraft flown by Lorne Ursel, No 18601, which was fitted with an afterburner as part of the Orenda Simplified Reheat programme in the CF-100 Mark 6 development.

On that momentous day in 1957, a small boy, George Foley, had come along with his mother and father to see the unveiling of the Arrow. He was as excited as all little boys can be on a special day, a day when he could go to see where his father, a tool and die maker, worked and, of course, to see the Avro Arrow. The crowds grew larger over the afternoon. 'As many as could fit came out to see it... There was a tremendous sense of pride in the beauty of the aircraft at that stage of time,'[20] recalled Stanley Cohen, one of the computer engineers.

At the speaker's platform, two dozen dignitaries were assembled. These included Avro Aircraft executives, government leaders and members of the RCAF and Canadian military as well as representatives from the USAF One of the most celebrated guests was John D McCurdy, the pioneer aviator who had been the chief designer and pilot of the 'Silver Dart', Canada's first aircraft. The first speaker was Fred Smye, who brought greetings from the

[20] Chris Gainor, *Arrows to the Moon: Avro's Engineers and the Space Race* (Burlington: Apogee Books, 2001), 17.

company and reviewed the history of the project and its innovative design. He then spoke about the people whose talents and dedication were instrumental in bringing the Arrow to this point.

The next speaker was RCAF Air Marshal Hugh L Campbell, the new Chief of Air Staff, who described the primary mission of the Avro Arrow. His address clearly indicated that the role of a fighter interceptor was essential to the nation's defence. 'The planned performance of this aircraft is such that it can effectively meet and deal with any likely bomber threat to this continent over the next decade. We in the Air Force look upon this aircraft as one component of a complex and elaborate air defence system covering in the first instance the whole of the North American continent, extending from Labrador to Hudson Bay to the Queen Charlotte Islands.'[21]

At the reviewing stand the keynote speaker of the afternoon, the Hon George Pearkes, proclaimed:

> Much has been said of late about the coming missile age, and there have been suggestions from well intentioned people that the era of the manned aeroplane is over and that we should not be wasting our time and energy producing an aircraft of the performance, complexity and cost of the Avro Arrow. They suggest that we should put our faith in missiles and launch straight into the era of push-button war. I do not feel that the missile and the manned aircraft have, as yet, reached the point where they should be considered as competitive.
>
> They will, in fact, become complementary. Each can do things which the other cannot do, and for some years to come, both will be required in the inventory of any nation seeking to maintain an adequate 'deterrent' to war. However, the aircraft has this one great advantage over the missile. It can bring the judgment of a man into the battle and closer to the target where human judgment, combined with the technology of the aircraft, will provide the most sophisticated and effective defence that human ingenuity can devise.[22]

These remarks, although echoing the comments expressed by the

---

[21] Ibid, 15.
[22] *There Never Was an Arrow.*

other speakers that day, were to be later repudiated by his government's actions.

With his words ringing from the podium, Pearkes announced, 'I now have the pleasure of unveiling the Avro Arrow, Canada's first supersonic aircraft, a symbol of a new era for Canada in the air.'[23] He then pulled on a golden lanyard attached to the speaker's platform as the signal for the Arrow to be unveiled. Gold curtains bearing the name 'Avro Arrow' in a large elongated triangle parted. As each person strained to look at the hangar doors, a small white tow truck rolled out. Behind it a striking, delta-winged 'dart' was wheeled into public view. Spectators spontaneously began to applaud and to

Avro Arrow rollout. *(DND)*

scramble for a better view as the Arrow moved forward.

At the top of one of the hangars, electrician Ron Lowry had an impressive view of the Arrow being towed out of the hangar. Like others in the crowd, he was dazzled by its beauty and strength. The memory of that day is still with him. He remembers the jubilant and cheery outlook that all the company employees seemed to have. One in particular, he recalled, was always smiling: 'You could see that glistening smile even in the dark tunnel between the main buildings. It was Elwy Yost. He was just one of the happy employees that

[23] Ibid.
[24] Ron Lowry, conversation with the author, 2001.

seemed to be everywhere in those days.'[24]

Ellie Park, one of the writers on hand from *Macleans* magazine, recalled that the 'bird was beautiful but it seemed to have awful small feet for a bird this size.'[25] His thoughts seemed to reflect the one difficult design problem that the Arrow would have in testing – the strength and suitability of the undercarriage.

As the music surged with the band playing the RCAF Marchpast, the crowd cheered, and young George Foley gazed at the wondrous sight of the glistening white interceptor. Some time later that day, a photographer spotted him at the red rope barrier and took a photograph that became legend: a little boy gazing out at the giant aircraft. The newspapers grabbed the wire photo and, soon after, it appeared in many publications worldwide. The photograph was captioned as 'The future, looking at the future'.

If the photographer could have anticipated future events, the camera would have been aimed heavenward instead. Just at that moment, on 4 October 1957, a launch was taking place from Soviet Central Asia of a small instrument package into a low orbit of the Earth. The Sputnik satellite was a small silvery globe, a little larger than a basketball, weighing no more than 183lb and able to transmit only a simple signal, yet history changed that day. The world's first artificial satellite took about ninety-eight minutes to orbit the Earth on its elliptical path. Sputnik's launch not only marked the start of the space age but also ushered in new political, military, technological and scientific developments that reverberated worldwide. Politically, Sputnik created a perception of American weakness, complacency, and a 'missile gap', which led to bitter accusations, resignations of key military figures, and the US-USSR space race.

The worldwide reaction to Sputnik ranged from shock to amazement, and news agencies rushed to cover the story. The rollout of the Avro Arrow was relegated to a secondary position even in leading Canadian publications. Robert Lindley, who was driving two USAF generals back to the airport, heard the news on his car radio. He anguished, 'They destroyed our rollout.'[26] Avro engineer R Brian Erb heard the news at home. He too knew that 'it completely overwhelmed the Arrow rollout in significance for that day.'[27] Doug Garland, another

[25] Reed Park, conversation with the author, 2001.
[26] *Arrows to the Moon*, 17.
[27] Ibid.

of the young Avro engineers, remembers that many people in the company simply called the day 'Sputnik Day'. The tiny satellite's impact would eventually have a more telling effect on the Avro Arrow.

Flight testing begins

The RL-201 was the first of five Arrow Mark Is that would fly as developmental aircraft for the series of thirty-nine production examples. Although carrying interim Pratt and Whitney J75 engines, the initial batch of Mark Is was still a fascinating hint of the future. After the rollout ceremony, the first aircraft was sent to Repair and Overhaul for approximately six to eight weeks to be fitted with monitoring equipment and fittings that had not been completed prior to rollout. Actual performance data was recorded through on-board recorders and a telemetry system mounted in the Arrow's cavernous weapons bay. As the test programme continued, provision was made for specialised instrumentation to be mounted in the rear cockpit, configured to monitor each test flight. A solo pilot flew all of the initial Phase One test flights, but the use of a flight test observer monitoring the flight was anticipated in later tests. As Peter Watson, one of the flight crew, recently disclosed, a 'dummy' was utilised in the rear cockpit for weight balance. During one troublesome preparation for a test flight, the pressurisation of the rear cockpit could not be maintained. Watson checked the front cockpit, and there was no problem there. He bent over and shouted to Zura that there were problems with the rear cockpit pressurisation. Zura

CF-105 tests. *(Western Canada Aviation Museum archives)*

[28] Peter Watson, conversation with the author, 2002.

quickly quipped, 'We'll go. My observer won't mind.'[28]

The Arrow flight tests utilised state-of-the-art technology to gather crucial flight test data, sending it to a telemetry station in a trailer, which would then feed signals to an operations room at Avro. 'Sensors located throughout the aircraft in various systems sent data to the telemetry and recorders by signal wires terminating near the armament bay in a large patch panel. This panel allowed measurements to be selected for a given flight and patched into the recorders and telemetry. In the operations room, data was read out primarily on strip-chart recorders. The recorders were modified so that the paper with the data recorded on it, instead of just winding up in a roll, was drawn out along a long table. The various 'experts' gathered around the table and scrutinised the data as it appeared in real time.

'This real-time evaluation permitted the aircraft to proceed to probe further into the flight envelope without having to land and view the data before proceeding further. This facility was a major reason for the rapid progress in the flight test programme. Not only did the operations room have telemetry readout, but it had voice (radio) contact with the pilot in order to get his impressions in real time and to permit any desired changes in the flight plan to be transmitted to the pilot.'[29]

A radio contact was also made between the Operations room and a radar tracking station, RCAF Edgar, Ontario, which was part of the NORAD defences. Edgar provided tracking support to aid in navigation and in clearing air traffic out of test airspace. (On Zura's seventh flight on 18 April, he flew RL-201 on a high-speed run from Tobermory (between Georgian Bay and Lake Huron) to the Peterborough-Kingston area in southern Ontario, directly over RCAF Edgar. As Fred Matthews monitored flight communications back at Operations, the excited RCAF radar operator cut in with the exclamation, 'Look at that son of a bitch go! Will you look at that son of a bitch go!'[30] Zurakowski hit Mach 1.52 on that flight.

Utilising a complex fly-by-wire control, an advanced weapons system and remote ground-controlled operation, the Arrow was, arguably, the most advanced fighter interceptor of its day. The developed Arrow Mark 2 powered by Canadian-designed Iroquois engines would have been capable of Mach 2.5 speeds – remarkable

[29] Fred C Matthews, conversation with the author, 2002.
[30] Ibid.

Avro Arrow production line. *(Western Canada Aviation Museum archives)*

for 1959!

Flying the Avro Arrow

The first series of nine test flights fulfilled the contractor's airworthiness trials in Phase 1 by assessing the general handling qualities of the Arrow Mark I The tests specifically evaluated the flying control system and damping system, checked instrumentation and telemetry techniques, and investigated the measures of safety under adverse conditions. The first two pilot familiarisation flights of the Avro Arrow were subsonic, while Zura flew RL-201 at supersonic (Mach 1.4) speeds on the third flight on 3 April 1958, at a height of 39,000 feet. The flight envelope of the Arrow was extended to Mach 1.52 at 49,000 feet on the seventh flight. Zurakowski carried out the majority of the initial tests, although Potocki and Woodman each carried out an orientation flight to complete the first phase of testing. A total of five Mark I Arrows were completed and as each aircraft was cleared from the Experimental Division, a first flight was made and the aircraft joined the trials aircraft. All five Arrows then proceeded to Phase 2, the RCAF contractor compliance trials.

From Zura's reports, a flight in the Avro Arrow Mark I can be recreated. The ground crew prepared the aircraft at the run-up area while the pilot conducted an external check of controls and equipment. The pilot then entered the cockpit through the use of a tall boarding ladder, stepping in between the clamshell canopy panels. All of the Phase 1 test flights were completed with the pilot flying solo; if an observer accompanied the flight, the rear cockpit was occupied first. Once all cockpit checks were completed and the ground crew had removed and stowed the safety pins from the sears of the MB C5 ejection seat and canopy, a signal was made to the ground crew to plug in the external AC power supply and the ground starter cart. An elaborate series of cockpit switch settings was followed to initiate the starting procedure. After the 'ready to start' signal was given to the ground start operator, the throttle lever on one or both engines was set to idle position and the engine start switch was activated. The starboard engine was started first, and if the engine start was normal, the pilot would close the canopies, then engage nose wheel steering; with the throttle set at idle, the chocks would be removed and the brakes released. Steering through the taxi run was done through rudder pedals and careful use of braking to avoid a bouncing or 'porpoising' effect.

Taxi speeds were maintained at 50 knots or less and gradually decreased until the Arrow was lined up with the centre of the active runway. After disengaging the nose wheel steering, the pilot applied the brakes heavily as the engine's revolutions per minute were increased to ninety per cent of maximum military thrust. Normal take-off would not use afterburners. The aircraft nose tended to dip as the thrust increased. On a clearance signal from the control tower, Zura would release the brakes, starting the take-off roll. He explained further: 'The nose wheel can be lifted off by very gentle movement of the stick at just over 120 knots... Unstick speed is about 170 knots ASI with an aircraft attitude of about 11 degrees... Acceleration is rapid, with negligible correction required and no tendency to swing... Typical touch-down speed is a little over 165 knots... There is no indication of stalling in a maximum angle of attack at 15 degrees... In turns, stick force was moderate to light, but always positive, with no tendency to pitch-up or tighten.'[31]

The climb had to be very steep or the engines throttled back, as the undercarriage had to be retracted at a speed of less than 200 knots. Any directional stability problems inherent with the undercarriage retraction would be corrected by using normal gear-down damper on the control stick, eliminating yawing. The slight vibration felt in the airframe during the undercarriage retraction immediately ceased as smooth flight ensued.

In normal flight, the pilot trimmed the aircraft to fly without his putting any pressure on the controls prior to opening up the throttles. The climb out was at 300 to 350 knots until 25,000 feet altitude was reached. Although sensitive to pitch, low-speed manoeuvring was positive and effective. The transition from subsonic to supersonic speeds using afterburners tended to introduce some roll, which would be eliminated with damper control. Supersonic flight was smooth and steady as controls became generally less sensitive to inputs.

The actual flight plan was determined by Flight Operations in concert with Engineering. Each aspect of the flight was carefully laid out, including top speeds and altitudes, which left little room for improvisation by the test pilots. The exact details of the flight could involve mundane component and system evaluation, although the test flights were always concerned with handling and manoeuvrability. As the flight test programme advanced, the flight envelope of the Arrow was gradually increased, even though each of the five test aircraft was usually designated for a specific role in the trials. While one aircraft was instrumented for a performance evaluation, others were specially equipped for control and system development. Chase planes were assigned to the flights, and

[31] William Green, 'The Mighty Arrow', *RAF Flying Review*, Vol XIV, No 6 (1958), 18.

although the CF-100 Mark 5 and the Sabre Mark 6 were able to monitor the test flights, the majority of high-altitude and high-speed runs were accomplished by the Arrow alone. The chase planes would formate on the Arrow at the conclusion of the flight plan in order to provide a photographic record to supplement the telemetry

Test Flight of the Avro Arrow, piloted by Janusz Zurakowski. The aircraft is flying low over the Toronto outskirts. *(Avro Aircraft Ltd)*

data being sent real-time to a telemetry van at Malton Airport.

Descent would begin with the afterburners shut off, the throttles reduced to eighty per cent rpm and the air brakes extended. With speeds of Mach 0.8 to Mach 0.9 indicated, some intake rumble could be manifested by vibrational noise in the airframe. Speed reduction to 185 knots in a 'clean' condition resulted in a heavier feel in the controls. When the undercarriage was selected at 200 knots, the speeds dropped unless power was increased. With the gear down, approach speeds could now be reduced to 180 knots and held there as the runway was lined up. At an incidence of twelve to thirteen degrees, the beginning of the runway would just be visible over the nose of the aircraft about one mile out. Descending at a steady 1,000 feet per minute sink rate, the aircraft attitude was maintained with the use of throttles. Elevator and aileron control throughout descent was positive and smooth. As the aircraft approached the runway, touchdown with the main wheels took place, and then the pilot lowered the nose wheel gently but firmly. If no 'porpoising' took place, together with heavy braking, the parabrake was extended. If the aircraft made any swinging motions, differential braking would correct the landing roll. When the aircraft cleared the runway, the parabrake was jettisoned on the taxiway.

Zurakowski disclosed that the Arrow was easier to fly than the Convair F-102 or the Gloster Javelin, the two other delta-winged fighters he had flown. Other test pilots, who highly praised the handling of the CF-105, would later confirm this. Zurakowski complained about the high workload in the cockpit despite the sophisticated automatic flight control system (AFCS); on the other hand, the electronic systems were more reliable than expected, although they weren't infallible. William L 'Bill' McNamara, who worked at the Structural Test Department, housed next door to the test pilots, recalled: 'One incident that I remember hearing about was the first flight involving testing of the Arrow's fly-by-wire system. At that time electronics were in their infancy, and Jan was noted for his meticulous checking of the engineering design parameters before a test flight. After he had cleared the runway, he switched on the control system and the aircraft immediately tried to roll; Jan, with his finger still on the switch, disabled the control system and recovered level flight, thus saving the aircraft and his own life. Later investigation reportedly found that a circuit had been wired ninety degrees out of phase.'[32] A near catastrophe over the Etobicoke subdivision had been avoided by Zura's lightning reactions and quick thinking. When he ascended to a safe altitude, accompanied by Peter Cope in the chase plane, Zurakowski repeated the AFCS test with similar results. The problem was eventually traced to a connector that had been installed improperly.

On Zura's eleventh flight in RL-201 on 11 June 1958, during the landing approach the starboard landing gear leg did not deploy fully, nor did it rotate to the correct alignment. The landing gear indicator had not shown any problems, but as soon as Zurakowski touched down, the aircraft began to skid wildly. Believing that the braking

---

[32] William L. 'Bill' McNamara, conversation with the author, 2002.

parachute had fouled, he immediately released it, but there was no appreciable effect on the slewing aircraft. As RL-201 skidded off the runway, the starboard landing gear broke off completely, and the Arrow ended up tilted on its belly. A fault in the chain linkage that pulled up the rotating gear could be traced to binding of the plating within the retractor sleeve. Once Dowty Equipment carefully adjusted manufacturing tolerances in this assembly, a revised Mark II undercarriage was fitted. The new landing gear components were more robust and were scheduled to be retrofitted to all the Mark I Arrows. The damage to the underside of the aircraft was not extensive, and on 5 October it flew again.

Meanwhile, on 1 August RL-202 had joined the flight test programme, and took over the majority of flights for the upcoming Phase 2 trials. At the conclusion of the twenty-second flight of the aircraft on 11 November 1958, the landing gear of RL-202 failed as Potocki landed. Although he could not recall using the elevators, a momentary lifting of the aircraft on touchdown had resulted in the wheels locking when brake pressure was applied. All four tyres on the main gears blew, and consequently the aircraft skidded off the runway, snapping off the port undercarriage leg. The initial RCAF evaluation of pilot error had dumbfounded Potocki as he was sure that he had braked lightly. Zura was the first to note that the report had not taken into consideration data from the telemetry on board or photographs taken by three young teenagers who had sneaked into the airport. The data confirmed by the photos showed the elevators in the full down position, although Potocki was sure he hadn't used the elevators. Zura attributed the accident to a failure in the automatic control system. The landing gear continued to be a troublesome area, but with time the engineering staff knew they would solve the nagging problems that plagued this vital component. The more robust Mark 2 undercarriage, designed by Dowty and Avro, was scheduled to be retrofitted to all the Arrow flying examples by the end of 1959.

Zurakowski flew the first three Arrows on all of their inaugural flights; he flew RL-202, the second Mark I, on 1 August 1958, and while in RL-203 on 22 September 1958 he exceeded the speed of sound on its first flight! Potocki made the first flight in Arrow RL-204 on 27 November 1958, and the first and only flight in Arrow RL-205 on 11 January 1959. In the end, Zura made twenty-two flights in the RL-201, RL-202 and RL-203 Arrows, for a total of

23hr 45min. Zurakowski reviewed his flights: 'I test flew the Arrow Mark I on twenty-two flights, including the first flight. My highest speed was Mach 1.89, achieved on the twentieth flight. My deputy test pilot, Spud Potocki, reached Mach 1.98 on flight number forty-four. I think the aircraft could have reached Mach 2.1 or 2.2 with the J75 at 40,000-50,000 feet. We expected to do Mach 2.5 with the Orenda Iroquois.' The true potential of the Avro Arrow Mark I was realised on the seventh flight of RL-201 on 23 August 1958, when Zurakowski exceeded Mach 1.52, 1,600kph (994mph) at an altitude of 50,000 feet in a climb, while still accelerating. Test flights indicated that, with the proper engines, the plane could well be the world's fastest and most advanced interceptor.

The Avro Arrow was a magnificent thing in the sky, and all who saw it marvelled. George Foley, who was only a child at the time, used to run out into the yard when he heard it fly. 'I loved watching it go. I can remember it still.'[33] Reporter June Callwood remembered: 'It was the most beautiful plane I will ever see... When it lifted straight up into the sky, a slim white arrowhead, it was poetry. I never saw it take-off without my eyes stinging.'[34] Ken Cooke in Flight Test Engineering recalled that he would receive a phone call regularly 'from Bob Rice who had a garage down the road from the airport, and he used to ask me, 'Is it taking off today?' and I would say 'Yeah.' 'What time?' 'I don't know, probably about 10 o'clock.' He would be out in front of the garage with his people. He wouldn't serve anybody gas. He would be waiting for the airplane to take-off to open the gas station.'[35]

Demise of a dream

A curious incident was recently related by Vern Morse of the Avro Photographic Unit. He had been dispatched by Lou Wise to the Canadian National Exhibition in August 1958 to take some 'glam' photographs of Zurakowski, Flight Lieutenant Woodman and the Silver Dart replica that had been unveiled to mark Canada's Fiftieth Anniversary of Flight. While Morse was setting up, a harried Avro public relations type breathlessly informed him that he was not to include anyone from the reviewing area in his shots. As the

---

[33] George Foley, conversation with the author, September 1999.
[34] June Callwood, 'Requiem for a Dream', *Macleans* (13 January 1997), 56.
[35] *There Never Was an Arrow*.

photographer glanced over his shoulder, he recognised the unmistakable countenance of Prime Minister Diefenbaker glowering at the scene of Zurakowski and the Silver Dart. Relations had become definitely strained between Avro and the government. Morse respectfully honoured the request and created a set of media photographs of Zura and the replica flyer but nowhere did the Prime Minister appear in the images. Zurakowski never got to meet the Prime Minister. He commented later, 'I don't think such a meeting

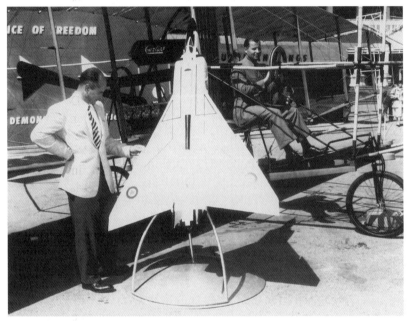

Janusz Zurakowski and F/L Jack Woodman at the 1958 Canadian National Exhibition. *(Zurakowski collection)*

would have been pleasant.'[36]

Other events were now to overtake A V Roe Canada. At their epicentre was the remarkable yet enigmatic John George Diefenbaker, the leader of the Progressive Conservative Party and, of late, the newly elected Prime Minister of Canada. His rise to power from his background as a fiery Prairie lawyer to Leader of His Majesty's Opposition was as unexpected as it was monumental. 'Dief's' populist message had stirred more than party loyalists and was the basis of two extraordinary electoral wins. The first, in 1957, unseated the post-war Liberal dynasty. During

[36] Melady, *Pilots*, 236.

his first term Diefenbaker began to establish his credentials on both the world stage and in Canada. As a fiscal manager, Dief had a vision that was decidedly unique; he distrusted the 'Bay Street Boys', who had prospered for years as part of C D Howe's grandiose projects and schemes. The prospect of dealing with Howe's creation, A V Roe Canada, as well as with its hand-picked Chief Executive Officer, Crawford Gordon, was now complicated by the conflicting evidence that he was gathering about the Arrow programme. Relying heavily on the advice of George Pearkes, his Minister of Defence, Diefenbaker decided early in his tenure to resolve the dilemma of the Avro Arrow.

On 23 September 1958 the Prime Minister made a five-page announcement to the press. He said, in part, that in recent weeks the Canadian air defence system had been fully reviewed by the government. The statement began on an optimistic note for Avro. Diefenbaker declared: 'Canadians are proud of what the Canadian aircraft industry has accomplished for defence. The Arrow supersonic plane has already thrilled us with its performance, its promise and its proof of ability in design and technology. The Iroquois engine, too, is a fine technical achievement, and its development had led to many industrial advances. Excellent scientific and technical teams had been created for these projects. In common with Canadians, the government recognises the accomplishments and technical quality of the work done, but to continue vast expenditures on aircraft and equipment which military and other expert opinion does not support as the best way to achieve the defence essential to our security would not only be wasteful but unjustifiable.'

> It is regrettable that, in Canada's contribution to a full and effective part in the air defence of the North American continent, adaptation to changing techniques and the nature of potential threat to this continent makes necessary, from time to time, changes in the requirements of deterrent power.
>
> However, it will be recognised, I believe, that as the age of missiles appears certain to lead to a major reduction in the need for fighter aircraft, Canada cannot expect to support a large industry developing and producing aircraft solely for diminishing defence requirements.[37]

[37] 'Here's the Ottawa text on Air Defence Programme', *Financial Post*, 27 September 1958.

The USSR's launch of Sputnik and advances in intercontinental ballistic missiles (ICBMs) were raising doubts about the significance of the Soviet bomber threat. Since the Avro Arrow project began, the government said, revolutionary changes had taken place that required a review of the programme in the light of anticipated conditions when the aircraft would come into service use.

Diefenbaker summed up his remarks with this ominous statement: 'The government had concluded that missiles should be introduced into the Canadian air defence system and that the number of supersonic interceptor aircraft required for the RCAF Air Defence Command would be substantially less than could have been foreseen a few years ago, if, in fact, aircraft would be required at all in the 1960s, because of the rapid strides being made in missiles by both the United States and the USSR'[38]

The Canadian government had decided to introduce the Boeing IM-99 Bomarc missile into the Canadian air defence system to be used against hostile bombers. The government's decision to integrate a missile defence appeared 'to parallel the British 1957 defence White Paper, which foreshadowed the replacement of manned aircraft by missiles for Britain's air defence.'[39] In light of these changes in defence priority, the government had decided that the development programme for the Arrow aircraft and the Iroquois engine would be continued until March 1959, when the situation would be reviewed again. The government believed, however, that it would be unwise to abruptly discontinue the development of the Arrow and its engine because of the effects upon the Canadian aviation industry. (An earlier incident had alerted the government to the economic implications of cancelling an aviation programme. In 1957, Donald Fleming, the Minister of Finance, had been enraged by the pressure exerted by Avro in the wake of the cancellation of the CF-100 Mark 6, an advanced high-altitude, missile-carrying version. In order to placate the company and delay the offset of anticipated lay-offs, a small order for Mark 5s had been placed.)

Although the entire programme was not cancelled outright, the costly and protracted development of the CF-105 was still a matter of concern. Specifically, the Astra flight and fire control system for the CF-105 and the Sparrow II air-to-air missile contracts were to be

[38] Ibid.
[39] 'For Canada's Defence', *The Aeroplane* (10 October 1958), 546.

terminated immediately. With suitable aplomb, the Prime Minister stated: 'The government deeply regrets the unemployment that will be involved in the termination of the Astra and Sparrow projects and in the Avro plant at Malton. It is hoped that our defence industry will be able to share effectively with the United States industry in one part or another of the major programmes in the air defence of the North American continent and thereby provide alternative employment in the field of missiles and electronics.'[40] The Avro design team had always advocated the adoption of the proven Hughes system, and Fred Smye had even proposed this change to the government via the Department of Defence Production. The important savings achieved by cancelling the Astra and Sparrow programmes and substituting the alternatives already in production would amount to roughly $330 million for a completed programme of 100 aircraft.

As part of the decision to proceed with only the development phase of the Arrow/Iroquois, the question of the high price of the project was raised. 'The total cost to the Canadian government of developing the Arrow aircraft and its associated elements, up to the beginning of September 1958, was around $303,000,000. To finish the development of the CF-105 and its components, including the Astra and the Sparrow, and to produce enough for 100 aircraft for squadron use, would cost about another billion and a quarter dollars, approximately $12,500,000 per usable aircraft. By substituting the alternate fire control system and missile for the Astra and Sparrow, the cost would be reduced to about $9,000,000 each.'[41]

With this public statement, Diefenbaker had laid out his arguments about cancelling the Avro Arrow. However, at A V Roe Canada, Gordon managed to convince himself that a final decision had not been made, despite a bizarre episode just days before when he had personally confronted Diefenbaker in a stormy meeting. On 17 September a fuming 'half-cut' Gordon had barged into the Prime Minster's office, reeking of Scotch and brandishing a cigar. To the dismay of the startled Diefenbaker (who not only did not smoke or drink, but also held a low opinion of those who did), the bullying and blustering simply confirmed the obvious – Gordon was not a man with whom Diefenbaker could negotiate. Although both antagonists would in future years deny that the impact of the

[40] *Financial Post*, 27 September 1958.
[41] Ibid.

meeting was significant, a close confidant of the Prime Minister, Grattan O'Leary, recalled, 'I was sitting in the anteroom when this fellow came out and he was white as a sheet. I was next in, and Dief said, 'I have just told him that the thing is off.''[42] It was all over with that meeting – nothing would reverse the government's decision to cancel the Arrow from that time on.

In the meantime, modifications to the CF-105 would be made during its development to permit the use of the Hughes fire control and weapons system that was already in production for United States interceptors. The Canadian government renewed its efforts to sell the aircraft to the United States, at the same time that the US had been promoting a new defence-sharing agreement. Pearkes himself headed up an effort to convince the US to come in on the Avro Arrow programme. With the strong influence of an American industrial-military complex, it would have been difficult to 'sell' a foreign military project like the Arrow in the United States. The subject was raised briefly, but the Canadian government's lacklustre pitch was politely but decidedly rejected.

More importantly, the Canadian Chiefs of Staff had already effectively doomed the Arrow programme with a negative review of its costs and repercussions on future equipment procurement for other military needs. At a meeting with members of the newly constituted Arrow Project Office in Ottawa, Zurakowski was unnerved by the reaction that he and John L Plant, the President of Avro Aircraft Limited, were receiving. 'There were about fifty Air Force officers present, and when Plant asked if there were any questions, there was silence until one of the officers said he was under explicit instructions not to ask anything about the Arrow. Now this was a very, very unpleasant moment for me. It was then I realised something was wrong.'[43]

Retirement from flying

When he reached the age of forty-four, Zura seriously considered an end to active flying. Although the Hawker Siddeley Group had not specified a termination date for test pilots, due to insurance restrictions and other considerations pilots had been advised to

[42] Peter Stursberg, *Diefenbaker: Leadership Gained 1958-62* (Toronto: University of Toronto Press, 1975), 122.
[43] *Shutting Down the National Dream*, 227.

consider retirement at the age of forty. For a number of days, Zurakowski deliberated about the decision to retire. Considering his decision carefully, he handed in his notice ten days after his birthday and ended his career in test flying. At the beginning of October 1958 Zura became a staff engineer with Avro Aircraft, working in the Flight Test Office as a liaison engineer with responsibilities in technical design. He explained that his new job kept him close to test flying. 'My duties were to transmit requests from technical designers for flight tests and see they were carried out. On a test flight, I was in the Operations room where records show what the aircraft is doing, After the flight, I was in the briefing where the pilot reported.' He held this position for five months.

Only four pilots ever flew the Arrow: Zurakowski, Cope, Woodman and Potocki. Lorne Ursel had joined the flight test team in late 1958 and had progressed to taxiing the Arrow at high speed just below take-off speed. Shortly after he had begun this testing, Ursel was sent to the Flight Test School at Edwards Air Force Base in the United States. Flight Lieutenant Norm Ronaasen, one of the RCAF Project team on the CF-105 Arrow, began to taxi the Arrow during the same period in 1958. Ronaasen recalled taxiing No 25203 and lifting the nose wheel off the ground before he detected a 'shimmy' in the nose wheel steering. He quickly aborted the taxi run and rolled back to the factory for adjustments, which were scheduled to last at least until the next day. A slow-down in the test-flying schedule late in the year meant that Ronaasen was never to have the chance to fly the Arrow. Flight observer D E 'Red' Darrah became the only aircrew member to fly, when he was aboard No 25203 on 19 February 1959 with Potocki.

From his office in the plant, Zurakowski could only commiserate with his fellow pilots and their fierce love of the Arrow. 'It was the experience of a lifetime. It lived up to everything a pilot could ever want in a fighter plane. I used to take the job very seriously, though. So much was riding on that plane, so many jobs and so on, that I didn't want to jeopardise anything. But then, in the end, I guess it didn't matter.'[44]

With the news of Zurakowski's retirement released to the public, a flurry of news media descended on the Avro Public Relations Department. Typically, Zura took all the attention in his stride, but

[44] Melady, *Pilots*, 236.

Avro Arrow test pilots. Left to right: Spud Potocki, Peter Cope, F/L Jack Woodman
and Janusz Zurakowski. *(Western Canada Aviation Museum archives)*

he good-naturedly participated in a slate of interviews including a
lengthy CBC interview carried out by news editor Ron LePlant. He
was touched by the genuine expressions of affection shown by his
fellow test pilots, who hosted a party to celebrate his time at Avro.
Other acknowledgements were more formal. On 25 November,
Mayor Nathan Phillips invited Zurakowski, accompanied by Arthur
Stewart, Avro's Public Relations Manager, and Spud Potocki, his
successor as Chief Development Pilot, to the Toronto City Hall for a
special presentation to commemorate Zura's contribution to test
flying. During the ceremony he was presented with gold cuff links
engraved with the official City of Toronto crest, and asked to sign
the Mayor's personal visitors' book. When Zura signed the guest
book, Phillips remarked that he should be sure to put down 'Zura'
too, since he was most familiarly known everywhere by his
nickname. Zura smiled and complied. Phillips's comments on that
occasion were heartfelt and paid Zurakowski an ultimate
compliment as a new Canadian. In part, he said, 'It is a very great
honour for me as Mayor of Toronto to receive you, Zura, and pay
this tribute to you as a great Canadian. You have made Canada your
home by choice, not by birth, and we are honoured that you have

done so. You have brought fame to this nation through your contributions to the advancement of Canadian aviation, and we are all very proud of you – Canada and the City of Toronto.'[45]

Later, at a reception at the Toronto Men's Press Club, Zurakowski was again the guest of honour and was asked to sign the Press Club's book for special guests. The gathering included representatives of all media in the Greater Toronto Area – newspapers, wire services, radio, television and magazines – which had followed Zurakowski's exploits over the years. At the reception he was asked to make a few comments. When he spoke, Zura deftly deflated the serious tone of the event. Don Rogers, who joined the Avro entourage at the reception, recalled that when Jack Marks, the President of the Press Club, innocently inquired how it felt to fly the Arrow at 'terrific speeds', the inscrutable Zurakowski quipped, 'It's this way. It's like driving slow. Only faster.'[46] The large audience roared.

'Black Friday'

The period from September 1958 to February 1959 was a disquieting time at the Avro and Orenda plants in Malton, Ontario. Despite the recent negative editorial commentary in the press and the icy reception by both military and government officials, the company busied itself with new submissions to the government regarding the outstanding issue of costs in the Avro Arrow programme. Even a 'fly-away' price of $3.3 million for the anticipated 100 production aircraft had been proposed. With the deadline for review of the Arrow and its Iroquois engine looming, it was difficult to conceal the anxiety experienced at the plants. Yet the top executives continued to insist that it would be inconceivable for the programme not to continue. Zurakowski reflected that at worst a slow-down in production may result. He recalled, 'People expected that the government could not cancel the project after seeing the results [of test flying].' Many people at Avro held the same opinion.

In Ottawa, Prime Minister Diefenbaker rose in the House to deliver a fateful announcement on 20 February 1959 (known as 'Black Friday' at Avro). The premature pronouncement on the Arrow programme in the House of Commons came nearly six weeks prior to the announced date for review of the programme. As

[45] Jim McLean, 'Each Move Experimental', 9.
[46] Jim McLean, 'Toronto's Mayor and Press Club Pay Tribute to Zura at Functions', *Avro Newsmagazine*, 4, No 17 (5 December 1958), 3.

reported in Hansard, the Prime Minister stated: 'The government has carefully examined and re-examined the probable need for the Arrow aircraft and Iroquois engine known as the CF-105, the development of which has been continued pending a final decision. It has made a thorough examination in the light of all the information available concerning the probable nature of the threats to North America in future years, the alternative means of defence against such threats, and the estimated costs thereof. The conclusion arrived at is that the development of the Arrow aircraft and the Iroquois engine should be terminated now.

'Formal notice of termination is being given now to the contractors. All outstanding commitments will of course be settled equitably. Having regard to the information and advice we have received, however, there is no other feasible or justifiable course open to us. We must not abdicate our responsibility to assure that the huge sums which it is our duty to ask Parliament to provide for defence are being expended in the most effective way to achieve that purpose.'[47]

With those words, the Prime Minister signalled the end of the Avro Arrow. A stunned House of Commons barely reacted. The official notice of cancellation had not yet been drafted, but reporters began to scramble from the session to file their stories.

Zurakowski was still seen as the heart and soul of the Avro Aircraft test-flying operation, and he was quickly contacted by the media for his reaction. 'The day of the cancellation, one of the reporters of a now non-existent newspaper, the *Telegram*, called me and said, 'Do you know the Arrow, the programme of the Arrow, has been cancelled just now by the Prime Minister in Parliament?' Of course, this was a shock; nobody would believe it, at least initially.'[48]

Zura checked with company officials; no one from the government had contacted the company.

> But in half an hour, official confirmation of this arrived. Of course, this was a shock for the people [of Avro] because a number of the people had been working for five to six years on this programme and the programme was successful. So, cancellation was really a complete surprise. Everybody expected that maybe because of

[47] House of Commons, *Debates* (20 February 1959).
[48] Bramh Rosensweig, 'Avro Arrow' [online], cited 28 June 1999: http://exn.ca/flightdeck/arrow/.

some economic or political pressure, the number of aircraft in production will decrease. But to cancel everything unexpectedly was really shocking.

What's more, in England, for example, at the end of the war, when a number of the aircraft in production and design they didn't need, then always the government considered the aircraft industry as a national asset, not a private venture. So even if a cancellation was taking place, then logically the government was trying to find means of employing the people when they cancelled the programme. But here the Prime Minister just declared, 'Sorry, I have no other jobs for these people.' Fourteen thousand people, by the way.

So, that's what was the second shock for everybody concerned... Of course, a number of people were highly upset. They had to change their life completely. In the instructions that arrived from the government, it said 'You have to stop all work immediately, inform subcontractors' so nobody could work anymore on the project.[49]

Friday 20 February was pay day at Avro and it was also the date when an agreement (which the company had just signed with two unions) would go into effect, providing a 2.5 per cent wage increase. After a protracted huddle with the executive officers, President John Plant closed the shops that morning and went on a public address system to break the news to the workers. To a hushed and stunned audience he solemnly pronounced: 'There will be no work after this date. Employees may return to remove their tool boxes Monday, Tuesday and Wednesday next week. Severance pay and vacation books will be mailed out shortly.'[50] Plant said that a few employees would be kept for maintenance and security duty and that seniority would decide that placement. Hundreds of workers who had just arrived in the night shift now made their way home. Bill Hayes, an Avro engineer, recalled, 'We were told to leave the building within an hour.'[51] As the first workers walked out into the teeth of an incipient blizzard, no one knew what to expect next.

[49] Ibid.
[50] Avro workers react to massive layoffs, 1959 [online], cited 13 October 2003: http://archives.cbc.ca/400d.asp?id=1- 75-275-1406.
[51] Jim Robb, 'The Avro Arrow', *The Ottawa Citizen*, 14 January 1989.

High above the Avro plant, test pilot Stan Haswell was carrying out a production check on No 18791, which was the second-to-last CF-100 delivered. As he phoned into the mobile unit, he received the distressing news that the plant had shut down. He couldn't believe it, but the message was, 'That's it. We've had it. We're all out!'[52] The first news reporters arrived at the factory gates and tried to buttonhole any of the workers who passed. Bill Beatty of CBC Radio was at the plant to witness 'a funeral procession of hundreds of cars, lined up bumper-to-bumper, carrying toolmakers, engineers and office workers from the plant for the last time.'[53] An unidentified office worker revealed her anguish to the reporter: 'Everyone's just shocked, just stunned!'[54] Frank Dickson, a structural assembly worker, was almost at a loss for words. He blurted out, 'It was a dirty trick.'[55] He and scores of friends in the plant were heavily committed to an instalment plan to purchase homes. More than 1,500 staffers had been enrolled in a payroll deduction plan. They were about to lose their homes as well as their livelihoods.

Reporter Bob Bergen's father, a machinist at Avro Orenda, came home drunk that night, cursing Diefenbaker for his decision to scrap the Iroquois. Bergen remembers his mother was in tears as well.

Zura left the Avro plant that day, not knowing if he would ever return.

The Avroites

That morning the giant plants that made up the Avro and Orenda works fell silent. The usual tapping of typewriters, noise of machinery and roar of jet engines were no more. It would never be the same again. To the executives such as A V Roe Canada President Crawford Gordon Jr and Avro Aircraft Limited Vice-President and General Manager Fred Smye, the Arrow and its mighty Iroquois engine were not just examples of new technology but the dreams of a future for the company. They were about to lose it all.

After the Arrow was cancelled, most of the ex-Avro employees began to move out. James C Floyd, Vice-President of Engineering, recalled, 'They didn't leave to seek better opportunity; they moved out because they were shunned by their country. Many people were

---

[52] Haswell, 'Test Flying the CF-100', 88.
[53] Avro workers react to massive layoffs, 1959 [online].
[54] Ibid.
[55] Ibid.

dismayed that the Arrow was cancelled and that they were going to lose not just national prestige but some very close friends.'[56] The exact number of employees in the tightly knit community of Avro Canada, collectively known as 'Avroites', who lost their jobs that dreary February day is hard to determine. Various sources have given the figures as anything from 13,860 to 14,528. Company records are imprecise, although the number fell below the 1955 figure of 15,000 employees. Lay-offs, attrition and the closing down of the CF-100 production line had accounted for the gradual reduction. What is more difficult to determine is the number of employees of the approximately 600 sub-contractors that supplied the parts and equipment who were equally affected by the Black Friday announcement. Conceivably, between 15,000 and 35,000 workers had their lives changed on Black Friday. Some Avroites were to come back within days; others looked for work in their speciality and were fortunate to find something, often far afield. Most found that employment in their trade or skill was nearly impossible to obtain and left their homes and the company forever.

Avroites were part of an enterprise that operated in many ways like a small city. The many thousands of Avro employees were served by a hospital, security force, fire department, training facilities, water and sewage systems, as well as services such as cafeteria/restaurants, mail, photography and printing/publication departments that are now common to many modern companies. These facilities and services were essentially duplicated at both Avro Aircraft Limited and the neighbouring Orenda Engine plant. The company was at work twenty-four hours a day, seven days a week (albeit with a reduced staff on Sundays). The extent of the operation required an immense parking area, and the largest traffic jams in Canada occurred as employees jockeyed around at the shift changes. The prominent locations of the Avro and Orenda companies in the village and (later town) of Malton led to a symbiotic relationship. One significant example was that the Avro plant supplied water to both Malton and the airport that Avro shared with the city of Toronto. More than ninety per cent of the tax assessment of Malton came from the Avro and Orenda facilities.

Although many of its employees lived nearby (with the largest group, more than 7,000, in Metropolitan Toronto), a wide area of

[56] Floyd, 2001.

southern Ontario was populated by Avro families. Brampton, Chinguacousy and Peel County each had more than 1,000 employees, while smaller centres such as Acton, Bolton, Caledon, Georgetown, Milton, Orangeville, Port Credit and Streetsville each had more than 200 Avroite residents. In small municipalities like Streetsville, almost every second home held an Avro employee. For more than a decade the company had built more than a thousand homes in Malton and the surrounding areas. In the harrowing months following the Arrow's cancellation, many embittered and angry Avroites simply walked away from their homes and began a new life elsewhere in Canada. Others left the country for good. By the end of the weekend, like other Avroites, Zura had begun to consider his options.

The end of the Arrow

A V Roe Canada's company directors, led by Crawford Gordon, had immediately laid off nearly 14,000 employees. However, approximately 1,500 senior engineers and technicians were rehired within a few weeks for work on other projects handled by Avro Aircraft Limited and Orenda Engines Limited, including the revolutionary Avrocar research vehicle. A further 1,000 employees made their way back in the next months.

The lay-offs were received by Prime Minister Diefenbaker and other members of the Cabinet as an attempt to embarrass the government. For the immediate period, the visible impact of the Arrow's cancellation was seen as mainly an Ontario problem, with media and public opinion generally favouring the government's decision. When Opposition members finally arose in the House of Commons to challenge the actions, the government replied with a curious new twist to the rationale for cancelling the Avro Arrow. On 23 February 1959 the Minister of National Defence explained: 'During 1958, when it was becoming obvious that neither the United States nor the United Kingdom would be interested in purchasing the CF-105, very extensive studies were carried out to see what alternatives might be adopted, how many of the CF-105s we could possibly afford to purchase and how many would be required to meet the diminishing threat. There was some concern at that time about the range of the CF-105. We had been informed then that the ranges were 238 nautical miles flying supersonically and 347 nautical miles flying subsonically.'[57] The stage was thus set for

[57] House of Commons, *Debates* (23 February 1959).

future debate on the cancellation of the Arrow.

Zurakowski was out of work, but so was almost everyone else in Avro Canada. He reflected: 'Lots of people started thinking what to do next. Of course, a number of people went to the United States, a few to the United Kingdom, but a number of people changed jobs completely. We had three flight engineers in the Experimental Flying Section, who decided they would never work in the aviation industry. They went to university and now they are dentists. One excellent aerodynamicist changed over to be a dentist. That's a colossal waste of manpower and knowledge and education, but that's what happened.'

Some of the returning workers ultimately were given the task of cutting up the five completed Arrows (RL-201 to RL-205 had already flown) and the other semi-completed Arrows on the production line, for on 18 April 1959 the government had ordered all plans and aircraft to be destroyed. David Mackechnie, son of Avro's Chief Photographer, Hugh Mackechnie, in a 1999 correspondence noted: 'On the day the destruction began, Defence Minister Pearkes was asked by the press if it was true that the Arrows were being destroyed. He answered no. That very day, my father, Hugh Mackechnie, came home from work with photographs of the aircraft being destroyed! The next day Pearkes rose in the House of Commons to correct himself and say that yes, it was true, the Arrows were being cut into scrap. In truth, much more than that was happening. Crews were going all over the plant gathering plans, drawings, photographs, negatives and films – anything relating to the Arrow – to be destroyed. There was to be no record left that the aircraft had ever existed.

'The destruction of all this material can be put this way. Looking back on this extraordinary event, the scrapping of the Arrow seems an act of either inspired malevolence or of criminal stupidity. A mocking epitaph to the work of the men and women who built her.'[58]

Grown men cried at the wanton destruction. Elwy Yost from Avro's Personnel Department vividly described the devastation.

> It was all shock. There was foreboding, but part of you would feel they're not going to destroy this incredible machine that was really the pinnacle of its art. People behaved as though their closest friend had died.
>
> I'll never forget one thing, the smell of acetylene

[58] David Mackechnie, conversation with the author, 1999.

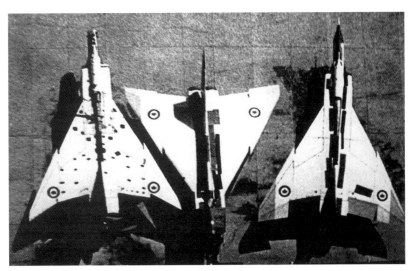

Avro Arrows cut up at the factory. *(Herb Nott)*

> torches that were being used to cut up the Arrows that
> had been completed. Word came through to us that
> Diefenbaker and his team didn't want so much as a
> set of blueprints left. I'll never in my life forget that
> acrid smell.[59]

Driving back from Malton on Thursday 25 April 1959, Zurakowski
was making his way slowly on the 401, southern Ontario's main
freeway. Co-workers had noted that Zura was a careful driver;
consequently it was not unusual for him that day to be passed on the
freeway by a large truck towing a flatbed trailer. When the truck
passed, he looked across at the stack of jagged white metal sections
tied down on the trailer. Not quite recognising what it was at first, he
looked again and was able to discern the numbers 2-0-1, in black
against the white metal. As the truck pulled away, he realised that
the pile of scrap metal was the Arrow. It was the last sight he had of
the Avro Arrow until years later when the remains of '206' were
displayed at the Science and Technology Museum in Ottawa.

A Hamilton scrapyard run by the Lax Brothers had purchased
the remains of the Arrow from Crown Assets for $300,000. The
purchase included all the aircraft and jigs in the plant. The job of

[59] Douglas Bell, 'Elwy Yost Remembers the End of the Arrow', *The Globe
and Mail*, 11 January 1998.

cutting up the aircraft was begun by Avro employees but it had been completed by the scrapyard.

From 1949, when the Avro CF-105 Arrow was initially proposed, until the Canadian government's controversial cancellation of the project in 1959, the Avro Arrow programme was one of great promise but unfulfilled objectives. The Arrow was undoubtedly one of the most advanced jet interceptors in the world, but owing to the prohibitive costs of development, it was an extremely expensive military venture for Canada. With the changing political and military policy considerations that emerged in the late 1950s, the Avro Arrow was doomed. Many Canadians bemoaned the cancellation of this incredible aircraft, the devastation of Canada's largest aerospace manufacturer and the resulting exodus of Avro Canada engineers and technicians. Most of these went to the United States to continue their work in the aerospace field, but it was a disaster for Canada's aviation industry, practically ensuring that future military aircraft would have to be purchased abroad.

Not only were the Arrow and the Iroquois dead, but the parent company was in dire trouble. A V Roe Canada's motto had been 'The Next Big Step'; regrettably, the next big step was with its shareholders across Canada.

Picking up the pieces of their lives

Efforts were made to keep the teams together in the event that work resumed at Avro. At the same time, aerospace companies from the United States brazenly went about the business of luring what General Lauris Norstad of NORAD had characterised as 'just about the best team that I have ever seen anywhere'.[60] Setting up shop at the Royal York Hotel in downtown Toronto, the recruiters did a turnstile business. Jim Floyd, Vice-President of Engineering, was one of the people trying to maintain some cohesion in the ranks of Avro's engineers. 'After the cancellation, I first of all went out to the West Coast to try and find jobs for my people, because I had 150 very qualified engineers and I had 1,500 other draughtsmen and engineers in the design office,' he remembers. 'I went out … and talked to a number of companies like Boeing and Lockheed so we could place teams of our people there, and get them back again when sense broke out and we got back into business at Avro, which of course we never did.'[61]

[60] Floyd, 2001.
[61] Bramh Rosensweig, 'Post-Arrow Brain-drain' [online], cited 28 June 1999: http://exn.ca/flightdeck/arrow/.

Floyd was offered several jobs in the US, although in the end he returned to his native Britain as Chief Engineer of the Advanced Projects Group (HAS/APG) at Hawker Siddeley Aviation, exploring supersonic transport designs. The HAS/APG supersonic transport feasibility programme also employed ex-Avro engineers in key roles: Joe Farridge in Project Analysis, John McCulloch in Aerodynamics, Pat McKenzie in Structures, and Colin Marshall as a System Specialist. This early supersonic transport (SST) study was the basis of the Anglo-French Concorde supersonic airliner. Floyd later established the consulting firm of J C Floyd Associates and, among many activities worldwide, from 1965 to 1972 he was a consultant on the Concorde – a fitting follow-up for the man whose designs included the Avro Jetliner and the Avro Arrow. He retired in 1980 and moved back to Canada with his family.

Many ex-Avro Canada engineers went to the United States. The most prominent was Jim Chamberlin, Chief Aerodynamicist on the Arrow. In April 1959 he and thirty-one other Avro engineers were recruited by the fledgling National Aeronautics and Space Administration (NASA). The 'Avro group', which eventually included twenty-six engineers, joined NASA's Space Task Group (STG), headed by Bob Gilruth at the Langley Research Center in Hampton, Virginia. The group later moved to Houston, Texas, to become the core of what is today the Johnson Space Center operation. Chamberlin was in charge of engineering on the Mercury and Gemini Projects, and Gilruth's chief advisor. One of his most important contributions to the Apollo missions was in advocating the use of the Lunar Orbit Rendezvous as a method of landing on and leaving the Moon.

Owen Maynard, another Arrow engineer, became Chief of the Systems Engineering Division of the Apollo programme at NASA Maynard was involved in the design of the lunar module and, in 1967, also conceived the influential 'A to G sequence' of missions prior to landing. He left NASA after the first two lunar landings and worked at Raytheon on solar energy and satellites.

Robert Lindley, the Chief Engineer at Avro, went to work at McDonnell Aircraft in St Louis. He became Production Manager on the Gemini project through McDonnell. Lindley joined NASA in 1969 as Director of Engineering and Operations for manned space flight just as the Space Shuttle was coming to life. Later, he went to the European Space Agency as a consultant for the Spacelab.

Of the Avroites who ended up working at Mission Control, the best known was John Hodge, who had worked on loads and flight tests for Avro. He served as a Flight Director through the Mercury, Gemini and Apollo programmes. He acted as Flight Director of Neil Armstrong's maiden space flight on Gemini 8 for the first docking of two spacecraft. The mission turned into the first emergency in space when one of the Gemini thrusters started spinning the capsule out of control. It was Hodge who ordered the crew back early and prevented a disaster. In 1967 Hodge was in the Flight Director's chair when the Apollo launch-pad fire took the lives of astronauts Roger Chaffee, Gus Grissom and Ed White. He subsequently left Mission Control and went into planning.

Mario Pesando, having served at Avro Aircraft as Chief Flight Test Engineer on the Jetliner and CF-100 and then as Chief of Project Research, was involved in some consultancy work in the immediate aftermath of Black Friday. Subsequently he moved to Massachusetts to work at RCA on the Operational Flight Control for NASA's Saturn V project. He later joined Avco in the Minuteman ICBM programmes before returning to RCA Pesando returned to Canada to work for Indac Technologies on helicopter landing systems for shipboard applications.

A number of other ex-Avro engineers also went on to make their mark at NASA and other aerospace firms. Bryan Erb, who was involved in aerothermodynamic analysis on the Arrow, became the Assistant Manager of the US-Canadian Space Station Project before moving to the Canadian Space Power Initiative as Manager. Formerly with Flight Test at Avro, C Frederick 'Fred' Matthews moved to NASA's Flight Monitor and Control as the Director and Backup Flight Director on the Gemini and Apollo programmes. Tecwyn 'Tex' Roberts, originally in Avro Engineering, joined the Trajectory Group in Mission Control Center as Flight Dynamic Officer, later becoming the head of the Space Task Group. John Sanford was the Director of Engineering, North American Aviation, Space Shuttle Launch System. Carl Lindow, formerly Engineering Project Manager on the Arrow, worked in Boeing as the Development Programme Manager, Space Programmes. Other Arrow alumni included Frank Brame, who was also at Boeing as the Chief Project Engineer on the Supersonic Transport (SST), 767 and 777 projects, and Ken Cooke, who was a Landing Gear Designer on the NASA Space Task Group and the Concorde airliner. Another Avroite, Alan Buley, became the Vice-President of Fokker Aviation.

A group of ex-Avro employees did find work close to home. de Havilland Canada, located at Downsview, Toronto, employed a group of Arrow engineers. Tom Higgins, Arrow engineer and Chief Designer on the WS-606A Flying Saucer, became the Senior Designer on the DHC5 Buffalo; Peter Martin from Project Design was the Project Engineer on the DHC2 Beaver and the DHC6 Twin Otter; while Don Whitley, Aerodynamicist on the CF-100, Arrow and Avrocar projects, became head of de Havilland Canada's 'blown-wing' projects. Don Rogers, formerly Avro Chief Test Pilot, joined de Havilland Canada as the test, demonstration and training pilot for the DH line of Short Take-off and Landing (STOL) aircraft.

Avro's large test pilots group was essentially broken up. Spud Potocki stayed on as Chief Test Pilot, overseeing the troublesome Avrocar flight-test programmes until 1962, when he left Avro to join North American Rockwell. Peter Cope continued until 1960 with Avro's Fight Test unit, mainly flying production testing on the last CF-100s. He left for Boeing to become part of the Customer Support Group on the 727, 737, 747 and 767 series. Mike Cooper-Slipper, who was carrying out the pre-flight inspection on the B-47/Iroquois test bed on Black Friday, retired from flying. Chris Pike continued flying for other companies, while Stan Haswell left Avro and flying for good. Lorne Ursel was on a course at the famed USAF Test Pilot School at Edwards Air Force Base when the news came down that the Arrow was finished. He telephoned Don Rogers to ask what to do. Rogers advised: 'Avro has paid for your course. Finish it and make something out of it.'[62]

He parlayed his technical experience into landing a job with Computing Devices, subsequently founding a ground breaking computer firm, Digital Methods Limited, which later became the Advanced Technology division of Canada Systems Group.

Following his termination, Zurakowski found himself as one of the most celebrated ex-Avro employees. The days after 20 February revolved around a number of options. Mario Pesando had an intriguing idea that involved collaboration on an engineering project. 'With Mario Pesando we were involved in a project known as the 'Paraplane'. Mr Bill Richardson (who made money on penny stock) was planning to put on the market the Paraplane, a light plane designed by Edward Lanier from Pennsylvania. The project

[62] Lorne Ursel, 2001.

was abandoned when a close evaluation of this aircraft's performance was found unsatisfactory.' The North American Rockwell Company also held out the possibility of returning to test flying. The project would be the incredible XB-70 Valkyrie supersonic bomber. Only a few test pilots of Zurakowski's calibre would be able to handle such an assignment.

He recently recalled the decision he had to make. 'After cancellation, I had some offers to work in the United States, but my wife decided that we would not leave Canada, that's all. I had to change and try to start a new life. Obviously, there was no future in my specialisation, which was high-speed development work in Canada. So I had to change completely. Previously I believed that to get anywhere, you have to specialise. Now I reversed everything. My friends considered I was crazy, but now I think they agree that my idea was quite right and I am quite happy.' After careful consideration, Zura turned down the offer from North American Rockwell and began to examine an opportunity that presented itself in the beautiful resort area where his family so enjoyed their summers.

The beginning of the end for Avro

Back at Avro Canada, the remaining employees worked on various projects, including fulfilling the existing maintenance contracts on the CF-100 and Orenda engines, as well as the sole remaining research and development programme that continued under US funding – the WS-606A with its Avrocar technology demonstration aircraft, which was now entering flight-test status. Attempts to interest the Canadian government in new aeronautical projects were futile; however, efforts to diversify into other ventures continued. Typical of its research projects was the unusual 'Big Wheel Transport'. The 200-ton capacity transporter was designed to 'negotiate 10-foot-deep holes and boulders as effortlessly as an automobile riding potholes.'[63] With four individual wheels, each 13 metres (50 feet) in diameter, the monster vehicle had its own living quarters, recreation room and more.

The first major programme in which the company invested its own capital was the manufacture of Richardson boats, built in co-operation with the Richardson Boat Company, an old-established US manufacturer from North Tonawanda, New York. Avro introduced

[63] 'Big Wheel Transport', brochure, A. V. Roe Canada Limited, c1961.

new construction techniques for the aluminium hulls, and although the boats were technically successful, the high costs of the luxury water cruiser, as well as the poor economic outlook for the Richardson company, resulted in cancellation of the project after only a few dozen boats had been completed. In a smaller but more successful venture, which was a near return to the original roots of the company in manufacturing steel pots and pans, Avro undertook the manufacture of vending machines under licence.

None of these new enterprises could bring the pride and the legacy that the Avro Arrow had brought. The people who were part of the Arrow programme worked not only to build an airplane but to put Canada in the forefront of aviation technology. In 1962, three years after the Arrow was cancelled, the once-booming aviation plant at Malton was renamed Hawker Siddeley Canada and its operations were wound down. Orenda Engines continued as an engine manufacturer, although its lone major contract of the 1960s was the licensed manufacture of the General Electric J79 engine that powered the CF-104 built by Canadair.

Chapter Ten

A New Life Begins

During the tumultuous months following the cancellation of the Avro Arrow, the award committee for the prestigious Trans-Canada Trophy named Janusz Zurakowski as the 1958 winner. Also known as the McKee Trophy, this award is the oldest aviation award in Canada, having been established in 1927. It recognises outstanding aerospace achievement by a Canadian citizen for a single exploit within the past year or a sustained high level of performance in recent years.

Ironically, on 15 April 1959 the award was announced by George Pearkes, Minister of National Defence, one of the men responsible for the fate of the Arrow and the company that gave it birth. In making the announcement, the Minister declared that the success of the initial Arrow flights was largely due to Zurakowski's untiring efforts to familiarise himself with the aircraft, together with his high degree of skill and judgment. The citation of the 1958 Trans-Canada Trophy further acknowledged Zurakowski 'in recognition of his outstanding contribution to experimental test flying of jet aircraft in Canada, and for his outstanding contribution to world recognition of Canadian aeronautical achievements.'[1]

Pierre Sevigny, Associate Minister of National Defence, presented the Trans-Canada Trophy on 28 October 1959 at the annual convention of the Air Industries and Transport Association held in Montreal. As a recognition and acknowledgement of his test flying, Zurakowski proudly considered the Trophy as a fitting end to his lifelong career in the air. By that time he had already set forth on a new endeavour – one that would take him back to the land, like his illustrious ancestors had done in his native Poland.

Both Janusz and Anna had resolved to remain in Canada after the end of the Arrow programme. His wife's interest in Polish traditions had led her to open the Lajkonik Gift Shop on Roncesvalles Avenue in Toronto in September 1957. The name 'Lajkonik' came from the Cracovian festival commemorating

---

[1] Sutherland, *Canada's Aviation Pioneers*, 248.

Poland's defeat of invading Tatars in the thirteenth century. The small hobby shop had sold mostly Polish handicrafts. In the same year, Janusz had become a Canadian citizen, giving up the British citizenship that he had retained since his time at Gloster. Now for both of them, it was time to look at the future. Choosing a new career as a tourist resort operator was an idea that had been formulating for a period of time. To some of his colleagues, the thought of Zura starting a new life in northern Ontario was not far-fetched. He was constantly talking about the summer vacations that Anna and the boys enjoyed. A rumour circulated in the plant that he flew various flight paths with the Arrow over the northern real estate that he was contemplating. This suggestion was jocularly denied by Zurakowski. 'The notion that a test pilot could control the conditions of a test flight has no basis in reality. We were told exactly where to fly and, besides, our family had already purchased the land for our new home in 1958.' For weeks, Zura had driven in the Ontario back country with his 1957 Chevrolet, and then travelled along northern lakes in his kayak, looking for the ideal location. He finally settled on Lake Kamaniskeg near Barry's Bay.

The Zurakowski family spent the fall and winter of 1959/1960 in preparation for their move north to make a new permanent home on the shores of Lake Kamaniskeg where a 125-acre tract had been purchased. Zura had previously studied building construction through a correspondence course at the Ontario Department of Education. He then enrolled in a drafting course at Ryerson College in order to design the lodge he had in mind. Skilfully he laid out the blueprints for a typical wooden zakopianski house. The design featured a small porch and a steep roof, which resulted in construction problems, but Zurakowski tackled the task and created workable solutions. He reflected later, 'We were stubborn, we wanted everything to look exactly like drawn on our paper sketches.' Two local workers were contracted as labourers, but Zurakowski undertook much of the construction by himself as he realised that the preliminary work of 'cutting the resort out of the wilderness' had to be completed before the winter. The arrival of the hunting season, one of the local traditions, meant that his construction crew would be unavailable for stretches of time, and Zura could not wait. Gradually during the summer the pine lodge was erected. The site chosen for the house was an outlook over the lake, near a sandy beach and sheltered by trees. The morning view from the bedroom windows would be spectacular.

For the rest of the family, the change in locale had been accepted in their stride. Anna helped wherever she could, but for the boys it was a great adventure. Their parents regarded that period as an idyllic one for their children. 'During this time our boys had a fabulous summer holiday; without a care in the world they played and ran around in the forest. When September came, it was time to register them in the local school, which was run by the Holy Sisters of St Jadwiga's Parish in Barry's Bay. To save me time, Hanka drove the boys to school by motorboat; it was exactly five kilometres across the lake.'

Kartuzy Lodge

Not only was the lodge nearing completion but the bush property was also starting to take shape. Using a tractor he nicknamed 'the elephant', Zurakowski cleared a rough roadway to the lodge. To this day the paths he had created are the basis of the lanes and roads of this area. Throughout the mild autumn, work proceeded on the new homestead, but soon, overhead, the first wondrous sight of geese foretold the approaching winter. On a frosty morning in the first week of November 1960, a cartage truck trundled up to the door of the newly completed home. Aboard were all the Zurakowski possessions: appliances, furniture, linens and sundry items that had been packed up in Toronto. As all the goods were discharged and brought inside, it was evident that there was still a lot of work to do. The interior walls were still not finished and black packages of insulation stuck out in odd spots. However, the essentials were there – electricity, heating and framed-in rooms. The rest would be completed over the long winter to come. For the first while, water came from the lake; it was pure and clean, although the operation necessitated a continual bucket brigade. The name selected for the lodge was 'Kartuzy', derived from the city of that name in Poland.

Kartuzy Lodge, with four rooms in the main lodge and supplemented by two additional cabins built nearby, was ready for visitors in 1961. With the assistance of young students from Barry's Bay, the Zurakowskis welcomed the first guests that summer. Anna became the director of the resort, sharing the duties of host with Janusz. Kartuzy Lodge, described by Zurakowski as 'a modest summer tourist resort which we continue to operate to this day,' became a part of the extraordinary Polish community of Ontario's 'Kaszuby' region. The area of Barry's Bay, Wilno and Round Lake – known as Madawaska Valley – was also named Kaszuby by its many

'Elephant' tractor. *(Zurakowski collection)*

Kartuzy Lodge. *(Bill Zuk)*

Polish-Canadian inhabitants. The rugged beauty of the forests, hills, lakes and rivers reminded the first Polish settlers of the Kaszuby region of Poland.

The Polish community in Canada

With the earliest French and British immigrations to the colonial holdings of New France and British North America came people of various other ethnic groups. The earliest recorded Polish settler in Canada was Dominek Barcz who arrived in 1752 to begin a new life in Montreal, although up to the middle of the nineteenth century only a few Poles had settled in Canada. Of special note was the contribution of Sir Casimir Gzowski, who had arrived in Ontario after taking part in the 1831 insurrection in Poland. He soon became involved in political, mercantile and military affairs in the colonies. Nominated as honorary aide-de-camp to Queen Victoria, who later bestowed a knighthood on him, Gzowski served as the Lieutenant-Governor of Ontario. Best known for his work as an engineer, he left a lasting legacy in the construction of roads and railways throughout Canada and is especially known for the building of the International Bridge across the Niagara River, connecting Fort Erie to Buffalo.

In the 1800s Polish territories were divided between Russia, Prussia and Austria, with civil authorities repressing Polish language and culture. Poles from the poorest farming regions fled the desperate poverty of their homelands, seeing the New World as a new beginning. Canadian agents promised these immigrants free land and free passage to Canada. What awaited them were overcrowded, poorly outfitted cargo steamers and a perilous ocean crossing. Many families arrived in Canada in mourning, with, as Anna described, 'The waves of the ocean closed forever over the bodies of their loved ones.' The second shock was the realisation that their new lives would start in a wild and untamed northern land. What lay ahead was the harsh rail trek into the barely charted wilderness and farm regions of Ontario and the West.

The first large-scale group of Polish settlers arriving in 1858 were the Kaszubs of northern Poland, who had escaped from Prussian oppression. Attracted by the beautiful Madawaska Valley in Renfrew County, Ontario, they founded the settlements of Wilno, Barry's Bay and Round Lake. By 1890 there were about 270 Kaszub families, primarily working in the lumber industry and farming along the Opeongo colonisation road in the Ottawa Valley. In the

beginning they were distrusted and ill-treated by others in the
Renfrew community because they were different and 'did not speak
the language'. Soon, the newcomers overcame this opposition
through their hard work and contribution to clearing the land in these
isolated communities. Like other Polish expatriates worldwide, they
dug in and established roots, relying on family, church and tradition.

After them came others who settled in the West. By 1911, Poles
living in Canada numbered 33,652, and twenty years later census
figures showed a thriving Polish community numbering 167,485.
This huge increase was attributable to not only the original settlers
but also a second influx of Polish immigrants during the period 1919
to 1931. This second wave was characterised by a change in the type
of Polish immigrant. While agricultural and semi-skilled labourers
still made up a considerable portion, this group also represented a
more cosmopolitan and educated worker. These immigrants
gravitated to the industrial centres in Canada and found success in a
variety of professional and technical vocations.

The third wave of immigration to Canada occurred in the post-
Second World War era as Polish refugees began to seek a new life
abroad. While the Polish nation struggled with the prospect of
resurrecting a new state under Communist leaders, many Poles
chose to remain as exiles. 'These were Poles whom wartime fate had
uprooted from their native land.' Most were members of the Polish
armed forces who had fought side by side with the Allies against the
Axis powers. Many of them came from England with a good
knowledge of the English language and higher education, and
integrated into mainstream society in Canada. Although culture and
traditions remained strong, many of these people and their children
are now very much a part of their adopted homeland. Nearly half of
the third wave of Polish immigration settled in Ontario and added to
what was now the seventh largest ethnic group in Canada. Janusz
Zurakowski and his family were part of this last wave, which
contributed a vital and vibrant facet of the Canadian mosaic.

As in the past, the beauty of the Kaszuby country and its vibrant
traditions have attracted many recent Polish immigrants. Scores of
summer cottages have been built, many permanent residences have
been established and youth camps have been organised, with
Kaszuby becoming the focus of Polish scouting in Canada. In 1986 a
group of Polish-Canadians founded The Polish Heritage Institute-
Kaszuby, a non-profit organisation. The aim of the Institute is to

Janusz Zurakowski repairing an outboard motor, 1988. *(Zurakowski collection)*

support the progress of the Kaszuby region and to preserve its traditions. In 1991 the organisation published *The Proud Inheritance: Ontario's Kaszuby*, edited by Anna Zurakowska, which described the region, its heritage and community life.

A new home

The first years at Kaszuby were alternately curious and wonderful. Zurakowski remembered that time. 'How were we accepted by the local population, of which the majority came from or had ancestors from the Kaszuby region in Poland? I have to admit that, like most post-war Polish immigrants, we encountered a certain share of suspicion. We were newcomers from a different world, representatives of a different social group, we spoke a different language. This 'difference' did for a while interfere with our interactions with the locals. But eventually people got used to us, and the local farmers would come up to me and give me a friendly slap on the shoulder and ask, 'How are you, Jan?' but in their pronunciation it sounded more like 'Jon'. The locals still did not appreciate our background and experiences. The news that we would be receiving electricity in our remote location led to a funny story. When Anna was asked to visit a local farmer, Pani Bleska, where we bought home-style cheese and fresh cream, she sat Anna down and patiently explained how a light switch worked.' With their gradual acceptance by the original residents, the Zurakowski family found that the community had a long and rich tradition.

In 1940 Zurakowski had been smuggled out of Romania in the guise of a forester. Prophetically, his future in northern Ontario took on the role of forest management. More than 120 acres of the property that the Zurakowski family owned, even after some small tracts had been sold to their neighbours, was forest land. The bush roads that were cleared allowed access to the lodge, but for the most part the forest was left as a pristine natural setting. One of the first observations Zurakowski noted was that the regeneration of the forest was ongoing. Lightning strikes and fires did not destroy the forest; rather they allowed it to flourish. While he watched surrounding timberlands wither from lack of culling, he nurtured his property by cutting down selected trees. When some of the neighbours complained that he was mismanaging his forest reserve, he pointedly indicated that where their trees 'had barely grown an inch in overcrowded conditions, my forest had a rich harvest.' In his final years, as Zurakowski proudly walked visitors through his brush and forest areas, he quietly indicated that his forest was still thriving due to his careful management.

Throughout the early 1960s, Zurakowski and his family constantly developed Kartuzy Lodge. Always mechanically minded, Zura had become a skilled carpenter and did much of the woodwork and construction required at the resort. To supplement the original accommodations, he added four cabins, and cleared areas for use as a campsite. Workshops, a garage and sheds were constructed over the years. A menagerie of pets, including two dogs, five chickens and a racoon that became Mark's constant companion, also became part of the household.

From the onset, Kartuzy Lodge attracted Polish families with its warm hospitality and spectacular vistas. The economics of running a summer resort were apparent, as Zura remarked in 1963: he had gone from a '$1,500 a month job to just getting by'.[2] Both of the proud owners saw the lodge as 'a labour of love, the kind of place that is a refuge for friends and family, not a business.'

As both older and younger guests found, the Zurakowskis were the quintessential Polish hosts, warm and affable and loving a good time. What began as a modest operation steadily grew over the years, with up to 300 visitors arriving for week-long and weekend holidays over a summer-autumn season. For seventeen years the

[2] Bill Montaigue, 'Arrow pilot running tourist camp', *The Ottawa Citizen*, 31 October 1963.

A Zurakowski sailboat in 1965. (*Zurakowski collection*)

lodge maintained an 'American plan', providing for lodging and meals that involved Anna in commanding a large staff of cooks and housekeepers who were temporary employees drawn from the nearby Barry's Bay community. The traditional fare was simple with uniquely Polish and European-style dishes. Three main meals were served: the morning sniadanie (breakfast), obiad (lunch) and the evening kolacja (dinner). The meals, with up to sixty people in attendance, were a joyous time at Kartuzy Lodge, where not only guests but also neighbours dropped by to share in the festivities.

With the demands of providing fifty to sixty meals three times a day, of housecleaning and of keeping a steady workforce, Anna decided on a change in the operation of the resort. 'Ten people were working here steadily, and the cooks were changing all the time, so it was impossible to keep the way of operation going. My idea was to go into a 'housekeeping cottage plan', which is now more popular than ever before.' To reduce the workload, Kartuzy Lodge has, since 1978, continued as housekeeping units with each individual cabin having its own kitchen. 'The lodge traditions remain with twice-weekly gatherings in the large parlour to which all guests and neighbours are invited.'[3] Guests have continued to enjoy hiking, games (an outdoor volleyball area is maintained), boating (using sailboats and kayaks), and water sports at the resort.

[3] S. Bernard Shaw, 'Jan Zurakowski', *The Country Connection*, No 21 (Spring 1994), 30-31.

The first few years saw a great number of Polish families renting cabins or rooms at the lodge. The first pleasant experiences continued over the next decades, with many guests making annual pilgrimages to the Kartuzy Lodge. With the returning visits, eventually second and third generations of guests came. Many of the visitors were Canadians, but Americans and travellers from further afield made the trek out to Lake Kamaniskeg. In 1961, Zurakowski's mother was able to spend her summer holiday with her son and his family. It was a bittersweet reunion as Zura and Anna had now made their home in Canada and there was no thought of going back home to the Communist-run Poland. Yet the ties from their ancestral homeland were strong, and Zura had continued to correspond with his family in Poland. A cousin had even travelled back to the family estate of Zytniki, now in Ukraine. He reported that the house was still in use as the foundations were very good, but only a solitary tree remained from the orchard of twenty walnut trees from Zurakowski's childhood.

When Bronislaw came to visit later, in 1976, a strong emotional link to the past was rekindled. His brother had been on a fact-gathering team sent by his company, PZL. Lately he had been reassigned to the Aircraft Division, especially redesigning the PZL-104 Wilga. However, as a trouble-shooter he was invaluable to the company in the Helicopter Division, and when initial problems with the Mi-2 project were being ironed out, he was constantly shuttling back and forth to and from Moscow. In North America he headed a small team of specialists who were investigating the licensed production of a Franklin helicopter engine and light helicopter from Piasecki Helicopters. The project did not amount to anything, but it did give Bronislaw a chance to visit Kartuzy Lodge.

Anna and Janusz resolved to travel to Poland when time permitted. Anna returned home to care for her ailing mother in 1967, but her post-war status was scrupulously reviewed before she was allowed back. The Polish authorities ultimately considered her unauthorised departure to be a thing of the past and did not impose any penalties. Both Anna and Janusz returned to their former homeland together in 1970. The conditions they found were not appealing. Polish military veterans had undergone harsh treatment, and the police-state mentality was widespread. Shortages and unrest among industrial workers prevailed. Later visits in 1990 and 1992, after the collapse of the Communist system and the election of Lech

Janusz Zurakowski in 1983. *(Zurakowski collection)*

Walesa as Prime Minister, revealed a change in the economic prospects for the nation that was also heightened by a different attitude in the citizens.

Zurakowski inventions

The one passion that emerged for Janusz at Kartuzy was boatbuilding, which led to a series of experimental boat designs. George Zurakowski described his father's inventions as a 'crash between experimental research and just plain tinkering'.[4] The skills acquired in clearing the land and building the lodge and its accompanying buildings were innate to Janusz's love of designing and working with his hands. Zura's first foray into watercraft was in the creation of a series of kayaks for his guests to use. Zura considered the canoe and the kayak as ideal designs from which to begin. 'I looked at the North American Indian canoe and compared it to the Eskimo kayak, which was narrower and faster in the water. I began with variations of anything possible... single-person, two-person, different seating positions, one hull, two hulls, long oars,

[4] *Straight Arrow*, 1998.

until I had a design I thought was efficient. The most economical design was a sixteen-foot-long kayak with oars that had spring-back features on supports. I continued to change the length of the kayak until I had the optimal design.'

As his knowledge and experience with fibreglass construction techniques increased, he began to experiment with unusual concepts including catamaran designs. With only rudimentary sketches and a sense of design aesthetics derived from his long career in aeronautical engineering, Zura built a sleek boat for the boys to use. The design featured a three-point hydroplane hull and shallow draft, but the catamaran was faster and more stable than conventional catamaran designs. Both Mark and George vied for captain's duties until Zura built a larger version. The two boats were equally speedy, even though the smaller unit used only a 100hp outboard compared to the larger boat, which used a 125hp motor. A series of unusual power boats and sailboats emerged from Zurakowski's garage workshop over the years. Through trial and error, inefficient models were quickly discarded and gradually a unique fleet of small watercraft was constructed.

During the winter, traversing the frozen lake provided a challenge to Zurakowski, but in typical 'garage-style engineering', he came up with an ingenious solution. Adapting a twin-hull kayak, he harnessed a motor and pusher propeller to make a 'landskimmer'. This practical and efficient design led to later versions that were more like blends of skis and aircraft pusher propulsion. The operator sat on an exposed sloped seat that had long runners attached to its sides. The craft looked like an ultralight without its wings and it was incredibly fast. Mark recalled that his arrival at school was an anticipated event as his 'friends were always wondering what kind of contraption he would arrive in next'.[5] The simple 'ice boats' developed into a more complex design that featured an all-encompassing, streamlined fibreglass body powered by a Volkswagen engine that was adapted to a pusher propeller at the back. The ice boats were equally adept over water, snow, ice and even rough ground.

As his imagination soared, Zurakowski looked at a marriage of aeronautical and hydrodynamic engineering to design a sailboat that could break the single-handed world sailing speed record. The current mark had been set by Australian Simon McKeon, whose catamaran *Yellow Pages* reached 46.52 knots in October 1992 at Sandy Point,

[5] Mark Zurakowski, conversation with the author, 1997.

'Wehicle' 1965. (*Zurakowski collection*)

Australia. The World Sailing Speed Record Council sets the rules for record attempts ranging from short-distance records (half a kilometre), recognised major races (for example, the Sydney-Hobart, Victoria-Maui), point-to-point and Around-the-World records.

The design that Zura had in mind was carefully sketched out, then submitted to a number of experts including Professor James DeLaurier of the University of Toronto, renowned for his work on the Project Ornithopter engine-powered piloted aircraft that took to the air in 1999. DeLaurier assessed the technology involved in the Zurakowski experimental sailboat and pronounced it sound. Although only a technical exercise, the design that resulted was and is a revolutionary concept.

To quote from his April 1995 submission, with an amendment in February 2001 to correct for pitching moment, Zurakowski proposed: 'A cross between a sailplane (glider) and a sailboat … (1) to obtain high efficient driving force, the sails are in the form of wings, with a structure stiff enough to retain proper sail profile and efficiency. (2) Sails are (at higher speed) of higher aerodynamic aspect ratio because the gap between the wing and the bottom of the sail is eliminated. (3) The sails produce strong heeling moments which have to be balanced. Balancing the boats by means of weight (heavy keel, or in the case of a catamaran, movable ballast or crew, etc) appears to be inferior to the wing-aileron aerodynamic balancing method. In this project, a wing is used for lateral control. At lower speeds, lift of the wing can decrease water resistance at over-the-hump speed. At highest speeds, only an angle-controllable pivoting centreboard (vertical hydrofoil) and small stabilising surfaces remain in the water. To decrease aerodynamic drag at high speed, the sailboat faces the apparent wind head-on (by virtue of the pivoting centreboard). By eliminating most of the hydrodynamic resistance and by introducing aerodynamic forces that are efficient at higher speed, a maximum boat speed three times the wind speed is possible.'

In practical terms, Zurakowski had evolved his concept of skimmers and sailboats to create an amazing hybrid, capable of theoretical speeds in the range of eighty knots per hour. The knowledge that a high-technology investment in computer and mechanical systems to make his sailboat feasible had not daunted Zurakowski in his dreams of taking on the world sailing record. For the time being, the project remains on hold but at least one reference source on hydrodynamics, *Sail Performance: Design and Techniques to Maximize Sail Power* by C A Marchaj (McGraw-Hill, 1996), has included the Zurakowski experimental sailboat.

The Zurakowski family legacy

The two Zurakowski boys gained a reputation in the Kaszuby area for their athletic prowess. Not only were they at home in the summer on the water, waterskiing, swimming and boating, but in the winter they took to the slopes. After completing studies at the University of Toronto, Mark eventually became a ski instructor in the area, before going on to a career in business. Whereas his parents considered themselves indifferent business people, Mark was an inveterate entrepreneur who turned his expertise in construction and commerce to the creation of Zuracon, a commercial, industrial and residential construction company. He also owns Home Hardware stores in Barry's Bay and Combermere, Ontario. George in some ways followed his father's path. First graduating from high school in Ottawa (since the Madawaska Valley District High School, which his younger brother, Mark, attended, was not built at the time), George went on to study engineering at Ottawa University. He recently retired as Director of the Certification and Engineering Bureau Laboratory at Industry Canada. Both boys married local girls and today Mark and his wife Susan have raised three girls, Robin, Tamara and Paige, while George and his wife Julie have two teenagers, Paul and Krysia.

Love of adventure led Mark and Susan to plan a round-the-world voyage in 1989. After designing and building their yacht, *The Sardak*, over a fourteen-month period, they were ready for an extended five-year world cruise. However, before they were able to embark, their yacht was destroyed by Hurricane Hugo while berthed near Puerto Rico. In typical Zurakowski fashion, Mark and Susan have persevered in their dream and have recently purchased a new boat in their winter home of Green Turtle Cay Island, Bahamas.

Janusz presented his granddaughter, Krysia, with her diploma when she received her pilot's licence at a ceremony in 2001. *(Zurakowski collection)*

Flying is also in the Zurakowski blood, as exemplified by Mark, an accomplished recreational pilot who owns a Lake LA4/200 Buccaneer amphibian. Another aviator has also emerged in the family. Zura's granddaughter Krysia achieved the rank of Flight Sergeant at the 211 Kiwanis Royal Canadian Air Cadet Squadron in Ottawa. In the summer of 2002 she became a gliding instructor and, in the autumn of that year, enrolled at Carleton University. Although she had first excelled as a gymnast at Nepean-Corona School of Gymnastics, an opportunity for a gliding course had led her to the Regional Gliding School (Pacific) at Comox, British Columbia. When she asked her grandfather for some advice on flying, he cautioned that she should keep her mind on her business. 'He told me not to think of boys when I was up in the air. He seems to have gotten into a little bit of trouble when he was up in the air thinking about his girlfriends.'[6] On 18 August 2000 Krysia graduated with the 'top student' award in the course. After she qualified on Schweitzer gliders, her award included more than a week of advanced soaring training at the company headquarters in Elmira, New York. The following summer Krysia qualified for her Private Pilot's Licence (Power Flying), and again won the flying scholarship award for the top cadet. In the graduation ceremony in August 2001, with her parents and brother and other members of her family also in attendance, she stood as a very proud Janusz Zurakowski pinned on her wings.

Recent honours

Throughout his later years, Janusz Zurakowski has been continually acknowledged through a series of awards and honours for his contributions to Canadian aviation. In 1973 he was named a member of Canada's Aviation Hall of Fame. The induction ceremony noted: 'The dedication of his aeronautical skills to the successful flight testing of Canada's first supersonic aircraft resulted in outstanding benefit to Canadian aviation.'[7] He was also made a Companion of the Order of Flight (City of Edmonton) at the same ceremony.

In March 1990 Janusz Zurakowski was the first recipient of the J C Floyd Award for lifetime achievement in Canadian Aerospace. The award was introduced and administered by the Aerospace Heritage Foundation of Canada. The Chairman Emeritus of the Foundation at that time was James C Floyd, who presented the honour in person at the Skyline Toronto Airport Hotel during the first annual dinner of the Foundation. Since leaving Avro, Zurakowski had become friends with Floyd and held this tribute in high esteem. The award was presented for three years but is no longer in effect.

In 1996 the Royal Canadian Mint issued new twenty-dollar coins in Part II of the Aviation Series, 'Powered Flight in Canada: Beyond World War II', begun in 1990. Overall, the series focused on aircraft designed, developed and/or manufactured in Canada that made a

[6] Captain Jeff Manney and Major Rob Wilson, 'All in the Family' [online], cited on 18 August 2000:
http://www.dnd.ca/menu/maple/vol_3/Vol3_32/airforce_e.htm.
[7] Mary Oswald, *They Led the Way* (Wetaskawin: Canada's Aviation Hall of Fame, 1999), 216.

significant contribution to both civil and military Canadian aviation. The twenty-four-carat, gold-plated cameos featured the likeness of an individual who was instrumental in the development of the aircraft shown on the coin. Part II covered the period from the late 1940s to the present. The third coin issued featured the Avro Canada CF-100 Canuck with an inset of Janusz Zurakowski, while the next coin was the Avro Canada CF-105 Arrow with a cameo of James A Chamberlin, Chief Designer.

The Western Canada Aviation Museum, at its Thirteenth Annual Pioneer Awards Dinner, recognised Janusz Zurakowski and Lorna de Blicquy, Canada's first woman bush pilot, for their remarkable achievements as 'Pioneers of Canadian Aviation'. Both were in attendance on 30 May 1997 at a ceremony that took place at the Holiday Inn Airport West in Winnipeg. Mark accompanied his father on that occasion. At the same ceremony, the museum's Award of Merit was presented to Team Canada, the first Canadian Team to win the William Tell Air-to-Air Combat Competition, and to George Richardson, on behalf of his family for their continued and generous support of the museum.

One of the finest tributes to Janusz Zurakowski came in the form of a television documentary, *Straight Arrow: The Janusz Zurakowski Story*, produced by White Pine Studio in 1998 and written and directed by George and Anna Prodanou. The documentary was part of a series, *A Scattering of Seeds: The Creation of Canada*, in which fifty-two documentaries recounted the stories of Canada's immigrant experience. The Prodanous took a personal interest in the story of Zurakowski and spent months collecting film footage that documented his aeronautical career. The production also spent two weeks with the Zurakowski family at Kartuzy Lodge and among residents in Barry's Bay. The documentary faithfully describes the life of a remarkable man and his contributions to his community and his country.

On 23 July 1999 CFB Cold Lake saluted Zurakowski when the Base's Aerospace Engineering Test Establishment was named in his honour. Acknowledged as the 'Dean of Canada's test pilots', he was back in his natural element and engaged in 'hangar flying' with some of the Cold Lake test pilots. Even though some were more than fifty years his junior, it was clear that things hadn't changed much among the people who put new airplanes through their paces. In an interview related to the award, his son George remarked that one of his father's greatest contributions to test flying was that he was 'very

Zurakowski speaking at the 40th anniverary of the Avro Arrow's first flight, 1998. *(Bill Zuk)*

meticulous and persistent in ensuring aircraft design ... from the pilot's point of view was done properly.'[8]

In September 2000 Zurakowski became an Honorary Fellow of the Society of Experimental Test Pilots. This international organisation, with headquarters in California, had previously honoured the elite of the aviation world. Zurakowski's name was placed there along with the likes of James 'Jimmy' Doolittle, Charles Lindbergh, Igor Sikorski and Air Commodore Sir Frank Whittle. His nomination had been made by 'his old mate', Neville Duke, and it was the first time that any Canadian or Polish pilot had received this honour. While the normal presentation of the award would have been made at a dinner in his honour, when Zura indicated that he would be unable to attend, special arrangements were made to fly the certificate bestowing his status as Honorary Fellow of the Society to Canada. Shawn Coyle, Chairman of the Canadian Test Pilots Association, flew a Bell Ranger helicopter to Kartuzy Lodge to make the presentation in person.

Colonel Zurakowski was accorded the privilege of presenting the

[8] George Zurakowski, 2001.

keynote address at the annual Battle of Britain ceremonies on Sunday 19 September 2001, in the National Aviation Museum, Ottawa. Zurakowski noted that 'the success of the Battle of Britain had a direct impact on freedom for most of the world and it is important that today's generation continues to learn about the battle and understand why it is so important.' The event specifically honoured the Polish fighter pilots who had fought in the Battle alongside Commonwealth pilots. The ceremonies included a flight of Polish veterans who took part in the parade, with members coming from some distance to participate. Dignitaries from the Polish Embassy were also in attendance at the ceremony.

Although until 2004 Janusz had still been extremely active in all his endeavours, his health had been fragile. He suffered from diabetes and had some blood disorders that necessitated careful medical supervision. Zura sometimes jokingly told friends and family that he was 'disintegrating'. The man some had called 'the great Zura' was now approaching his late eighties and had slowed appreciably. However, during a visit in 2001, Zura took pains to show his guest a favourite forest path nearby and briskly hiked through the bush. He also drove to town for some groceries in his four-wheel-drive Subaru station wagon. To belie the tale that he was terrified at the wheel of an automobile, Zurakowski deftly manoeuvred through the blind switchbacks and dirt roads that mark the route to Kartuzy Lodge.

At Kartuzy Lodge, Janusz and Anna still operated the summer resort, although the season was shortened in 2001 to accommodate a more leisurely pace. Anna became more of the caretaker of not only the lodge but also Zura himself. With his failing hearing, he found it difficult to converse easily on the telephone, requiring his wife to relay most messages. Even in the rustic settings of Kartuzy, the two Zurakowskis maintained a ready access to the outside world, with computers, fax machines, photocopier and the Internet as part of their lives. Throughout any encounter, they remained the consummate hosts, still vibrant and charming with a quaint European grace.

Since 1960 Zurakowski has become established as a local celebrity, and many of the locals are aware that the quiet elderly gentleman who did his shopping at the Barry's Bay IGA is considered a national icon by countless Canadians. Answering requests from young and old for his reflections about the Avro Arrow had been a nearly constant feature of Zura's life. It was also not uncommon for an old friend from the Avro days or a young

Anna and Janusz Zurakowski at the Kartuzy Lodge in 2001.
(Zurakowski collection)

researcher to drop in for coffee and a chat. Artists, authors, film-makers and historians have all sought out Zurakowski.

Anna continued to write after their marriage, contributing articles as a freelancer to the Polish press in Canada throughout the 1950s and 1960s. In recent years she helped her husband in writing his memoirs, a Polish text drawn from the extensive files that Zura has kept over the years, which is titled *Nie tylko o lataniu* (translated as *Not Only About Flying*) and was published by the Polish-Canadian Publishing Fund in 2002.

Epilogue

A Legend is Born

The story of the Avro Arrow did not die on that cold day in February 1959; instead, it has entered the realm of modern Canadian legend. The legend tells of a technological wonder that had its life cut short by partisan politics, a lack of military foresight and government intrigue. Even more symbolically, the Arrow represents a watershed in Canadian history, a time when the nation surrendered its role as an industrial and technological leader and shamefully destroyed all traces of its most glorious effort. Zurakowski once remarked, 'It was far ahead of its time, and it showed that this country was in the forefront in aircraft technology worldwide. There will never be another Arrow. When we were told that the plane was to be scrapped, I was totally dumbfounded and so shocked I could have cried.'[1]

The debate over the merits of the Arrow had begun even before the project was cancelled, fuelled partly by government statements, media speculation and the public's interest in the Arrow. Prime Minister Diefenbaker cited the case for terminating the Avro Arrow and Iroquois programmes in two policy statements on 23 September 1958 and 20 February 1959. The official positions revolved around two reasons: the mission or role of the aircraft being overtaken by the use of missile defence, and the lack of sales outside Canada. These were presented as seemingly compelling arguments; however, there were also unofficial reasons that may have been influential in the final decision.

Missile or man

Military strategists of the late 1950s responded strongly to a perceived 'missile age', heralded by the Soviet launch and orbit of the Sputnik satellite in 1957. In reaction to Soviet missile advances, Great Britain and the United States re-evaluated the use of manned fighters as a means of defence. The influential 1957 White Paper authored by British Defence Minister Duncan Sandys went further in advocating that manned aircraft be replaced by guided missiles,

[1] Melady, *Pilots*, 234-235.

resulting in the cancellation of fighter projects in development in the UK such as the Saunders Roe SR177. The United States similarly terminated the Convair F-106D and North American Rockwell F-108 Rapier programmes. Canada's response to the new Soviet threat was influenced by the NORAD Agreement, which dictated a combined role of Canadian and American armed forces in protecting North American airspace.

The Pentagon began to advocate new missile defences as part of mutual defence planning, thereby accelerating the deployment of point-defence missiles such as the Boeing IM-99 Bomarc as a replacement for the jet interceptor. Touted as the new line of defence for the United States and Canada, the Bomarc never lived up to its advance billing. One of the main failings in a missile defence is a limited range of protection. Bomarc bases in Canada at Lamacaza (Quebec) and North Bay (Ontario) were located near built-up centres and would only protect eastern Canada. (The two Canadian sites essentially filled in a gap in the ring of northern US missile bases.) The detection and warning time of a Soviet bomber attack was another problem. Warnings would be in the tens of minutes, necessitating a constant alert status at Bomarc bases. This status would further require a high commitment of service and maintenance hours as well as trained personnel. A final complication was that once fired, missiles could not be recalled or diverted, which also limited their usefulness when the threat was not readily confirmed.

The most serious deficiencies in the Bomarc were that it was not a precise weapon and it relied on a nuclear device to destroy attacking Soviet bombers. This situation was a particularly difficult one to resolve because Prime Minister Diefenbaker had publicly declared that Canada would not use nuclear weapons or have them housed on Canadian soil. The first Bomarcs were deployed with no weapons at all, with sandbags used as ballast. The eventual resolution of this issue was that nuclear weapons would be stored at the two Canadian bases but that American military personnel would have the ultimate responsibility for initiating a nuclear attack.

In choosing to equip Canada's defence forces with the Bomarc, the Diefenbaker government presented the case that the Arrow had been 'overtaken by events'. However, with the cancellation of the Avro CF-105, the CF-100 Canuck continued as Canada's contribution to NORAD defence. By the early 1960s the necessity of replacing the ageing CF-100 resulted in the Canadian government acquiring fifty-six two-seater F-101B Voodoo fighters, together with ten dual-control F-101Fs (essentially surplus USAF aircraft) in June 1961. Ironically, the Voodoo fighter that was initially rejected by the RCAF entered service exactly at the time when the Avro Arrow would have become operational. The final irony was that the Bomarc couldn't perform as advertised and that its use in Canada was short-lived. The Bomarcs were out of service after a short operational career, and any remaining examples were consigned to roles as gate guardians and museum displays. The Voodoo continued to serve for over thirty years.

Selling the Arrow

The poor prospect of foreign sales of the Avro Arrow was often quoted as a deciding factor in the decision to cancel the programme. The reality is that aircraft undergoing trials rarely generate sales; production or service types are most likely to be 'shopped around' to other countries. The real-world sales prospects would have been difficult to determine, but in the late 1960s Canada itself again became a customer for fighter aircraft. The military chose the Northrop F-5 Freedom Fighter and Lockheed F-104 Starfighter to fulfil its NATO and other commitments.

Citing a number of examples of aircraft, including the Meteor and CF-100, as being able to achieve foreign sales after proving themselves, Zurakowski described the process of marketing fighter aircraft and provided a more recent example. 'Around 1977, the Canadian government began searching for a replacement for its aging Voodoo, Starfighter and CF-5 aircraft. Initially, six foreign companies were bidding on a contract worth about $4 billion for more than 100 aircraft. (This was twenty years after the then Prime Minister, Diefenbaker, had declared that the age of the manned fighter was coming to an end and that even if the Arrow were in service by 1960, it would be obsolete.) The F-18 was ultimately the winner, with the average age of the six aircraft competing to fill Canada's needs (as calculated from the date of their first flights) being well over six years.' Other contemporary fighters such as the Eurofighter 2000 have gone down the same road. 'In light of the above, it is difficult to comprehend why most of our historians keep repeating the extraneous observations that Canada tried to sell the Arrow to the US and Europe but no one wanted it. Whatever the reasons, I must emphatically state that at the time of the programme's cancellation, it was premature to attempt marketing the Arrow (or the Iroquois engine) abroad. Even the best aircraft, such as the Arrow, cannot normally be expected to be marketable before being successfully pressed into domestic service.'

The one great sales prospect resulting from the technology in the Avro Arrow was the Avro Orenda Iroquois jet engine. In that period the Iroquois was one of the most powerful and fuel-efficient engines available in the Western world, with thrust in afterburner of 25,000lb (the interim J75s in the Arrow Mark I could only generate 18,500lb thrust). Orenda was negotiating with Curtiss-Wright in the United States for licensed manufacture, and Dassault was expressing serious interest in the purchase of 300 Iroquois engines for the new Mirage IV strategic bomber. These contracts were never fulfilled due to the cancellation of the Iroquois engine, which took place at the same time as the termination of the Arrow.

The rationale that the Arrow was obsolete and unwanted technology would have been sufficient to cause Diefenbaker's government to cancel the Avro Arrow; however, the underlying motives of various parties should be considered. These can be summarised as government and military concerns over prohibitive costs; political and issue-driven reasons; and personal animosity between the principals of A V Roe Canada and the government.

The cost of the Arrow

The production costs of the Arrow programme were a contentious issue in 1959 and were cited by the government as the underlying factor in the cancellation. The government had its own figures, ranging from around $7.8 million to $12.5 million per plane. These figures projected the most dire predictions of cost overruns and included money that had already been spent during the early research and development period. As a contrast, Avro Aircraft provided a figure of approximately $3.5 million per plane based on a total of 100 aircraft produced, reduced to in the region of $2.8 million per plane based on 200 aircraft produced.

Development costs of the Avro Arrow programme had been daunting. It began as a research and development project in 1954 for the construction of two prototypes at a total cost of roughly $26 million. At the time of the initial design, an off-the-shelf engine, the Rolls-Royce RB-106, was the power plant choice, but the cancellation of this engine and the subsequent replacement, the

Curtiss-Wright J67, forced A V Roe Canada to proceed with the development of its advanced Avro Iroquois engine. This choice of a new and untried engine then led to further costs in development.

The selection of an armament and avionic package also led to additional expenses. The first choice was a highly sophisticated Astra 1 guidance system that was matched to the Douglas Sparrow II missile. Each of these decisions was highly influenced by the Royal Canadian Air Force's specifications, AIR-73, which outlined the role and mission of the Avro Arrow. Even though the work was subcontracted to RCA Victor Canada for the Astra component and to the Douglas Company for the Sparrow missile, it meant that the main systems of the highly advanced interceptor – engines, weapons and avionics – were all new and untried. The consequent time and development of these key components made the entire project more expensive and risky. When Douglas suddenly abandoned the Sparrow II missile in 1956, Avro reluctantly stepped in to continue the development of the weapon, acting as a project manager, with Canadair Aircraft in charge of airframe and Westinghouse Canada in charge of radar and guidance control. By September 1958 the Astra/Sparrow II weapons system was abandoned, and Avro was able to revert to the Hughes MA-1/Falcon avionics and weapons combination that was first proposed

If the Avro Arrow had continued to operational status in NORAD squadrons, a heavy commitment of funds would have had to be made. Canadian Chiefs of Staff were faced with the prospect of a military budget being overwhelmingly apportioned to the Air Force for the foreseeable future, while the Canadian Navy and Army also needed to re-equip and re-arm. Financial concerns were the most serious consideration, with a momentous decision made in August 1958 to base future military fighter procurement on US aircraft. Concluding that a decreasing Soviet bomber threat combined with rapid progress in missile defence were decisive factors, although Air Marshall Hugh Campbell pleaded the case for continuation, the Chiefs of Staffs recommended that the government cancel the CF-105 programme. Defence Minister Pearkes forwarded this recommendation to Cabinet.

A political price to pay

That the Avro Arrow programme began as one of C D Howe's prize projects is part of its history. The Honourable Clarence Decatur

Howe, Canada's 'Minister of Everything', not only engineered the war effort of the nation but set in place post-war recovery. He was responsible for the creation of Trans-Canada Airlines, the Trans-Canada Pipeline and the St Lawrence Seaway in his various capacities as Minister of Transport and Minister of Reconstruction. He was also instrumental in the formation of the A V Roe Canada company, which by 1958 was one of Canada's largest industrial empires, owning twenty-nine companies with products ranging from coal, steel and rolling-stock to electronics. A new Conservative government coming to power could only look on the A V Roe company as one of the prime beneficiaries of Liberal largess.

The new government also had a decidedly parochial and provincial view of the nation. Its ideas and values could be traced to its fiery and messianic leader, John George Diefenbaker. 'Dief was a small-town and rural lawyer who had made it to the top of the political ladder in his party by espousing a nationalistic and populist message. He was for small business and against big business, for Canada but not against the US (he admired President Eisenhower, yet abhorred President Kennedy), and wanted a stable economy for the ordinary Canadian. In the midst of this jumble of political beliefs, dogmas and strained ideologies emerged a very partisan and opinionated 'politico'. Dief always went for the jugular of his political opponents and rarely was known for his tact or diplomacy.

Arrogance and animosity

To Dief, Avro Canada represented a flagrant abuse of power and trust. He saw it not only as a Liberal enclave but as one of C D Howe's 'stepchildren'. That its president was also an arrogant 'son of a —' did not bode well for future relations. Crawford Gordon Jr was one of C D Howe's 'boys' who had worked for him in the war years and was considered the boy wonder of Canada. He was personally recruited by Howe to take over the company at a critical juncture. When the new government came to power and began to make it clear that the Arrow was in trouble, Gordon reacted negatively. First he refused to accept the news that the company was in jeopardy. Then he aggressively stormed into a meeting with Diefenbaker, slamming his fist on the table in the Prime Minister's office and angrily demanding the continuation of the Arrow programme. For the very righteous and strait-laced Dief, the sight of this blustering, obviously drunk lout only reinforced the notion that

Avro was not going to be able to do the job. Gordon was shown the door, and the project was as good as dead from that point on.

The decision

The Avro Arrow was going to be cancelled, no matter what, as soon as Dief took power. He built up a case for its cancellation with the support of his trusted military advisors, the Canadian Chiefs of Staff. (The Air Chief naturally did not support the majority and felt that the government had been ill-advised in its decision.) The decision-making process in the Diefenbaker Cabinet was unusual, to say the least. One of his later ministers described the problems as paramount. 'One of the difficulties of the Diefenbaker approach was that there was no discussion of major government decisions in caucus. It was more or less a 'like-it-or-lump-it' approach. The Arrow issue was never raised in caucus before the government decision was made.'[2]

The lack of a technical background may have affected Diefenbaker's views; he relied heavily on advisors and experts in these areas. What he did not seem to consider was the considerable amount of talent already in the Conservative caucus. One of the backbenchers was Erik Nielsen, a former wartime bomber pilot and a bush pilot in the Yukon. Nielsen later lamented: 'Over the years from 1958 to 1962, my ideals slowly metamorphosed into disillusionment and finally crystallised into a deeply held cynicism about the whole process... That was the case with the development of the supersonic jet interceptor called the Avro Arrow, a technological wonder that was cancelled in 1959, after the expenditure of $310 million, notwithstanding the fact that anyone with a scintilla of understanding of the air industry could recognise the Arrow as one of the most outstanding aircraft in existence. We were told at the time that it would cost half a billion dollars to produce 100 jets, which in today's terms is 'peanuts'. The cancellation was a dreadful mistake – 14,000 employees of A V Roe were laid off and the aircraft industry in Canada suffered a devastating blow. I instinctively believed that at the time, and hindsight has convinced pretty well everyone else.'[3] Those who were not convinced included Diefenbaker and some of the principals in

[2] Erik Nielsen, *The House is Not a Home* (Toronto: Macmillan of Canada, 1989), 118.
[3] Ibid, 124.

the decision – Defence Minister George Pearkes; Pierre Sevigny, the Associate Defence Minister; and David Golden, the Deputy Minister for Defence Production.

Diefenbaker often referred to the Arrow cancellation as a critical factor in his government's eventual slide from power. The decision was the right one in his mind, but the repercussions of the cancellation of the Arrow were to haunt him and his government for years. For the most part, from his Minister of Defence, George Pearkes, to the lowliest member of Cabinet, he had support for his decision to cancel the Arrow. What he didn't have support for was the ultimate destruction of the aircraft, the production jigs and tools, and all the documentation concerning the programme. As to the actual orders to destroy and where they originated, it may have been the Cabinet, the Minister of Defence or the Chiefs of Staff who made the fateful decision to cut apart all the flying and production examples of one of the world's most impressive military projects. Ultimately Prime Minister Diefenbaker bore the responsibility for the ignoble act.

Evidence today tends to support the contention that the US was not responsible for the Arrow's cancellation in either colluding with the Canadian government or in directly influencing the final decision. One reason is that the US military defence of the continent would have been bolstered by the deployment of a first-rate fighter interceptor like the Arrow. Zurakowski contends that 'US support came in many forms. I was trained to fly on their supersonic fighters.'

In perhaps the most heated controversy of his career, Pearkes, as Minister of Defence at the time of the cancellation of the Arrow, never wavered in maintaining that he had made the correct, though very difficult, decision regarding Canada's defence system. Dr Reginald Roy recorded interviews with Pearkes and others involved in the Arrow's cancellation. Pearkes is quoted as saying, 'I thought to myself, well, I had to make these decisions; I know people blamed me for a lot of it; but I did what was right in my opinion.'[4] His Associate Defence Minister, Pierre Sevigny, claimed that the government was unfairly blamed for the Arrow cancellation and its effects, even advancing the astonishing view that Crawford Gordon deliberately destroyed the aircraft. David Golden went on record

[4] Dr Reginald Roy, 'Pearkes Discusses the Bomarcs, Interview #61, 5 April 1967. ACC 74-1 Box 6,' [online], cited on 20 October 2003: collections.ic.gc.ca/uvic/pearkes/plv5/pbomarc.html

about the decision in 1990 by stating, 'In my view, it is not one that one can be dogmatic about, but I would certainly come down on the side of saying, yes, painfully, regrettably, it was the right decision at the time, under all the circumstances, and I think so now, too.'[5]

There never was an Arrow

David Golden is equally famous for coining the phrase that typified the views of the backroom boys. He revealed to E K Shaw and others: 'If you mean by the Arrow, I take it as a fighting instrument of war which must include an aircraft, an engine and a sophisticated fire control system, then of course, there never was an Arrow... I think it's a mistake and gets people somewhat worked up when they ought not to, to talk about this great Canadian achievement when in fact ... at the time it was cancelled, it was too soon to say whether the hopes that everyone held out for it were to be realised or not.'[6]

For those who were there, like Jim Floyd who fathered the project and Janusz Zurakowski who made the Arrow soar, the cancellation of the Avro Arrow was undoubtedly the single most climactic event of their careers. Zurakowski reflected, 'Those were the times when Canada stood at the forefront of a niche technology and I am proud that I was part of it. The first flight of the Arrow was not my success. It was created by the thousands of enthusiastic and hardworking men and women.' The project was one of vision and daring that represented a vast undertaking in technology and research. In scope and commitment, the Arrow programme should be compared to the construction of the Canadian oil pipeline and the Great Lakes Seaway.

Three aspects alone of the Avro Arrow illustrate the cutting-edge technology that was integral to the design's unique characteristics. The Arrow was filled with electronics; its primary avionics and flight control systems were based on the latest computer programmes; and the pilot also flew with a groundbreaking fly-by-wire system that was only duplicated twenty years later by the Lockheed F-16 Falcon. The airframe was a combination of many exotic materials and included the extensive use of titanium, mirroring the type of composite structure found on modern fighter aircraft. The limiting factor in the Arrow's top speed was not its

---

[5] Shaw, *There Never Was an Arrow.*
[6] Ibid.

engine, but the thermal limits of the airframe. The final Arrows that were in design, the Mark 3 versions (and beyond), would fly so fast that the Arrow would actually be melting; the solution would probably have to be sought in the use of the high-ablative materials that were incorporated in the Lockheed SR-71 and Rockwell Space Shuttle. Another innovative element of its technology was the use of a buried weapons system that allowed the aircraft to fly without the drag-inducing external weapons stores. The Avro Arrow utilised a large missile bay that was located along the underside in the centre of the fuselage. Partly due to the changes in missile armament that took place during its development, the weapons bay represented a simple but elegant solution to weapons storage. Lockheed's F-117 Stealth and F-22 Raptor fighters now use a similar system.

Designed as a high-altitude Mach 2 interceptor to counter the current and proposed Soviet bomber force of the late-1950s era, the Avro Arrow never realised its promise, although every indication from flight testing had shown that it would have been one of the most capable interceptors available to the West. (Arrow Mark I, RL-202, using an interim Pratt and Whitney J75, achieved Mach 1.96 on 11 November 1958 at the hands of Avro Aircraft's test pilot, Spud Potocki.) In relative numbers, this performance was outstanding as it bettered the speeds of contemporary production interceptors in the West, such as the North American F-100, Convair F-102, Gloster Javelin and Dassault Mystere IV, which all had top speeds in the Mach 1 to 1.5 range. The Mach 2 performance of the definitive Arrow Mark 2 production model, using Avro Orenda Iroquois engines, was already being considered by the company as the basis of an attempt to set world altitude and speed records. The first Mark 2, RL-206 (No 25206), was scheduled to fly within days of the cancellation of the programme. Zura noted that the contemporary 'improved models of the MiG-31 started about twenty years after the Arrow, but with performance very similar to the Arrow, continue in service. The most recent trend is a delta-shaped wing with a small controllable wing ahead of the main wing (canard style). Best examples include the French Dassault Rafale, the Eurofighter 2000 and the Swedish Saab Gripen, all expected to be in use into the twenty-first century, over forty years after cancellation of the 'obsolete' Arrow and forty years after the declaration that 'the age of the manned fighter was over'.'

Dief proceeded with the conviction that the decision was the right one for the times, yet years later in his memoirs, *One Canada*, he could not adequately explain the rationale for cancellation of the Arrow. Ultimately costs were the deciding factor, and the popular press as well as many Canadian citizens not directly affected by the Avro lay-offs felt that cost-saving was a good thing. Only in recent times does the mythology of the 'one that got away' appear. It is a clear analogy of a great loss when the true assessment of what Canada lost is appreciated. The fact that a valuable piece of technology was thrown away was only one of the tragedies; the real loss was in the brain drain of one of the nation's leading industrial and technological giants.

The future sales resulting from the Avro Arrow programme can never be fully estimated, but a graver consequence to the company and Canada was the departure of experienced and skilled specialists who were immediately laid off on Black Friday. The lay-offs of approximately 14,000 employees of the Avro Aircraft and Avro Orenda factories could be weighed in with the job losses in the 600 or more sub-contractors directly tied to the Avro Arrow. In the entire nation, nearly 50,000 people lost their jobs, with the majority lost forever to Canada. The devastation in the Ontario 'Golden Triangle' was most acutely felt and resulted in the aviation industry in Canada being decimated for the next decade. Many former Avro Canada employees were recruited to go to other aviation concerns in the United States and abroad.

The death of the Arrow also sounded the death knell of Canada's military aerospace industry. At the time of the Arrow's cancellation, Canada was at the forefront of military and civilian aviation technology in many research and production areas. For the foreseeable future, Canada cannot afford to compete again as an indigenous aviation manufacturer in military applications. The government now relies on purchasing American aircraft, with offsetting Canadian subcontracting guarantees for portions of the aircraft systems. For example, when the Canadian Armed Forces selected the McDonnell-Douglas F-18 Hornet multi-purpose fighter in the late 1970s, part of the deal was an arrangement for main airframe components to be constructed in Canada at Canadair.

The Avro Arrow resurrected

Today the Avro Arrow only remains as a memory, although there are some vestiges of RL-206 (nose, front landing gear, wing panels and definitive Avro Iroquois engine) preserved in the National Aviation Museum in Ottawa. In a quirk of fate, the Arrow's remains sit near the chopped-up nose section of the Avro Jetliner, another unrealised dream of Canadian aeronautics. Visitors to the museum, viewing the stark cadaver of the Arrow, can see the jagged and burnt ends where the torches did their work. Nevertheless, the memories of this magnificent aviation project have not died away, due to the continuing fascination of the Canadian public. In countless books, documentary films and even a theatrical production, where a large-scale model of the Arrow dominated the stage, the legend of the Avro Arrow has been reborn. A CBC television mini-series, *The Arrow*, from Straight Arrow Productions (a joint production of Winnipeg's John Aaron Productions and Toronto's Tapestry Films and The Film Works), has also been responsible for a revived interest in the sensational and fanciful aspects of the story.

In recreating the era of the 1950s, the director chose Winnipeg as the primary site for location shooting. One of the 'stars' was a full-scale Avro Arrow prop that had begun its life as a shop project by Alan Jackson in Wetaskawin, Alberta. The wood and metal framework was completed by carpenters and prop-makers in Winnipeg and became a working model capable of taxiing under its own power. At the end of principal photography, the Arrow model was briefly displayed at the Western Canada Aviation Museum, then dismantled and returned to Jackson. After re-assembly in Alberta, the movie model was displayed at the Abbotsford Air Show before returning to its present home at the Reynolds-Alberta Aviation Museum.

Alberta is also the home of another Avro Arrow replica, albeit in one-fifth scale, which had its origins in the CBC mini-series. Doug and Donette Hyslip were responsible for the series of realistic radio control flying models featured in the production. Inspired by the achievements of the Avro company and its employees, the husband and wife team are the driving force behind the A V Roe Canada Heritage Museum located in Calgary, Alberta. The museum sponsored the Arrow 2000 Project that sought to recreate faithfully a one-fifth-scale Avro Arrow, which has already been flown successfully. The museum also houses an immaculate scale model of the Avro Jetliner.

Currently the Avro Arrow has been replicated at the Toronto Aerospace Museum. A dedicated group of volunteers built a non-flying replica of Avro Arrow No 203 and had plans to present it to the public with its original test pilot, Janusz Zurakowski, in the cockpit. The replica was constructed at Downsview Park, the former home of de Havilland Aircraft (Canada). The museum, in just over three years, has taken on a number of challenging projects revolving

Remains of Avro Arrow 26 at the Canada Aviation Museum. *(Bill Zuk)*

around the aviation heritage of the Toronto area, including the Curtiss-Wright, de Havilland (Canada) and A V Roe Canada operations. At the back of the hangar, a Canadian-built Avro Lancaster bomber is being restored after three decades of static display at Ontario Place, but the recreation of the Avro Arrow, led by Claude Sherwood and a team of volunteers including many ex-Avro Canada staff, remains as its most audacious project. The steel-framed replica has an accurate cockpit and nose section that were mated with fuselage, tail and various outer wing panels in 2006. One of the project dilemmas was the creation of blueprints and tooling from a handful of photographs and drawings. The project manager, Paul Cabot, stated that completion of the Arrow replica was an eight-year project with an estimated 600,000 man-hours.

A V Roe Canada, the once mighty company that gave the Avro Arrow life, was eventually sold. It continued in other guises, first in 1962 as part of the Hawker-Siddeley Group and renamed de Havilland Canada, although the main operation of the factory was shifted to the Downsview plant. In the late 1960s Douglas Canada Ltd acquired the massive factory space at Malton to build DC-9 wings. With the merging of Douglas and McDonnell as the McDonnell Douglas Corporation in 1967, its Canadian holdings were renamed McDonnell Douglas Canada Ltd. The workforce in the Toronto complex numbered 4,000, and their work continued on the DC-9, now renamed the MD 80 series. In 1997 Boeing merged with the McDonnell Douglas Corp, and the factory continued work on the re-badged Boeing 717, the modern reincarnation of the workhorse DC-9. Although work continues on wings, anodising components, and making spare parts, the numbers in the Boeing Toronto facility stood at a scant 400 in 2002. Only one employee still remains from the Avro years; the giant assembly bays, endless corridors of draughting boards and mesh of offices stand empty; yet the memory of what once was there remains. The current plans for the facility are indeterminate as seventy-eight acres of the Boeing Toronto site were recently sold to the Greater Toronto Airport Authority and projections call for the manufacturing areas to be downsized from 1,800,000sq ft to 400,000sq ft. A corresponding downsizing of staff is also anticipated.

On 4 October 2002 Boeing Toronto marked the forty-fifth anniversary of the rollout of the Avro Arrow. On the spot where more than 13,000 employees and guests had once cheered its birth, 300 'Avroites' returned to mark its passing. For the most part their numbers had dwindled, and although a few younger people were in the crowd as family members, those who had lovingly built the Arrow were now in their late seventies or early eighties. Set in the Arrow's final assembly bay, the event was marked by moving speeches by Jim Floyd, the Canadian Armed Forces' Historian, Don Pearsons, and Stephen J Fisher, the President of Boeing Toronto Ltd, who recalled the achievements of the Avro years. Jim Floyd remarked, 'Returning to this spot has awakened a lot of ghosts and memories.' The few Arrow artefacts that were assembled only poignantly reminded the audience of a time when the Arrow stood proudly in the sunlight. As of this writing, despite the efforts of a group of historians and concerned citizens in Toronto, the assembly bays of the Avro company have been demolished. Janusz Zurakowski had once written: 'It is impossible to destroy everything... Governments and torches can destroy an aircraft but they cannot destroy hope and aspiration, and the majesty of the questing spirit. In the hearts of the people, the dream lives on.'[7]

A final note

More significantly, the story of Janusz Zurakowski also lives on in the hearts of people all over the world, and especially in Barry's Bay, his home. Through the efforts of a dedicated team of volunteers, the Township of Madawaska Valley has recently unveiled a unique memorial to the life and achievements of its most famous resident. On 26 July 2003 Zurakowski Park was officially dedicated in a ceremony in Barry's Bay attended by more than 1,000 guests, including dignitaries from Canada, the United States, Germany, Romania and Poland. Scattered among the crowd of friends, neighbours and well-wishers was a group of his old Avro colleagues. The new park features a life-size granite statue of Janusz Zurakowski and an imposing one-quarter-scale Avro Arrow.

Although not in the best of health, Janusz, accompanied by his wife and sons (and their families), was present at the ceremony. In a drizzle that one wag quipped should remind Zura of his days in England, the throaty roar of a Supermarine Spitfire announced the arrival overhead of one of his favourite wartime fighters.

[7] Topham, 'Remembering the Arrow's first flight,' 1998.

Left to right: Anna, Janusz, Mark and George Zurakowski at the dedication
ceremony for Zurakowski Park in Barry's Bay, 26 July 2003. *(Bill Zuk)*

As he peered up into the clouds, in typical modesty, Janusz
announced, 'I don't think I deserve this, but I wish to dedicate this
park to the thousands of wonderful Canadians who built this excellent
aircraft,' and he glanced over to the Arrow model beside him. There
wasn't a dry eye in the crowd and that wasn't because of the rain.

Zurakowski Park is located on Kelly Street at the junction of
Highways 60 and 62 in an arrow-shaped corner site that can be seen
by visitors as they enter Barry's Bay from an eastern, western or
southern approach. The Avro Arrow model, depicted in flight
streaking high into the sky, will lead visitors to a future orientation
centre and museum on the site. Inside the centre, young and old will
view a multimedia display depicting the legacy of Janusz
Zurakowski. It is hoped that for generations to come, Zurakowski
Park will stand as a tribute to one of Canada's greatest legends.

Bibliography

Published books

Ascherton, Neal *The Struggles for Poland* (London: Michael Joseph, 1987)

Avery, D H and Feborowicz, J K *The Poles in Canada* (London: University of Western Ontario, 1971)

Bethell, Nicholas *The War Hitler Won: The Fall of Poland, September, 1939* (New York: Holt, Rinehart and Winston, 1972)

Bracken, Robert *Spitfire: The Canadians* (Erin: Boston Mills Press, 1995)

Brodniewicz-Stawicki, Margaret *For Your Freedom and Ours* (St Catharines: Vanwell Publishing, 1999)

Campagna, Palmiro *Storms of Controversy* (Toronto: Stoddart, 1992)

Campbell, Jerry L *Messerschmitt Bf 110 Zerstôrer in Action* (Warren, Michigan: Squadron/Signal Publications, 1977)

Clayton, Ken *Phantom 202* (fiction) (Baltimore: AmErica House, 2001)

Collier, Richard *Eagle Day: The Battle of Britain* (London: Pan Books, 1956)

Deighton, Len *Blood, Tears & Folly: In the Darkest Hour of the Second World War* (London: Jonathan Cape, 1993)

Dixon, Joan and Nicholas Kostyan Dixon *Made for Canada: The Story of Avro's Arrow* (Calgary: A V Roe Canada Heritage Museum, 2001)

Dow, James *The Arrow* (Toronto: James Lorimer, 1979)

Duke, Neville *Test Pilot* (1953, reprinted London: Grub Street, 1997)

Dugelby, Thomas B 'Arrowplans' (fiction, based on the author's earlier series, *The Avro Arrow*, self-published, 1999)

Fleming, Donald M *So Very Near: The Political Memoirs of the Honourable Donald M Fleming*, Vol 1, *The Rising Years* (Toronto: McClelland and Stewart, 1985)

Floyd, James C *The Avro Canada C102 Jetliner* (Erin: Boston Mills Press, 1986)

Fraser, Blair *The Search for Identity: Canada: Postwar to Present* (Toronto: Doubleday Canada, 1967)

Gainor, Chris *Arrows to the Moon: Avro's Engineers and the Space Race* (Burlington: Apogee Books, 2001)

Garnett, Graham Christian *Against All Odds* (London: The Rococo Group, 1990)

Gething, Mike *Test Pilots* (Vero Beach: Rourke Enterprise, 1988)

Gretzyngier, Robert *Poles in Defence of Britain* (London: Grub Street, 2001)

Halliday, Hugh *The Tumbling Sky* (Stittsville: Canada's Wings, 1978)

Haute, André Van *French Air Force* Vol 1, *1909-1940* (London: Ian Allan, 1974)

Hough, Richard and Richards, Denis *The Battle of Britain*
    (London: Hodder and Stoughton, 1989)

James, Derek N *Gloster Aircraft Since 1917*
    (London: Putnam Aeronautical Books, 1971)

Johnson, Brian *Test Pilot* (London: Guild, 1986)

Jones, Barry *The Gloster Meteor* (Ramsbury, England: 1998)

Kaplan, Philip and Collier, Richard *Their Finest Hour: The Battle of Britain*
    Remembered (New York: Abbeville Press, 1989)

Kent, J A *One of the Few: Gp Capt J A Kent* (London: Corgi Books, 1971)

Koniarek, Dr Jan *Polish Air Force 1939-1945*
    (Carrolton, Texas: Squadron/Signal Publications, 1994)

Kos-Rabcewicz-Zubrowski, Ludwik *The Poles in Canada*
    (Ottawa: Polish Alliance Press, 1968)

Kusiba, Marek *Janusz Zurakowski: From Avro Arrow to Arrow Drive*
    (Toronto: Adres Press, 2003)

Lambermont, P *Helicopters and Autogyros of the World*
    (London: South Brunswick, 1970)

Leslie, R F (ed) *The History of Poland Since 1863*
    (Cambridge: Cambridge University Press, 1980)

Leversedge, T F J (ed) *The Arrow: Avro CF-105 Mk1 Pilot's Operating*
    Instructions and RCAF Testing/Basing Plans
    Erin: Boston Mills Press, 1999)

Liss, Witold *P Z . P-11: Aircraft in Profile*, Vol 4 (New York: Doubleday, 1970)

Makowski, William *The Polish People in Canada*
    (Montreal: Tundra Books, 1987)

Marchaj, C A *Sail Performance: Design and Techniques to Maximize*
    Sail Power (New York: McGraw-Hill, 1996)

McCauley, Martin *The Russian Revolution and the Soviet State 1917-1921*
    Documents (New York: Barnes & Noble Books, 1975)

MacNaughton, Monique Renee *Arrowflight: The Well and the Whaler's Cat,*
    Part 1 (fiction) (New Maryland, NB: Coydog Press, 1995)

Arrowflight: The Well and the Whaler's Cat, Part 2 (fiction)
    (New Maryland: Coydog Press, 1996)

Arrowflight: He Crossed His Neck with Thunder, Part 1 (fiction)
    (New Maryland: Coydog Press, 2001)

Melady, John *Pilots: Canadian Stories from the Cockpit, from First Flights to the Jet Age* (Toronto: McClelland and Stewart, 1989)

Middleton, Don *Test Pilots: The Story of British Test Flying, 1903-1984* (London: Collins Willow, 1985)

Milberry, Larry *The Avro CF-100* (Toronto: CANAV Books, 1981)

Canada's Air Force at War and Peace, Vol 3 (Toronto: CANAV Books, 2001)

Nicholson, Patrick *Vision and Indecision: Diefenbaker and Pearson* (Don Mills: Longmans Canada, 1968)

Nielsen, Erik *The House is Not a Home* (Toronto: Macmillan of Canada, 1989)

Organ, Richard; Page, Ron; Watson, Don; and Wilkinson, Les *Arrow*, 2nd ed (Erin: Boston Mills Press, 1993)

Oswald, Mary *They Led the Way: Members of Canada's Aviation Hall of Fame* (Wetaskawin: Canada's Aviation Hall of Fame, 1999)

Page, Ron D *CF-100 Canuck: All-Weather Fighter* (Erin: Boston Mills Press, 1981)

Peden, Murray *Fall of An Arrow* (Toronto: Stoddart, 1978)

Polish Air Force Association *Destiny Can Wait: The Polish Air Force in the Second World War* (London: Polish Air Force Association, 1949)

Ramsey, Winston (ed) *The Blitz Then and Now*, Vol 1 (London: Battle of Britain Prints International, 1987)

Rimell, Ray *Battle of Britain Aircraft* (Hemel Hempstead: Argus Books, 1990)

Robinson, Anthony *RAF Fighter Squadrons in the Battle of Britain* (London: Brockhampton Press, 1999)

Robinson, Robert R *Scrap Arrow* (fiction) (Don Mills: PaperJacks, 1975)

Rose, W J *Poland* (London: Penguin Books, 1939)

Rossiter, Sean *The Chosen Ones: Canada's Test Pilots in Action* (Vancouver: Douglas & McIntyre, 2002)

Sevigny, Pierre *This Game of Politics* (Toronto: McClelland and Stewart, 1965)

Shacklady, Edward *The Gloster Meteor* (London: Macdonald, 1962)

Shainblum, Mark and Dupois, John (ed) *Arrow Dreams: An Anthology of Alternate Canadas* (fiction) (Winnipeg: Nuage Editions, 1997)

Shaw, Edith Kay 'The Arrow' (original treatise written 30 April 1959 to become the basis of the book *There Never Was an Arrow*)

There Never Was an Arrow (Brampton: Steel Rail, 1981)

Shirer, William L *A Native's Return: 1945-1988* (Boston: Little, Brown and Company, 1990)

Smith, Denis *Rogue Tory: The Life and Legend of John G Diefenbaker* (Toronto: Macfarlane, Walter and Ross, 1995)

Smye, Fred 'Canadian Aviation and the Avro Arrow'
    (1985; short-run publication by Randy Smye, 1989)
Stewart, Greig *Arrow Through the Heart: The Life and Times of Crawford
    Gordon and the Avro Arrow* (Scarborough: McGraw-Hill Ryerson, 1998)
Shutting Down the National Dream, 2nd ed
    (Scarborough: McGraw-Hill Ryerson, 1997)
Stursberg, Peter *Diefenbaker: Leadership Gained 1958-62*
    (Toronto: University of Toronto Press, 1975)
Sutherland, Alice Gibson *Canada's Aviation Pioneers: 50 Years of McKee
    Trophy Winners* (Toronto: McGraw-Hill Ryerson, 1978)
Ulam, Adam *Understanding the Cold War: A Historian's Personal
    Reflections* (Charlottesville: Leopolis, 2000)
Waterton, W A *The Quick and the Dead* (London: Frederick Mueller, 1958)
Wernick, Robert (ed) *Blitzkrieg* (New York: Time-Life Books, 1976)
Whitcomb, Randall *Avro Aircraft and Cold War Aviation*
    (St Catharines: Vanwell Publishing, 2002)
Willis, John *Churchill's Few* (London: Michael Joseph, 1985)
Wood, Derek and Dempster, Derek *The Narrow Margin: The Dramatic Story of
    the Battle of Britain and the Rise of Air Power: 1930-1940*, revised ed
    (New York: Paperback Library, 1969)
Wyatt, Daniel *The Last Flight of the Arrow* (fiction)
    (Toronto: Ballantine Books, 1990)
Zamoyski, Adam *The Forgotten Few: The Polish Air Force in the Second
    World War* (New York: Hippocrene Books, 1995)
Zebrowski, Walter *In Search of Freedom: Tales of World War Two*
    (Whistler, British Columbia: Whistler Ventures, 1995)
Ziegler, Frank H *The Story of 609 Squadron: Under the White Rose*
    (London: Crécy Books, 1993)
Zuk, Bill *Avrocar: Canada's Flying Saucer: The Story of Avro Canada's
    Secret Projects* (Erin: Boston Mills Press, 2001)
Zurakowska, Anna (ed) *The Proud Inheritance: Ontario's Kaszuby*
    (Ottawa: The Polish Heritage Institute-Kaszuby, 1991)
Zurakowski, Janusz *Janusz Zurakowski: Nie tylko o lataniu*
    (Toronto: The Polish-Canadian Publishing Fund, 2002)
Zuuring, Peter *The Arrow Scrapbook: Rebuilding a Dream and a Nation*
    (Ottawa: Arrow Alliance Press, 1999)
    Arrow Countdown: Rebuilding a Dream and a Nation
    (Kingston: Arrow Alliance Press, 2001)

Technical papers

Anderson, R K 'Production of an All-Weather Long Range Fighter',
A V Roe Canada Limited, 24 Oct 1954.

'Arrow Quarterly Technical Report 70/ENG PUB/5 for Period Ending
31 December 1957', A V Roe Canada Limited.

'70/ENG PUB/11 for period ending 30 September 1958',
A V Roe Canada Limited.

'Design Study of Supersonic All-Weather Interceptor Aircraft in Accordance
with RCAF Spec Air 7-3 Report No P/C-105/1',
A V Roe Canada Limited, May 1953.

'Orenda Training School Notes OEL-1140 (Iroquois engine)',
A V Roe Canada Limited, c1959.

Perley, Daniel R 'The Need for Defence Oriented Science and Technology
Policies in Smaller NATO Countries: The Canadian Avro CF-105
Arrow as a Case Study', International Exposition and Conference for
Defence Industries, Chicago, 8-11 February 1979.

Woodman, Jack 'Flying The Avro Arrow', Canadian Aeronautics and Space
Institute Symposium, Winnipeg, 16 May 1978.

Magazine articles

Adams, Russell 'For the Record', *Pinion* (Gloster's house magazine)
(Summer 1957), 24-26.

'Arrow Development Programme Will Be Continued as Canada's Air
Defence Policy is Reviewed', *Avro Newsmagazine*, 4, No 13
(26 September 1958), 3-4.

'Arrow Exceeds 1,000mph – RCAF', *Avro Newsmagazine*, 4, No 5
(24 April 1958), 3, 7.

'The Arrow Revealed', *Aircraft* (October 1957), 31-34.

Avro Newsmagazine, Special First Flight Edition (2 April 1958), 2-11.

Bentham, Richard P 'Empire Test Pilots School, 1963', *AirForce*
(Summer 2000), 52-55.

Bliss, Michael 'Arrow that doesn't fly', *Macleans* (20 January 1997), 49.

Callwood, June 'Requiem for a Dream', *Macleans* (13 January 1997), 56-57.

'Canada's Gain is Britain's Loss: Appreciation of S/L Zurakowski as Test
Pilot and Aerial Photographers' Target', *Flight* (25 April 1952), 487.

Champion, Chris 'The Arrow Myth Still Flies', *AirForce* (Winter 1997), 3.

Cope, Peter R 'The Zurabatic Cartwheel', *Flying* (May 1956), 69.

Cynk, Jerzy B 'Pictorial Museum of Polish Aviation', *Air Progress*
(May 1959), 63-72.

'Farnborough: The Opening Phases', *Flight* (September 1951), 344-348.

'Festival Farnborough', *The Aeroplane* (September 1951).

Floyd, James C 'Avro Arrow Design', *The Aeroplane* (10 October 1958),
566-568.

'Avro C102 Jetliner', *SAE Quarterly Transactions*, 5, No 2 (April 1951),
217-235, 272.

'The Avro Story', *Canadian Aviation* (June 1978), 52-53, 56, 58, 60,
126-127, 130-131.

'The Canadian Approach to All-Weather Interceptor Development',
The Journal of the Royal Aeronautical Society, 62, No 576
(December 1958), 845- 866.

'For Canada's Defence', *The Aeroplane* (10 October 1958), 546-565.

Gale, John 'Farnborough Newcomer', *Jet Age* (Autumn 1955), 1-3.

Garrett, Gilbert D S (ed) 'Aircraft Development in the Commonwealth',
Hawker Siddeley Review, 3, No 2 (June 1950), 11.

Green, Gerald J 'Readers' Letters', *Aeroplane*, 30, No 10, Issue 354
(October 2002), 21.

Green, William 'The Mighty Arrow', *RAF Flying Review*, XIV, No 6
(1958),18-21.

Haswell, Stan 'Test Flying the CF-100', *CAHS Journal* (Fall 1983), 86-89,
92-93.

'He did it', *Aircraft* (April 1958).

'I shot an Arrow...', *Hawker Siddeley Review* (June 1958), 36-37.

Isinger, Russell 'Flying Blind: The Politics of the CF-105 Avro Arrow
Programme', *Western Canada Aviation Museum Aviation Review*, 22,
No 4 (December 1966), 23-30.

Johnson, Brian D 'Raising the Arrow: A TV mini series conjures up a
stratospheric dream', *Macleans* (13 January 1997), 48-52.

Lamb, Ken (ed) 'Wit matches Speed at 650mph', *Shell News*, 7, No 3
(March 1954), 3-5.

Lukasiewicz, Julius 'Canada's Encounter with High-Speed Aeronautics',
CASI Log Carnet de L'IASC, 8, No 5 (October 2000), 8-26.

Maloney, Sean M 'Canada's Glory Days', *Macleans* (21 January 2002), 16-18.

McCaffrey, Margaret 'A Flawed Plane and an Inept Corporation? The Historian's
View', *Engineering Dimensions* (September/October 1988), 50.

'Setting the Record Straight: The Designer's View', *Engineering Dimensions* (September/October 1988), 52-53.

McLean, Jim 'Each Move Experimental on Arrow's First Flight', *Avro Newsmagazine*, 4, No 4 (2 April 1958), 2, 10.

'Toronto's Mayor and Press Club Pay Tribute to Zura at Functions', *Avro Newsmagazine*, 4, No 17 (5 December 1958), 4.

'Zura Makes News While Flying... and It's News When He Quits', *Avro Newsmagazine*, 4, No 17 (5 December 1958), 9.

Meadows, Jack 'The Auxiliary Tradition', *Aeroplane Monthly* (June 1987), 285-289.

Mellberg, Bill 'Too Good to be True', *Air Enthusiast*, 54 (1994), 52-57.

'Mr Martin's Memorable MB 5', *Air International* (February 1979), 73-80.

Neil, Tom 'Boscombe Down Memories: Reflections of an A&AEE Test Pilot', *Air Enthusiast*, 54 (Summer 1994), 36-42.

Norris, Geoffrey 'Impossible, of Course!', *RAF Flying Review*, XIV, No 8 (April 1959), 28-30, 42.

Orwovski, J S 'Polish Air Force versus Luftwaffe', *Air Pictorial*, Part One (September 1959), 378-382, 388; Part Two (October 1959), 394-400, 418.

Painter, John F 'Showing Off the CF-100', *Aeroplane Monthly*, Part One (January 1998), 36-41; Part Two (February 1998), 42-48.

'Zura: Turning Cartwheels in the Sky', *Aeroplane Monthly*, Part One (January 2002), 24-30; Part Two (February 2002), 22-27; Part Three (March 2002), 62-67.

Rogers, Don 'Testing the Jetliner', *The CAHS Journal* (published by the Canadian Aviation Historical Society), 10, No 1 (Spring 1972), 16-22, 32.

Shaw, S Bernard 'Jan Zurakowski', *The Country Connection*, No 21 (Spring 1994), 30-31.

Stevens, James Hay 'Canada's CF-100s at Farnborough', *Aircraft* (November 1955), 17.

'Farnborough '51', *Air Pictorial and Air Reserve Gazette* (September 1951), 313-315.

Stewart, Arthur 'First Flight New Blankets World', *Avro Newsmagazine*, 4, No 4 (2 April 1958), 6-7, 8-9, 10-11.

Stewart, Oliver 'News from Britain', *Canadian Aviation* (October 1955), 55, 38.

Stinton, Darrol 'Test Pilot', *Airforce Monthly* (August 1988), 52-54.

Stratford, H Ralph 'Feather-weight Feet for 30-ton Giant: Designing the Landing Gear for the Avro Arrow', *Canadian Aviation* (February 1958), 53-55, 87.

'There and Back to see how near it is!', *Hawker Siddeley Review*, 3, No 4 (December 1950).

Thistle, Rick 'Canada's Supersonic Fighter Fiasco', *Aviation History* (January 1998), 34-40.

Williams, Paul 'First test pilot has gone fishing', *The Mississauga Times* (23 April 1980), 4, 10, 13.

Witkowski, Ryszard 'Rotorcraft in Poland's Civil Aviation History', *Aerospace* (January 1981), 12-19.

Young, Scott 'The Way Up: An Account of the 10-year History of A V Roe Canada Limited', *Jet Age* (Winter Issue 1957), 5-12, 16-25.

Zuk, Bill 'The Avro Arrow on Centre Stage: CBC Recreates a Dream', *Airforce* (Winter 1997), 4-11.

'Zurabatic Cartwheel', *Hawker Siddeley Review*, 4, No 4 (December 1951).

Zurakowski, Jan 'Horizons Unlimited', *Jet Age* (Summer 1952), 10-11.

'Test Flying the Arrow and Other High Speed Jet Aircraft', *The CAHS Journal* (published by the Canadian Aviation Historical Society) 17, No 4 (Winter 1979), 100-112.

'Zurabatic Cartwheel in a Meteor', *Wingspan* (1986), 4-7.

'Zurakowski's Retirement', *The Aeroplane* (10 October 1958), 548.

Newspaper articles

Allen, Helen 'Jan's Wife had Pressing Job, Too', *Toronto Telegram*, 25 March 1958.

'Arrow', *Toronto Daily Star*, 25 March 1958.

Bell, Douglas 'Elwy Yost Remembers the End of the Arrow', *The Globe and Mail*, 11 January 1998.

Bergen, Bob 'Movie blurs line between fact, fiction', *Calgary Herald*, 14 January 1997.

Conologue, Ray 'Arrow play falls short of Target', *The Globe and Mail*, 17 February 1990.

Dunwoody, Derm 'Inventor of Zurobatic [sic] Cartwheel Joins Avro as Test Pilot', *Toronto Telegram*, 24 April 1952.

'Here's the Ottawa Text on Air Defence Programme', *Financial Post*, 27 September 1958.

Hornick, James 'New Arrow Flies Exactly to Avro Plan', *The Globe and Mail*, 28 March 1958.

Hum, Peter 'The Man Who Flew the Arrow', *The Ottawa Citizen*, 9 January 1997.

'Inventor of Zurabatic Cartwheel Joins AVRO as Test Pilot', *The Telegram*,
24 April 1952.

'Jet Ace Hurt, Aide Killed but Save Homes from Crash', *Toronto Daily Star*,
24 August 1954.

Kingsley, Justin 'Pilot still mourns Arrow's death', *Canadian Press*,
23 March 1998.

Montaigue, Bill 'Arrow pilot running tourist camp', *The Ottawa Citizen*,
31 October 1963.

'Orenda Crew here to learn B-47 handling', *Boeing Plane Talk*, 14, No 38,
20 September 1956.

'Picturebatics Tough in CF-100', *Toronto Star*, c1955.

'Polish Air Force in the Battle of Britain', *The Ottawa Citizen*, 20 September 1999.

Redekop, Bill 'High Flyers honoured for pioneering efforts',
Winnipeg Free Press, 31 May 1997.

Robb, Jim 'The Avro Arrow', *The Ottawa Citizen*, 14 January 1989.

Stamplecoski, Ray 'Canadian aviation history died after just 11 glory
months', *The Eganville Leader,* 23 March 1988.

Thompson, John 'Captains of the Clouds: Remembering that day 40 years
ago when the Arrow first took flight', *Toronto Sun*, 21 March 1998.

Topham, Bill 'Remembering the Arrow's first flight', *Brighton Independent*,
6 October 1998.

West, Bruce 'Zura Lands: Test Pilot Cold-eyed Small Man',
The Globe and Mail, 1 December 1952.

Zurakowski, Jan, as told to Phyllis Griffiths 'In the Life of Zura',
Toronto Telegram, 2-14 May 1959.

Related material (textual)

'Big Wheel Transport', A V Roe Canada, brochure, 1961.

Fighting Talk No 5, RAF pilot's notes, 1942.

House of Commons, *Debates*, 20, 23 February 1959.

'*The Legend Lives on…*', Zurakowski Park brochure, February 2003.

McCourt, Mike 'Pioneer of Flight', Western Canada Aviation Museum
presentation, 1997.

McShane, Tim 'In the Loop', e-mail correspondence with R C Hangar,
16 February 2000.

Smye, Fred Personal correspondence with Janusz Zurakowski, 1952 and 1955.

Stebbings, Ray *A Short History of No 234 Squadron, Royal Air Force, 1917-1955*.

Ursel, Lorne 'Types of Test Flying', Handout, 2001.

Zurakowski, Jan 'Flying the Arrow', *The 35th Anniversary Celebration of the Roll-Out of the 'Avro Arrow' CF-105*, souvenir booklet, 1992.

Audiovisual resources

Arrow: From Dream to Destruction, ed Jim Lloyd (60-minute videocassette) (Burlington: A-V Studio, 1992)

The Arrow, directed by Don McBrearty (four-hour mini-series) (Toronto: CBC/Filmworks, 1997)

Straight Arrow: the Janusz Zurakowski Story, directed by George and Anna Prodanou (22-minute videocassette) (Toronto: White Pine Pictures, 1998)

There Never was an Arrow, produced by George Robertson (44 minutes) (CBC Film Production, 1980)

Virtual resources

Avro workers react to massive layoffs, 1959 [online], cited 13 October 2003: http://archives.cbc.ca/400d.asp?id=1-75-275-1406.

Bartoszewski, Wladyslaw 'Britain and Poland: Allies in NATO, Partners in Europe', address by Mr Wladyslaw Bartoszewski, Minister of Foreign Affairs of the Republic of Poland, London, cited 12 March 2001: www.msz.gov.pl/english/polzagr/20010317bartoszewski_uk.html.

Center for Defence & International Security Studies 'Ballistic Missile Threats', current and historical perspectives on defence issues, cited 9 April 2002: http://www.cdiss.org/v2.htm.

Davis, Kristina 'Avro Arrow test pilot honoured at Cold Lake', Department of National Defence, Canada, cited 21 March 2000: www.dnd.ca/menu/maple/vol_2/Vol2_15/.

Eldridge, Jason 'AVROLAND', a site dedicated to the people and aircraft of AVRO Canada and Orenda Engines Limited, 2001-2002: http://www.avroland.ca/al-vz9.html.

Farnborough Air Science Trust Newsletter No 14, December 1998, cited 2001: http://www.fasta.freeserve.co.uk/fasta.htm.

Jobson, Robert 'Prince ends Enigma of Poles' role in bringing war to end', cited 19 September 2000: www.LineOne.net.

Kusiba, Marek 'ZURA' Opisanie Janusza Zurakowskiego (an interview and biography of Janusz Zurakowski in Polish), cited October 2001: http://www.math.ualberta.ca/~amk/zwoje18/text10.htm.

Mackechnie, David 'Avro Canada Archive on the Web', David
    Mackechnie's tribute to his father, Hugh Mackechnie, former Avro
    Canada photographer, cited 15 August 2001:
    http://www.odyssey.on.ca/~dmackechnie.

Manney, Captain Jeff and Wilson, Major Rob 'All in the (flying) family', Maple
    Leaf (Department of National Defence, Canada), cited 18 August 2000:
    http://www.dnd.ca/menu/maple/vol_3/Vol3_32/airforce_e.htm.

Payne, Stephen R, Curator, Aeronautical Technology, and Shortt, A J,
    Director, Collections and Research 'Technical Aspects of the Avro
    CF-105 Arrow', National Aviation Museum, Ottawa, cited 28 June
    1999: http://exn.ca/FlightDeck/Arrow/words.cfm?ID=19990628-69.

Postowicz, Robert 'Polish Aviation History Page' [online], cited
    16 September 2001: http://www.s-studio.net/polavhist/.

RAF662 CFSG (Royal Air Force 662 Combat Flight Sim Group), cited
    23 September 2001: http://www.dynotech.com/bravo/fighters34.html.

'Ramrod Books Book Launch of Kaleidoscope III', photographic record of
    the Battle of Britain by Dilip Sarkar, Ramrod Books, Worcester,
    England, cited 2 September 2000:
    http://www.battleofbritain.net/ramrodbooks/booklaunch.html.

Rosensweig, Brahm 'Avro Arrow', cited 28 June 1999:
    http://exn.ca/flightdeck/arrow/.

'Post-Arrow Brain Drain', cited 6 July 1999:
    http://exn.ca/flightdeck/arrow/braindrain.cfm.

Roy, Dr Reginald 'Pearkes Discusses the Bomarcs, Interview #61, 5 April
    1967. ACC 74-1 Box 6' [online], cited 20 October 2003:
    collections.ic.gc.ca/uvic/pearkes/plv5/pbomarc.html.

Schmidt, R Kyle 'Homage to the Avro Arrow', an excellent reference source
    including a historical summary, illustrations and other links, cited
    2002: http://www.avro-arrow.org/.

'SETP (The Society of Experimental Test Pilots)', cited 2001:
    http://www.setp.org/contactingsetp.htm.

Salski, Andrzej M The Summit Times, TST, 2, No 5-6/1994. Excerpts from a
    speech by Mr Joseph Jedd during a conference in San Francisco.
    'An Intelligence Perspective and Commemoration of the 50th
    Anniversary', dedicated to the 50th anniversary of the CIA Cited 9
    April 2002: http://www.dnai.com/~salski/No05-06Folder/Jedd-
    Poland-Contribution.htm.

303 Squadron (Polish) 'Kosciuszko', RAF Regulations, cited 21 October
    2001: www.raf303.org/regulations/.

Worsley, John Howard 'Incident at Ashey', Riddle Raveller with Little-Pearl
    Publishing and Art Gallery, John Howard Worsley, in the series
    'Echoes of the Home Front', depicting the first victory of Janusz
    Zurakowski over the Messerschmitt Bf 110 on the Isle of Wight, 15
    August 1940, cited 21 June 2002:
    http://www.warbirdart.demon.co.uk/aechoes.html.

Zuk, Bill 'My Home Page', excerpts from articles on Avro Canada, cited 21
    September 2001: http://www.autobahn.mb.ca/~billzuk/.

Index